I0820674

ANGLISTISCHE FORSCHUNGEN
Band 451

Begründet von
Johannes Hoops

Herausgegeben von
Rüdiger Ahrens
Heinz Antor
Klaus Stierstorfer

"... that I wished myself a horse"

The Horse as Representative of Cultural Change in Systems of Thought

Edited by
SONJA FIELITZ

Universitätsverlag
WINTER
Heidelberg

Bibliografische Information der Deutschen Nationalbibliothek
Die Deutsche Nationalbibliothek verzeichnet diese Publikation in der Deutschen Nationalbibliografie; detaillierte bibliografische Daten sind im Internet über *http://dnb.d-nb.de* abrufbar.

COVER ILLUSTRATION
© Jens Krüger

ISBN 978-3-8253-6425-0

Dieses Werk einschließlich aller seiner Teile ist urheberrechtlich geschützt. Jede Verwertung außerhalb der engen Grenzen des Urheberrechtsgesetzes ist ohne Zustimmung des Verlages unzulässig und strafbar. Das gilt insbesondere für Vervielfältigungen, Übersetzungen, Mikroverfilmungen und die Einspeicherung und Verarbeitung in elektronischen Systemen.

© 2015 Universitätsverlag Winter GmbH Heidelberg
Imprimé en Allemagne · Printed in Germany
Druck: Memminger MedienCentrum, 87700 Memmingen

Gedruckt auf umweltfreundlichem, chlorfrei gebleichtem und alterungsbeständigem Papier

Den Verlag erreichen Sie im Internet unter:
www.winter-verlag.de

Introduction

Sonja Fielitz
University of Marburg

In recent years, animal studies have doubtlessly become established as an important interdisciplinary field of research. Cultural and literary studies have dealt in various ways with the discourse on animals in order to proceed beyond, as well as find alternatives to, the traditional method of *Motifgeschichte*. It is in this context that our collection of essays is designed to offer fresh insights into a particular and hitherto largely neglected field of animal studies, that is, 'horse studies'.

Since the classical myths of Pegasus and the centaurs, mankind in the Western word has shared a deep relationship with horses. In ancient Greece, the good-natured quadrupeds were employed as warhorses and racehorses, and they also prominently featured as Olympic victors. The Romans could not have established and defended their Empire without their cavalry, and the *ludi circenses* throughout the Roman Empire are widely documented in literary and legal sources, as well as mosaics. In the Middle Ages, horses played a major part in codes of chivalric imagination, inherent, for instance, in the interrelationships between the knight, his lady, and his steed. The early modern period abounds with references to horses which were ubiquitous as means of travel and transportation in everyday life. From the late 17th century on, a flood of paintings and prints testifies to the noble and physically majestic appearance of horses in aristocratic sport. With the technical innovations of the 19th century and the desire to return to the more sensual aspects of life and thus also newly define the balance between body and mind, horses gained a new cultural status. They were less and less required in matters of travel and transport and became increasingly important in the discipline of sports and, in literary texts, as symbols of majestic energy and creativity (see below). Leisure time, once a privilege of the upper classes, now became a promise for all citizens, and it may be no coincidence that *Turnvater Jahn* established the vaulting horse as a gymnastic apparatus.

All in all, throughout the ages, horses have fulfilled various roles as a means of labor, travel, and transportation as well as being willing servants in times of war, and partners in modern sports. The horse's obedience has been seen all the more valuable for being ungrudgingly offered by a proud, powerful creature capable not only of strong attachment but of righteous resentment of injuries. Horses have thus proved themselves to be a central part in the life of humans in many ways (and especially Britons of all ranks have been known for their love of horses).

Body and Mind

As mentioned above, this collection of essays does not see itself in the field of *Motivgeschichte*. The interest which lies behind rather is the dichotomy between horses and humans, and this with a particular focus on the dichotomy of 'body' and 'mind'. From antiquity onward, horse and man have been portrayed as representatives of passion and drive, on the one hand, and reason and control, on the other. The so-called *Arbor Porphyriana* (3rd century AC) considers man as the climax of creation because he is gifted with *ratio*. Porphyry still used various animals like horses, dogs, and sheep in order to illustrate his thesis. The well-known representation of the early modern period, i.e. the woodcarving by Carolus Bovillus (1510), however, symbolized the level below (sentient and pensive) man by exclusively focusing on the (sentient) horse. What reasons lie behind this decision? As will become evident in this volume, literature of the 16th and 17th centuries, such as dramas and poems by William Shakespeare and his contemporaries, abound with references to the relationship and also hierarchy between humans and horse, and thus discuss this very question of superiority. At the end of the 17th century, John Locke in his *Essay Concerning Human Understanding* (1689) claims the absolute rational superiority of mankind over horses. "Reason stands for a Faculty in Man, […] that Faculty, whereby Man is supposed to be distinguished from Beasts, and wherein it is evident he much surpasses them." In the 18th century and dawning Romanticism, this attribution of (human) rationality and (equine) instinct is radically questioned, however, when Gulliver meets the Yahoos and Houyhnhnms. The dichotomy is defined anew in the 19th century when the horse becomes as a symbol of poetic creativity. In *Don Juan*, for instance, Lord Byron allows the Icarian man of the Romantic period to strive on the wings of Pegasus to infinity. In hardly any other picture than that of the falling Pegasus do the images of creative genius and utter failure unfold more obviously. In the middle of the 19th century, Charles Darwin transcended the existing hierarchy in his work *The Origin of Species* (1859) by arguing that man's intellect and body descended directly from animals, thereby finally closing the gap between the notion of the rational (?) man and the irrational (?) horse that had existed up until then.

"… that I wished myself a horse"

It was against this intellectual context that the conference *"... that I wished myself a horse" The Horse as Representative of Cultural Change in Systems of Thought* held at the University of Vechta, Germany, from 14 to 16 November 2013 took place. The introductory quotation goes back to Sir Philip Sidney's late-16th century *A Defense of Poesie* which so prominently begins with the management of horses. Sidney and his friend, Sir Edward Wotton, have learned all about horses, horseman, and horsemanship at the court of the Holy Roman Emperor Maximilian II. Their instructor, John Pietro Pugliano, a squire of the Emperor's stable, said so much in praise of horses and horsemanship that Sidney confesses, "if I had not beene a peece of a Logician before I came to him, I thinke he would have persuaded me to have wished myself a horse." This quotation perfectly indicates the discussion of the above-mentioned separation of the domains of humans as the rational being, and the former obviously being overwhelmed by emotions while listening to Pugliano praising horses.

The conference, hosted and organised by Prof. Dr. Norbert Lennartz (University of Vechta) and myself, was designed to foster innovative enquiries into 'horse studies' from the Middle Ages to the present. It aimed at providing a forum for the exchange of ideas between widely-known professors and famous specialists in their respective fields of inquiry on the one hand, and postgraduates on the other hand, but also reflected upon the necessity to do so in a broader national and international context. In its fostering of critical dialogues, it also allowed various kinds of border crossings within different cultural frameworks. Not only did the topic explore the cultural construct of the horse in various cultures, it also traversed time, space, and medial representations.

The essays gathered in this volume represent selected papers presented at the conference, as well as essays by scholars who were personally invited to contribute.

In the opening essay of the section devoted to *Authors and Texts*, **Stanley Wells and Paul Edmondson** (Stratford-upon-Avon, UK) "canter through the almost inexhaustible topic 'Shakespeare and the Horse' by first thinking about horses as Shakespeare came to know them from his boyhood. In his days, horses certainly were ubiquitous, and they appear to have had a profound impact on his artistry." By referring to and extensively quoting from the sonnets, *Venus and Adonis* as well a plethora of the Bard's plays, Wells and Edmonson reflect about "the artistic function or some of the myriad mentions of horses in Shakespeare's works, thus revealing his own specialist knowledge of equine terminology". As they demonstrate in their (inevitably compressed) survey, "we cannot escape the dimension of 'horses' when dealing with Shakespeare's works. Whenever you open your copy of the Complete Works, horses are liable to gallop and curvet in front of you in all their local, classical, vivid, energetic, uninhibited and rhetorically heightened glory." All in all, the Wells and Edmonson, who gave the opening keynote lecture of the Vechta conference, demonstrate that "to understand the horse in relation to Shakespeare is to enter into a fuller understanding of his overall artistry and imagination."

Erich Poppe (Marburg, Germany) as the expert on Celtic Studies takes on the scattered evidence for equestrian sports in medieval Ireland's legendary past and the so-called *Ulster Cycle* as well as the *Finn Cycle*. By repeatedly crossing borders between the fields of linguistics and literary studies, Poppe in his richly annotated essay delineates how various types of horse-fight were designed in medieval Ireland. He comes to the conclusion that "horse-racing appears to have been a constituent part of the ideal image of assemblies of the legendary Irish past, a literary motif, and a cultural emblem of this social space."

Roy Eriksen (Kristiansand, Norway) focuses on Shakespeare's contemporary, Christopher Marlowe, and his use of equine imagery. With reference to the two *Tamburlaine* plays as well as *Dr Faustus*, he develops that "the equine metaphors deployed by Marlowe in *Tamburlaine* indicate the potential range and complexity of meanings attributed to horses and myths in which the animal is vital." What is more, Eriksen also opens up a biographical dimension in his survey by suggesting that "the dramatist draws on conventional and heterodox ideas from various sources. Horses acquire functions exceeding what was to be expected not least when we consider their crucial role in a myth that was to become his (Marlowe's) personal myth to the extent that he even signed himself 'phaeton' in his dedicatory sonnet to John Florio's *Second Fruites* (1591)."

Kirsten Juhas (Münster, Germany) invites us to a border crossing from drama to poetry, and here, verse-satire of the 17th century. Taking as her starting point the equestrian statues of Charles I (1633) and his son Charles II (1672), which both evoked a number of poetic responses, she focuses on three poems, i.e., "The Statue in Stocks-Market", "The Statue at Charing Cross", and "The Dialogue between The Two Horses" (all three most likely written by Andrew Marvell). In her text-based and richly annotated essay, Juhas lines out the satirical dimension of these poems, interestingly uttered through horses. "In their seditious talk", she argues, "the horses not only criticize the Monarchs on moral grounds, but also on their costly life style, the corruption at Court and in Parliament, as well as the royal tax policies."

Hermann Josef Real (Münster, Germany) as the expert of Swift studies and one of the keynote speakers at the Vechta conference first reflects on the Dean's personal preoccupation with riding who regarded "horses not only a welcome but indispensable means of transportation and travelling but also of as status symbols." Swift was very good on equine breeds, too, he lines out, and in *Gulliver's Travels*, "he was drawing from a fund of knowledge when delineating the hierarchical, non-egalitarian structure of Houyhnhnm society in Book Four." Despite his affinity to horses, however, "it is not (yet) sufficient evidence to account for that perennial teaser why the Dean when elaborating the thereophilic paradox of Book Four opted for horses rather than, say, foxes of shunks." By turning the traditional relationship between Man and Horse in the ontological order upside down in Book Four of *Gulliver's Travels*", Real argues, "Swift reverted to a strategy familiar throughout his career as a satirist from its inception, that is, the strategy of inversion." By doing so "he does not only challenge prevailing assumptions, conventions and norms, but also surprises, provokes and confuses." For Real, it is inevitable to see Book Four as a constituent part of a larger context, because it is by no means complete in itself, but rather "the logical culmination of the preceding journeys, the meaning of the Houyhnhnms (and that of the Yahoos) must be implicit not in Book Four, but in Books One to Three. The specific function of Book Four is to make this meaning explicit." Real comes to the conclusion that the houyhnhnms are "incarnations of what the 'orthodox' of Swift's age envisaged men to be, rational creatures. Their sole function is to remind Gulliver of his own ideal, his own standard. Swift's standard is double-edged: in a first cut, he shows that Man does not measure up to his own standard; in a second, that his self-fashioned standard is not for Man. As the conclusion of the *Travels* proposes, it is neither possible nor desirable for Gulliver to qualify for a rational community."

Francesca Orestano (Milano, Italy) ties in with the genre of narrative texts and proceeds into Victorian and early twentieth-century British literature. She deals with the cultural shift occurring in those decades with the rise of a 'new girl', when she discusses Charles Dickens' *Hard Times* (1854) and Enid Bagnold's *National Velvet* (1935), in which the horses "offer their full support to the weak, timid, ugly girls they escort in to life, and victory." As Orestano lines out, there is a gendered world of facts and emotion, of reality and imagination. According to the empiricist agenda and crude logic and figures of Coketown, the horse is a hard fact. As Sissy Jupe, the circus girl, is concerned, however, horses also evoke sublime wonder and affect the senses." What Dickens suggests in his novel, Orestano argues, is "the poetical lightness of an equestrian show will alleviate the gravity of facts." As an outlook, she briefly touches upon Anna Sewell's *Black Beauty* (1877) and other children's books of the 19th to 21st centuries, as well as the 1944 movie of *National Velvet* starring Elizabeth Taylor and Mickey Rooney.

Susanne Peters (Magdeburg, Germany) makes a related point about popular and / or adolescent fiction and also questions of gender. She looks at how these stories "manage to elicit reader response and encourage empathy in both groups of addressees", that is, youngsters but grown-ups as well. For her purpose, she chooses Anna Sewell's *Black Beauty* (1871-1877), " a book that has suffered countless adaptations for the television screen as well as the cinema", and Michael Morpurgo's *War Horse*, written roughly a hundred years and two world wars later (1982). It is Peters' critical interest (other than Müller's; see below) to identify the narrative perspectives of the two novels. In Sewell's novel, Peters argues, "the message is limited, yet clear: mend ignorance and stop cruelty, and in Malpurgo's text, the message is foremost an anti-war one, a call for the fair treatment and honouring of the horse veterans of war. Although they are to be seen in the context of the time in which they were written, they point towards some greater understanding that may only be achieved in the future." In both cases, the individualised horse is an eloquent messenger with a voice that may help bridge the human-animal divide, if only tentatively. The literary horse is situated in the text to negotiate subject as well as object positions, an ideological construct grounded in biological nature that allows us to rethink our relations to nonhuman animals in theriotopological terms."

Other than Peters, **Anja Müller** (Siegen, Germany) puts her focus on Michael Marpurgo's novel for children *War Horse* (1982) in its medial representations, that is, the printed text, the stage adaptation, and the movie screen. Müller discusses Marpurgo's "rather conventional horse biography" together with Nick Stafford's stage version (first premiered in the National Theatre's Olivier auditorium on 9 October 2007) and the movie by Steven Spielberg of 2011.

Müller's overall interest lies "with how 'horseness' is embodied on page, stage and screen, how the figure of the horse is juxtaposed with human beings, and to what effect this happens." She thus reflects on the (non-speaking) horse as a reflector of moral implications (in the novel), as well as the stage-representation of the horses as abstract puppets with almost life-like movements which effectively contributes to the highly emotional response of audiences to the play. Spielberg in his movie, in contrast, uses an anthropomorphized life horse as the alter ego of his human protagonist. As Müller develops, the three versions of *War Horse* reflect on different cultural meanings and significances of the relationship between horse and man. In Marpurgo's novel, the horse as a focalizer "provides a vision of the shattered worlds left by World War I, in which the aesthetic quality of the horse contrasts sharply with the degradation and corruption of human beings that has come to fore in the destructiveness of the War. The life-size puppets (each operated by three players) of the stage version do not disneyfy anthropomorphism but rather achieve to create true 'horseness' on stage. "The horses thus communicate on stage with a language of their own that is rendered accessible to the audience, and which is purely theatrical." Spielberg's employment of the horse in his movie, to the contrary, results largely in the sentimental effect which both novel and stage production tried to avoid."

Martin Kuester (Marburg, Germany) crosses the Atlantic and offers a case study on Robert Kroetsch's Canadian novel *The Studhorse Man* (1969). Kuester thus opens up a postmodern and postcolonial dimension of 'horse studies' by tracing the role of the horse as symbol of social change in Canadian culture. In his contribution, he shows that horses "stand for social and medical change in mid-twentieth-century Canadian society. Rather than standing for the traditional lifestyle of the agrarian West, the horse in Kroetsch's novel "stands for one of those epistemic breaks that Kroetsch sees as central elements of the decentring movement of postmodernism, that is "not only for the innovation and epistemological change that liberated sexuality means for the role of women but also for the shift from traditional conservative to a more liberal (perhaps even promiscuous) society, for Canada's move from [...] Victorian into Postmodern without ever having been modern." The horse in *The Studhouse Man* "may well be seen as a symbol of epistemic change from realism to postmodernism."

The second part of this essay collection, *Aesthetics*, is opened by **Barbara Ravelhofer** (Durham, UK), who also belonged to the keynote speakers of the Vechta conference. She argues that Equestrian Ballet can be seen as a representative of the epistemological changes in Europe between 1500 and 1700. How did, she asks, poets, philosophers, and equestrian experts relate to horses? By referring to the Court of Dresden, and, most of all, to William Cavendish, Duke of Newcastle and England's foremost equestrian expert at the time, she opens up the field of European performance culture by taking a closer look on man being equally interested in spectacle, drama, and cross-communication between humans and animals, i.e., horses. She concludes on the note that "equestrian ballet was the perfect form to enact, in a harmonious vision, early modern notions of a human self that was collective, interpersonal, and viscerally physical – a self that defined itself also in relation to the animal world and communicated with it."

Sonja Fielitz (Marburg, Germany) takes up on Ravelhofer's topic of 'horse ballet' and crosses the boundaries between theory and practice by focussing on the dimension of 'presence' in Freestyle Dressage (*Dressur Kür*). Why are, she asks, spectators 'touched' by a performance in Freestyle Dressage while perceiving it with their eyes and ears, but (other than the rider) without touching anything physically with their hands? Fielitz finds the answer to these questions partly in Bruce Smith's, and mostly in Hans Ulrich Gumbrecht's (scientifically, respectively philosophically, based) theories. In Freestyle Dressage, she argues as a scholar and an active rider, "a human and an equine body produce presence effects for the rider by touching each other in their harmonious swaying to the musical score of their performance by which they become one bodily and aesthetic entity." In Freestyle Dressage, presence effects happen with, through, and to the bodies of two performers, i.e., an animal and a human being. For the spectators, "presence effects are not only created by two individual bodies (equine and human) becoming one, but by the oscillation between the technical and artistic sections. By this interplay of technical excellence on the one hand, and aesthetic movements and impressions on the other hand, horse and rider establish a particular intimate connection of their two bodies by the constant phenomenon of (aesthetical) movement as registered in music, as well as (technical) precision in figures." By a constant oscillation between positions of detachment and intimacy, rider and horse evoke a pattern of (rational) reflection and (sensual) fascination in their audience and thus provide a narrative of bodily experience."

Rolf Lessenich (Bonn, Germany) provides the more general frame for the section on *Aesthetics* by presenting an overview of neoclassical poetics and the art of horsemanship. Taking Xenophon as his starting point and Laurence Sterne as his closing one, Lessenich traces various methods of training horses (among them the ones by Pluvinel, and William Cavendish, Duke of Newcastle) as well as their representations in literary texts. All in all, he delineates that "throughout all history, changes in the breeding and training of horses, as well as in the art of dressage riding, were representative of wider cultural changes in systems of thought."

The fourth and last part of this volume is dedicated to *Linguistics*. **Rolf Kreyer** (Marburg, Germany) explores the depiction and conceptualisation of horses in English literature from early modern times to the present from a distinctly linguistic point of views. His method of choice is that of corpus linguistics with its extremely broad perspective, respectively, bird's-eye view, on the use of the lexeme *horse* and its (near-)synonyms (e.g. *steed* or *mare*) over the centuries. For his overview, two corpora were built: The first represents writing of 58 authors ranging from Sir Thomas More to Virginia Woolf, containing 124 texts and a total of approximately 13 million words. The first corpus was supplemented by the imaginative prose section of the British National Corpus, which contains roughly 16.5 million words. All in all, the findings reported in Kreyer's contribution are based on almost 30 million words. As he develops, "the way that authors use the word *horse* reflects changes in the conceptualization of horses over the centuries, and, in addition, the way horses are described and, hence, conceptualized becomes narrower and less diversified." It is remarkable within this development, Kreyer concludes, "that two semantic fields show a slight increase of use in the modern data, namely the fields of 'temperament' and 'breaking'. It might be argued that the horse, rampant but reigned in, is still as valid a symbol of the eternal struggle of passion and reason today as it was 400 years ago, even though the power of this symbol does not necessarily show in its instantiation in one particular piece of art but in the way the word *horse* is used in the language of literature."

Christoph Schubert (Vechta, Germany) closes this volume by tracing the uses of the lexeme *horse* in its large number of figurative uses in English-speaking cultures. By founding his analysis on the Conceptual Metaphor Theory (CMT), Schubert provides "a cognitive-semantic analysis of the lexeme *horse* and its compounds with regard to their occurrence in English phraseology, concentrating on idioms, similes, proverbs, and winged words." By tracing numerous phraseological units he shows "that phraseological units pertain mainly, albeit not exclusively, to positive and desirable qualities of horses, such as physical strength and material value. In addition, superior intellectual qualities and features such as industriousness are attributed to horses. Many winged words stress similar merits of energy, ability, and value, but here also negative and undesirable aspects are quite noticeable," All in all, Schubert concludes, "although equine cultural models have obviously changed over the centuries, phraseology and metaphor act as preservers of diachronic cultural knowledge, which is thus perpetuated in idiomatic usage such as bodily excretion, illness, stupidity, as well as war and death.

This points to the fact that the cultural model of HORSE is by no means one-sided but rather multi-faceted."

Acknowledgements

My special thanks are due to Prof. Dr. Martin Winter, Vice-Principal of the University of Vechta, for his kind and informed welcome address at the conference. Katharina Genn-Blümlein (*Stabstelle Presse- und Öffentlichkeitsarbeit*) most kindly and indefatigably provided extremely helpful support in various fields, among them matters of funding. Sabrina Daubenspeck (*Stabstelle Presse- und Öffentlichkeitsarbeit*) designed the splendid posters and flyers for the conference. Dr. med. vet. Hermann Josef Genn arranged for us an exclusive and unforgettable guided tour of Paul Schockemöhle's estate. My warmest thanks are to him and his team for their time and extremely generous hospitality. My greatest debt is to our Marburg/Vechta organisational team without whose efforts and support the conference would not have run as smoothly as it in fact did. This was first of all due to my co-convener, Norbert Lennartz, and his assistants Swantje van Mark and Oliver Schmidt, and on the Marburg side, Liza Bauer and Imke Kimpel. I should like to express my warmest thanks to all of them.

The present volume was made possible by the extraordinarily diligent editing and formatting by Amelie Käßer B.A – a very hearty and most grateful "thank you" to her. Christian Pauls M.A. patiently kept providing technical support when I was lost in the wilderness of modern media. Last, but by no means least, my thanks are to the editors of *Anglistische Forschungen*, and to Dr. Andreas Barth of *Universitätsverlag Winter* who kindly accepted the volume for publication and most efficiently guided us in bringing it on its way. All possible shortcomings are at my responsibility only of course.

May this book be dedicated to Countess M and her peers.

Marburg, October 2014 Sonja Fielitz

Shakespeare and the Horse

Paul Edmondson and Stanley Wells
The Shakespeare Institute, Stratford-upon-Avon

"Let us on your imaginary forces work." Those words from the Prologue to *Henry V* invite the audience to project on to the bare stage of Shakespeare's theatre the movement and image of horses "printing their proud hooves i' th' receiving earth." (Chorus 1, 27) We should like to begin this essay by asking you, our readers, too, to exercise your imaginations. The scene is a summer's day, let's say 21 July 1589, precisely a year since English forces led by Sir Francis Drake engaged with the invading Spanish Armada off Plymouth. Shakespeare, now 25, has just arrived in London – probably on foot (he couldn't yet afford a horse of his own) – and has started work in the world of the emerging professional theatre. He has with him an almost completed play (*The Two Gentlemen of Verona*) but he needs to earn his living somehow and has found gainful employment holding horses for playgoers attending performances at The Theatre and The Curtain. Samuel Johnson was the first to write about this, in 1765:

> Many came on horseback to the play, and when Shakespeare fled to London from the terror of a criminal prosecution, his first expedient was to wait at the door of the playhouse and hold the horses of those who had no servants, that they might be ready again after the performance. In this office he became so conspicuous for his care and readiness that in a short time every man as he alighted called for Will Shakespeare and scarcely any other waiter was trusted with a horse while Will Shakespeare could be had.[1]

Of course, this account may be entirely fictional. What is important for our purposes is its appropriateness. This image of Shakespeare holding horses outside the London playhouses provides us with an opportune starting-point for our canter through this almost inexhaustible topic, "Shakespeare and the Horse."

Let us first think about horses as Shakespeare came to know them from his boyhood onwards in his daily life in Stratford-upon-Avon. What did they mean to him culturally as well as artistically? We want then to think about the artistic function of some of the myriad mentions of horses in Shakespeare's works. References to horses and riding occur in every single one of the plays and memorably, of course, in the narrative poem *Venus and Adonis* (1593). So, as we speak, keep allowing your minds to drift back to the image of Shakespeare, newly arrived from Stratford-upon-Avon, looking after horses for members of a paying London audience.

[1] Samuel Johnson: *Johnson on Shakespeare*, ed. by Arthur Sherbo, Yale Edition of the Works of Samuel Johnson, vol. 7, New Haven and London 1968, p. 115.

Part One: "So that I wished myself to be a horse"

The quotation that sets the scene for our collection of essays alludes closely to the beginning of Sir Philip Sidney's *A Defence of Poetry*. Sidney, an excellent horseman whose very name Philip – phil-hippos – is the Greek for "love of horses" – recalls a long and detailed conversation with John Pietro Pugliano, the horseman of the Holy Roman Emperor. Pugliano, says Sidney, explained that

> no earthly thing bred such wonder to a prince as to be a good horseman; […] Then would he add certain praises, by telling what a peerless beast the horse was, the only serviceable courtier without flattery, the beast of most beauty, faithfulness, courage, and such more, that if I had not been a piece of a logician before I came to him, I think he would have persuaded me to have wished myself a horse.[2]

Sidney is speaking from an aristocratic perspective, but the affinity with horses and horsemen which he admires and recognises from speaking with Pugliano is one which permeated English society at every level.

Shakespeare was familiar with horses and with how they behaved from his earliest days. They could be dangerous. We learn from the Stratford-upon-Avon Corporation Records for 1578, when he was thirteen years old, about a four year old boy who "had his left ear disfigured with a horse."[3] The poor lad could have been a playfellow of Shakespeare and his siblings.

Horses were so much a part of everyday life that in the following year the civic authorities thought it necessary to decree that "no person within this borough shall keep above one horse, gelding or mare in and upon Bancroft upon pain and forfeiture for every time that any shall offend."[4] The Bancroft is an area by the river, close to the site of the current Royal Shakespeare Theatre. Townsfolk could use it for common grazing.

The Corporation accounts include many payments for the hire of horses and for their upkeep. In 1608, for example, the hire of two horses for twenty days cost 16 shillings.[5] Similarly we know how much horses cost to buy from the toll-book "of horses, geldings, mares and colts sold or exchanged in the open fair holden in Stratford-upon-Avon in the county of Warwick the third day of May in the 44th year of our sovereign Lady Elizabeth" – 1602 – under the supervision of Shakespeare's friend Richard Quiney who was Bailiff at that time: "*a black nag, three white warts on the near ear, underhaft on the fur ear* [that's a handle-shaped marking], *ambling* [how the horse

[2] Sir Philip Sidney: *A Defense of Poesie,* in *Miscellanous Prose of Sir Philip Sidney*, ed. by Katherine Duncan-Jones and Jan van Dorsten, Oxford 1973, p. 73.

[3] *Minutes and Accounts of the Corporation of Stratford-upon-Avon and Other Records*, 1553-1609, Vols I-VI, ed. by Edgar I. Fripp and others, Dugdale Society, 1 (1921), 3 (1924), 5 (1926), 10 (1929), 35 (1990), 44 (2011) (hereafter *Minutes and Accounts*), vol. 3, p 9. Quotations from this source are modernized.

[4] *Minutes and Accounts*, 2.73.

[5] *Minutes and Accounts*, 6, 438.

moved], *price £5 8s, toll 4e.*"[6] The prices range from 30s to over £5. It is irresistible to compare this kind of information with the much more elaborate and technically detailed, virtuoso description that Shakespeare puts into the mouth of the comic servant Biondello describing the horse on which his master Petruccio rides to the church to marry Kate in *The Taming of the Shrew.*

> his horse hipped with an old mothy saddle and stirrups of no kindred, besides, possessed with the glanders and like to mose in the chine, troubled with the lampass, infected with the fashions, full of wingdalls, sped with spavins, rayed with yellows, past cure of the fives, stark spoiled with the staggers, begnawn with the bots, weighed in the back and shoulder-shotten, near-legged before and with, a half-checked bit and a head-stall of sheep's leather which, being restrained to keep him from stumbling, hath been often burst and now repaired with knots; one girth six times pieced and a woman's crupper of velure, which hath two letters for her name fairly set down in studs, and here and there pieced with packthread. (3.2.48-61)

This description is shot through with technical vocabulary which is still a challenge to modern editors. The language is remote and has caused some to resort to emendation. "Glanders" (a runny nose), "lampas" (swollen gums) and "windgalls" (swollen fetlocks) are all reasonably straightforward equine conditions. But "mose in the chine" ["chine" means spine], H. J. Oliver comments in his note to l. 50 in his Oxford edition, "is nowhere else recorded in the context of equine disability." This passage is highly revealing of Shakespeare's own specialist knowledge of equine terminology. In its own way it is not only dazzling in its range and detail but often leads to a virtuosic delivery by actors, finding comedy in reeling off the complicated list of various horse diseases at breakneck speed.

Richard Quiney, whose son Thomas was to marry Shakespeare's younger daughter, Judith, travelled frequently between Stratford and London on civic business, and did so on horseback. When he was in London negotiating a loan of £30 from Shakespeare, his father, Adrian, knowing how important his horses were to him, wrote to Richard on 29 October, 1598:

> your mare hath been in Luddington ground and is well amended for the time; but she is now at home and shall be well kept. Your colt is well and is put in your brother Sturley's ground, but will not tarry there but breaketh into Master Perry's ground. I hope I shall get pasture for him, or you may send to Simon Biddle to get him into Clopton Park.

All the places he mentions are within the neighbourhood of Stratford-upon-Avon and it is interesting and touching to note that Quiney is sending his son news of the horses as though they were members of the family. The letter goes on:

[6] *Minutes and Accounts*, 6, 194.

> If you bargain with William Shakespeare or receive money there [i e from him] bring your money home that you may buy such wares as you may sell presently to [i.e. at a] profit.[7]

Presenting his accounts of expenses for repayment, Richard mentioned

> my own diet in London eighteen weeks in which I was sick a month; my mare at coming up 14 days,[8]

And we can deduce how long the journey from Stratford-upon-Avon to London took on horseback from the following:

> another I brought there to bring me home seven weeks; and I was six days going thither and coming homewards

– in other words the journey took him three days in each direction.[9]

During his second period as Bailiff, in 1601, Richard went to London again on 5 November, staying at Oxford on the first night, then at Uxbridge, arriving in London on the third day in time for dinner – probably at the Bell on Carter Lane, near St Paul's, from where he wrote his famous letter to Shakespeare -– where he and his companions had a fire lit in their chamber. They started their return journey on Friday 13 November, paying 9s 9d for horse food and ostlers, for the chamberlain and other servants 5s. 6d, and for dinner before setting off 20d. The roads were so hard with frost that their horses' hooves had to be frost-nailed for reinforcement and greater protection.[10] This time they reached Aylesbury by nightfall, on Saturday they paused at Banbury then went on almost to Wellesbourne – not far from home – and they reached home on Sunday. Again a journey of three days.

In her book *Travelling Players in Shakespeare's England*,[11] Siobhan Keenan provides helpful information about how players travelled with their costumes and props while on tour. Whilst it is usually assumed that the actors walked along with a horse and wagon, Keenan points out that "civic money was spent on horse meat and beer for the Queen's Men when they visited Fordwich in 1591-2"[12], suggesting that the actors themselves were mounted. There is strong evidence that in his early years Shakespeare was a member of the Queen's Men as a writer and possibly as an actor. In 1598 a payment to Lord Derby's players is followed by a payment "for their horsemeat three nights and lading."[13]

Details such as these help to evoke the horse culture in which Shakespeare lived and breathed. Little wonder, then, that horses and horsemanship had a profound impact on

[7] *Minutes and Accounts*,6, 145
[8] *Minutes and Accounts,* 6, 69.
[9] *Minutes and Accounts* 6, 160.
[10] *Minutes and Accounts* 6. 187.
[11] Keenan, Siobhan: *Travelling Players in Shakespeare's England*, Basingstoke 2002.
[12] Ibid. p. 20.
[13] Keenan, Siobhan: *Travelling Players in Shakespeare's England*, Basingstoke 2002, p. 76.

his artistry. Perhaps the most influential English literary antecedent to Shakespeare in which horses play a significant role is Chaucer's *The Canterbury Tales*, still widely read and reprinted during Shakespeare's lifetime. *The Knight's Tale* is a source for Shakespeare's *A Midsummer Night's Dream* and, especially, for the collaborative *The Two Noble Kinsmen*, but more on that later. The imagined context of storytellers on horseback allowing their stories and confessions to unfold as they plod on their way as pilgrims adds creative impetus to Shakespeare's own practice.

Two of his sonnets take place, as it were on horseback. In Sonnet 50, Shakespeare's unhappiness at being separated from someone he loves is compared to the suffering of the spurred horse that is carrying him ever further away. There is much argument about whether Shakespeare's sonnets are autobiographical or written from invented experience, but surely this sonnet, at least, shows us him writing in his own person:

How heavy do I journey on the way,
When what I seek – my weary travel's end –
Doth teach that ease and that repose to say
"Thus far the miles are measured from thy friend."
The beast that bears me, tired with my woe,
Plods dully on to bear that weight in me,
As if by some instinct the wretch did know
His rider loved not speed, being made from thee.
The bloody spur cannot provoke him on
That sometimes anger thrusts into his hide,
Which heavily he answers with a groan,
More sharp to me than spurring to his side;
For that same groan doth put this in my mind:
My grief lies onward, and my joy behind.

Sonnet 50 is the first of a pair and the next sonnet continues where that left off.

Thus can my love excuse the slow offence
Of my dull bearer when from thee I speed:
"From where thou art why should I haste me thence?
Till I return, of posting is no need."
O what excuse will my poor beast then find
When swift extremity can seem but slow?
Then should I spur, though mounted on the wind;
In wingèd speed no motion shall I know.
Then can no horse with my desire keep pace;
Therefore desire of perfect'st love being made,
Shall rein no dull flesh in his fiery race;
But love, for love, thus shall excuse my jade;
Since from thee going he went wilful-slow,
Towards thee I'll run, and give him leave to go.

In understanding this difficult and contorted poem, Katherine Duncan-Jones' summary is useful: "the horse continues to move slowly as he takes the speaker away from his friend; but on the return journey the poet hopes to fly at the speed of love, outstripping or abandoning his slow-paced steed."[14]

We should like to notice here a buried allusion to Book 2 of Ovid's *Metamorphoses* in lines 11 and 12. The horse's "fiery race" links with Juliet's "fiery-footed steeds" which are, of course, the tragic Phaeton's horses of the sun; "jade" in the following line links the thought here to Richard II's self-comparison to Phaeton "wanting the manage of unruly jades" (*Romeo and Juliet*, 3.3.178). The desire that Shakespeare is expressing in Sonnet 51 is no less powerful than that of Phaeton's horses who ultimately drive him out of all control.

Bruce R. Smith interestingly relates the movement and motion of the horse to the basic metrical patterns of Shakespearian verse:

> Let us not underestimate the importance of horses' three gaits – walk (four beats), trot (two beats), canter (three beats) – for most people's experience of rhythm before the advent of the steam engine and railroads. […] The thumps of the hooves mark the stresses of English verse.

Smith points to lines in *As You Like It* which suggest that Shakespeare was fully conscious of the relationship between the rhythms of horse-riding and the metrical effects available to him as poet. Quoting Touchstone's mocking of Orlando's overly short lines – "this is the very false gallop of verses" – Smith explains:

> a gallop because a rhyme every seven or eight syllables makes the verse move along rapidly, false because Orlando's four hooves don't mount the air as they would in a true gallop […] but hit the ground with a clump when a syllable is wanting or there is one too many.

He goes on to comment that Rosalind and Celia take up the conceit in lines which follow:

> CELIA That's no matter; the feet might bear the verses.
> ROSALIND Ay, but the feet were lame and could not bear themselves without the verse, and therefore stood lamely in the verse. (*As You Like It*, 3.2.164-7)[15]

The ubiquity of the horse in Shakespeare's daily life clearly underpins not only what he chose to write about but the actually techniques of his versification.

[14] *Shakespeare's Sonnets*, ed. by Katherine Duncan-Jones, revised edition, Arden Shakespeare, Bloomsbury 2010, p. 51.

[15] Bruce R. Smith: *Finding Your Footing in Shakespeare's Verse*, in: *The Oxford Handbook of Shakespeare's Poetry,* ed. by Jonathan F. S. Post, Oxford 2013, pp. 323-339 (324 and 325).

Part Two: The Horse in Shakespeare's Works

As we have mentioned, references to horses and riding occur throughout Shakespeare's works, and a whole book could be written on the subject. We can mention only in passing the kinds of horse to which Shakespeare refers: the ambler, the courser, the coal-black horse, the dancing horse, the footcloth horse, the great horse, the hackney, the hunting nag, the pack horse, the fill horse, the running horse, the trotting horse, the Barbary nag, the Galloway nag, the High Almain, the Flanders mare, the Neapolitan horse, the English horse, and the Irish hobby. But let us point to four different ways in which horses figure substantially in Shakespeare's works.

First, we should like to remind you of a plot device in *The Merry Wives of Windsor* involving German travellers and horses. In act four, scene three Bardolph asks the Host of the Garter Inn if three German visitors may borrow three of the Host's horses to meet a visiting Duke. The Host asks if they speak English, which they do, so he agrees, seeing in the moment an opportunity to get some of his money back from the German visitors. He complains that they have been in his house for a week, ordering everyone around, and that he's had to turn away other guests. Later the Host discovers that the Germans have escaped, "for so soon as I came beyond Eton, they threw me off from behind one of them in a slough of mire, and set spurs and away, like three German devils, like three Doctor Faustuses." But the Host wants to believe the best of them and replies "They are gone but to meet the Duke, villain. Do not say they be fled. Germans are honest men." (*The Merry Wives of Windsor*, 4.5.62-7) This apparently insignificant episode is often cut in performance, but it is revealing of Shakespeare's artistry. He is simultaneously indulging his interest in horses and creating plot parallelism, the Germans' trick echoing the gulling of Master Ford and Falstaff.

A second feature of Shakespeare's writing about horses is his practice of conjuring their presence on stage as though they were real, bodied-forth entities in their own right. It was not possible to bring real horses onto the stages of Shakespeare's time.[16] If he had had available to him the resources of film, then there are many occasions when he might well have written real horses into the action. From time to time we are asked to imagine that horses are present, or within reach but just off stage. We have mentioned the Prologue to *Henry V*. At the beginning of act four, scene two of this play we see members of the French army behaving as though their horses were actually present. "*Monte cheval*! My horse!", "Hark how our steeds for present service neigh." (*Henry V*, 4.2.2 and 8) The moment is comparable to Richard III's first words as he awakes from his nightmare, "Give me another horse! Bind up my wounds" (*Richard III*, 5.5.131) as well as his command as he goes into battle to "bustle, bustle! Caparison my horse." (5.6.19) Later Richard instructs the gentlemen and yeomen of England to "Spur your proud horses hard, and ride in blood" (5.6.70). Richard III is famous for the desperation of his repeated, dying cry "A horse! A horse! My kingdom for a horse!" (5.7.7 and 13). His own horse whom he names earlier as White Surrey is now lost on the field, and any horse will do.

[16] The mysterious, anonymous manuscript play *Thomas of Woodstock,* however, appears to call for one, though it may have been represented by a hobby horse.

In *Henry IV Part One* we hear about the packing of horses at Eastcheap to carry turkeys, bacon and ginger as far as Charing Cross. This process is embellished with vivid details such as "I prithee, Tom, beat cut's saddle, put a few flocks in the point. Poor jade is wrung in the withers out of all cess." (2.1.5-7) We can imagine that Shakespeare longed here for the opportunity to bring real horses onto the stage. This fascinating little scene ends with the line "bid the ostler bring my gelding out of the stable. Farewell, you muddy knave." In the next scene, the robbery at Gadshill, Shakespeare excuses the fact that horses are not present with the First Traveller's line: "Come, neighbour, the boy shall lead our horses down the hill. We'll walk afoot a while and ease their legs." (2.2.76-8) Prince Harry and Poins have stolen the horses of Falstaff and his companions, forcing them to run away. Falstaff "lards the lean earth as he walks along" (2.3.17), and the Prince and Poins, who have robbed them of their stolen booty, are able easily to make their escape: "Got with much ease. Now merrily to horse." (2.3.12)

To these examples we might add, among many other instances, Achilles' command about the dead Hector: "Come, tie his body to my horse's tail" in *Troilus and Cressida* (5.9.21); the First and Third Murderers in *Macbeth* observing that just off stage Banquo and Fleance have dismounted from their horses and will walk the last mile to the palace gate (3.3); the interrupted joust between Henry Herford and Thomas Mowbray in *Richard II* (1.2.), and the procession of knights preparing for the tournament in *Pericles* (scene 6) who, as Shakespeare knew, would have been on horseback as they presented their impresa. In 1613, Shakespeare and Richard Burbage devised just such an impresa to be carried by the mounted Earl of Rutland at the Accession Day tilt for King James I.

A third feature of Shakespeare's creative interest in horses and horsemanship is his causing characters to talk about them in expert detail. In *The Merchant of Venice*, Portia quips that her would-be suitor the Neapolitan Prince "doth nothing but talk of his horse" (1.2.39-40). The same might almost be said of Shakespeare. His fascination with horses manifests itself, for example, through Grumio's comic account of Kate and Petruccio's journey from their wedding reception to Petruccio's house:

> GRUMIO We came down a foul hill, my master riding behind my mistress.
> CURTIS Both of one horse?
> GRUMIO What's that to thee?
> CURTIS Why, a horse.
> GRUMIO Tell thou the tale. But hadst thou not crossed me thou shouldst have heard how her horse fell and she under the horse; thou shouldst have heard in how a miry a place, how she was bemoiled, how he left her with the horse upon her, how he beat me because her horse stumbled, how she waded through the dirt to pluck him off me, how he swore, how she prayed that never prayed before, how I cried, how the horses ran away, how her bridle was burst, how I lost my crupper, with many things of worthy memory which now shall die in oblivion, and thou return unexperienced to thy grave. (*The Taming of the Shrew*, 4.1.59-75).

When we picture the catastrophe that Grumio recounts we find in it a jumble of horse and human injury and misfortune. The horses wander away, lost; the humans are left in states of high emotion – swearing, praying – with a broken bridle and a missing crupper (the strap that attaches the back of the saddle to the underside of a horse's tail).

In sharp contrast to this slapstick-style comic episode is the mock-poetic eulogy of the Duke of Bourbon who in act three of *Henry V* enjoys boasting about his horse to the Constable of France and the Duke of Orléans. The Constable says that Orléans' is "the best horse of Europe." The Duke of Bourbon begs to differ and claims that his horse is the best:

> He bounds from the earth as if his entrails were hares – *le chaval volant*, the Pegasus *qui a les narines de feu*! When I bestride him, I soar, I am a hawk; he trots the air, the earth sings when he touches it, the basest horn of his hoof is more musical than the pipe of Hermes. (3.7.13-18)

The boasting continues and climaxes with Bourbon's claim that "I once writ a sonnet in his praise and began thus: 'Wonder of nature! –'." The Duke of Orléans punctures Bourbon's hyperbole with "I have heard a sonnet begin so to one's mistress." And Bourbon, unabashed, replies "my horse is my mistress." (3.7.39-41 and 43)

Horses figure in moments of high tragedy, too. The Groom who visits Richard II in prison talks about the usurping Henry Bolingbroke's coronation procession:

> GROOM
> O, how it earned my heart when I beheld
> In London streets that coronation day,
> When Bolingbroke rode on roan Barbary,
> That horse that thou so often hast bestrid,
> That horse that I so carefully have dressed!
> KING RICHARD II
> Rode he on Barbary? Tell me, gentle friend,
> How went he under him?
> GROOM
> So proudly as if he disdained the ground.
> KING RICHARD II
> So proud that Bolingbroke was on his back.
> That jade hath eat bread from my royal hand;
> This hand hath made him proud with clapping him.
> Would he not stumble, would he not fall down –
> Since pride must have a fall – and break the neck
> Of that proud man that did usurp his back?
> Forgiveness, horse! Why do I rail on thee,
> Since thou, created to be awed by man,
> Wast born to bear? I was not made a horse,
> And yet I bear a burden like an ass,
> Spur-galled and tired by jauncing Bolingbroke. (5.5.76-94)

Richard is incredulous that his favourite horse, Roan Barbary, appeared proud to be bearing his enemy, Bolingbroke. But Richard regains self-control by asking his horse for forgiveness and acknowledging that he is only a beast of burden after all, rather like Richard himself, who bears his burdens "like an ass", wounded by the spurs of Bolingbroke.

A fourth aspect of Shakespeare's use of horses is to evoke them for symbolic and emotional effects. He shows strong awareness of this possibility early in his career. In *Venus and Adonis* he parallels Venus' attempted and eventually successful seduction of Adonis with Adonis' horse's rampant, uncontrollable and immediately successful sexual pursuit of a mare. In this poem, as in *The Taming of the Shrew*, Shakespeare describes the horse in close and technically detailed language. He has clearly been reading his treatises on horsemanship, such as Thomas Blundeville' *The Four Chiefest Offices Belonging to Horsemanship* (1565-6). Has he even been doing so because of his interest in the young dedicatee of his poem, Henry Wriothesley, the Earl of Southampton, whose expertise in horsemanship would be demonstrated in 1595 when he rode in Queen Elizabeth I's Accession Day tilt? And the Earl of Essex appointed Wriothesley Master of the Horse in 1599. The episode in the poem takes up 78 lines –all of them crackling with frustrated, sexual energy. "A breeding jennet, lusty, young and proud" spies Adonis' horse who rushes towards her. Adonis' male horse breaks his reins and his girth, crushes the iron bit between his teeth, breathes and pants heavily and hotly. In short he behaves in completely the opposite way to his inhibited master. Adonis' horse, Shakespeare tells us, is exceptional in the perfection of all its features – much more so than any idealized painting could achieve:

> Round-hoofed, short-jointed, fetlocks shag and long,
> Broad breast, full eye, small head and nostril wide,
> High crest, short ears, straight legs and passing strong;
> Thin mane, thick tail, broad buttock, tender hide –
> Look what a horse should have he did not lack,
> Save a proud rider on so proud a back. (lines 294-300)

Shakespeare's description is grounded in his source material, Thomas Blundeville's adaptation, in his *The Four Chiefest Offices belonging to Horsemanship*, of Federico Grisoni's *Gli Ordini di Cavalcare* (1550):

> Round hooves, short pasterns with fewter locks, broad breast, great eyes, short and slender head, wide nostrils, the crest rising, short ears, strong legs, crisp mane, long and bushy tail, great round buttocks. (Blundeville, 8 recto-9 verso)

Shakespeare varnishes the description with a sexual allusion in the repetition of the word "proud", meaning "sexually aroused" – "proud rider on so proud a back." The horse is sexually aroused even if his master Adonis is not.

Shakespeare's poetic adaptation of Blundeville bursts at the seams with rhythmic energy. The trochaic compound adjectives with nouns dominate the lines leaving almost no room for anything else. The horse's body fills everything. The words carry such rhetorical and visual force that Shakespeare's style here can be compared to that of Gerard Manley Hopkins' sprung-rhythm and instress three centuries later. Shakespeare is revelling in poetic virtuosity and exhibiting his knowledge of technical aspects of horsemanship at one and the same time to convey, as it were, the essence of a horse, the thing itself. The details in this passage are comparable in Shakespeare's works only to Biondello's description of Petruccio's horse in *The Taming of the Shrew*, written at around the same time. Had Shakespeare been reading up about horses and their riders especially with his exciting and glamorous new patron in mind?

The horse is also a passionately sexual image for Cleopatra who envies the horse that bears Antony's weight as she herself has so often done during their sexual encounters.

> O, Charmian,
> Where think'st thou he is now? Stands he, or sits he?
> Or does he walk? Or is he on his horse?
> O happy horse, to bear the weight of Antony!
> Do bravely, horse, for wot'st thou whom thou mov'st? –
> The demi-Atlas of this earth, the arm
> And burgonet of men. (1.5.21-24)

In another late play, *The Winter's Tale*, horses are also evoked in the context of sexuality, for example when Hermione imagines Leontes making love to her in terms of riding:

> You may ride's
> With one soft kiss a thousand furlongs ere
> With spur we heat an acre. (1.2.96-98)

A little later Leontes picks up Hermione's imagery when he refers to her as a "hobby-horse" (1.2.278), a play-thing to be used for illicit sex. He goes on to imagine both Hermione and Polixenes riding the same hobby-horse and being physically close together with its pole sexually prominent between both their legs, "Horsing foot on foot." (1.2.290)

Horses have happier sexual connotations in *Cymbeline* when Innogen expresses her longing to follow her husband on his journey to Milford Haven: "O for a horse with wings!" (3.2.48) In the Pegasus imagery here there is a longing not only for a swift journey, but also for a magical escape.

Shakespeare surpasses himself with the horse imagery he uses when Macbeth, contemplating King Duncan's virtues says that they:

> Will plead like angels, trumpet-tongued against
> The deep damnation of his taking-off,
> And pity, like a naked new-born babe,
> Striding the blast, or heaven's cherubin, horsed
> Upon the sightless couriers of the air,
> Shall blow the horrid deed in every eye
> That tears shall drown the wind. I have no spur
> To prick the sides of my intent, but only

Vaulting ambition which o'erleaps itself
And falls on th'other. (1.7.19-28)

These lines dazzle us for many reasons, but one striking feature is the way Shakespeare transforms "horse" into a verb at the end of the fourth line, pushing the speaker towards the "sightless couriers" at the beginning of the next and pulling a personified Pity and cherubin behind it. The image caught the fancy of William Blake who in 1795 produced the now famous print on paper in ink and watercolour.

The Blake scholar Martin Butlin comments that this is one of the most inspired literal representations of a text in the whole history of art.[17] Blake's picture presents a pictorial commentary and gloss on Shakespeare's richly dense and compressed image. And it is the moment in the play which marks the opportunity for the actor playing Macbeth to show the angel in the man – which not every actor can do. The image Macbeth uses has a profound effect on his language up to the end of the speech. The quasi-heavenly horses continue to be present in his use of horsemanship metaphor: the spur that he lacks to goad himself forward, his ambition which like a horserider seeks to vault nevertheless into action, and even so might fall at the first hurdle because like a horse it jumped too high.

We also find in this passage an echo of an earlier, medieval world which Shakespeare conjured so vibrantly in *Henry IV Part One*. In that play Vernon describes the newly reformed Prince Harry:

I saw young Harry with his beaver on,
His cuishes on his thighs, gallantly armed,
Rise from the ground like feathered Mercury,
And vaulted with such ease into his seat
As if an angel dropped down from the clouds
To turn and wind a fiery Pegasus,
And witch the world with noble horsemanship. (4.1.105-111)

As in *Macbeth*, horses are associated with angels, but classical imagery is also used here to bring dignity to the characterization. Here the reformed Prince Harry, like Macbeth, has something bewitching about him. Later, as a result of King Duncan's murder, we learn in an exchange between the Thane of Ross and an anonymous Old Man that:

Duncan's horses – a thing most strange and certain –
Beauteous and swift, the minions of their race,
Turned wild in nature, broke their stalls, flung out
Contending 'gainst obedience, as they would
Make war with mankind.
OLD MAN 'Tis said they ate each other.
ROSS They did so, to th'mazement of mine eyes
That looked upon't. (2.4.14-20)

[17]Martin Butlin: *The Evolution of Blake's Large Color Prints of 1795*, in: *William Blake: Essays for S. Foster Damon*, ed. by Alvin Rosenfeld, Providence 1969, p. 109.

The moment is surreal and profoundly disturbing, all the more because Ross has actually seen the horses cannibalizing one another. It's almost as if Shakespeare, in trying to convey the horror of what has happened, transfers the worst possible violation of human nature to his most-prized of animals, and also the "minions of their race", that is the most cared-for and most cherished. The surrealism of the image allows Shakespeare to convey the emotional reality of the perversion which has taken place with the murder of King Duncan. The violation is so powerful that it has torn through the barriers between the human and the animal kingdoms.

Finally, our inevitably compressed survey of the ways in which horses figure in Shakespeare's works would be incomplete without our quoting one of the most extraordinary speeches he ever wrote. Pirithous' account of Arcite falling from his horse in the co-authored *The Two Noble Kinsmen* provides an artistic climax to Shakespeare's constant deployment of his expert knowledge and experience of horses. No one but he at the end of his career could have written so intensely compressed a narrative description. In it, Shakespeare makes a new departure in the writing of innovative, introverted blank verse, finding an early seventeenth-century linguistic equivalent to a film in slow motion. This account of a horse and its rider also serves to support our biographical view that Shakespeare was experimenting to the end of his writing career in some of the very last lines he was to write.

Pirithous is speaking to Palamon and his three knights who are all bound as prisoners and guarded by a jailer and an executioner. Palamon himself is awaiting execution with his head on the block when Pirithous brings news of Arcite's tragic fall from his horse:

List, then: your cousin,
Mounted upon a steed that Emily
Did first bestow on him, a black one owing
Not a hairworth of white--which some will say
Weakens his price and many will not buy
His goodness with this note; which superstition
Here finds allowance-- on this horse is Arcite
Trotting the stones of Athens, which the calkins
Did rather tell than trample; for the horse
Would make his length a mile, if't pleased his rider
To put pride in him. As he thus went counting
The flinty pavement, dancing, as 'twere, to th' music
His own hooves made – for, as they say, from iron
Came music's origin) what envious flint,
Cold as old Saturn and like him possessed
With fire malevolent, darted a spark,
Or what fierce sulphur else, to this end made,
I comment not--the hot horse, hot as fire,
Took toy at this and fell to what disorder
His power could give his will; bounds, comes on end;
Forgets school-doing, being therein trained,
And of kind manèe; pig-like he whines

At the sharp rowel, which he frets at rather
Than any jot obeys; seeks all foul means
Of boist'rous and rough jad'ry to disseat
His lord, that kept it bravely. When naught served,
When neither curb would crack girth break, nor diff'ring plunges
Disroot his rider whence he grew, but that
He kept him 'tween his legs, on his hind hooves
On end he stands –
That Arcite's legs, being higher than his head,
Seemed with strange art to hang: His victor's wreath
Even then fell off his head; and presently
Backward the jade comes o'er and his full poise
Becomes the rider's load. Yet is he living,
But such a vessel 'tis that floats but for
The surge that next approaches. He much desires
To have some speech with you - lo, he appears.
(5.6.48-85)

Pirithous' speech represents the culmination of Shakespeare's journey on horseback throughout his career, but it also coincides with Shakespeare's development of a new form of footing in his verse style.

We have drawn attention to significant stages of a journey that takes Shakespeare from his formational years in Stratford-upon-Avon, through to his patronage by the Earl of Southampton, and far beyond. Thinking about Shakespeare and the horse invites us to journey with him and to understand more about how he wrote and what he was interested in writing; it allows us to connect with one of the most important spurs to his imagination. Wherever you open your copy of the Complete Works, horses are liable to gallop and curvet in front of you in all their local, classical, vivid, energetic, uninhibited and rhetorically heightened glory.

We hope that in this contribution we have presented a compelling case that to understand the horse in relation to Shakespeare is to enter into a fuller understanding of his overall artistry and imagination. Shakespeare may or may not have wished himself a horse, but he certainly could not have written as he did without his profound knowledge and deep love of horses and horsemanship.

Bibliography

Butlin, Martin: *The Evolution of Blake's Large Color Prints of 1795*, in: *William Blake: Essays for S. Foster Damon*, ed. by Alvin Rosenfeld. Providence 1969.

Duncan-Jones, Katherine (ed.): *Shakespeare's Sonnets*, revised edition, Arden Shakespeare. Bloomsbury 2010.

Fripp, Edgar I and others (eds.): *Minutes and Accounts of the Corporation of Stratford-upon-Avon and Other Records*, 1553-1609, Vols I-VI, Dugdale Society, 1 (1921), 3 (1924), 5 (1926), 10 (1929), 35 (1990), 44 (2011), vol. 3.

Johnson, Samuel: *Johnson on Shakespeare*, ed. by Arthur Sherbo, Yale Edition of the Works of Samuel Johnson, vol. 7, New Haven and London 1968.

Keenan, Siobhan: *Travelling Players in Shakespeare's England*. Basingstoke 2002.

Sidney, Philip: *A Defence of Poesie*, in *Miscellaneous Prose of Sir Philip Sidney*, ed. by Katherine Duncan-Jones and Jan van Dorsten. Oxford 1973.

Smith, Bruce R.: *Finding Your Footing in Shakespeare's Verse*, *The Oxford Handbook of Shakespeare's Poetry,* ed. by Jonathan F. S. Post. Oxford 2013.

Equestrian Sports and their Social Space in Medieval Ireland

Erich Poppe
University of Marburg

My exploration of equestrian sports and of their social – and (inevitably) literary – space in medieval Ireland will begin with a short passage that takes us into the prehistoric, legendary past of Ireland. The narrative from which the excerpt is taken, *Noínden Ulad* or 'The Debility of the Ulstermen', was probably composed in the first half of the ninth century; it belongs to the so-called 'Ulster Cycle' of texts, which according to medieval Irish learned traditions are set in the time around the birth of Christ. The excerpt focuses on an *óenach* (or 'assembly'), and the horse races, as well as the chariot races that are conducted there:

> Now the Ulidians [or Ulstermen] used to hold great and frequent encampments and assemblies [*dúnada et óenaige*]. All the people of Ulidia [the province of Ulster], both men and women of those who could go to it, used to go to the assembly. [...] The assembly [*óenach*] was splendid, including people and horses and costumes. At the assembly were held horse-races [*graifne*], combats [*or* jousts, *tressa*], casting and shooting matches, chariot-races, and processions. In the mid-afternoon the king's chariot [*carpat ind ríg*] was brought to the course, (and) his horses gained the victory of the assembly.[1]

In a poetic version of the same story, a *dindshenchas* (place-name lore) poem about the origin of the place-name Ard Macha, the setting of the assembly, and the races are described as following: "Then they bring, pacing proudly, / two horses, whose like I see not, / to the warriors' horse-race [*i n-ech-thress curad*] – hide it not! – / held at that season by the king of Ulaid."[2] This then is the scene for a final race between the king's horses and Macha, a pregnant Otherworld woman, brought about by the unwise boasts

[1] Vernam Hull: *Noínden Ulad: The debility of the Ulidians,* in: *Celtica* 8 (1968), pp. 36-37, 28; for 'jousts' as a possible meaning of *tressa* here cf. Hull, 'Noínden Ulad', p. 39. I am still unclear about the basis for Hull's translation 'chariot-races', the word 'rémenn' (nom.pl. < *réimm*) seems to mean 'going, movement'. For some general background to the 'Ulster Cycle' cf. Barbara Hillers: *The heroes of the Ulster Cycle of Tales,* ed. by J.P. Mallory & Gerard Stockman, Belfast 1994.

[2] Edward Gwynn: *Metrical Dindshenchas*, vol. iv, Dublin 1903, repr. Dublin 1991, pp. 127, 126. *Dindshenchas* 'lore of places' is "a popular genre of early Irish literature that purported to explain the origin of well-known Irish placenames" (Nollaig Ó Muraíle: *Dinnshenchas*, in: *Medieval Ireland. An Encyclopedia,* ed. by Seán Duffy, New York & London 2005, p. 132).

of her human husband;[3] Macha inevitably wins the race, gives birth to twins, and curses the Ulstermen – these details, however, need not concern us here. What I am interested in is the assembly, or fair, – the *óenach*, pl. *óenaige* – as a site of equestrian sports in medieval Ireland, captured in the two excerpts in the terms *grafand* and *ech-thress* respectively, and in the reference to the chariot race.[4] In the texts about Macha there is a slight uncertainty about the actual format of the race. In the version of the prose tale in the Book of Leinster (which was produced in the second half of the twelfth century), Macha races against the king's chariot, "Then she raced against the chariot, and when the chariot reached the end of the green [she gave birth]." In the prose version and in the poetic version quoted above, Macha is said to race against the (two) horses of the king, but a late version of the story may imply that both horses and boys were racing, though not necessarily against each other.[5] I will come back later to possible motivations for these ambiguities.

I will first look at some evidence for horse-racing at medieval Irish assemblies, but before I present some factual information about such events I will quote another, exaggerated description of a horse-race (*grafand*) which is conducted by demonic giants. It is found in a literary text belonging to the genre of voyage-tales or *immrama*, *Immram curaig Máele Dúin* 'The Voyage of Máel Dúin'.[6] The horse-racing watched by

[3] Summarized in the next quatrain of the poetic version: "Though their like was not found among the horses of Mag Da Gabra, Cruind [Macha's husband], eager and shaggy, said that his wife was swifter, though heavy with child" (Edward Gwynn: *Metrical Dindshenchas*, ed. cited, vol. iv, pp. 127, 126).

[4] Many of my examples develop the references to horse-racing given by Fergus Kelly: *Early Irish Farming*, Dublin 1997, p. 99. For a useful general survey of the horse in pre-historical and medieval Ireland cf. Finbar McCormick: *The horse in Early Ireland,* in: *Anthropozoologica* 42.1 (2007), pp. 85-194, and for some further discussion of literary and mythological aspects cf., for example, Próinséas Ní Chatháin: *Traces of the cult of the horse in Early Irish sources,* in: *The Journal of Indo-European Studies* 19 (1991), and William Sayers: *Conventional descriptions of the horse in the Ulster Cycle,* in: *Études Celtiques* 30 (1994), pp.233-249. For a comparative perspective on horses in medieval Welsh literature, cf. the relevant chapters in Sioned Davies & Nerys Ann Jones: *The Horse in Celtic Culture,* in: *Medieval Welsh Perspectives,* Cardiff 1997, but horse-racing does not seem to play a social or cultural role there.

[5] Cf. R.I. Best & M.A. O'Brien: *The Book of Leinster*, vol. ii, Dublin 1956, p. 467: "Comluid iarum frisin carpat. & in tan roanic in carpat cend na blae [...]"; Vernam Hull, 'Noínden Ulad', ed. cited, pp. 37 ("To race with the two steeds of the king"), 29, and Edward Gwynn, *Metrical Dindshenchas*, vol. iv, ed. cited, pp. 128, 129 ("the horses were brought beside her", "the king's horses were over-slow"); Rudolf Thurneysen: *Tochmarc Cruinn orcus Macha,* in: *Zeitschrift für celtische Philologie* 12 (1918) , pp. 252, 253-254 ("Ihre Pferde liefen zur Wette und ihre Knaben. 'Die sind gar nicht zu loben', sagte Cruinn; 'ich habe eine schwangere Frau, die würde die Pferde und die Knaben hinter sich lassen'. [...] Sie sprang mit den Pferden um die Wette und liess sie hinter sich.").

[6] A voyage tale "may be defined as a story which describes a visit to an otherworld region or regions, reached after a sea journey" (John Carey: *Voyage literature*, in: *Celtic Culture. A Historical Encyclophedia,* ed. by John T. Koch, Santa Barbara, Denver, Oxford 2006, p. 1743). In another text of the *immram* genre, *Immram Brain*, racing is introduced in passing as an activity of the happy otherworld: "The host race along Mag Mon, / a beautiful game which is not feeble"

Máel Dúin and his companions during their sea-voyage takes place on an island inhabited by giants, and in spite of its imaginative and fantastic quality I find it worth quoting here since it would appear to reflect the excitement and drama associated with horse-racing in medieval Ireland:

> Large was its [this island's] size and its breadth and they saw therein a long wide green [*faichthi*] and enormous hoofmarks of horses in it. The mark of the hoof of every horse was as big as the sail of a ship. [...] They were afraid then after seeing what they saw and they all went swiftly and hastily into their boat. When they had gone a little from land they saw a large host along the sea(shore) to the island and they held a horse-race [*grafaind*] after reaching the green of the island and swifter than the wind was each horse and loud was their noise and their outcry and their shouting; and then the blows of the whips at the meeting were heard by Máel Dúin and moreover he heard what each of them was saying: "Bring the grey horse." "Drive the dun horse there." "Bring the white horse." "My horse is faster." "Better is my horse's leap."[7]

According to Fergus Kelly, the "most prestigious colour for a horse seems to have been white, and the poetic term *gabor* is used especially of a white or partly white horse."[8] The king's outstanding horses in *Noínden Ulad* which race against Macha, are said to be such white ones.[9] The three horses racing in *Immram curaig Máele Dúin* reflect a triadic

("Graibnid in slóg íar Maig Mon, / clu(i)che n-áland nád indron"), (Séamus Mac Mathúna: *Immram Brain. Bran's Journey to the Land of the Women,* Thübingen 1985, pp. 50, 37).

[7] H.P.A. Oskamp: *The Voyage of Máel Dúin. A Study in Early Irish Voyage Literature followed by an Edition of Immram curaig máele Dúin from the Yellow Book of Lecan in Trinity College, Dublin*, Groningen 1970, pp. 113, 112; the prose version is followed by a verse account: "At length thereafter they went to an island [...]. [//] A couple walked into that plain, great was its fierceness, with tracks of horses; they see unmistakably a gathering for a horse-race [*cet(i) ngraifne*]. [//] The size of boat-shaped cauldrons or large cups – honour with luxury – [or] a sail by itself is the hoofmark of every horse that was in the gathering. [//] They went back in painful flight, a deed without fierceness; quickly a host of demons spread out along the sea(shore). [//] They held a horse-race [*grafaind*], their voices were heard, shouting with fury; when they saw this in dust they were certain it was a host of demons."

[8] Fergus Kelly: *Early Irish Farming*, ed. cited, pp. 91-92. In late medieval times, the hierarchy of colours appears to have changed somewhat and become much more differentiated; texts containing veterinary lore about horses written between *c.* 1469 and *c.* 1527 state: "Brown horses with white heads are the best colour. The black is soft and given to sweating. Light is a good colour. The swarthy (horse) is strong. Red horses are bad and the yellow is worse. The best horses are those with a black streak along their back. Dun-coloured horses are good. The grey is seldom praiseworthy. The dark-swarthy black is good; and dappled horses are often good. And the white-headed brindled horse is good." (Brian Ó Cuív: *Fragments of two mediaeval treatises on horses,* in: *Celtica* 2.1 (1952), p. 119), but a second similar group of texts says that the "white is a good colour" (Brian Ó Cuív: *Fragments of two mediaeval treatises on horses,* in: *Celtica* 17 (1958), p. 55, and cf. p. 43). For an instructive discussion of medieval Irish views on the proper qualities of horses cf. Patricia Kelly, Téchta eich*: the proper qualities of a horse,* in: *Saltair Saíochta, Sanasaíochta agus Seanchais. A Festschrift for Gearóid Mac Eoin,* ed. by Dónall Ó Baoill, Donncha Ó hAodha, Nollaig Ó Muraíle, Dublin & Portland 2013.

[9] Vernam Hull: *Noínden Ulad*, ed. cited, p. 29 ('da gabair ind ríg').

hierarchy of colour and quality – triadic arrangements being frequent in Irish texts and thinking –, the first horse is grey (*glass*), perhaps with a speckled mane,[10] the second horse is partly white (acc. *in gabair n-uidir*), and the third then is brilliantly white (acc. *in gabuir ngil*).[11]

The intimate connection between an *óenach* – the annual assembly or fair of a kingdom normally held in early August[12] – and horse-racing is indicated in passing in the legal tract *Di Astud Chirt ⁊ Dligid* 'On the Establishing of Right and Entitlement', in a gloss on the phrase 'aenach n-aiditan' ('an acknowledged fair'), which says "do denam graithfne and .i. aenach naititin, cia tiasa dia cluithi ind" ("to hold horse-racing there, that is, [at] an acknowledged fair, if one comes to a game there").[13] More detailed, even if arguably idealizing, information about the activities at medieval Irish assemblies

[10] Fergus Kelly: *Early Irish Farming*, ed. cited, p. 92.

[11] H.P.A. Oskamp: *Voyage*, ed. cited, p. 112, and cf. Fergus Kelly, *Early Irish Farming*, ed. cited, p. 92. However, the two horses of the outstanding hero of the Ulster Cycle, Cú Chulainn, do not observe this hierarchy of colours: their names denote their colours, namely Liath Macha 'the Grey One of Macha' and Dub Sainglenn 'the Black One of Sainglenn', cf., for example, Rudolf Thurneysen: *Die irische Helden- und Königsage bis zum siebzehnten Jahrhundert*, Halle 1921, pp. 91, 269.

[12] Cf. Fergus Kelly: *Early Irish Farming*, ed. cited, pp. 458-460; Francis John Byrne: *Irish Kings and High-Kings*, London 1973, pp. 30-31, as well as Catherine Swift: Óenach Tailten, *the Blackwater Valley and the Uí Néill kings of Tara,* in: *Seanchas, Studies in Medieval Irish Archaeology, History and Literature in Honour of Francis J. Byrne,* ed. by Alfred P. Smyth, Dublin & Portland 2000, p. 118, cf. also pp. 116-118, and compare N.B. Aitchison: *Armagh and the Royal Centres in Early Medieval Ireland, Monuments, Cosmology and the Past,* Woodbridge & Rochester 1994, pp. 61-66; Charles Doherty: *Exchange and trade in early medieval Ireland*, in: *Journal of the Royal Society of Antiquaries of Ireland* 110 (1980), pp. 81-84, emphasizes the economic functions of such assemblies. For a useful summary of the historical developments cf. Elva Johnston: *Literacy and Identity in Early Medieval Ireland,* Woodbridge 2013, pp. 77-79. The assembly at the beginning of August is related to the festival of Lugnasad, a "major agricultural festival of the year in Irish tradition" (Fergus Kelly, *Early Irish Farming*, ed. cited, p. 459), and compare Máire MacNeill: *The Festival of Lughnasa,* Dublin 1982, for a detailed discussion of the folklore traditions surrounding this event. *Lebor Gabála* claims that Lug established games [*cluiche*] in pre-historic times in honour of his foster-mother Tailte/Tailtiu and that he was the first who brought "chess-play and ball-play and horse-raching [*echlaisc*] and assembling [*oenach*] into Ireland" (R.A. Stewart Macalister: *Lebor Gabála Érenn. The Book of the Taking of Ireland,* part iv, Dublin 1941 (=Irish Texts Society, XLI) pp. 128, 129). However, the word *echlasc* seems to denote "a rod for driving horses" or a "temporary tether" (Fergus Kelly, *Early Irish Farming*, ed. cited, p. 495), but could perhaps be used metaphorically for an event at which horses are driven with a rod – I wish to thank Axel Harlos for bringing the passage in *Lebor Gabála* to my attention. For an interesting account of horse-racing in water, attested for the early years of the nineteenth century in the context of a fair held on the first Sunday of August by Lough Owel in county Westmeath, cf. Philip Dixon Hardy: *Legends, Tales, and Stories of Ireland*, Dublin 1837, pp. 290-309, with an illustration between pp. 304 and 305.

[13] D.A. Binchy: *CorpusIuris Hibernici,* 6 vols, Dublin 1978, pp. 241-242, on the tract cf. Liam Breatnach: *A Companion to the Corpus Hibernici,* Dublin 2005, pp. 293-294; according to Breatnach, p. 294, the phrase 'aenach naiditan' occurs in a list of "actions or occurrences which incur liability on no-one."

is provided by an eleventh-century *dindshenchas* poem about the triennial fair at Carmun in the province of Leinster.[14] The assembly would last for a week, and every day horse-races were held: "On the kalends of August free from reproach / they would go thither every third year: / they would hold seven races [*secht ngraifne*], for a glorious object, / seven days in the week."[15] The prose version similarly reports: "There were seven horse-races [*Secht ngraifne*] there, and a week for promulgating the judgments and laws of the province."[16] The poem emphasises the presence of race-courses as an outstanding feature of the site: "Carmun, gathering place of a hospitable fair [gen. *óenaig*], / with level sward for courses: – / the hosts that used to come to its celebration / conquered in its bright races [*a glan-graifni*]."[17]

In all the examples quoted so far, the term *grafand* is employed to denote horse-racing.[18] A fragment of a legal tract provides the term *echréim* as the name of one of the competitive games, perhaps a 'para-military game played by youths', but no further information about it seems available.[19] Another term used in the *dindshenchas* poems

[14] For the retrospective and antiquarian character of the poem cf. D.A. Binchy: *The Fair of Tailtiu and the Feast of Tara,* in: *Ériu* 18 (1958), p. 125, and Charles Doherty: *Exchange*, ed. cited, p. 81, who suggests that "[t]his poem is a piece of antiquarian lore, since provincial fairs had virtually ceased by the early tenth century"; Edward Gwynn: *The Metrical Dindshenchas*, vol. iii, Dublin 1913, repr. Dublin 1991, p. 471, suggests that the poem may have been composed after 1040, and perhaps in 1079, when the *óenach* was revived after a gap in time. On *Óenach Carmain* cf. also Máire MacNeill: *The Festival*, ed. cited, pp. 339-344, and Alfred P. Smyth: *Celtic Leinster. Towards A Historical Geography of Early Irish Civilization A.D. 500-1200,* Blackrock 1982, pp. 34-35; for a discussion of the location of the site cf. Diamuid Ó Murchadha: *Carman, site of Óenach Carmain: a proposed location,* in: *Éigse* 33 (2002).

[15] Edward Gwynn: *Metrical Dindshenchas*, vol. iii, ed. cited, pp. 19, 18.

[16] Whitles Stokes: *The prose tales in the Rennes dindshenchas [I],* in: *Revue Celtique* 15 (1894), pp. 314, 312.

[17] Edward Gwynn: *Metrical Dindshenchas*, vol. iii, ed. cited, pp. 3, 2. The second line could be translated more literally as"'with a very level green (*faithche*) possessing [race-]courses[?]", and the horse-racing in *Immram curaig Máele Dúin* is also conducted on such a green. Fergus Kelly provides another example of horse-racing on a green, from a poem by Cináed úa hArtacáin (d. 975) set in the Irish legendary past: "One day as they held deedfully their sports [*graiphni*] upon the ample lawn of the *liss* [*ar faidchi in liss*], they spoke with rash malice to fair and active Óengus" (Lucius Gwynn: *Cináed úa hArtacáin's poem on Brugh na Bóinne,* in: *Ériu* 7 (1914), pp. 233, 224), cf. Fergus Kelly, *Early Irish Farming*, ed. cited, pp. 369-370, for a discussion of the various uses of these 'greens', and also Catherine Swift, '*Óenach Tailten*', ed. cited, pp. 113-114.

[18] Edward Gwynn: *Metrical Dindshenchas*, vol. iii, ed. cited, p. 18, lines 221-224, seems to imply that the time of the races ('la graifne') is a time of peace. However, Sayers, 'Games', p. 115, suggests to retain the manuscript reading and to see here a compound with *dréim* 'climbing': 'Perhaps mounting horses on the run is meant, perhaps breaking untrained animals, i.e., mounting for the first time'. I wish to thank Dagmar Bronner for bringing Sayers' paper to my attention.

[19] D.A. Binchy: Mellbretha, in: *Celtica* 8 (1968), pp. 149 (with emendation of MS 'echdreim), 151, and compare Kelly: *Guide*, pp. 150-151.

on Carmun and on Ard Macha is *echthress*,[20] a compound of *ech* 'horse' and *tress* 'contention, fight'. This term is also used in other texts to denote an event at an assembly,[21] and I think it is therefore likely that *echthress* denotes 'horse-racing' in these contexts. However, on the basis of a passage in *Immram curaig Máele Dúin* 'The Voyage of Máel Dún', from which I quoted earlier, Whitley Stokes believed that horse-fights were also conducted in ancient Ireland, which "corresponded with the *hestavig* of the Icelanders", and he believes that *echtress* is a term for such a horse-fight.[22] The passage in question reads (and note that no term to denote the horses' activities is used):

> It was not long thereafter then that they found another high island: it was delightful, and therein was a multitude of big animals like horses. Each of them would take a piece out of the side of another and carry it away with its skin and its flesh, so that streams of bright blood were pouring out of their sides so that the ground was full of it.[23]

Fergus Kelly refers to a statement in a medieval Irish legal tract which says that "a horse fight is the exemption of horses" ("blaí ech echthres"); the accompanying commentary explains that "the horse-fight they fight among themselves, is an exemption for horses."[24] This seems to refer to accidental fights between horses, not to formal horse-fights arranged by their owners for competition. The compound *ech-thress* may therefore denote either a horse-race or a fight between horses depending on the situation.[25]

[20] Edward Gwynn: *Metrical Dindshenchas*, vol. iii, ed. cited, pp. 22 ('ech-thress Ossairge'), 23 ('horse-racing of Ossory'); cf. also Whitley Stokes: *The prose tales*, ed. cited, pp. 312 ('echtres Osraige'), 314 ('Ossory's horse-contest').

[21] Cf. Edward Gwynn: *Metrical Dindshenchas*, vol. iii, ed. cited, pp. 350 ('ic gním óenaig ech-thressa'), 351 ('holding a meeting for horse-races'); Rudolf Thurneysen: *Die irische Helden- und Königsage bis zum siebzehnten Jahrhundert,* Halle 1921, p. 616, who renders *ech-thressa* in a poetic version of *Tochmarc Étáine* as 'Pferdekämpfe'; Ernst Windisch: *Irische Text emit Wörterbuch*, Leipzig 1880, p. 128 ("co n-dernad óenuch ocus echtressa leo ann" ["and an assembly and horse-racings were held by them there"]) in the parallel passage in a prose version of *Tochmarc Étáine*; Edward Gwynn: *Metrical Dindshenchas*, vol. iv, ed. cited, pp. 126, 127, in the poem about the origin of the place name Ard Macha quoted earlier. For an unspecified prohibition of the king of Ulster to attend "the horse-race ['echthress'] of Ráith Lini among the warriors of Dál nAraide", cf. Myles Dillon: *The Taboos of the Kings of Ireland,* Dublin 1951 (=*Proceedings of the Royal Irish Academy,* 54 C 1), pp. 18, 19.

[22] Whitley Stokes: *The Voyage of Mael Duin)I),* in: *Revue Celtique* 9 (1888), p. 473.

[23] H.A. Oskamp: *Voyage*, ed. cited, p. 119, for a brief comment, which endorses Stokes' views, cf. p. 71. George Henderson: *Fled Bricrend. The Feast of Bricrui,* London 1899, pp. 190-191, argues for a difference between Irish horse-racing and Icelandic *hestavíg*, but draws attention to horse-racing in nineteenth-century Uist, on which cf. also Svale Solheim: *Horse-Fight and Jorse-Race in Norse Tradition,* Oslo 1956, pp. 79-109.

[24] Fergus Kelly: *Early Irish Farming*, ed. cited, p. 179, and D.A. Binchy: *Corpus*, ed. cited, p. 290.

[25] The simplex *tress* in *Noínden Ulad* in the first quotation seems to denote an activity unrelated to equestrian sports.

The Icelanders' horse-fight, *hestavíg* or *hestaat*, on the other hand, is a formal and competitive fight between two horses in which the owners may interfere and urge them into action.[26] Svale Solheim, in a detailed study of horse-fights and horse-racing in Norwegian and Icelandic traditions, points out that such accounts are characteristic of medieval Icelandic Family Sagas and that the focus here

> was not the manner of proceedings and the fate of the horses which were fighting, and not at all the way the horsefights were arranged, but the presentation of the individuals who took part in the horsefights, the 'heroes' in the Sagas, who set them going and gave them substance. Out of the horsefights grew antagonism and enmity among the principals in the Sagas. During the horsefights old antagonisms ripened, secret enmity and concealed hatred erupted, and, as a result of this, the horsefights became the great dramatic turning points in the events and accounts in the Sagas.[27]

Solheim suggests that the "picture, which the Family Sagas give of the horse combats, is – in the main – quite similar to what actually happened" and that we can assume "that, in all probability, these descriptions satisfactorily correspond to actual horse matches": "the horsefight, as a factual motif in actual life, was reflected as a literary motif in Family Sagas."[28] The social space of horse-fighting in medieval Iceland was "entertainment during Tings and other public gatherings, [...] and the horsefight was largely an institution which the chieftains used as a social measuring-rod, for social comparison."[29] Horse-racing, on the other hand, would appear to have been uncommon.[30]

Icelandic-style horse-fights do not seem to be attested in medieval Ireland, nor in texts about the legendary Irish past. Horses at assemblies appear to have constituted a risk all the same, since a medieval Irish legal regulation concerning liabilities of horses at an assembly states that "an assembly is an exemption for horses", further enlarged upon in the commentary that "a horse-owner is not normally liable for injuries inflicted by his horse at a fair, nor is he entitled to compensation if his horse is itself injured."[31]

[26] For a useful discussion and collection of examples of horse-fighting in Iceland Family Sagas cf. Svale Solheim: *Horse-Fight*, ed. cited, pp. 51-78; compare also Hans Kuhn: *Das alte Island*, Köln 1978, p. 81.

[27] Svale Solheim: *Horse-Fight*, ed. cited, pp. 56-57, cf. also pp. 54-55, and Lena Rohrbach: *(Nur) Ein Spiel? Spieltheoretische Überlegungen zu den Pferdekämpfen der Sagaliteratur,* in: *Sport und Spiel bei den Germanen. Nordeuropa von der römischen Kaiserzeit bis zum Mittelalter*, ed. by Matthias Teichert, Berlin & Boston 2014, pp. 470-472.

[28] Svale Solheim: *Horse-Fight*, ed. cited, pp. 57, 59, cf. also pp. 64-67, and Lena Rohrbach: *(Nur) Ein Spiel?*, ed. cited, pp. 467-468.

[29] Svale Solheim: *Horse-Fight*, ed. cited, pp. 70-71. For Norwegian traditions of the seventeenth to nineteenth centuries cf. ibid. pp. 28-50.

[30] Ibid. pp. 71-78.

[31] Fergus Kelly: *Early Irish Farming*, ed. cited, p. 153; cf. D.A. Binchy: *Corpus*, ed. cited, p. 265: "Bla ech aenach .i. islan donti beires int ech leis isin naenach" ("an assembly is an exemption for horses, that is, he is exempt who brings the horse with him into the assembly"). For some exceptions from this exemption, which entails the owner's responsibility for his horse, cf. Fergus Kelly, *Early Irish Farming*, ed. cited, p. 153.

Kelly also points out that "by attendance at a fair (*óenach*) a person is evidently felt to have willingly exposed himself to the risk of being killed or injured by horses or chariots, and there is consequently no recompense for such accidents."[32] It is not clear whether these injuries are caused by equestrian sports, by unintended accidents involving horses and chariots, or by both. The possibility of violence connected with horse racing at assemblies seems implied, however, in the early medieval wisdom tract *Audacht Morainn* 'The Testament of Morann', whose original form is dated to around 700: it says with reference to the just ruler – the model of the good king in early medieval Ireland – that one of his "three immunities of violence at every assembly" is specifically "the racing of horses at assemblies" ("án ech n-óenag").[33]

This brings me back to horse-racing at assemblies or fairs. I have already discussed the importance of horse-racing in the idealizing lore about the fair of Carmun in the province of Leinster; another such ancient fair was the Fair of Tailtiu (Teltown), or *Óenach Tailten*, in county Meath.[34] A legendary story in the Book of Leinster about the holding of the fair by the sixth-century king Diarmait mac Cerbaill, in the year in which he took the kingship of Ireland (about 544), links games and horse-racing as a matter of course: "games were celebrated, and the races of the fair ["graifni ind Oenaig"] were performed."[35] The races at this fair even motivated a miracle: In the retrospective Life of the seventh-century saint Colmán mac Lúacháin, angels are said to have run "three races of an assembly" (or perhaps "the three races of the Fair", ".iii. grafne óenaich"), for him and his monks who were sad because they were unable to attend the fair of Teltown.[36]

An elegy for the death of king Aed Finnliath in 879, which is transmitted in the seventeenth-century *Annals of the Four Masters*, mourns Aed specifically as the "master of the horse-races of fair-hilled Tailtiu" ("graifnidh Tailten telglaine")[37] – *graifnid* 'master of horse-racing' being the agentive noun derived from *grafand* 'horse-racing'. The *dindshenchas* poem on Tailtiu, "written to celebrate the holding of the Fair

[32] Kelly: *Guide*, p. 150, with reference to D.A. Binchy, *Corpus*, ed. cited, pp. 265 (quoted in the preceding note), 283: "Bla carbat aenach .i. Slan donti beires in carbat isin naenach" ("an assembly is an exemption for chariots, that is, he is exempt who brings the chariot into the assembly"), cf. also Fergus Kelly, *Early Irish Farming*, ed. cited, p. 153.

[33] Fergus Kelly: *Audacht Moriann,* Dublin 1976, pp. 9, 10, 11, xiv (for the date); reference to the racing of horses is found in only one of the two recensions of the text, compare Maxim Fomin: *Instructions for Kings. Secular and Clerical Images of Kingship in Early Ireland and Ancient India,* Heidelberg 2013, pp. 120, 121, 122. In a *dindshenchas* text a legendary king is praised as a 'rider ('graiffnech') over Femen-mag' (Edward Gwynn: *Metrical Dindshenchas*, vol. iii, ed. cited, pp. 203, 202); the adjective *graiffnech* 'fond of horse-racing' is used as a noun here.

[34] Compare for further background N.B Aitchison: *Armagh*, ed. cited, pp. 63-66, D,A, Binchy 'The Fair', ed. cited, pp. 115-127, Catherine Swift: '*Óenach Tailten*', ed. cited,, and Máire MacNeill: *The Festival*, ed. cited, pp. 311-338, and cf. footnote 12.

[35] R.I. Best & M.A. O'Brien: *The Book of Leinster, formerly Lebar na Núachongbála*, vol. v, Dublin 1967, p. 1204: "Agtair cluicheda ⁊ ferthair graifni ind Oenaig".

[36] Kuno Meyer: *Betha Colmáin maic Lúacháin. Life of Colmán son of Lúachan,* Dublin & London 1911, pp. 85, 87.

[37] Máire MacNeill: *The Festival*, ed. cited, p. 328.

by Maelsechlainn in 1066, for the first time after an interval of seventy-nine years", does not mention horse-racing.[38]

Horse-racing appears to have been a constituent part of the ideal image of assemblies of the legendary Irish past, a literary motif and a cultural emblem of this social space. The length of another such assembly, the Feast of Tara or *Feis Temra*, is explicitly characterised in a text from the Ulster Cycle in terms of the duration of its horse-races: "the fair-races were run by them for a fortnight and a month" ("cor cuiread graifne in aenaich leo co cend caecaisi ar mis").[39] Note the collocation *graifne in óenaich* "the races of the fair, fair-races" here and in the stories about Diarmait and Colmán respectively quoted earlier. Racing at a further, fourth assembly, the *óenach* of Crúachain in the province of Connacht, is mentioned in passing, and as a matter of course, in another tale from the Ulster Cycle, *Fled Bricrend* or 'The Feast of Bricriu', when its three heroes Cú Chulainn, Conall Cernach, and Lócgaire Búadach, travel through the province: "They travel on, after running races at the assembly of Crúachain, and Cú Chulainn won the victory of the assembly three times" ("Lotar iarom rompa iar cor graphand doib i n-óenach na Cruachna ocus ruc Cuchulainn buaid ind óenaig fo thri").[40] Three victories are specified here, and the special heroic status of Cú Chulainn requires that he wins all races possible, as in all other competitions in this tale, and we can therefore posit three races, as in the story about Colmán and the three races run by the angels for him and his monks. Here, however, we encounter a problem of logistics, since the preferred means of transport for the heroes of the Ulster Cycle is the chariot harnessed to a team of two horses.[41] It remains unclear whether the race at Crúachain is a horse-race or a chariot-race, and I think that the authors' realization of the importance of chariots in the Ulster Cycle motivated the ambiguities in the descriptions of Macha's race quoted at the beginning of this paper. Medieval legal texts stress the importance and social status of the riding horse, and implicitly of riding as a normal way of travelling: "Throughout the written sources, the horse is associated in particular with men of high rank, and much stress is laid on their possession of ornate riding equipment."[42] David Stifter has suggested that up to some time perhaps in the ninth century "the chariot is a high-status, prestige vehicle for transport purposes" and that it then "came out of use and became an object of the collective memory of the Irish."[43]

[38] Edward Gwynn: *Metrical Dindshenchas*, vol. iv, ed. cited, pp. 413, 146-163. Ruaidrí Ó Conchobair held the fair of Tailtiu in 1168, as "an artifical revival" (D.A. Binchy: *The Fair*, ed. cited, p. 126), and the *Annals of the Four Masters* mention for this occasion "a ngraifne agus a marcsluagh" (probably "their horsemen and their soldiers"), cf. Máire MacNeill: *The Festival*, ed. cited, p. 335.

[39] Joseph O'Neill: *Cath Boinde,* in: *Ériu* 2 (1905), pp. 179, 178.

[40] George Henderson: *Fled Bricrend*, ed. cited, p. 84, cf. also pp. 190-191.

[41] Compare, for example, J.P. Mallory: *The world of Cú Chulainn: the archaeology of* Taín Bó Cúailnge, in: *Aspects of the Táin,* ed. by J.P. Mallory, Belfast 1992, pp. 147-151, and George Henderson: *Fled Bricrend*, ed. cited, pp. 54-65, for an elaborate description of the three heroes approaching Crúachain in chariots.

[42] Fergus Kelly: *Early Irish Farming*, ed. cited, p. 89

[43] David Stifter: *The Old Irish chariot and its technology,* in: *Kelten am Rhein. Akten des dreizehnten internationalen Keltologiekongresses. Zweiter Teil. Philologie. Sprachen und Literaturen,* ed. by Stefan Zimmer, Mainz 2009, pp. 279, 282. The *Annals of Ulster* note that in

Three races and three available prizes of the assembly – as in the case of the race at Crúachain in *Fled Bricrend* – are also mentioned in an eleventh-century poem preserved in the Book of Leinster about another character of the legendary Irish past, Finn mac Cumaill – the main character of the so-called Finn Cycle located in the third century A.D.[44] The setting is an assembly by Lough Gur in county Limerick.[45] The relevant quatrains read:

> (It was) Oenach Clochair that Find greatened, / And the champions of Ireland on every hilltop, / Munstermen from the plain greatened it, / And Fiachu son of Eogan. //
> The champions' horses ['eich na fían'] were brought, it is known, / And the Munstermen's horses ['eich Mumnech'], into the great contest. / They ran three clear races ['tri graffne'] /
> On the green ['for faichthe'] of Mairid's son. //
> A black horse ['Ech dub'] belonging to Díl son of Two-Raids / Was in every game ['cluchi'] that he played. / Unto the rock over Loch Gair / He won the three prizes of the meeting ['trí lanbuada ind oenaig'].[46]

In this passage there is no reference to chariots, but to horses alone, and the winning horse is black. More importantly, however, the stanzas show that horse-racing was emblematic for fairs as a social space, arguably with three races on the green as conventional, and conventionalised, constituent elements.

The Irish adaptation of Statius' *Thebaid*, *Togail na Tebe* 'The Destruction of Thebes', mentions three races ('tri graifni') as part of the funeral games for Archemorus. The funeral games are significantly called "a fair in honour of that boy" ("aenaich [acc.] in n-onoir in mic sin"). These three races reflect Statius' description of seven squadrons which circle the pyre of Archemorus three times.[47]

There is a road back here from the Irish version of Statius to horse-racing at assemblies as a real social space in medieval Irish. *Cormac's Glossary* – or *Sanas*

811 the "fair of Tailtiu was prevented from being held on Saturday under the aegis of Aed son of Niall, neither horse nor chariot ["ech na carpat"] arriving there" (Séan Mac Airt & Gearóid Mac Niocaill: *The Annals of Ulster (to A.D. 1131),* Dublin 1983, pp. 266, 267.

[44] For a survey cf. Joseph Falaky Nagy: *Fiannaíocht,* in: *Celtic Culture. Histroical Encyclopedia,* ed. by John T. Koch, Santa Barbara, Denver, Oxford 2006.

[45] Cf. Máire MacNeill: *The Festival*, ed. cited, p. 50.

[46] Whitley Stokes: *Find and the Phantoms,* in: *Revue Celtique* 7 (1886), pp. 291, 290.

[47] George Calder: *Togail na Tebe. The Thebaid of Statius,* Cambridge 1922, pp. 144, 145, and Statius: *Thebaid, Books 1-7,* ed. & transl. by D.R. Shackleton baily, Cambridge Mass. & London 2003, pp. 342, 343. In the races conducted afterwards in honour of Arsemaris / Archemorus chariots are used; for a discussion cf. David Vessey: *Statius and the Thebaid,* Cambridge 1973, pp. 211-218. Horse-races are also conducted at the funeral of Achall by the heroes of Ulster, cf. Edward Gwynn: *The Metrical Dindshenchas*, vol. i, Dublin 1903, repr. Dublin 1991, pp. 47, 46: "The nobles of Ulster came / round Conchobar of the champions; / they held races ['graffaind'] bright and pure / for Achall over against Temair." Cf. also the tradition about the establishment by Lug of games in honour of his foster-mother Tailte mentioned in footnote 12.

Chormaic, an early, in origin perhaps tenth-century glossary[48] – has an article dealing with various kinds of roads, which *inter alia* mentions three times at which roads are cleaned, one of them being the "time of horse-racing" ("aimser echrúathair").[49] Another sentence then states the reasons for cleaning, namely "that they [the roads] may not soil chariots going on a [coshering or guesting] and that they may not soil steeds going to an assembly ["arná éilnet echrada oc techt do óenuch"]."[50] Binchy suggests that here "*[ó]enach* [assembly] obviously corresponds to *echrúathar* [horse-racing] in the former sentence, for horse-racing was one of the most important features of an *óenach*."[51] Medieval Irish legal tracts provide some further factual information, regarding terms for race-horses and their special legal status at a time when races are due. The tract *Bretha im Fhuillemu Gell* 'Judgements concerning Pledge-Interests', which "deals with the complex regulations on the payment of interest for articles belonging to various ranks and professions",[52] implies that special conditions obtain for a race-horse, *ech aige* (lit. 'a horse of impelling/racing'), when the festival of Lugnasad or a meeting of the territory are about to take place.[53] In *Cormac's Glossary* the etymological derivation – by meaning and sound – of the word *mag* 'plain' as 'greater its impelling/racing' ('mó a aighe') is associated with and explained by 'its racing of horses' ('a graifne ech'),[54] thus establishing a conceptual chain *mag* 'plain' – *aige* 'impelling, racing' – *graifne ech* 'horse-racing'. The same glossary explains the word *óenach* 'assembly' with 'driving/ racing of horses' ('áine ech'),[55] and thus creates a further important conceptual chain between assemblies and horse-racing.

The collocation *ech aige* is also used in a poetic comparison 'swifter than a racehorse' ('luaithe ech aighe'), and the accompanying explanation links the swiftness of the horse to its being driven, or perhaps raced, "at the fair in the middle month of Summer": "int ech innṡaighther isin aenach a mí medhonach int sámraid."[56] Another term for a (winning) race-horse is *ech búada* ('a prize horse', lit. 'a horse of victory'), and a legal tract on livestock not to be distrained states: "A prize horse ['ech búada'], while it is racing it does not even bear liability for its own offence", indicating that it cannot be distrained in this situation.[57] The collocation *ech búada* is found used

[48] For some background to this text cf. Paul Russell: *Sanas Chormaic*, in: *Celtic Culture. A Historical Encyclopedia,* ed. by John T. Koch, Santa Barbara, Denver, Oxford 2006.

[49] D.A. Binchy: *Aimser chue*, in: *Féil.sgríbhinn Eóin Mhic Néill. Essays and Studies Presented to ProfessorEoin MacNeill,* ed. by John Ryan, Dublin 1940, p. 19.

[50] Ibid. p. 20.

[51] Ibid. p. 20.

[52] Kelly: *Guide*, p. 166, cf. also Liam Breatnach: *Companion*, ed. cited, p. 296.

[53] A.D. Binchy: *Corpus*, ed. cited, p. 471, and Kelly, *Early Irish Farming*, ed. cited, p. 99.

[54] Kuno Meyer: *Sanas Cormaic,* Halle & Dublin 1912 (= *Anecdota from Irish Manuscripts,* ed. by O.J. Bergin, R.I Best, Kuno Meyer, J.G. O'Keeffe, vol, iv), p. 78.

[55] Kuno Meyer: *Sanas Cormaic*,ed. cited, p. 86, *aige* and *áine* are different forms of the verbal noun of the verb *aigid* 'drives, impels'.

[56] Liam Breatnach: *The Caldron of Poesy,* in: *Ériu* 32 (1981), pp. 66, 67.

[57] Fergus Kelly: *Early Irish Farming*, ed. cited, pp. 523, 522, and cf. p. 528: "A prize horse cannot be distrained while it is racing [...]. Presumably this refers to the day – or period of days – when the horse is due to race".

metaphorically in a religious poem, in order to denote a man who strives after God's kingdom, and he is also compared to a chariot under a victorious king:

> He is a race-horse over a smooth plain ['ech buada tar mag réid'], / the man that strives after the kingdom of great God; / he is a chariot that is seen / under a king that bears off victories [...][58]

The reference to the victorious rider of a chariot may be taken as an indication that chariot-races were conducted in medieval Ireland. Another, similar collocation occurs in an Old Irish legal text, also in an apparently metaphorical usage: "the chariot which gains the victory at an assembly" ("carbad beireas buaidh aonaigh").[59] Here a link between chariot-races and assemblies appears to be established – but note that both passages speak *metaphorically* about chariot-races.

When in conclusion we survey the scattered evidence for equestrian sports and horse-racing in medieval Ireland, and the different contexts of the references, we encounter a methodological problem for 'Realienkunde' and cultural studies. Many of the references occur in texts about the legendary Irish past, of the Ulster Cycle or of the Finn Cycle, or in other retrospective accounts, such as the *dindshenchas* texts. In the cultural memory of the medieval Irish preserved there, the social space of horse-racing (*grafand*) was the assembly or fair (*óenach*) – itself very much an idealized social space of the past. These texts may of course project elements of their own contemporary social experience into the past. References in legal texts indicate that horse-racing had a place in medieval life ('Sitz im Leben') and that it was associated with fairs and assemblies. Important evidence is provided by *Cormac's Glossary* and its conceptual association of an *óenach* with the driving or racing of horses. The emblematic importance of horse-racing is reflected in a poem assessing the traumatic experience of the Flight of the Earls in 1607, which begins with "To-night Ireland is desolate, the banishment of her true race hath left wet-cheeked her men and her fair women",[60] and then describes Ireland as bereft of central cultural and social assets, which would include the racing of horses:

> No gaming, no banqueting, no pastime; no commerce or horse-racing ['gan ghraifne greagh', lit. 'without racing of horses'] or deeds of daring. // No reciting of poems of praise, no relating of stories at sleeping time, no interest in consulting books, no hearkening to genealogies.[61]

[58] Whitley Stokes: *Félire Óengusso Céli Dé, The Martyrology of Oengus the Culdee,* London 1905, pp. 156, 157.

[59] Fergus Kelly: *Early Irish Farming*, ed. cited, p. 99.

[60] Eleanor Knott: *The Flight of the Early,* in: *Ériu* 8 (1916), p. 193, for the author cf. Caball, *Poets*, p. 177; for the Flight of the Earls and the reaction of the Irish poets cf., for example, Joep Leerssen: *Mere Irish and Fíor-Ghael. Studies in the Idea of Irish Nationality, its Development and Literary Expression prior to the Nineteenth Century,* Cork 1996, pp. 190-194.

[61] Eleanor Knott: *The Flight*, ed. cited pp. 194, 192.

A similar image is employed in a poem attributed to Lochlainn Ó Dálaigh which reflects the Jacobean plantations of Ulster in the aftermath of the Flight of the Earls; it was composed about 1610 and states that "they (the strangers) practise not to gather together their horses for the race ["gan dál graifni"]."[62] Fear Flatha Ó Gnímh complains in much the same vein in his poem beginning "Woe, how the Irish are", written shortly after the launch of the Ulster plantation in 1609-10:

> The men of Fódla [= Ireland] have reason for dejection, / cruel oxen ploughed, / in the place of the races of their nimble horses ['i n-áit graifne a ngroigheadh seang'], / every green within the country of Ireland.[63]

And finally, in a "verse farewell to Ireland and her people" of *c.* 1615 Brian Mac Giolla Phádraig expresses sorrow at leaving "the racing of our sharp-hoofed stud of horses" ["graifne ar ngreagh n-inginghéar"].[64] Horse-racing thus emerges as a powerful cultural and social emblem in the medieval and early modern Irish system of thought, and as a marker of political and cultural change, even though we cannot now capture all details of this form of equestrian sports.[65]

Bibliography

Aitchison, N.B.: *Armagh and the Royal Centres in Early Medieval Ireland. Monuments, Cosmology, and the Past.* Woodbridge & Rochester 1994.

Best, R.I. & M.A. O'Brien: *The Book of Leinster, formerly Lebar na Núachongbála*, vol. ii. Dublin 1956.

Best, R.I. & M.A. O'Brien: *The Book of Leinster, formerly Lebar na Núachongbála*, vol. v. Dublin 1967.

Binchy, D.A.: *Aimser chue*, in: *Féil-sgríbhinn Eóin Mhic Néill. Essays and Studies Presented to Professor Eoin MacNeill*, ed. by John Ryan. Dublin 1940, pp. 18-22.

Binchy, D.A.: *Corpus Iuris Hibernici*, 6 vols. Dublin 1978.

Binchy, D.A.: Mellbretha, in: *Celtica* 8 (1968), pp. 144-154.

Binchy, D.A.: *The Fair of Tailtiu and the Feast of Tara*, in: *Ériu* 18 (1958), pp. 113-138.

Breatnach, Liam: *'The Caldron of Poesy'*, in: *Ériu* 32 (1981), pp. 45-93.

Breatnach, Liam: *A Companion to the Corpus Iuris Hibernici.* Dublin 2005.

Byrne, Francis John: *Irish Kings and High-Kings.* London 1973.

[62] Standish Hayes O'Grady: *Catalogue of Irish Manuscripts in the British Library*, reprint Dublin 1992, pp. 375, 374; for the date and some background cf. Marc Caball: *Poets and politics, Reaction and Continuity in Irish Poetry, 1558-1625*, Cork 1998, p. 97.

[63] Ó Rathile: *Measgra Dánta II*, p. 145; for the date and some background cf. Marc Caball: *Poets*, ed. cited, p. 106.

[64] Thomas Ó Rathile: *Measgra Dánta II*, reprint Cork 1927, p. 138, and Cuthbert Mhág Craith: *Brian Mac Giolla Phádraig*, in: *Celtica* 4 (1958), p. 116; for the date and some background cf. Marc Caball: *Poets*, ed. cited, p. 130. I wish to thank Meidhbhín Ní Úrdail for her help with the translation of the quatrain.

[65] David Stifter: *The Old Irish chariot*, ed. cited, p. 280-281, similarly reminds us that "it was not necessary for the authors to refer explicitly to charioteering or to elaborate on specific features of the complex, but the audience was able to supply all necessary connotations".

Caball, Marc: *Poets and Politics, Reaction and Continuity in Irish Poetry, 1558-1625*. Cork 1998.
Calder, George: *Togail na Tebe. The Thebaid of Statius*. Cambridge 1922.
Carey, John: *Voyage literature*, in: *Celtic Culture. A Historical Encyclopedia*, ed. by John T. Koch. Santa Barbara, Denver, Oxford 2006, pp. 1743-1746.
Davies, Sioned & Nerys Ann Jones: *The Horse in Celtic Culture. Medieval Welsh Perspectives*. Cardiff 1997.
Dillon, Myles: *The Taboos of the Kings of Ireland*. Dublin 1951 (= *Proceedings of the Royal Irish Academy*, 54 C 1).
Doherty, Charles: *Exchange and trade in early medieval Ireland*, in: *Journal of the Royal Society of Antiquaries of Ireland* 110 (1980), pp. 67-89.
Fomin, Maxim: *Instructions for Kings. Secular and Clerical Images of Kingship in Early Ireland and Ancient India*. Heidelberg 2013.
Gwynn, Edward: *The Metrical Dindshenchas*, vol. i. Dublin 1903, repr. Dublin 1991.
Gwynn, Edward: *The Metrical Dindshenchas*, vol. iii. Dublin 1913, repr. Dublin 1991.
Gwynn, Edward: *The Metrical Dindshenchas*, vol. iv. Dublin 1924, repr. Dublin 1991.
Gwynn, Lucius: *Cináed úa hArtacáin's poem on Brugh na Bóinne*, in: *Ériu* 7 (1914), pp. 210-238.
Hardy, Philip Dixon: *Legends, Tales, and Stories of Ireland*. Dublin 1837.
Henderson, George: *Fled Bricrend. The Feast of Bricriu*. London 1899.
Hillers, Barbara: *The heroes of the Ulster Cycle*, in: *Ulidia. Proceedings of the First International Conference on the Ulster Cycle of Tales*, ed. by J.P. Mallory & Gerard Stockman. Belfast 1994, pp. 99-106.
Hull, Vernam: *Noínden Ulad: The debility of the Ulidians*, in: *Celtica* 8 (1968), pp. 1-42.
Johnston, Elva: *Literacy and Identity in Early Medieval Ireland*. Woodbridge 2013.
Kelly, Fergus: *A Guide to Early Irish Law*. Dublin 1988
Kelly, Fergus: *Audacht Morainn*. Dublin 1976.
Kelly, Fergus: *Early Irish Farming*. Dublin 1997.
Kelly, Patricia: Téchta eich: *the proper qualities of a horse*, in: *Saltair Saíochta, Sanasaíochta agus Seanchais. A Festschrift for Gearóid Mac Eoin*, ed. by Dónall Ó Baoill, Donncha Ó hAodha, Nollaig Ó Muraíle. Dublin & Portland 2013, *pp.* 83-87.
Knott, Eleanor: *The Flight of the Earls*, in: *Ériu* 8 (1916), pp. 191-194.
Kuhn, Hans: *Das alte Island*. Köln 1978.
Leerssen, Joep: *Mere Irish and Fíor-Ghael. Studies in the Idea of Irish Nationality, its Development and Literary Expression prior to the Nineteenth Century*. Cork 1996.
Mac Airt, Seán & Gearóid Mac Niocaill: *The Annals of Ulster (to A.D. 1131)*. Dublin 1983.
Mac Mathúna, Séamus: *Immram Brain. Bran's Journey to the Land of the Women*. Tübingen 1985.
Macalister, R.A. Stewart: *Lebor Gabála Érenn. The Book of the Taking of Ireland*, part iv. Dublin 1941 (= Irish Texts Society, XLI).
MacNeill, Máire: *The Festival of Lughnasa*. Dublin 1982.
Mallory, J.P.: *The world of Cú Chulainn: the archaeology of* Taín Bó Cúailnge, in: *Aspects of the Táin*, ed. by J.P. Mallory. Belfast 1992, pp. 103-159.
McCormick, Finbar: *The horse in Early Ireland*, in: *Anthropozoologica* 42.1 (2007), pp. 85-194.
Meyer, Kuno: *Betha Colmáin maic Lúacháin. Life of Colmán son of Lúachan*. Dublin & London 1911.
Meyer, Kuno: *Sanas Cormaic*. Halle & Dublin 1912 (= *Anecdota from Irish Manuscripts*, ed. by O.J. Bergin, R.I. Best, Kuno Meyer, J.G. O'Keeffe, vol. iv).
Mhág Craith, Cuthbert: *Brian Mac Giolla Phádraig*, in: *Celtica* 4 (1958), pp. 103-204.
Nagy, Joseph Falaky: *Fiannaíocht*, in: *Celtic Culture. A Historical Encyclopedia*, ed. by John T. Koch. Santa Barbara, Denver, Oxford 2006, pp. 744-746.

Ní Chatháin, Próinséas, 'Traces of the cult of the horse in Early Irish sources', *The Journal of Indo-European Studies* 19 (1991), pp. 123-131.

Ó Cuív, Brian: *Fragments of Irish medieval treatises on horses*, in: *Celtica* 17 (1985), pp. 113-122.

Ó Cuív, Brian: *Fragments of two mediaeval treatises on horses*, in: *Celtica* 2.1 (1952), pp. 30-63.

Ó Muraíle, Nollaig: *Dinnshenchas*, in: *Medieval Ireland. An Encyclopedia*, ed. by Seán Duffy. New York & London 2005, pp. 132-133.

Ó Murchadha, Diarmuid: *Carman, site of Óenach Carmain: a proposed location*, in: *Éigse* 33 (2002), pp. 57-70.

Ó Rathile, Tomás: *Measgra Dánta II*. Reprint Cork 1927.

O'Grady, Standish Hayes: *Catalogue of Irish Manuscripts in the British Library*. Reprint Dublin 1992.

O'Neill, Joseph: *Cath Boinde*, in: *Ériu* 2 (1905), pp. 173-185.

Oskamp, H.P.A.: *The Voyage of Máel Dúin. A Study in Early Irish Voyage Literature followed by an Edition of Immram curaig Máele Dúin from the Yellow Book of Lecan in Trinity College, Dublin*. Groningen 1970.

Rohrbach, Lena: *(Nur) Ein Spiel? Spieltheoretische Überlegungen zu den Pferdekämpfen der Sagaliteratur*, in: *Sport und Spiel bei den Germanen. Nordeuropa von der römischen Kaiserzeit bis zum Mittelalter*, ed. by Matthias Teichert. Berlin & Boston 2014, pp. 467-480.

Russell, Paul: Sanas Chormaic, in: *Celtic Culture. A Historical Encyclopedia*, ed. by John T. Koch. Santa Barbara, Denver, Oxford 2006.

Sayers, William,: 'Games, Sport, and Para-Military Exercise in Early Ireland', in: *Aethlon: The Journal of Sport Literature* 10.1 (1992), pp. 105-123.

Sayers, William: *Conventional Descriptions of the Horse in the Ulster Cycle*, in: *Études Celtiques* 30 (1994), pp. 233-249.

Smyth, Alfred P.: *Celtic Leinster. Towards a Historical Geography of Early Irish Civilization A.D. 500-1200*. Blackrock 1982.

Solheim, Svale: *Horse-Fight and Horse-Race in Norse Tradition*. Oslo 1956.

Statius: *Thebaid, Books 1-7*, ed. & transl. by D.R. Shackleton Baily. Cambridge Mass. & London 2003.

Stifter, David: *The Old Irish chariot and its technology*, in: *Kelten am Rhein. Akten des dreizehnten Internationalen Keltologiekongresses. Zweiter Teil. Philologie. Sprachen und Literaturen*, ed. by Stefan Zimmer. Mainz 2009, *pp.* 279-289.

Stokes, Whitley: *Félire Óengusso Céli Dé. The Martyrology of Oengus the Culdee*. London 1905.

Stokes, Whitley: *Find and the Phantoms*, in: *Revue Celtique* 7 (1886), pp. 289-307.

Stokes, Whitley: *The prose tales in the Rennes dindshenchas [I]*, in: *Revue Celtique* 15 (1894), pp. 272-336.

Stokes, Whitley: *The Voyage of Mael Duin [I]*, in: *Revue Celtique* 9 (1888), pp. 447-495.

Swift, Catherine: Óenach Tailten, *the Blackwater Valley and the Uí Néill kings of Tara*, in: *Seanchas. Studies in Early and Medieval Irish Archaeology, History and Literature in Honour of Francis J. Byrne*, ed. by Alfred P. Smyth. Dublin & Portland 2000, pp. 109-120.

Thurneysen, Rudolf: *Die irische Helden- und Königsage bis zum siebzehnten Jahrhundert*. Halle 1921.

Thurneysen, Rudolf: *Tochmarc Cruinn ocus Macha*, in: *Zeitschrift für celtische Philologie* 12 (1918), pp. 251-254.

Vessey, David: *Statius and the Thebaid*. Cambridge 1973.

Windisch, Ernst: *Irische Texte mit Wörterbuch*. Leipzig 1880.

Marlowe's Horses: Vehicles of Desire and Change

Roy Eriksen
University of Agder, Kristiansand, Norway

> Holla, ye pampered jades of Asia!
> What, can ye draw but twenty miles a day,
> And have so proud a chariot at your heels,
> And such a coachman as great Tamburlaine, / [...]
> *2 Tamburlaine the Great*, 4.3.1-4[1]

> *O lente, lente, currite noctis equi!*
> *Doctor Faustus* (B),[2] 5.2.147

The verses above are the most frequently quoted examples of Marlowe's reference to horses. But what do they really tell us about his use of equine imagery? Do they merely reflect early modern English symbolism of horses in general, or can they tell us something more specific about Marlowe's engagement with the rich connotations aggregated around images of the horse in literary, philosophical and religious discourse from Antiquity to the Early Modern period? His activation of such nexuses, narratives involving mythical figures like Phaeton, Hippolytus, and King Aegeus, is sufficiently rich in implication, I propose, to suggest a particular personal interest, particularly evident in his references to the myth of Phaeton. First, however, I wish to consider how he relates to the more common early modern representations of horses, before turning to the role in his more complex personalised expressions of *libido transgrediendi*, his desire to transgress.

It may be surprising that Leon Battista Alberti, the author of innovative theoretical treatises in various fields, should have written a treatise on such a mundane topic like horses and horse breeding, *De aequo animante* (1443), but to modern readers it is easy to forget that horses were important members and living "implements" in early modern society. Horses were considered noble animals on the basis of their valuable role in war

[1] I quote the play from Christopher Marlowe: *The Complete Plays*, ed. J. B. Steane, Harmondsworth 1969.

[2] Unless otherwise specified, I quote the play from *Doctor Faustus. A- and B texts (1604, 1616)*, eds. David Bevington and Eric Rasmussen, The Revels Plays. Manchester 1993.

and peace, a gift of kings and token of their wealth and power. The humanist Alberti fully recognized this fundamental fact. In his dedication to the Duke of Ferrara he sees beyond aesthetics and seeks "scientific knowledge [...] in his definition of optimal typologies" (Franco Borsi, 1975: 25). Alberti explains:

> Mi venne in mente di riflettere più diligemente non sulla bellezza e sui lineamenti ma sulla natura e comportamento dei cavalli. M'interessava quali fossero i cavalli per tutti gli usi pubblici e private preparati per lo sforzo bellico insieme agli ornamenti della pace. [...] gli uomini moltissimo si servono dell'aiuto e dell'opera di questi animali, tanto che non penso si possa ottenere senza il loro sostegno né salute né dignità"[3]

Men could not, suggests Alberti, keep their health or dignity, without the assistance and support of horses. It is almost as if Alberti, who always had a practical end in mind, was writing a treatise on the dignity ("dignità") of the horse, projecting the highest moral qualities into the species. Of course, there is an additional moral and philosophical dimension to horses due to Plato's explanation of the soul and its struggle between reason and conscupiscence in terms of a chariot drawn by winged horses of noble and ignoble breed.[4] This figurative use of horses came to influence both Lucretius and Ovid and, as I will argue, decisively coined what gradually became Marlowe's personal myth, the Phäeton myth.

Belonging to a later century, but being an heir to the humanist culture that Alberti's work and example fostered, Marlowe has rightly been called "modern" in his approach to and reconfiguration of received ideas of that tradition. Of course, he too like his contemporaries refers to horses in several of his plays, as a common means of transport and a crucial resource in warfare, witnessed not least in his play abut the warrior king, *Tamburlaine the Great*, where in accordance with royal protocol, Tamburlaine promises Zenocrate that "A hundred Tartars shall attend on thee, / Mounted on steeds swifter than Pegasus" (1.2.93-94). Also, Mycetes took special pleasure in his rare "milk-white steeds" (1.1.77-78). However, more typical of our author is his transformation of well-established images for special effects and to his personal ends.

For rather than underscoring the dignity of horses, he reduces nobility –emperors and kings– to mere animals of traction. He pits nobility by birth against nobility by individual worth and personal virtue. Critics frequently underscore the cruelty exhibited by Tamburlaine, but often miss the point that Marlowe makes it clear that Tamburlaine's opponents are no less cruel and merciless than their conqueror, as when Bajazeth prophesizes that

> Ambitious pride shall make thee fall as low,
> For treading on the back of Bajazeth
> That should be horsed on four mighty kings (4.2.76-78).

[3] Leon Battista Alberti: *De aequo animente*, in: *Inedita* etc. Ed. by G. Mancini, Firenze 1890, p. 238.

[4] Plato: *Euthphro, Apology, Crito, Phaedo, Phaedrus*, trans H.N. Fowler, Cambridge and London 1914; 1953, 246.25A:470-71.

The feeble and effeminate Persian ruler Mycetes constitutes no exception, who longs to see Theridamas return from battle "That I may view these milk-white steeds of mine / All loaden with the heads of men" (1.1.77-78). These are the same horses that are "foaming gall with rage and high disdain" (63) some verses earlier in the scene. Marlowe seems to turn the Persian king's costly "milk-white" horses into extensions of the ineffectual character's nature and feeble performance. This goes for his characterization of Tamburlaine, too, "the great Tartarian" (3.3.171) who wishes:

> To march upon the slaughtered foe,
> Trampling their bowels with our horses' hoofs,
> Brave horses bred on the white Tartarian hills. (3.3.149-51)

Bajazeth behaves no surprise in the very same way when wishes the forces, and horses, of darkness to strike Tamburlaine with terror:

> Let ugly darkness with her rusty coach, / [...]
> Smother the earth with never-ending mists,
> And let her horses from their nostrils breathe
> Rebellious winds and dreadful thunder-claps
> That in this terror Tamburlaine may live, / [...] (5.1.294; 296-99)

And we note that here as later in the endings of both *Doctor Faustus* and *Hero and Leander*, the horses of the night that haunt both Faustus and Hero.[5]

Cruelty and the use of horses to execute the violence seem to be common to the rulers in the Tamburlaine plays, but the unflinching and absolute resolve to perform the acts of torture and death exceeds that of his opponents, and makes even the horses accustomed to bloody battles react and refrain from carrying them. Zenocrate laments the death of the guiltless Babylonian virgins and describes how the inherent nobility of horses and their reverence for beauty hold them back:

> For every fell and stout Tartarian steed,
> That stamp'd on others with their thundering hoofs,
> When all their riders charg'd their spears,
> Began to check the ground and rein themselves,
> Gazing upon he beauty of their looks. (5.2.269-73)

The horse reveals an inherent nobility of mind of the kind Alberti describes, a quality that enables them to restrain themselves and that even surpasses that of their murderous riders. Tamburlaine, too, lacks not only that capability when resolutely exercising his absolute will, he also seems to possess a nature-given and Lucretian will to pursue

[5] At the end of the poem, in which he also openly refers to the Phaeton myth, Marlowe brings in Apollo and "day's bright-bearing car" (I.330) to mock "ugly Night/Till she, o'ercome with anguish, shame, and rage, / Dang'd down to hell her loathsome carriage." (II.332-34). I quote *Hero and Leander* from Christopher Marlowe: *The Poems,* ed. Millar MaClure, London 1968, pp. 40-41.

"knowledge infinite" to achieve his goals, a theme that is more fully developed in *Doctor Faustus*.

The use of horse-imagery is continued and also prominently expanded in *2 Tamburlaine* as part of a strategy to humiliate and dehumanize his defeated opponents, while aggrandizing himself:

> Holla, ye pampered jades of Asia!
> What, can ye draw but twenty miles a day,
> And have so proud a chariot at your heels,
> And such a coachman as great Tamburlaine,
> But from Asphaltis, where I conquer'd you,
> To Byron here, where I honor you?
> *2 Tamburlaine*, 4.3.1-23

In fact in *2 Tamburlaine* systematically reduces the conquered kings to animals of traction, as when the Scythian's three vice-roys comment on the protesting prisoners: Techelles asks Tamburlaine to "Rein their lavish tongues" (*1 Tamburlaine*, 4.3.67), Theridamas suggests that Tamburlaine

> get some bits for these,
> To bridle their contemptuous cursing tongues
> That like unruly, never-broken jades
> And pass their fixed bounds exceedingly. (4.3.43-47)

Usumcasane follows suit and continues to dehumanize his master's victims, urging him "to restrain / These coltish coach-horse tongues from blasphemy." (52-3)

Marlowe does not content himself to use horses in a strategy to demean Tamburlaine's enemies, he also seizes on the image of the charioteer to add a significant mythological dimension to his protagonist's character and actions, when he firmly associates himself with the sun god Apollo. He refers to "the horse that guide the golden eye of heaven" (4.3. 1; 7), and states that he will "ride in golden armor like the sun, […]"(4.3.114-15). Such high-blown language fires Amyras, who Phaëton-like asks his father:

> Let me have coach, my lord, that I may ride
> And thus be drawn with these two idle kings. (4.3.27-28)

Apollo who had thoughtlessly promised his son to grant him whatever he wished for, kept his promise but warned Phaëton about his "non tuta […] voluntas" ("unsafe wish"). Tamburlaine more providently answers his son: "Thy youth forbids such ease my kingly boy" (4.3.29), revealing how closely the dramatist follows Ovid's *Metamorphoses*, II. 54-55, at this point:

Magna petis, Phaëthon, et quae nec viribus istis
Munera conveniant nec tam puerilibus annis.
(Thou askest too a great boon, Phaëthon, and one
which does not befit thy strength and those boyish years.)

Tamburlaine at this point in the action denies Amyras a chariot, but the scene prepares us for the transition of imperial power to Amyras in the death-bed speech, in which he more directly compares himself to Apollo (Phyteus) and his son to Phaëton:

So, reign my son; scourge and control those slaves,
Guiding thy chariot with thy father's hand.
As precious is the charge thou undertak'st
As that which Clymene's brain-sick son did guide,
When wandering Phoebe's ivory cheeks were scorched,
And all the earth, like Aetna, breathing fire.
Be warned by him; then learn with aweful eye
To sway a throne as dangerous as his;
For if thy body thrive not full of thoughts
As pure and fiery as Phyteus' beams,
The nature of these proud rebellious jades
Will take occasion by the slendrest hair
And draw thee piecemeal, like Hyppolitus,
Through rocks more steep and sharpe than Caspian cliffs.
The nature of thy chariot will not bear
A guide of baser temper than myself,
More than heaven's coach the pride of Phaeton.
Farewell, my boys! My dearest friends, farewell!
(*Tamburlaine, Part Two*, V, iii, 228–45)

Here Marlowe combines the metaphors of men as horses, "these proud rebellious jades" (238) and the figure of Phaëton, traditionally emblematic of youthful pride.[6] The dangers involved in the "precious" charge Tamburlaine bestows on Amyras would have been clear to many of the play's audiences and readers, who had read about Phäeton in one of the fashionable emblems collections inspired by Andrea Alciati, like Jeffrey Whitney's *A Choice of Emblems* (1586). Death by fire awaits Tamburlaine's young heir.

The equine metaphors deployed by Marlowe in *Tamburlaine* indicate the potential range and complexity of meanings attributed to horses and myths in which the animal is vital. The metaphors also seem to conglomerate into personal myth in his imagination, when they surface and are combined in *Doctor Faustus*, the play that in particular dramatizes the question of the freedom of will. This emphasis is different from that

[6] Andreae Alciati: *Emblematum liber* (1531), Emblem LVI, p. 264, "In temerarios:" II. PHAETON filius Solis & Clymenes Nymphae, iuuenis maximè temerarius, qui arroganter ac importunè a patre efflagitans, vt currum & equos, quibus Sol vehitur, die vno gubernare permitteretur: impetrauit, sed oneri difficilissimo impar."

found in Marlowe's two-part play which in particular underscores the ruler's absoluteness of will and unflinching resolve to carry out precisely what he had threatened to do, and without mercy. There is, however, in *Tamburlaine, Part One*, an indication that that resolve is rooted in a more complex system of thought according to which the aspiring force of the will is inborn and parallel to the forces at work in nature itself. Harrry Levin said that "Marlowe could have brought the authority of Lucretius [...] to the support of his hero's restlessness", but he – not unreasonably – reminded his readers that "Giordano Bruno was in England during his lifetime."[7] However, Lucretius was a major influence on Bruno and his London dialogues, as the Nolan openly admits when he quotes "l'epicureo poeta" at various points. In fact, one of the passages that best show this dual influence on Marlowe is the speech from which Levin quotes a only a part (21-29):

> The thirst of reign and sweetness of a crown
> That caus'd the eldest son of heavenly Ops,
> To thrust his father from his chair
> And place himself in the emperial heaven,
> Mov'd me to manage arms against thy state.
> What better precedent than mighty Jove?
> Nature that fram'd us of four elements
> Warring within our breasts for regiment,
> Doth teach us all to have aspiring minds.
> Our souls, whose faculties can comprehend
> The wondrous architecture of the world;
> And measure every wandring planet's course,
> Still climbing after knowledge infinite,
> And always moving as the restless spheres,
> Wills us to wear ourselves and never rest,
> Until we reach the ripest fruit of all
> That perfect bliss and sole felicity,
> The sweet fruition of an earthly crown. (2.7.17-29)

Tamburlaine's speech with its emphasis on "element warring" and "restless spheres" reveals an awareness of Lucretius presentation of Epicurean philosophy and its sources in Plato's definition of the soul and its power in *Phaedrus* and also his cosmological interpretation of the Phaeton myth in *Timaeus*.[8] Marlowe absorbes the philosophical content in Lucretius, but here like elsewhere he also draws on Ovid's description of

[7] Harry Levin: *Christopher Marlowe: The Overreacher*, London 1961, 3rd ed. 1973, p. 56.

[8] Like Lucretius later (*De rerum natura*, 5. 396-419), Plato dismisses the legend and explains the message within the legend. Sara Myers points out that "Ovid's Phaeton episode at *Metamorphoses* 1.1-400, for example, incorporates many echoes of Lucretius' passage at *De Rerum Natura* 5.396-410 which is pointedly directed against such mythological accounts." in: *Ovid's Causes. Cosmogony and Aetiology in the Metapho,* Chicago 1994, p. 55.

Phäeton in *The Metamorphoses*, Book Two.[9] In its emphasis on the nature-given war of the elements within each human,[10] we remember Lucretius' presentation of the restlessness and force of nature that also prompts the freedom of the will. In fact, to underline the force of the will in *De rerum natura*, Lucretius systematically uses imagery from horse racing: horses yearning to burst free of the *carceres*[11] in the circus:

> ex infinito ne causam causa sequatur,
> Libera per terras unde haec avolsa voluntas,
> Unde est haec, inquam, fatis avolsa volutas,
> per quam progredimur quo ducit quemque voluptas
> Declinamus item motus nec tempore certo
> Ncc regione loci certa, sed ubi ipsa tulit mens?
> nam dubio procul his rebus sua cuique voluntas
> principium dat et hinc motus per membra rigantur.
> Nonne vides etiam patefactis tempore puncto
> Carceribus non posse tamen prorumpere equorum
> Vim cupidam tam de subito quam mens avet ipsa?
> Omnis enim ttum per corpus materiai
> Copia conciri debet, concita per artus
> Omnis ut stadium mentis conixa sequator;
> Ut videas initum motus a corde creari
> Ex animique volutate per totum corpus et artus. (252-271)

> [...] if cause forever follows,
> In infinite sequence, cause–where would we get
> This free will we have, wrested from fate,
> By which we go ahead, each one of us,
> Wherever our pleasures urge? Don't we also swerve
> At no fixed time and place, but as our purpose
> Directs us? There's no doubt each man's will
> Initiates action, and this prompting stirs
> Our limbs to movement.

9 K. Sara Myers points out that "Ovid's Phaeton episode at *Metamorphoses* I.1-400, for example, incorporates many echoes of Lucretius' passage at *De Rerum Natura* 5.396-410 which is pointedly directed against such mythological accounts."

10 Cf. Lucretius: *De rerum natura*, Book Five:

> With the elements
> Fighting their fierce and fraticidal wars,
> Can't you imagine there will be some day
> An ultimate truce? (5.380-83)

11 The particular metaphors used are "carceres", which are the cells or compartments used to control horses and chariots before the beginning of the race, and the verbs and verb forms "refrenavit", "refrenatur" and "flecti", and other implicit references to horseracing, cf. M.F. Smith's note in *Hermathena* 102 (1966), pp.76-77.

When the gates fly open,
No racehorse breaks as quickly as he wants to,
For the whole body of matter must be aroused,
Inspired to follow what the mind desires;
So, you can see, motion begins with will
Of heart and mind, from that will moves on
Through all the framework.

It is easy to understand that Lucretius' emphasis on the nature-given freedom of the will to aspire *ad infinitum*, and unbound by fate, would have inspired Marlowe, as it indeed had inspired Bruno in *De gli eroici furori* (London, 1585). Then, too, it is precisely "what the mind desires" and the quest for "knowledge infinite" that fire Faustus' mind, too, turning him into an overreacher. In fact, the two mythical overreachers Icarus and Phäeton, who both are rebellious sons whose actions have been aligned at least since Ovid, are alluded to in the Prologue and the Epilogue, respectively. The fall of Faustus is implicitly compared to that of Icarus in the Prologue:

Till swollen with cunning of a self-conceit,
His waxen wing did mount above his reach,
And melting heavens conspired his overthrow. (20-22)

The lines which bring to mind Whitney's well-known Icarus emblem (*in Astrologos*)[12] are perhaps indicative of Marlowe's response to the new medium of the emblem book. However, more relevant is that Marlowe activates the image of Faustus as a Phäeton-like charioteer and fool-hardy son of Apollo not only in the Epilogue, but also in the Second Chorus:

Learnèd Faustus
To find the secrets of astronomy
Graven inthe book of Jove's high firmament,
Dismount him up to scale Olympus' top,
Where, sitting in a chariot burning bright
Drawn by the strength of yokèd dragons' necks,
He views the clouds, the planets, and the stars,
The tropics, zones, and quarters of the sky,
From east to west his dragons swiftly glide
Within the concave compass of the pole, / […] (1-10)

Here, then, we find Faustus riding in a chariot, that true enough is not drawn by winged horses, but "yokèd dragons." At this stage he apparently manages quite well, not least by the help of Mephostophilis. His actions however are described in phrases that are parallel to those used by Ovid's Apollo when he informs his son about the dangers of

[12] Jeffrey Whitney: *A Choice of Emblems*, London 1586, p. 28.

driving his golden chariot across the heavens (II. 70-78; 128-32).[13] The allusive transformation of Apollo's horses into dragons adds an ominous aura to the tale.

Before turning to the last part of the play, it needs be pointed out that a comic version of the quest for secrets and forbidden knowledge focussed on horses surfaces in the scene with the Horse-Courser. He buys a horse from Faustus, but is sternly warned against riding the animal into the water, which he nevertheless stupidly does. The episode is a slight one, but it picks up the main theme of seeking forbidden knowledge. "O what a cozening doctor was this", exclaims the Horse-Courser,

> I riding my horse into the water, thinking some hidden mystery had been in the horse, I had nothing under me but a little straw and had much ado to escape drowning.
> (4.4.1-52)

The scene that fulfils the conventional role of a comic parallel action in this way anticipates Faustus' attempt to dissolve into water drops in the final soliloquy, where the treatment of this material is more sophisticated and serious. In the climactic midnight soliloqy "the Lucretius of the English language"[14] returns to what almost appears to have been somewhat of a personal myth.

Even though discussed by all major Marlowe scholars, the Lucretian subtext for the final soliloquy has received less attention than it deserves. In one of the most stimulating studies of Marlowe's oeuvre to date Harry Levin noted that

> If Marlowe learned the lyric mode from Ovid and the epic mode from Lucan, it may well have been Lucretius who schooled him in tragic discernment of the nature of things.[15]

Oddly, Levin does not see how his own insight into the dramatist's use of Lucretius in general or in particular in *Tamburlaine, Part One* (2.7.17-29), applies in the final soliloquy, too. The speech cited above does in fact serve as the subtext for Faustus' soliloquy, repeats in several steps the main elements in the earlier speech, albeit differently charged. Faustus no longer is in control of the opposite forces rivaling within his soul[16] and the visions of punishment that oppress him. Faced with prospect of imminent divine judgement and hellish torture, Faustus has reached a state of emotional and intellectual impasse, wishing to hault the passage of time and desperately bids the spheres

[13] Ovid: *The Metamorphoses*, ed. cited, 1:64.

[14] Christopher Marlowe: *Tamburlaine the Great*, ed. by Una Ellis-Fermor, London 1930, p. 34.

[15] Harry Levin: *The Overreacher*, ed. cited, p. 190.

[16] Plato: *Euthphro, Apology, Crito, Phaedo, Phaedrus*, trans. H.N. Fowler, Cambridge and London 1914; 1953, 246.25A:470-71.

> Stand still, you *ever-moving spheres of heaven*,
> That time may cease and midnight never come.
> Faire nature's eye, rise, rise again, and make
> Perpetual day: …
> *O lente lente currite noctis equi*!
> The stars move still: time runs; the clock will strike; […]

Faustus wants to prevent the completion of the compact and the imprisonment of his soul in hell. This is, however, impossible for according to Lucretian theory of the human souls and the will where the soul is "always moving as the restless spheres":

> Our souls, whose faculties can comprehend
> The wondrous architecture of the world;
> And measure every wandring planet's course,
> Still climbing after knowledge infinite,
> And *always moving as the restless spheres*,
> Wills us to wear ourselves and never rest […].

Within the Lucretian model, "perpetual day" is impossible. The panic-stricken Faustus nevertheless appeals to the sun, "fair nature's eye", which is ironically both a reference to Christ as *sol iustitiae*[17] on Judgment Day and to the sun, Apollo, whose chariot is to drive across the heavens starting at the break of dawn. Hence the appeal to the dark horses of the night ("noctis equi") also stirs our awareness of Phäeton and his fate caused by the failure to control the horses of day.

The escape into what Lucretius terms "the fratricidal elements" is even evoked as a wish to be "dissolved in elements" recalling Tamburlaine's lines about "Nature that fram'd us of four elements / […] / Doth teach us all to have aspiring minds." (2.7.23; 25) and his wish that "our bodies turn to elements, / And both our souls aspire celestial thrones" (1.2.236-37). Marlowe appropriately ends Faustus' speech by importing lines from his epicurean contemporary, Giordano Bruno, from the night sequence in his most famous London dilalogue, *De gli eroici furori* (1585), in which the escape into the elements of nature constititutes the climax. When facing the deity, Bruno's Cesarino explains, "The weakness of the human mind, which […] in divine enterprises risks finding itself suddenly engulfed in the abyss of an incomprehensible excellence"(215). That is why:

> Il senso […] che non sapendo passar avanti, né tornare a dietro, né dove voltarsi, svanisce e perde l'eser suo; non altrimente che *una stilla d'acqua che svanisce nel mare, o un picciol spirito che s'attenua perdendo la propria sustanza nell'aere* spacioso e immenso. (2.1.461)

[17] Roy Eriksen: *The Forme of Faustus Fortunes: A Structural and Thematic Analysis of* The Tragedie of Doctor Faustus (1616), Atlantic Highland CT and Oslo 1987, p. 49.

> "Not knowing where to turn, equally incapable of going forwards or backwards, the mind vanishes and loses its being *like a small drop of water that disappears into the ocean, or a little spirit that fades away when losing its proper substance in the vast and spacious air.* (Author's translation and emphases)

This in Marlowe's rendering becomes

> Now, body, turn to air,
> Or Lucifer will bear the quick to hell.
> O soul, be changed to little water drops,
> And fall into the ocean, ne'er be found (5.2.193-96)

While Faustus is at an impasse being paralysed by panic, wavering between divine wrath and death by devils, Marlowe imports some crucial lines from a Lucretian-inspired text into the finale, and thus hints at text a way out.[18] At this point "enter the Devils" to drag him off and the audience would be in no doubt to believe that death awaits him, whose last line of repentance is "come not, Lucifer! / I'll burn my books! Ah, Mephostophilis!" (5.2.199-200), placing the emphasis on his failed, bookish quest for knowledge infinite, and thus on intellectual pride.

Falling does not constitute the end in Lucretius and Bruno, however, being a part of the process of infinite motion and recreation in nature. It is therefore not surprising that in the following discovery scene the First Scholar would underscore precisely creation; "For such a dreadful night was never seen / Since first the world's creation did begin" (5.3.2-3). The scholars soon discover his body "[a]ll torn asunder by the hand of death" (7) and they decide to give him "due burial" (17) in memory of his "wondrous knowledge" (17). These words still ring in the audience's ears when "Enter Chorus" to recite the Epilogue and reintroduce the Phäeton myth in the play.

The metaphors of its opening lines "Cut is the branch that might have grown full straight / And burned is *Apollo's* Lawrell bough" rework the opening line of Petrarch's plaintive sonnet 269 ("Rotta l'alta colonna e 'l verde lauro"), but interestingly it also provides a strong allusion to Phäeton. As the son of Apollo, and his "branch" as it were, and a mythical figure who overreached, was scorched and fell to his death, Phäeton does indeed match Faustus, as the "burned" and daring offshoot of Apollo Musagetes. I believe the parallel was prepared for and strengthened by the Phäeton allusions in the Second Chorus, where Faustus goes on a chariot ride to prove cosmography, that matches the "currus" of Phaeton. For all his criticism of Lucretius, Ovid, too, stressed that Phäeton was not entirely to be blamed, but also commended Clymenes' son for his daring.

[18] That is why Bruno emphasizes that at the moment of illumination and revelation, Phäeton will once again meet Apollo. Cf. *De gli eroici furori*, in: *Opere italiane*, 2 vols., ed. by Giovanni Gentile, Bar 1925-27, II, 5.

> HIC SITVS EST PHAETON CURRVS AVRIGA PATERNI
> QVEM SI NON TENVIT MAGNIS TAMEN EXCIDIT AVSIS
> (HERE PHAETON LIES. IN PHOEBUS' CAR HE FARED
> AND THOUGH HE GREATLY FILED, MORE GREATLY DARED.)
> (*Metamorphoses*, II.327-28; 82-83)

The mood similar to that in these lines resurfaces in the Epilogue of *Doctor Faustus*, even though the balance is tipped towards an emphasis on the unlawfulness of Faustus' enterprise. Jeffrey Whitney's contemporary emblem "Temeritas" in *A Choice of Emblemes* (1587) illustrates and underlines the moral lesson that concludes Marlowe's play:

> The waggoner, behoulde, is hedlonge throwen,
> And all in vaine doth take the raine in hande,
> If he be drawen by horses fierce vnknowen,
> Whose stomacks stowte, no taming vnderstande,
> They praunce, and yerke, and out of order slinge,
> Till all they breake, and vnto hauocke bringe.
>
> That man, whoe hath affections fowle vntamde,
> And forwarde runnes neglecting reasons race,
> Deserues by right, of all men to bee blamed,
> And headlonge falls at lengthe to his deface,
> Then bridle wil, and reason make thy guide,
> So maiste thow stande, when others doune doe slide. (p. 6)

Behind the moralizing poem in which images of horsemanship abound we inevitably detect not only Plato's account as that it came to colour Lucretius' and Ovid's interpretations of the myth about the fate of Apollo's overreaching son.

What this brief survey of Marlowe's use of horses suggests, is that the dramatist draws on conventional and heterodox ideas from various sources. Horses acquire functions exceeding what was to be expected not least when we consider their crucial role in a myth that was to become his personal myth to the extent that he even signed himself "Phaeton" in his dedicatory sonnet to John Florio's *Second Fruites* (1591).[19]

[19] Cf. *D. Nicholas Ranson: A Marlowe Sonnet*? in: *Publications of the Arkansas Philological Associations,* 1979, vol. 5: 1–8; and Roy Eriksen: *Entering the Garden: Marlowe and "Phaeton to his Friend Florio"* in: *Shakespeare en devenir* No 4 (2010), available at: http://shakespeare.edel.univ-poitiers.fr/index.php?id=472.

Bibliography

Alberti, Leon Battista: *De aequo animente*, in:, *Inedita* etc., ed. by G. Mancini. Firenze 1890.

Alciati, Andreae: *Emblematum liber* (1531), Emblem LVI (p. 264), "In temerarios:" II.

Eriksen, Roy: *Entering the Garden: Marlowe and "Phaeton to his Friend Florio"*, in: *Shakespeare en devenir* 4 (2010), available from: http://shakespeare.edel.univ-poitiers.fr/index.php?id=472.

Eriksen, Roy: *The Forme of Faustus Fortunes: A Structural and Thematic Analysis of* The Tragedie of Doctor Faustus (1616). Atlantic Highland CT and Oslo 1987.

Gentile, Giovanni (ed.): *De gli eroici furori*, in: *Opere italiane*, 2 vols. Bari 1925-27, II, 5.

Levin, Harry: *Christopher Marlowe: The Overreacher*. London 1961, 3rd ed. 1973.

Lucretius: *De rerum natura*, Book Five.

Marlowe, Christopher: *Doctor Faustus. A- and B texts (1604, 1616)*, ed. by David Bevington and Eric Rasmussen, The Revels Plays. Manchester 1993.

Marlowe, Christopher: *Hero and Leand*, in *The Poems*, ed. by Millar MaClure. London 1968.

Marlowe, Christopher: *Tamburlaine the Great*, ed. by Una Ellis-Fermor, London 1930.

Marlowe, Christopher: *The Complete Plays*, ed. J. B. Steane. Harmondsworth 1969.

Myers, K. Sara: *Ovid's Causes. Cosmogony and Aetiology in the Metaphor.* Chicago 1994.

Ovid: *The Metamorphoses*, 1:64.

Plato, *Euthphro, Apology, Crito, Phaedo, Phaedrus*, trans H.N. Fowler, Cambridge and London: Harvard University Press and Heinemann, 1914; 1953, 246.25A.

Ranson, D. Nicholas: *A Marlowe Sonnet?* In: *Publications of the Arkansas Philological Associations* 5:1-8 (1979).

Smith, M.F: note in *Hermathena* 102 (1966).

Whitney, Jeffrey: *A Choice of Emblems*. London 1586.

Swift Horsing Around: or, The Madness of Reason

Hermann Josef Real
Westfälische Wilhelms-Universität, Münster

I think it helps to be a little crazy,
as long as you don't overdo it.
Sam Savage, *Firmin: Adventures of a Metropolitan Lowlife*

I

"Swift, I discover", Her Majesty the Queen tells her royal servant, Sir Claude Pollington, in Alan Bennett's *The Uncommon Reader*, "is very good about horses."[1] It is easy to agree with Her Majesty: indeed, he is, and this is no surprise. The Dean was a habitual rider throughout his life, and his letters (including the *Journal to Stella*) are studded with references to horses and riding.[2] Predictably, perhaps, travelling on horseback was an activity first of all affording intense joy to Swift. In October 1711, for example, while at Windsor, a proud and sartorially advanced Jonathan, perhaps remembering Francis Osborne's "Advice to a Son" (I) that "next to Cloaths, a *good Horse*, becomes a Gentleman",[3] borrowed riding equipment and horse to accompany "a noble caravan" of courtiers and maids of honour in Windsor Great Park on a fine day, enjoying "much conversation" with the Duchess of Shrewsbury in the forest during the dozen miles of the ride.[4] But 'joy-riding' occasions always seem to have had a lower priority for Swift than riding as a necessity of physical exercise, which helped him battle, and mitigate, the debilitating effects of labyrinthine vertigo, the attacks of deafness and giddiness known as Menière's syndrome, which tormented him from his early twenties.[5] "I want Air and Riding," he grumbled to Stella after a year and a half in

[1] Alan Bennett: *The Uncommon Reader,* London 2007, p. 97.
[2] Cf., for example, *The Correspondence of Jonathan Swift*, ed. by David Woolley, 5 vols, Frankfurt am Main 1999-2014, II, 97, 127, 154, 163, 573; III, 245, 308, 334, 355.
[3] In: *The Works of Francis Osborn, Esq; [...] in Four Several Tracts*, 9th ed. London 1689, par. 25.
[4] *Journal to Stella*, ed. by Harold Williams, 2 vols, Oxford 1948, II, 376; cf. also I, 329-30, 363.
[5] Cf. Irvin Ehrenpreis: *Swift: The Man, his Works, and the Age*, 3 vols, London and Cambridge, MA 1962-83, II, 298-300; III, 319-20. For a fuller account of Swift's medical case history, cf. Wanda Creaser: *"The Most Mortifying Malady": Jonathan Swift's Dizzying World and Dublin's Mentally Ill*, in: *Swift Studies*, 19 (2004), pp. 27-48. The traditional diagnosis of Swift's disease as Menière's syndrome has more recently been questioned by medical specialists, who have proposed various other hypotheses instead (for a good survey, cf. Marjorie Lorch: *Language and Memory Disorder in the Case of Jonathan Swift: Considerations on Retrospective Diagnosis,* in:

London, and, as a result, he showed himself "resolved to be a great Rider this Summer [of 1712] in Ire[lan]d," his "riding in Ireland [keeping him] well."[6] Sadly, Swift never managed to return to Ireland before the summer of 1713 when tired of the Dublin 'party madness' he escaped to Trim, his "Country Parish", where he spent his time "riding every Day for [his] Health", and, predictably, riding [in Laracor] for life" on that occasion *did* make him feel "something better."[7] Two years earlier, in June 1711 on hearing that Stella was in the country, and in good health, too, Swift grew almost ecstatic visualizing his beloved "ride, and ride, and ride", but even so found it impossible to resist the temptation of an exhortatory gesture on this occasion: "Now, madam Stella, what say you? [*reading a letter from Stella in bed in the morning*] You ride every day; I know that already, sirrah; and if you rid every day for a twelve-month, you would be still better and better."[8] And Vanessa was no exception to this rule. When she confessed to being in the spleen in the summer of 1722, an inexorable Cadenus had some therapeutic advice: "We differ prodigiously in one Point, I fly from the Spleen to the worlds end, You run out of your way to meet it [...] The use I have made of [the bad weather] was to read I know not how many diverting Books of History and Travells. I wish you would get y^r^ self a Horse, and have always 2 Servants to attend you, and visit your Neighbors, the worse the better."[9] Later in life, the Dean reportedly chid his former protégé, the (not-so-)Reverend Matthew Pilkington and husband of the equally flirtatious Laetitia, that he was "a Fool [...] to marry [her], for he could have afforded to keep a Horse for less Money than [she] cost him", and that, besides, the horse "would have given him better Exercise and more Pleasure than a Wife", a judgement which, Laetitia sensed, perhaps ill fitted the bachelor Dean.[10] As a sexagenarian, Swift told his old friends Lord Oxford and Alderman John Barber that he would "ride a dozen miles two or three times a week."[11] Taken literally and computed in (longer) Irish miles, whose 2.048 metres were equated with the 1.638 metres of the English mile in the seventeenth century,[12] the Dean rode a staggering 75 kilometres a week. In May 1713, when he had to return from London to Ireland to take up his deanery, Swift averaged on his "good for nothing" mare Bolingbroke, presumably named in honour of the giver, Secretary of State Henry St John,[13] some 35 miles per diem in five days, arriving in Chester, 181 miles from London one way, on the morning of the sixth day, admittedly

Brain, 129 [2006], 3127-37). Cf. also the bibliography of studies on Swift's medical case history by Hermann J. Real and Ulrich Elkmann: *From Madness to Ménière's to Alzheimer's: A Bibliography of Studies on Jonathan Swift's Medical Case History*, in: *Swift Studies*, 28 (2013), pp. 148-50.

[6] *Journal to Stella*, ed. cited, II, 520, 496; I, 177.

[7] *Correspondence*, ed. cited, I, 517, 513.

[8] *Journal to Stella*, ed. cited, I, 300-1.

[9] *Correspondence*, ed. cited, II, 424.

[10] *Memoirs of Laetitia Pilkington*, ed. by A. C. Elias, Jr, 2 vols, Athens, GA and London 1997, I, 35.

[11] Swift to Lord Oxford, 2 September 1735, in: *Correspondence*, ed. cited, IV, 170; Swift to John Barber, 21 March 1734/5, in ibid. 62: "I ride a dozen miles as often as I can." Cf. also III, 355 and n5, 403, 494, 498, 546, 619, 707 and n3; IV, 172, 203, 260, 354, 365, 432.

[12] Cf., for example, ibid. II, 429 and n5, 553 and n1; III, 355 and n5; IV, 100n4, 155 and n3.

[13] Ibid. I, 502 and n5; II, 83 and n2.

"terribly weary", but, he was convinced, after a journey "good for [his] Health."[14] Riding, the Dean assured Pope, was "the only remedy against encreasing ill health", and he accordingly encouraged his "dear and honoured Friend", Alderman John Barber, too, "to buy and keep a horse, and ride every tolerable day twenty miles", twenty-five kilometres every tolerable day, that is.[15] The list is almost endless.

At the same time, he boasted when comparing the advantages of life in Ireland with the attractions of visiting Harley in England: "I have here a large convenient house, [and] I can afford to keep *three* horses."[16] Ostensibly, the Dean regarded horses not only as a welcome, indeed indispensable means of transportation and travelling, but also as status symbols. In a similar manner, he warded off pressing invitations from Mary Caesar, née Freeman, the wife of the Jacobite Tory MP Charles Caesar, and Mary Delany, née Granville, who married Swift's friend and future biographer, Dr Patrick Delany, by putting forward demands for a visit which he knew his prospective hostesses were unable to satisfy. In addition to a large house, two or three servants, and a decent supply of wine,[17] the Dean, unashamedly, requested "*three* horses."[18] At one stage, in May 1719, the usually parsimonious Swift was self-indulgent enough to spend an astonishing £26 on a horse, more than the semi-annual salary of a curate in the Church of Ireland,[19] which he himself admitted to be "a great Price" but which was to enable him "to ramble extensively in the following summer months."[20] By contrast, the well-to-do Knightley Chetwode in 1715 refused to pay £16 for a "strong, young, tolerably handsome & sound [gelding which] trott[ed] well [and had] good spirits" because he thought the price too high.[21] Concurrently, his *Account Books* testify that Swift was prepared to "allow for" considerable sums on keeping his horses: "In 1702-3, probably a typical early year in Swift's Irish residence", the editors of his account books tell us, "he totalled £13 10s 6d1/2 [...] Of this over £6 went for hay [...] oats, straw, and grass. Incidental expenses were for mending saddles and bridles, shoeing, gelding, and grazing", not to mention the costs for smiths and vets.[22]

Although the Dean was not averse to travelling in a coach at times,[23] when, for example, he was suffering from an ailment, the piles, he felt to be "incommodious for Riding",[24] he would as a rule reject an offer of it. In October 1714, he told Knightley

[14] *Correspondence*, ed. cited, I, 498 and n2; cf. also I, 497n1; III, 469 and n5; *Journal to Stella*, ed. cited, II, 670. Cf. also I, 502 and n5; IV, 133n6.

[15] *Correspondence*, ed. cited, III, 284; IV, 532-33. Cf. also II, 290.

[16] Swift to Lord Oxford, 2 September 1735, ibid. IV, 170.

[17] For Swift's (annual) consumption of wine, cf. Michael DePorte: Vinum daemonum*: Swift and the Grape*, in: *Swift Studies*, 12 (1997), 56-68.

[18] *Correspondence*, ed. cited, III, 677; IV, 59. Cf. also Swift to Pope, 23-31 March 1733, III, 616; IV, 15.

[19] Louis A. Landa: *Swift and the Church of Ireland,* Oxford 1954, p. 114. Cf. also *Correspondence*, ed. cited, IV, 598.

[20] Ibid. II, 301 and n2, 333 and n3.

[21] Ibid. p. 117.

[22] Cf. *The Account Books of Jonathan Swift*, ed. by Paul V. Thompson and Dorothy Jay Thompson, Newark and London 1984, pp. lxxxv-lxxxvii.

[23] *Correspondence*, ed. cited, II, 384, 385.

[24] *Correspondence*, ed. cited, I, 253 and n1.

Chetwode that he scorned the squire's coach, finding "upon Tryall" that he could ride, and, in 1733, he "utterly renounced" Lord Orrery's coach "being not used to that vehicle for many years."[25] Occasionally, the Dean's preoccupation with riding even led him to picture himself as a horse, which, or rather who, he told Pope after a parlous bout of illness in August 1729, "though off his mettle, can trot on tolerably", and "this comparison", he hastened to admonish his coach-riding (and accident-prone) friend, "puts me in mind to add that I am returned to be a rider, wherein I wish you would imitate me."[26] In fact, the comparison seems perilously reminiscent of a progressively auto-intoxicated Gulliver falling "into the Voice and manner of the *Houyhnhnms*" and imitating "their Gait and Gesture", which grows into such a habit that his "Friends often tell [him] in a blunt Way, that [he] *trots like a Horse*" (XI, 278-79 [IV, x, 4]). Among the friends telling Gulliver-Swift off may have been the pert Laetitia Pilkington, who would occasionally smile at the Dean's "odd Gait": "I thought to myself, he had written so much in Praise of Horses, that he was resolved to imitate them as nearly as he could."[27]

Of course, a lover of horses like Her Majesty would have immediately recognized that Swift was 'very good' on equine breeds, too, and that he was drawing from a fund of knowledge when delineating the hierarchical, non-egalitarian structure of Houyhnhnm society in Book Four of *Gulliver's Travels*, even though the Dean's expertise was not only rooted in "human experience with natural horses", but also in "a matrix of ideas and literary allusions."[28] Thus, Gulliver's aristocratic Master, a Dapple Grey, made the traveller observe "that among the *Houyhnhnms*, the *White*, the *Sorrel*, and the *Iron-grey*, were not so exactly shaped as the *Bay*, the *Dapple*-grey, and the *Black*; nor born with equal Talents of Mind, or a Capacity to improve them; and therefore continued always in the Condition of Servants, without ever aspiring to match out of their own Race" (p. 256 [IV, vi, 15]). As a result, the Master belongs to the family of 'noble horses' which on account of their colours, conduct, and pose have traditionally figured in (sublime) classical epics and pictorial representations since the Renaissance. By contrast, in making "white and [mouse] dun [...] the 'worst' colours for horses", Swift repeated, and disseminated, advice from Virgil's *Georgics* and Pliny's *Natural History*, which was endorsed by the foremost seventeenth-century authority on horsemanship, Gervase Markham, a copy of whose *Master-Piece* was on the Dean's library shelves.[29] Markham subscribed to humoral pathology, and in his

[25] Ibid. II, 85; III, 628-29.

[26] Ibid. III, 245. For a description of the accident, in which Pope's coach overturned when going through a river in the middle of the night, cf. ibid. 28 and n6, 30 and n3.

[27] *Memoirs of Laetitia Pilkington*, ed. cited, I, 35.

[28] For this, and some of what follows, I am indebted to Gene Washington: *Natural Horses > The Noble Horse > Houyhnhnms*, in: *Swift Studies*, 3 (1988), 91-95 (91, 92).

[29] Dirk F. Passmann and Heinz J. Vienken: *The Library and Reading of Jonathan Swift: A Bio-Bibliographical Handbook*, 4 vols. Frankfurt am Main 2003, II, 1197-98. The bibliography of Markham titles is probably one of the most complicated ones in the whole of seventeenth-century history. Regrettably, it is unknown which edition exactly Swift owned, there being some 17 editions of *Markham's Master-Piece* between 1610 and 1710. Quotations are from the copy in the library of the Ehrenpreis Centre, Westfälische Wilhelms-Universität, Münster: *Markham's*

system of correspondences, he correlated the 'worst' colours with melancholy, the most pernicious temperament.[30] Conversely, like others before and the Dean after him, Markham took Dapple Greys to be partaking of a "fifth Constitution", described as a "mixture of Complexions", which on account of its harmonious balance of the humours – "in due proportion, none being greater or lesser than another" – "of all other is the best, and most perfect." Dapple Greys, he concluded, are "of Nature most excellent, most Temperate, Strongest, Gentlest, and most Healthfull [...] and naturally inclined to no Disease",[31] all qualities anticipating Houyhnhnm aristocratic status.

II

But then, Dapple Grey was not only an emblem of beauty and a symbol of status; it was also a metaphor of poetic perfection. This is particularly evident in Swift's early odes and early satires like *A Tale of a Tub* and *The Battle of the Books* (both published in 1704).[32] In *The Battle of the Books*, for example, Virgil, in addition to appearing "in shining Armor, completely fitted to his Body", was "mounted on a dapple-grey Steed, the slowness of whose Pace was an Effect of the highest Mettle and Vigor", a description which mirrors the seventeenth-century debate on the comparative positions of Homer and Virgil in the generic hierarchy. In this contest, Virgil was frequently victorious because, as the century progressed, he came to be regarded as the more perfect poet: "[He] brought green *Poesie* to her perfect Age; / And made that *Art* which was a *Rage*", Cowley praised Virgil in "The Motto";[33] a judgement which Swift's patron, Sir William Temple, and Dryden, among many others, were to endorse.[34] That indefatigable rhymer, Sir Richard Blackmore, whose *Prince Arthur* Swift read at Moor Park in 1697/8, likewise struggled "to form [himself] on *Virgil*'s *Model*, which [he] look[ed] on, as the most *just* and *perfect*."[35] Naturally, a hero of such distinction has to be mounted on a Dapple Grey, the most eminent of contemporary horse breeds. After all, in epic poetry as in mock epic, its counterpart, the hero's horse is as important to him as his armour, the most important thing about it being its pedigree: "Just as heroes

Master-Piece Revived: Containing All Knowledge [...] touching the Curing All Diseases in Horses London 1675, pp. 7-8.

[30] For this, and some of what follows, cf. Richard Nash *Of Sorrels, Bays, and Dapple Greys*, in: *Swift Studies*, 15 (2000), 110-15 (110, 111).

[31] *Markham's Master-Piece Revived*, ed. cited, pp. 18-19.

[32] For this, and some of what follows, cf. Michael DePorte: *Swift's Horses of Instruction*, in: *Reading Swift: Papers from The Second Münster Symposium on Jonathan Swift*, ed. by Richard H. Rodino and Hermann J. Real, with the assistance of Helgard Stöver-Leidig, Munich 1993, pp. 199-211.

[33] *Poems,* London 1656, p. 2. Passmann and Vienken, I, 475-76.

[34] *Sir William Temple's Essays "Upon Ancient and Modern Learning" und "Of Poetry": eine historisch-kritische Ausgabe mit Einleitung und Kommentar*, ed. by Martin Kämper, Frankfurt am Main 1995, pp. 50-51 and 256-57; *Preface to Fables Ancient and Modern*, in: *The Poems of John Dryden*, ed. by James Kinsley, 4 vols. Oxford 1958, IV, 1448.

[35] *Prince Arthur: An Heroick Poem,* London 1695, sig. c1v; Jonathan Swift: *"The Battle of the Books": eine historisch-kritische Ausgabe mit literarhistorischer Einleitung und Kommentar*, ed. by Hermann Josef Real, Berlin and New York 1978, pp. 128-30.

are superior to other men through their lineage, so their horses are superior to other horses by their birth and resemble their masters in a divine origin."[36] By contrast, Virgil's foe, the sadly equipped Dryden, his translator, appears "upon a sorrel Gelding of a monstrous Size," all his aspirations for magnificence notwithstanding. According to *Markham's Master-Piece*, a sorrel, which in his humoral system has a choleric temper, is "seldome of any great strength",[37] with the upshot that Markham's views on equine complexion in Swift's covert handling are being turned into a wicked jest at the expense of Dryden's feeble versification.[38] Last but not least, unlike Virgil's stallion, his translator's gelding is a "castrated horse" (OED), so that in this respect the battle between the Ancients and the Moderns becomes a symbolical contest between fertility and impotence – with a predictable outcome.[39]

However, despite all this 'affinity' between Swift and his horses, it is not (yet) sufficient evidence to account for that perennial teaser why the Dean when elaborating the theriophilic paradox of Book Four opted for horses rather than, say, foxes or skunks.[40] Remarkably, none of the non-human republics belonging to the generic matrix of *Gulliver's Travels* is ruled by horses; they are ruled by sheep, birds, and dogs instead.[41] There are two facets to this question, both interrelated in some respects: the first relates to Swift's *source*, or *sources*; the second to what these add up to for the *meaning* of the Houyhnhnms. In my view, it is this second question, the meaning of the Houyhnhnms, which is central to *Gulliver's Travels* (to the extent that anything can at all be *central* to an 'infinite' literary cosmos). Should Swift's readers succeed in finding a 'rationale,' a convincing answer to this, all other questions which accompany it – that of the meaning of the Yahoos, the function of Don Pedro de Mendez, the conclusion of Book Four, or the 'ending' of Gulliver, and, finally, that of the overall meaning of the *Travels* – fall into place and answer themselves.[42]

[36] C. M. Bowra: *Heroic Poetry,* London and New York 1966 [1952] p. 157.

[37] *Markham's Master-Piece*, p. 17, Passmann and Vienken II, 1197.

[38] *Of Sorrels, Bays, and Dapple Greys*, ed. cited, p. 112.

[39] Cf. also Ronald Paulson: *Theme and Structure in Swift's "Tale of a Tub",* New Haven 1960, p. 202; cf. also Swift: *"The Battle of the Books"*, ed. by Real, pp. lxviii-lxx.

[40] Cf., for example, Conrad Suits: *The Rôle of the Horses in* A Voyage to the Houyhnhnms, in: *University of Toronto Quarterly*, 34 (1964-65), 118-32 (p. 127); Hermann J. Real and Heinz J. Vienken: *Jonathan Swift, "Gulliver's Travels",* München 1984, pp. 110-11.

[41] Cf. the persuasive essay on this issue by Ann Cline Kelly: *Biting the Hand that Feeds them: The Abuse of Humankind in Houyhnhnmland and Other Animal Republics*, in: *"The first wit of the age": Essays on Swift and his Contemporaries in Honour of Hermann J. Real*, ed. by Kirsten Juhas, Patrick Müller, and Mascha Hansen, Frankfurt am Main 2013, pp. 267-79.

[42] These questions are of course the ones that have (unsuccessfully) exercised both 'hard' school adherents and 'soft' school supporters. For the distinction, cf. James L. Clifford: *"Gulliver's Fourth Voyage": 'Hard' and 'Soft' Schools of Interpretation*, in: *Quick Springs of Sense: Studies in the Eighteenth Century*, ed. by Larry S. Champion, Athens, GA 1974), pp. 33-49. Cf. also Richard H. Rodino: *Swift Studies, 1965-1980: An Annotated Bibliography,* New York and London 1984, pp. xxx-xxxvi.

III

"I desire you and all my Friends will take a special care that my [Dis]affection to the World may not be imputed to my Age", the Dean told Pope in his second-most celebrated letter, that of 26 November 1725, when trying to justify his ostensibly misanthropic convictions to his friend. "For I have Credible witnesses ready to depose", he continued, "that it hath never varyed from the Twenty First to the f–ty eighth year of my Life (Pray fill that Blank Charitably)." Much as we would like to oblige the Dean of St Patrick's, "fill[ing] that Blank Charitably" seems hardly possible: at the moment of writing, he was four days away from his 58th birthday."[43] "Twenty First" when Swift dates the inception of his "[Dis]affection to the World", is more useful, however, taking us back to 1688, his final months at Trinity College, Dublin, and the outbreak of the troubles in Ireland,[44] in the wake of which he was forced to embark for England, "probably by the end of January 1689."[45] Swift had never been particularly happy while at Trinity, and although he "did passably well" in his studies, he certainly did not distinguish himself.[46] As he later told the story in his autobiographical fragment, "Family of Swift", he rebelled against the College's scholastic curriculum. In addition to the "Provost's Logic", Provost Narcissus Marsh's manual on the *Institutiones Logicæ in usum juventutis Academicæ Dubliniensis*, first published in 1679 and revised and reprinted in 1681,[47] which, as Trinity's Caroline (that is, Laudian) statutes stipulated in Latin, had to be "read through at least thrice" during the first year,[48] students were treated to liberal doses of Aristotle's *Organon* in the second, and of the *Physics*, *Metaphysics* and *Nichomachean Ethics* in the third and last years.[49] "[While at the University at Dublin], he was so discouraged and sunk in his Spirits", he remembered, "that he too much neglected his Academical Studyes, for [*in the margin* some parts of] which *he had no great relish by Nature*, and turned himself to reading History and Poetry." With few exceptions, biographers of the Dean have taken delight in quoting the consequences in Swift's own words: "So that when the time came for taking his degree of Batchlor [...] he was stopped of his Degree, *for Dullness and Insufficiency*, and at last hardly admitted in a manner little to his Credit, which is called in that Colle[d]ge

[43] *Correspondence*, ed. cited, II, 623 and n6.

[44] For a useful collection of essays on the personal and political as well as religious, military, and economic aspects of the troubles, cf. *Kings in Conflict: The Revolutionary War in Ireland and its Aftermath, 1689-1750*, ed. by W. A. Maguire, Belfast 1990.

[45] Ehrenpreis: *Swift*, ed. cited, I, 88.

[46] Ibid. 62.

[47] Cf., in addition to M. Pollard: *The Provost's Logic: An Unrecorded First Issue*, in: *Long Room*, NS 1 (1970), 38-40, James A. W. Rembert: *Swift and the Dialectical Tradition,* Houndmills, Basingstoke, Hampshire, and London 1988, pp. 63-72; and Muriel McCarthy: *Marsh's Library: Dublin: All Graduates & Gentlemen,* Dublin 2003, pp. 15-16 and n6.

[48] Robert Bolton: *A Translation of the Charter and Statutes of Trinity-College, Dublin, 1760,* Dublin 1760, pp. 70-71.

[49] Cf. E. J. Furlong: *The Study of Logic in Trinity College, Dublin,* in: *Hermathena*, 60 (1942), 38-53; Constantia Maxwell: *A History of Trinity College, Dublin, 1591-1892,* Dublin 1946, pp. 49-53.

Speciali gratia."[50] Sadly, though, in the late 1720s when he was probably jotting down these notes,[51] Swift would no longer have felt comforted by Archbishop William King's understanding and compassion. Commenting on "some abuses in the training up of our youth" a few years earlier, his Lordship lamented that academic education in Ireland still began "with inculcating the dull, crabbed, system of *Aristotle*'s Logic", and at a time, King continued, when [the young people] were "least capable of applying that to any valuable purpose."[52] Indeed, it is no surprise that, in his final year, Swift's mark in philosophy was *male*.[53]

To extrapolate from hindsight, what exasperated the young Jonathan most about the "Provost's Logic" was perhaps less the fact that it was required reading, or rather cramming, for all junior freshmen at the time but that he encountered in it the maxim which enunciated 'the doctrine of the schools', the boastful belief in the essential rationality of Humankind – *homo animal rationale* – the conviction that made reason "God's defining gift to Man", the "noblest creature in the world",[54] which the mature Dean was to run down in *Gulliver's Travels*. As he told his friend Pope in what is probably the most famous of all his letters, that of 29 September 1725:

> I have got Materials Towards a Treatis proving the falsity of that Definition animal rationale; and to show it should be only *rationis capax*. Upon this great foundation of Misanthropy … the whole building of my Travells is erected.[55]

What is more, the "Provost's Logic" also contained a diagram of the *Arbor Porphyriana*, or Porphyry's tree, an ontological pyramid of the Creation named after the third-century Neoplatonist Porphyry (AD 233-*c*.305), in which the dichotomy between rational and irrational animals was illustrated by the specific instances not of Man and Lion, as in earlier models,[56] but of Man and Horse.[57]

[50] *The Prose Works of Jonathan Swift*, ed. by Herbert Davis, *et al.*, 16 vols. Oxford 1939-68, V, 192 (emphasis added).

[51] Cf. Hermann J. Real: *The Dean's Grandfather, Thomas Swift (1595-1658): Forgotten Evidence*, in: *Swift Studies*, 8 (1993), 84-93 (91 and n36).

[52] William King: *An Essay on the Origin of Evil: Translated from the Latin, with Notes, by Edmund [Law], Lord Bishop of Carlisle*, 5th, London and Cambridge 1781, p. xviii. This criticism was also endorsed by Matthew Prior (*The Literary Works of Matthew Prior*, ed. by H. Bunker Wright and Monroe K. Spears, 2nd ed., 2 vols, Oxford 1971, II, 1007).

[53] Ehrenpreis: *Swift*, ed. cited, I, 279.

[54] Howard D. Weinbrot: *"'Tis well an Old Age is out": Johnson, Swift, and his Generation*, in: *Reading Swift: Papers from The Sixth Münster Symposium*, ed. by Kirsten Juhas, Hermann J. Real, and Sandra Simon, Munich 2013, pp. 595-620 (603 and n16).

[55] *Correspondence*, ed. cited, II, 607 and n7

[56] Cf., for example, Margaret T. Hodgen: *Early Anthropology in the Sixteenth and Seventeenth Centuries*, Philadelphia 1971 [1964], p. 401; Uwe Ruberg: *Vom Aufstieg im Mittelalter: das Konzept der Himmelsleiter in Text und Bild*, in: *Geisteswissenschaften wozu? Beispiele ihrer Gegenstände und ihrer Fragen*, ed. by Hans-Henrik Krummacher, Wiesbaden 1988, pp. 211-44 (232-33).

[57] Cf. the seminal essay by R. S. Crane: *The Houyhnhnms, the Yahoos, and the History of Ideas*, in: *Reason and the Imagination: Studies in the History of Ideas, 1600-1800*, ed. by J. A. Mazzeo,

While it is still safe to assume that Marsh's *Institutiones Logicæ* was *among* Swift's targets,[58] it seems more safe, in the light of new evidence, to assume that the Dean was aiming not at *individual*, identifiable sources but at the *whole* school of 'orthodox' thought according to which Reason "stands for a Faculty in Man, That Faculty, whereby Man is supposed to be distinguished from Beasts",[59] and of which Marsh was but *one* representative.[60] I no longer agree with the once widely disseminated view that, in *Gulliver's Travels*, the Dean was grinding his axe against his old College Provost, whose head, as he acerbically noted in "A Character of Primate Marsh", was packed with "other mens thoughts" anyway.[61] Remarkably, Swift's massive two-volume edition of Aristotle's *Opera omnia* of 1629 contained the *Institvtiones Porphyrii*, in which the ontological order, or tree diagram, was described in these words: "Substantia est & ipsa genus. sub ea est corpus, & sub corpore, animatum corpus: sub quo animal. sub animali autem, rationale animal: sub quo homo. sub homine autem Socrates, & Plato, & particulares homines."[62] Likewise, the horse as a specific instance of an irrational creature was commonplace long before the "Provost's Logic" was composed.[63] Not to mention Aristotle's *Categories* and *Topica*, both of which are studded with comparisons

New York and London 1962, pp. 231-53 (243-52); endorsed by Irvin Ehrenpreis: *The Meaning of Gulliver's Last Voyage*, in: *A Review of English Literature*, 3, no 3 (1962), 18-38 (pp. 23-24).

[58] For the reason, cf. Hermann J. Real and Heinz J. Vienken: *Vistas of Porphyry's Tree*, in: *Eighteenth-Century Life*, 8 (1983), pp. 92-94.

[59] John Locke: *Essay concerning Human Understanding,* ed. by Peter H. Nidditch, Oxford 1979 [1975]), p. 668 (IV, xvii, §1).

[60] I agree with Ian Campbell Ross, who argues that Swift was not attacking Marsh, but was rather "concerned to indicate his personal resistance to the folly and pride of humans who, for over a thousand years had perpetrated the notion that human essence could be captured confidently and unproblematically in the formulation that man is a rational being" (*"No Horse is a Rational Being": Jonathan Swift, Provost Marsh and* Gulliver's Travels, in: *Treasures of the Mind: A Trinity College Dublin Quartercentenary Exhibition*, ed. by David Scott, Dublin 1992, pp. 109-17 [114]). Conversely, J. A. Downie has more recently argued that "Swift is indeed remembering a specific writer's treatment of the subject in Gulliver's fourth voyage, and that that writer is Locke" (*Gulliver's Fourth Voyage and Locke's* Essay concerning Human Understanding, in: *Reading Swift: Papers from The Fifth Münster Symposium on Jonathan Swift*, ed. by Hermann J. Real, Munich 2008, pp. 453-64 [459]).

[61] *The Prose Works of Jonathan Swift,* ed. cited, V, 211-12 (212).

[62] *Opera omnia quae extant, Graece et Latine*, ed. Guilelmus Du Val, 2 vols. Paris 1629, I, 1-14 (sigs A1v-B1v) (p. 3 [A2r]); cf. also Chapter XII: "semper enim Socrates *est* rationalis, & semper Socrates *est* homo" (p. 11 [A6r] [Real and Vienken: *The Library and Reading of Jonathan Swift*, ed. cited, I, 85-86]). As Irvin Ehrenpreis has noted in a manuscript gloss inserted into his own copy of *Gulliver's Travels*, ed. by Davis (*Prose Works*, ed. cited, XI), now at the Ehrenpreis Centre for Swift Studies, Westfälische Wilhelms-Universität, Münster (EC 389), "in manuals of logic, the man-horse contrast is normal" (p. 219).

[63] In a wide-ranging essay on the role and function of logic, in the eighteenth century still "the art of the arts," Clive T. Probyn points out that "in Europe between the Restoration in 1660 and the end of the eighteenth century a book about logic appeared, on average, once every three weeks" (*Swift and the Human Predicament,* in: *The Art of Jonathan Swift*, ed. by Clive T. Probyn, London 1978, pp. 57-80 [57 and n1, 58]).

between Man and Horse,[64] the French humanist Carolus Bovillus (Charles Bouillé) used it in his *Liber de sapiente* of 1510[65] to illustrate the *differentia specifica* between man and brute, as did Dean Henry Aldrich, of Christ Church, Oxford, in his *Artis logicæ compendium* of 1691,[66] also written for the students of his college, and dedicated to one of Aldrich's young protégés, Charles Boyle,[67] the unacknowledged 'hero' of Swift's *Battle of the Books*. Whereas it is unknown whether Swift ever saw Aldrich's *Compendium*, he would certainly have spotted the Porphyrian-tree diagram, a most elaborate "Tabvla Svbstantiae [Table of Gradation]", in a bulky anthology of Hermetic writings, published at Cologne in six volumes in 1630, of which he had a copy in his library before 1715 and which he may already have mined for his satire on occultism in *A Tale of a Tub*. Here, too, the horse figures as the supreme exemplar of individual members in the species of animals.[68] And this is most certainly not to ignore the *Arbor Porphyriana* in John Guillim's "large Folio of Heraldry", entitled *A Display of Heraldry*, an edition of which Swift saw in, or before, 1712 (presumably because it paraded his Uncle Godwin's coat of arms)[69] and in which "Reasonable MAN" is pitted once more against "Unreasonable Animals", among them, "Terrestrial, Four-footed, Living Creatures" which are also "Whole footed, [such] as the Elephant, Mule, Ass, [and] Horse."[70]

However, knowledge of the horse as the embodiment of (irrational) animals not necessarily has to rely on book learning; it also turns out to have been embedded in people who had no university education whatsoever, such as the Digger Gerrard Winstanley, who at times thought of the horse as a paradigm of *un*reason, thereby provoking the question whether the *un*reasonable horse does not 'naturally' lend itself to comparison with reasonable Mankind, all the more so to a man who was as preoccupied with horses as Swift, and whether, in other words, the comparison was not simply 'in the air'. In Winstanley's *Truth Lifting up its Head above Scandals* of 1649, this dialogue occurs:

> Qu. *What Reason is to be seene in a Horse?*
> *Ans*. Reason carries him along to eate his meat, that he may doe worke for the use of man.
> Qu. *But the horse doth not know this Reason that rules him?*

[64] Cf., for example, *Topica*, V, 1, in *Opera omnia quae extant, Graece et Latine*, ed. Du Val, I, 226 (T5v): "Exempli gratiâ, in omnibus & semper: vt hominis cum equo comparati *proprium est esse* bipedem. homo namq; & omnis & et semper est bipes: at equus nullus vmquam est bipes."
[65] Real and Vienken: *Jonathan Swift, "Gulliver's Travels"*, ed. cited, p. 32; cf. also Bernhard Groethuysen: *Die kosmische Anthropologie des Bovillus*, in: *Archiv für Geschichte der Philosophie*, 40 (1931), pp. 66-89.
[66] Henry Aldrich: *Artis logicæ compendium,* Oxford 1691.
[67] W. G. Hiscock: *Henry Aldrich of Christ Church, 1648-1710,* Oxford 1960, p. 50.
[68] *Divinus Pymander Hermetis Mercurii Trismegisti*, 6 vols (in one), Cologne 1630, VI, 58 (Passmann and Vienken: *The Library and Reading of Jonathan Swift*, II, 833-34).
[69] *Journal to Stella*, ed. cited, II, 497 and nn8, 10. Cf. also Hermann J. Real and Heinz J. Vienken: *Swift and "The Herald*", in: *American Notes and Queries*, 1, no 1 (1988), pp. 14-16.
[70] Cf. also Nic Panagopoulos: *Gulliver and the Horse: An Enquiry into Equine Ethics*, in: *Swift Studies*, 21 (2006), 56-75 (p. 60).

> *Ans.* No: Neither hat any creature that priviledge to see and know that Reason rules him, but man. Therefore he is said to be the Lord of creatures, because he knowes how to govern them by reason that is within himselfe.
> Qu. *But all men doe not see and know Reason to rule in them?*
> *Ans.* No: Therefore some are called unreasonable men and though they are in the shape of men, yet their actings are like horses, and they know the spirit that rules them, no more then their horses.[71]

Whichever the case, it has become clear by now that Swift, in turning the traditional relationship, or rather opposition, between Man and Horse in the ontological order upside down in Book Four of *Gulliver's Travels*, reverted to a strategy familiar throughout his career as a satirist from its inception, the strategy of 'inversion'. Deposing Man from his position as 'Lord of the Creation', the Dean, as was its wont, argues *contra opinionem*, he challenges prevailing assumptions, conventions, and norms, and, in doing so, he surprises, provokes, *and* confuses. But this is not enough by way of explanation, if only because we are still unclear about the 'true' *meaning* of the Houyhnhnms.

IV

When holding forth on the *meaning* of Swift's Horses, critics are in the habit of focusing on Book Four of *Gulliver's Travels*. *Pace* my many distinguished predecessors, no matter whether 'hard-school' devotees or 'soft-school' supporters, this is a grave misjudgement, with grave consequences into the bargain. In my view, Gulliver's last voyage has no meaning. In other words, to try to speak about Book Four of the *Travels* alone would be as daft as to try to expatiate on, say, the word "leg" without knowing whether the word "leg" belongs to a "table" or a "human being." I can see you wince at being reminded of this trite commonplace, probably the tritest of all commonplaces. After all, many of us experienced what is fashionably called a 'paradigm change' in hermeneutics, the theory of interpretation which is concerned with the problems of understanding the meaning, or meanings, of texts, and we are all agreed now that understanding, in ordinary life as in literary criticism, is predicated upon the interdependence of part and whole: "The whole can be understood only through its parts, but the parts can be understood only through the whole."[72] Since Book Four, the Voyage to the Country of the Houyhnhnms, is a part, a constituent part, of a larger, more comprehensive unit originally entitled, *Travels into Several Remote Nations of the World* (1726), which controls, or rather should control, our understanding of its individual parts, it seems mandatory to look at the close-knit fabric to which Book Four belongs."[73] One distinct context of Book Four, I humbly submit, is Books One to Three (I-III), including their varying sub-contexts, of course. In my view, neither Books One plus Two (I+II) and Three plus Four (III+IV) cohere in the overall design of the *Travels* nor do Books One plus Three (I+III) and Two plus Four (II+IV). Book Four differs

[71] *The Works of Gerrard Winstanley*, ed. by George H. Sabine, New York 1965 [1941], p. 110.
[72] E. D. Hirsch, Jr: *Validity in Interpretation,* New Haven and London 1978 [1967], p. 76.
[73] Ibid. p. vii.

radically from Gulliver's earlier voyages, it is true, yet it is by no means set apart, and it is by no means complete *in itself*. Formally, in their surface structure, the voyages may seem discrete, separable, and repetitive, perhaps even mechanical, but thematically, in their deep structure, they are as incremental and interrelated as they are progressive and organic.[74] In the criticism of *Gulliver*, as well as in the critical history of Swift studies generally, we tend *not* to heed the most important mandate of modern hermeneutics, to search for (legitimate) *wholes*; instead, we see too much of quotation-mongering and wrenching of passages from their *con*-texts; we see too many interpretative snippets, too many *disjecta membra* and explanatory *quodlibetica*, of readings, in short, which present too many parts too fast to produce a sense of what the whole work is actually like.[75] Tending to ignore the fact that *Gulliver's Travels* consists of four voyages, not one (Book Four), critical practitioners, in short, tend to go about their business as if a paradigm change in theory had never happened, engaging as they do in an aesthetics of the fragment.

At this point, you may well feel, as Sterne did in *Tristram Shandy*, that "Heat is in proportion to the want of true knowledge" (IV, 0, p. 315), but before you proceed to endorse this dictum, give me a chance to sketch out a comprehensive formula (or rather, what I take a comprehensive formula to be) which will allow us to make unified sense of otherwise chaotic data; to sketch out, in other words, the 'pivotal centre' which makes the world of *Gulliver's Travels* cohere.[76]

V

The first thing to be insisted on in analysing the structure of *Gulliver's Travels* is that its first-person narrator, through whom alone the reader observes, feels, and thinks, is an average Englishman ("MY Father had a small Estate in *Nottinghamshire*; I was the Third of five Sons"; p. 19 [I, i, 1]),[77] 'mediocre' in every respect, of middling quality, neither good nor bad, both intellectually and morally at the disposal of others. "Like Dr Watson in *Sherlock Holmes*", one reader has noted, "Gulliver can understand the obvious or that which is carefully explained to him, but is deficient in perceiving subtleties. He is still more so in applying the moral lessons he learns to the conduct of his own life."[78] In short, Gulliver is the embodiment of *l'homme moyen*, the allegorical

[74] As will have become obvious, I entirely disagree with Pat Rogers: *The Augustan Vision,* London 1974, p. 193.

[75] I endorse wholeheartedly the position proposed by John Irwin Fischer in a review of David M. Vieth's *Essential Articles for the Study of Jonathan Swift's Poetry,* Hamden, CT 1984: "I think that most of us most of the time serve Swift's verse best by recovering the social, religious, and literary history that verse responds to, records, and transforms" (*The Scriblerian*, 18, no 2 [1986], 195-97 [p. 197]).

[76] In what follows, I partly draw on my essay, *The Structure of* Gulliver's Travels, originally delivered at The First Münster Symposium on Jonathan Swift in 1984 and subsequently reprinted in *Securing Swift: Selected Essays,* Dublin, Oxford, and Bethesda 2001, pp. 283-97. I have revised, and improved, I hope, my earlier conclusions on Gulliver's 'ending'.

[77] All quotations from *Gulliver's Travels* are from the edition by Herbert Davis in: *Prose Works*, ed. cited, XI.

[78] Huntington Brown: *Rabelais in English Literature,* New York 1967 [1933], pp. 162-63.

representative of Humankind. His *Travels into Several Remote Nations of the World* are the memoirs of Mr Everyman.

As in some illustrious fellow-travellers, Ulysses or Raphael Hythlodaeus,[79] Gulliver's most distinguishing trait is his thirst for knowledge, his curiosity, "one of the strongest and most lasting Appetites implanted in us", as Addison pointed out in the *Spectator* (no 237),[80] yet, at the same time, the impulse which was the cause of Man's original sin, the illegitimate desire for knowledge which made him blind. After his return from Lilliput, Gulliver spends but two months with his family: "My insatiable Desire of seeing foreign Countries", he explains, "would suffer me to continue no longer" (p. 80 [I, viii, 11]). Before he sets out on the journey which eventually takes him to Laputa, he confesses that not even the remembrance of his past misfortunes could abate his curiosity: "The Thirst I had of seeing the World, notwithstanding my past Misfortunes, [continued] as violent as ever" (pp. 153-54 [III, i, 2]). In the countries he is visiting, Gulliver is always eager "to see the Curiosities" (p. 167 [III, iii, 1]), and he feels contempt for people who do not appear "to be curious in any Part of Knowledge" (p. 173 [III, iv, 1]). In short, he is "condemned by Nature and Fortune to an active and restless Life" (p. 83 [II, i, 1]). As *homo curiosus*, Gulliver is goaded on by an indomitable wanderlust, the characteristic feature of the traveller; as *homo curiosus*, he transgresses the frontiers of uncharted intellectual and moral territory.

Although Gulliver visits fantastic, imaginary countries, he never leaves the 'real' world, the world to which he belongs, and to which he always returns. The accounts Gulliver gives of these voyages invite readers to compare favourably and unfavourably the prevailing conditions of his native country with the ones reflected in the truthful memoirs of the 'foreign' lands. The alternative worlds Gulliver chances upon are alternative versions of England; paradoxically, he is a foreigner who visits his own country. In other words, his travels are but superficially voyages into the contemporary present; in reality, they are allegorical voyages into the past, the surface structure of characters, actions, and events being superimposed upon a 'real' structure of "discernible historical particulars." In seventeenth-century dictionaries like the *Glossographia Anglicana*, allegory is defined as "a Figure in Rhetorick, consisting of one continued Metaphor running thro' the whole Discourse";[81] like metaphor, it is, thus, a trope of transference in which an unknown, or imperfectly known, is described in terms of a known.

Gulliver-Everyman journeys into England's past no less than three times. On his first journey, he re-experiences the most significant events in a period of English political history which was of particular importance to Swift. To a large extent, 'Gulliver in Lilliput' is a satirical vivisection of the intellectual and moral shortcomings of Whig politics between approximately 1708 and 1715. Whatever the differences in detail, in this reading Flimnap, for example, recalls Walpole, Bolgolam, the High Admiral of Lilliput, Marlborough; Gulliver's fire-extinguishing feat refers to the Tories'

[79] Cf. Hermann J. Real: *Voyages to Nowhere: More's* Utopia *and Swift's* Gulliver's Travels, in: *Eighteenth-Century Contexts: Historical Inquiries in Honor of Phillip Harth*, ed. by Howard D. Weinbrot, Peter J. Schakel, and Stephen Karian, Madison, WI 2001, pp. 96-113 (98-99).

[80] *The Spectator*, ed. by Donald F. Bond, 5 vols. Oxford 1965, II, 420.

[81] *Glossographia Anglicana Nova,* ed. by Thomas Blount, London 1719, s.v.

ending of the War of the Spanish Succession, and the impeachment of Gulliver 'parallels' the prosecution of the Tory leaders by the Whigs after the Death of Queen Anne, to name but a few.[82] On Gulliver's second voyage, this dissection of English political history is supplemented by a satirical anatomy of the corruptions in the English system of government, its legislature, executive, and judiciary; an anatomy, which is a very serious indictment of Walpole's system of government and which raises issues of political morality, such as parliamentary corruption, election rigging, mercenary standing armies, and national debt.[83] Neither English history nor England's constitution live up to the standards set by the political philosophy and practice of ancient Sparta and Rome and as exemplified in Brobdingnag.[84] On his third trip into the past, Gulliver-Everyman travels into the realms of science. In a country called the 'United Kingdom', he experiences a cascade of follies committed in the name of science, its inane futility and tyrannical hubris, its anti-human and anti-divine nature. More particularly, Swift showers contempt on its 'Baconian' obsession with theory, its preoccupation with 'otherness', and its indifference towards application. Rather than being utilitarian, as Bacon had postulated throughout his writings, the telos of scientific research in Laputa and Lagado is not operational, neither "for the use and benefit of man" nor for "the relief of man's estate." And rather than being conducive to the "therapy of human disquietude", the prospect of which Baconian science had also held out, scientific discoveries generate fear, and increase human anxiety there.[85]

In other words, it is in history, more particularly, the history of recent English politics and science, that Gulliver-Everyman encounters Man and his actions, Man and his accomplishments. On three allegorical excursions into the past, Gulliver is confronted with the vast discrepancy between Man's assessment of himself as a rational being and Man's achievement. The human pretence to be *animal rationale*, which was driven home to young Jonathan in his early years at Trinity College as the generally accepted and approved doctrine of the nature of Man, which the old Dean rejected imperiously in his letter of 29 September 1725 to Pope, [this human pretence] is refuted by the historical record. However, although Gulliver has the opportunity to see how

[82] The reader will rightly have gathered at this point that I unreservedly endorse the position advanced by the *ad hominem* school on the nature of the satirical allegory in *Gulliver's Travels*, represented by, among others, Sir Charles Firth, Arthur E. Case, and Irvin Ehrenpreis, rather than that of the 'generalists', such as J. A. Downie, F. P. Lock, and Phillip Harth. The whole issue is unresolved. For a survey, and a compromise solution, cf. Brean S. Hammond: *Applying Swift,* in: *Reading Swift: Papers from The Second Münster Symposium on Jonathan Swift*, ed. by Rodino, Real, and Stöver-Leidig, pp. 185-97.

[83] J. A. Downie: *Political Characterization in* Gulliver's Travels, in: *Yearbook of English Studies*, 7 (1977), 108-20 (pp. 118-119).

[84] Cf. Ian Higgins: *Swift and Sparta: The Nostalgia of* Gulliver's Travels, in: *Modern Language Review*, 78 (1983), pp. 513-31.

[85] Cf., for the definition of 'Baconian', Hermann J. Real: *The Dean and the Lord Chancellor: or, Swift Saving his Bacon*, in: *Britannien und Europa: Studien zur Literatur-, Geistes- und Kulturgeschichte. Festschrift für Jürgen Klein*, ed. by Michael Szczekalla, Frankfurt am Main 2010, pp. 95-111 (110-11).

corrupt human nature is, he does not recognize it; history does not teach him anything: "In Book IV, [Gulliver] is three books behind the reader's awareness."[86]

If the lesson of Gulliver's excursions into history is not to be lost, somebody will have to 'enlighten' Gulliver. After all, even after having been marooned in the Country of the Horses, he professes philanthropic convictions: "There were few greater Lovers of Mankind, at that time, than myself" (p. 230 [IV, ii, 5]). The historical *exempla* of Books One to Three, then, need interpreting; they have to be supplemented by a concise statement, a moral, in which the lesson of history is driven home to Gulliver, 'mediocre' representative of Humankind that he is. This moral is presented in Book Four, which presents the bill, or balance, of Everyman's journeys throughout the 'vulgar errors' of Man, the view of Man *sub specie historiae*. Thus, the dichotomous macro structure of *Gulliver's Travels* combines the rhetorical forces of historical experience with those of philosophical reason, to unite the historian's examples (Books One to Three) with the philosopher's precept (Book Four): *homo non est animal rationale sed rationis capax.*
If it is correct to assume that Book Four is to be read in the light of Books One to Three, there are important implications for the interpretation of Book Four. The most significant of these is that the moral of this book, or thesis of the fable, cannot be brought home to the reader through the story itself. The most vexing question in interpreting Book Four is that of the meaning of the Houyhnhnms (with that of the Yahoos closely following on its heels), for which more than a dozen differing, and largely mutually exclusive, readings have been proposed.[87] If, however, Book Four is *not* a new beginning, but the continuation of Gulliver's travels, if Book Four, in fact, is the logical culmination of the preceding journeys, the meaning of the Houyhnhnms (and that of the Yahoos) must be *implicit* not in Book Four but in Books One to Three. The specific function of Book Four is to make this meaning *explicit.*

Book Four may be divided into two main sections, each of which is subdivided into two parts. In the first, an introductory part, describing at some length Gulliver's struggle for physical and spiritual survival, and concluding with "*a more particular Account of himself*" (pp. 221-43 [i-iv, 4]), is followed by Gulliver's conversations with the Principal of the Horses, his Houyhnhnm Master (pp. 245-67 [v-viii, 7]), in which "[Gulliver's] great business is talking and listening, telling his master about Europe and hearing the master's reflections."[88] These conversations, which deal with "*the State of* England", as the chapter headings remind readers (pp. 245, 251 [v and vi]), are the rhetorical *conclusio* of the *Travels*, a recapitulation of Gulliver's earlier voyages. Here, the familiar themes recur, occasionally enlarged by an illustration (p. 248 [v, 12]): the inner constitution of the *res publica*, the common weal, its powers and classes, the flaws and defects of its principal professions and institutions, above all that of princes and aristocrats, of ministers and politicians, of judges, lawyers, and physicians. Having "arrived at a competent Knowledge of what human Nature in our Parts of the World is capable to perform" (p. 244 [iv, 7]), the Houyhnhnm Master is able to explain to

[86] Philip Pinkus: *Jonathan Swift*, Gulliver's Travels, in: *Studies of Major Works in English*, ed. by John Orrell, Toronto 1968, pp. 137-72 (144).
[87] For the details, cf. the survey by Clifford: *"Gulliver's Fourth Voyage*, ed. cited, pp. 33-49.
[88] Irvin Ehrenpreis: *The Styles of* Gulliver's Travels, in: *Literary Meaning and Augustan Values,* Charlottesville 1974, p. 104.

Gulliver the baseness of the motives which have guided Humankind's actions in history. At the same time, he is eager to illustrate human (mis)demeanour with parallels drawn from the life of the bestial Yahoos and vice versa

> My Master said, he could never discover the Reason of this unnatural Appetite [for certain *shining Stones* of several Colours], whereof the *Yahoos* are violently fond]; but now he believed it might proceed from the same Principle of *Avarice*, which I had ascribed to Mankind (pp. 261, 260 [vii, 7]).

In contrast to what he, as "a Creature pretending to Reason" (p. 248 [v, 8]), assumes of himself, Gulliver gradually perceives that human history has been nothing but an uninterrupted series of acts *against* reason. Put more succinctly, humans have tended to act in history not like rational beings but like brutes. As a consequence, Gulliver leaves off fighting the Houyhnhnms' insistence of identifying him with the Yahoos: "It was easy to apply the Character [my Master] gave of the *Yahoos* to myself and my Countrymen" (p. 265 [viii, 1]). The sexual assault of the Yahoo female does away with whatever hope Gulliver may have had of possessing a reasonable nature. Gulliver's physical experience of Man's Yahoo nature is immediately followed by his intellectual awareness of it. Shaking with disgust at himself, Gulliver confesses the end of his humanity: "For now I could no longer deny, that I was a real *Yahoo*" (p. 267 [viii, 7]). The meaning of the Yahoos becomes plain through Swift's satirical strategy, then. At the beginning of Book Four, (the philanthropic) Gulliver is a man without memory. He only learns his lesson after having been instructed by the Houyhnhnm Master about Man's 'true' nature. Man's claim to be a rational being is parried, and refuted, by a counterproof for which Gulliver's Master recruits his evidence from the arsenals of the defendant himself, the history of Humankind. Gulliver, the allegorical representative of man, has to admit the failure of his species *on his own terms*. On recognizing himself in the mirror of history, he realizes with shock and despair: *Homo est Yahoo*.

Up to this point, the course of argumentation resembles that of Gulliver's conversations with the King of Brobdingnag. In both cases, it proceeds in three steps. An apparently innocuous conversation about the state of England, Gulliver's "dear native Country" (p. 127 [II, vi, 6]), is imperceptibly transformed into a trial-like enquiry, which their 'Honours' end by passing a verdict on the animal nature of Man, the defendant. While Gulliver's instruction by the King of Brobdingnag is of no consequence for the visitor, however, an 'enlightened' Gulliver suffers a shock of recognition with the Houyhnhnms. He decides to end his days "among these admirable *Houyhnhnms*", those incarnations of reason pure and unalloyed, whose description comprises the first part of Section Two (pp. 274-82 [viii, 8-x]): "I contracted such a Love and Veneration for the Inhabitants, that I entered on a firm Resolution never to return to human Kind" (p. 259 [vii, 2]).

In parading the Houyhnhnms, the epitome of virtue and rationality, before and for Gulliver, Swift exhibits the ideal which the philosophy of the schools, the 'orthodox' anthropology of the age, claimed for *Man*'s nature. While the bestial Yahoos are an emblem of Man as he has documented himself within history, the rational horses image Man as he appears in his own view, as he should be in his own assessment of himself. It is not at all surprising that Gulliver tries to identify himself as completely as possible with the Houyhnhnms, going so far as to imitate "their Gait and Gesture" (p. 279 [x, 4]): he believes to have found in the horses what he had (mis)taken for his own nature. The Houyhnhnms, therefore, are incarnations of what the 'orthodox' anthropology of Swift's age envisaged men to be, rational 'creatures'. Their sole function is to remind Gulliver of his own ideal, his own standard. If the Yahoos' task is to present Gulliver with the devastating balance sheet of Humankind's presumed historical accomplishment, the satirical thrust gains momentum if the accomplishment does not in the least measure up to the standard which Man boasted he was capable of achieving. But there is more than meets the eye.

Swift's satire is double-edged. In a first cut, he shows that Man does not measure up to his own standard; in a second, that this self-fashioned standard is not for Man. As the conclusion of the *Travels* proves, it is neither possible nor desirable for Gulliver to qualify for a rational community. When Gulliver tries to live a life of reason, the results are disastrous. In his pride of reason, his self-complacent hauteur, he barely recognizes the Portuguese captain, Don Pedro de Mendez, ostensibly a Marrano Jew, who may have been chosen "to play the role of the compassionate man for the same reason that the [biblical] parable features a Samaritan, not a priest or a Levite",[89] not to mention his wife and his children. The ending of the travels is also the 'end' of self-banished, non-repatriated Gulliver, if not physically, at least emotionally, morally, and intellectually. "The education Gulliver undergoes [in Houyhnhnmland]", the most recent critic of the episode writes, "is a crash course in dehumanizing, the eradication of any sentiments or instincts that can be recognized as remotely human."[90] Seen as a 'Roman model', Books One to Three are identical with the 'destructive' A-Part, the satiric scene; Book Four, the community of the rational horses, is not a 'utopia' but the 'constructive' B-Part, the satiric norm.

However, it is crucial to remember here that a satire's norms are *relative to the object of its attack*, not necessarily relative to its author. As a result, the norms of Gulliver/*Gulliver* need not be identical with those of *Swift*. In fact, the Dean's stance is not at all straightforward. The most one can say is that his position is a negative one: the definition of Man as a reasonable animal is *not* commensurate with his nature. But this 'truth' does not remain unquestioned at the end, either, for two reasons: first, although Gulliver is taught history's lessons, his illumination results in darkness. Since history teaches Gulliver nothing, he continues to worship the ideal which his travels should have taught him only rational *animals* are able to live. Second, Swift nowhere speaks *in propria persona*; all informations, and accompanying judgements, are transmitted through Gulliver, *unreliable* narrator that he is or progressively becomes. The panegyric of reason into which Gulliver bursts is spoken by somebody who has obviously lost his wits or no longer is in his right mind. The embodiment of *l'homme moyen*, the allegorical representative of Humankind, Gulliver resents being treated as a human being. In *Gulliver's Travels*, Swift writes a new and paradoxical, that is, heretical

[89] Maurice A. Géracht: *Pedro de Mendez: Marrano Jew and Good Samaritan in Swift's* Voyages, in: *Swift Studies*, 5 (1990), pp. 39-52 (49-50).

[90] Allan Ingram: *Gulliver's Travails: Labour and Self-Loathing in Several Remote Nations of the World*, in: *"The first wit of the age": Essays on Swift and his Contemporaries*, ed. by Juhas, Müller, and Hansen, pp. 257-68 (267).

anthropology. Its central tenet is that philosophy does Humankind no favour by defining him as *animal rationale*. "I tell you after all", Swift told Alexander Pope in his second-most celebrated letter of 26 November 1725, "that *I* do not hate Mankind, it is *vous autres* who hate them because you would have them reasonable Animals, and are Angry for being disappointed."[91] In other words, Gulliver's fate reveals that Man cannot live by reason alone. Preferring to live with equine companions, his stallions, rather than with his family, he is, by any recognizable standard, mad. Paradoxically, if Gulliver needed medical treatment, he would have to seek treatment not from a psychiatrist but from a vet.[92] Man's desire to be regarded as reasonable, then, is a symptom of madness. *Gulliver*, not *Swift*, is 'mad' for reason. In the character of Gulliver, Swift 'makes' a man who is mad enough to believe in his reasonable nature: in order to cope with madness, he adapts to it. *Voilà*!

One element common to all types of paradox – rhetorical and logical, epistemological and theriophilic[93] – is the fact that paradoxes never 'hold' positions; they never 'assert' views; and they never commit themselves to anything. It is the privilege of 'nonsense', Swift knew, "neither to affirm [nor] to deny."[94] As in the early stroke of genius, *A Tale of a Tub* (1704), the collapse of norms seems to be complete. Where is *Swift*?

Where is Swift? I do not know, nor do I know anybody who does, alas. But even if it were possible to ask the Dean *in propria persona* (having succeeded in locating his present whereabouts) would he answer, I wonder? A sentence he wrote to Vanessa, poor, unfortunate, unhappy Esther Van Homrigh, in a letter of August 1720, provides as good a guess as any: "I am glad my writing puzzles you, for then your time will be employd in finding it out."[95]

Bibliography

Aldrich, Henry: *Artis logicæ compendium.* Oxford 1691.

Bennett, Alan: *The Uncommon Reader.* London 2007.

Blount, Thomas (ed.): *Glossographia Anglicana Nova.* London 1719.

Bolton, Robert: *A Translation of the Charter and Statutes of Trinity-College, Dublin, 1760.* Dublin 1760.

Bond, Donald F. (ed.): *The Spectator*, 5 vols. Oxford 1965.

Bowra, C. M.: *Heroic Poetry.* London and New York: 1966 [1952].

[91] *Correspondence*, ed. cited, II, 623 (my italics)

[92] I am indebted to Allan Ingram for this thought; cf. his *Doctor at Sea: Gulliver and Medical Perception*, in: *Reading Swift: Papers from The Sixth Münster Symposium*, ed. by Juhas, Real, and Simon, pp. 495-503 (502).

[93] For this taxonomy, cf. Rosalie L. Colie: *Paradoxia Epidemica,* Princeton, NJ 1966; cf. also Rmbert: *Swift and the Dialectical Tradition*, pp. 190-93.

[94] *Prose Works*, ed. cited, II, 78. Cf. also Hermann J. Real: *The Dean's European Ancestors: Swift and the Tradition of Paradox*, in: *La Grande-Bretagne et l'Europe des Lumières*, ed. by Serge Soupel, Paris 1996, pp. 135-42 (141-42).

[95] *Correspondence*, ed. cited, II, 340. I thank Ulrich Elkmann, Ehrenpreis Centre for Swift Studies, Westfälische Wilhelms-Universität, Münster, for his dedicated support.

Brown, Huntington: *Rabelais in English Literature.* New York 1967 [1933].

Bunker Wright, H. and Monroe K. Spears (eds.): *The Literary Works of Matthew Prior*, 2nd ed., 2 vols. Oxford 1971.

Campbell Ross, Ian: *"No Horse is a Rational Being": Jonathan Swift, Provost Marsh and* Gulliver's Travels, in: *Treasures of the Mind: A Trinity College Dublin Quartercentenary Exhibition*, ed. by David Scott. Dublin 1992, pp. 109-17.

Clifford, James L.: *"Gulliver's Fourth Voyage": 'Hard' and 'Soft' Schools of Interpretation*, in: *Quick Springs of Sense: Studies in the Eighteenth Century*, ed. by Larry S. Champion. Athens, GA 1974, pp. 33-49.

Colie, Rosalie L.: *Paradoxia Epidemica.* Princeton, NJ 1966.

Crane, R. S.: *The Houyhnhnms, the Yahoos, and the History of Ideas*, in: *Reason and the Imagination: Studies in the History of Ideas, 1600-1800*, ed. by J. A. Mazzeo. New York and London 1962, pp. 231-53.

Creaser, Wanda: *"The Most Mortifying Malady": Jonathan Swift's Dizzying World and Dublin's Mentally Ill,* in: *Swift Studies*, 19 (2004), 27-48.

Davis, Herbert, *et al.* (eds.): *The Prose Works of Jonathan Swit*, 16 vols. Oxford 1939-68.

DePorte, Michael: *Swift's Horses of Instruction*, in: *Reading Swift: Papers from The Second Münster Symposium on Jonathan Swift*, ed. by Richard H. Rodino and Hermann J. Real, with the assistance of Helgard Stöver-Leidig. Munich 1993, pp. 199-211.

DePorte, Michael: Vinum daemonum*: Swift and the Grape*, in: *Swift Studies*, 12 (1997), 56-68.

Divinus Pymander Hermetis Mercurii Trismegisti, 6 vols (in one). Cologne 1630, VI, 58. Cited from: Dirk F. Passmann and Heinz J. Vienken: *The Library and Reading of Jonathan Swift*, II, 833-34.

Downie, J. A.: *Political Characterization in* Gulliver's Travels, in: *Yearbook of English Studies*, 7 (1977), pp. 108-20.

Du Val, Guilelmu: *Opera Omnia quae extant, Graece et Latine.* 2 vols. Paris 1629.

Du Val, Guilelmus (ed): *Topica*, V, 1, in: *Opera omnia quae extant, Graece et Latine*, I.

Du Val, Guilelmus (ed.): *Opera omnia quae extant, Graece et Latine*, 2 vols. Paris 1629. Quoted from: Passmann and Vienken: *The Library and Reading of Jonathan Swift*, I, 85-86.

Ehrenpreis, Irvin: *Swift: The Man, his Works, and the Age*, 3 vols. London and Cambridge, MA 1962-83.

Ehrenpreis, Irvin: *The Meaning of Gulliver's Last Voyage*, in: *A Review of English Literature*, 3, no 3 (1962), pp. 18-38.

Ehrenpreis, Irvin: *The Styles of* Gulliver's Travels, in: *Literary Meaning and Augustan Values.* Charlottesville 1974.

Elias, A. C., Jr (ed.): *Memoirs of Laetitia Pilkington*, 2 vols. Athens, GA and London 1997.

Fischer, John Irwin: Review of David M. Vieth's *Essential Articles for the Study of Jonathan Swift's Poetry.* Hamden, CT 1984. Cited from: *The Scriblerian*, 18, no 2 [1986], pp. 195-97.

Furlong, E. J.: *The Study of Logic in Trinity College, Dublin*, in: *Hermathena*, 60 (1942), 38-53.

Géracht, Maurice A.: *Pedro de Mendez: Marrano Jew and Good Samaritan in Swift's* Voyages, in: *Swift Studies*, 5 (1990), pp. 39-52.

Groethuysen, Bernhard: *Die kosmische Anthropologie des Bovillus*, in: *Archiv für Geschichte der Philosophie*, 40 (1931), pp. 66-89.

Hammond, Brean S.: *Applying Swift*, in: *Reading Swift: Papers from The Second Münster Symposium on Jonathan Swift*, ed. by Richard H. Rodino, Hermann J. Real, and Helgard Stöver-Leidig, pp. 185-97.

Higgins, Ian: *Swift and Sparta: The Nostalgia of* Gulliver's Travels, in: *Modern Language Review*, 78 (1983), pp. 513-31.

Hirsch, E. D., Jr: *Validity in Interpretation.* New Haven and London 1978 [1967].

Hiscock, W. G.: *Henry Aldrich of Christ Church, 1648-1710.* Oxford 1960.

Hodgen, Margaret T.: *Early Anthropology in the Sixteenth and Seventeenth Centuries.* Philadelphia 1971 [1964].

Ingram, Allan: *Doctor at Sea: Gulliver and Medical Perception*, in: *Reading Swift: Papers from The Sixth Münster Symposium*, ed. by Kirsten Juhas, Hermann J. Real, and Sandra Simon, pp. 495-503.

Ingram, Allan: *Gulliver's Travails: Labour and Self-Loathing in Several Remote Nations of the World*, in: *"The first wit of the age": Essays on Swift and his Contemporaries in Honour of Mermann J. Real*, ed. by Kirsten Juhas, Patrick Müller, and Mascha Hansen. Frankfurt am Main 2013, pp. 257-68.

J.A. Downie: *Gulliver's Fourth Voyage and Locke's* Essay concerning Human Understanding, in: *Reading Swift: Papers from The Fifth Münster Symposium on Jonathan Swift*, ed. by Hermann J. Real. Munich 2008, pp. 453-64.

Kämper, Martin ed.): *Sir William Temple's Essays "Upon Ancient and Modern Learning" und "Of Poetry": eine historisch-kritische Ausgabe mit Einleitung und Kommentar*. Frankfurt am Main 1995.

Kelly, Ann Cline: *Biting the Hand that Feeds them: The Abuse of Humankind in Houyhnhnmland and Other Animal Republics*, in: *"The first wit of the age": Essays on Swift and his Contemporaries in Honour of Hermann J. Real*, ed. by Kirsten Juhas, Patrick Müller, and Mascha Hansen. Frankfurt am Main 2013, pp. 267-79.

King, William: *An Essay on the Origin of Evil: Translated from the Latin, with Notes, by Edmund [Law], Lord Bishop of Carlisle*, 5th ed. London and Cambridge 1781.

Kinsley, James (ed.): *Preface to Fables Ancient and Modern*, in: *The Poems of John Dryden*, 4 vols. Oxford 1958.

Landa, Louis A.: *Swift and the Church of Ireland.* Oxford 1954.

Locke, John: *Essay concerning Human Understanding,* ed. by Peter H. Nidditch. Oxford 1979 [1975].

Lorch, Marjorie: *Language and Memory Disorder in the Case of Jonathan Swift: Considerations on Retrospective Diagnosis*, in: *Brain*, 129 [2006], pp. 3127-37.

Maguire, W. A. (ed.): *Kings in Conflict: The Revolutionary War in Ireland and its Aftermath, 1689-1750.* Belfast 1990.

Markham's Master-Piece Revived: Containing All Knowledge ... touching the Curing All Diseases in Horses. London 1675.

Maxwell, Constantia: *A History of Trinity College, Dublin, 1591-1892.* Dublin 1946.

McCarthy, Muriel: *Marsh's Library: Dublin: All Graduates & Gentlemen.* Dublin 2003.

Nash, Richard: *Of Sorrels, Bays, and Dapple Greys,* in: *Swift Studies*, 15 (2000), pp. 110-15.

Panagopoulos, Nic: *Gulliver and the Horse: An Enquiry into Equine Ethics*, in: *Swift Studies*, 21 (2006), pp. 56-75.

Passmann, Dirk F. and Heinz J. Vienken: *The Library and Reading of Jonathan Swift: A Bio-Bibliographical Handbook*, 4 vols. Frankfurt am Main 2003.

Paulson, Ronald: *Theme and Structure in Swift's "Tale of a Tub".* New Haven 1960.

Pinkus, Philip: *Jonathan Swift, Gulliver's Travels*, in: *Studies of Major Works in English*, ed. by John Orrell. Toronto 1968, pp. 137-72.

Pollard, M.: *The Provost's Logic: An Unrecorded First Issue,* in: *Long Room*, NS 1 (1970).

Probyn, Clive T. (ed.): *Swift and the Human Predicament*, in: *The Art of Jonathan Swift*. London, 1978, pp. 57-80.

Real, Hermann J. and Heinz J. Vienken: *Jonathan Swift, "Gulliver's Travels".* München 1984.

Real, Hermann J. and Heinz J. Vienken: *Swift and "The Herald"*, in: *American Notes and Queries*, 1, no 1 (1988).

Real, Hermann J. and Heinz J. Vienken: *Vistas of Porphyry's Tree*, in: *Eighteenth-Century Life*, 8 (1983).

Real, Hermann J. and Ulrich Elkmann: *From Madness to Ménière's to Alzheimer's: A Bibliography of Studies on Jonathan Swift's Medical Case History*, in: *Swift Studies*, 28 (2013).

Real, Hermann J.: *The Dean and the Lord Chancellor: or, Swift Saving his Bacon*, in: *Britannien und Europa: Studien zur Literatur-, Geistes- und Kulturgeschichte. Festschrift für Jürgen Klein*, ed. by Michael Szczekalla. Frankfurt am Main 2010, pp. 95-111.

Real, Hermann J.: *The Dean's European Ancestors: Swift and the Tradition of Paradox*, in: *La Grande-Bretagne et l'Europe des Lumières*, ed. by Serge Soupel. Paris 1996, pp. 135-42.

Real, Hermann J.: *The Dean's Grandfather, Thomas Swift (1595-1658): Forgotten Evidence*, in: *Swift Studies*, 8 (1993), pp. 84-93.

Real, Hermann J.: *The Structure of* Gulliver's Travels, originally delivered at The First Münster Symposium on Jonathan Swift in 1984 and subsequently reprinted in *Securing Swift: Selected Essays*. Dublin, Oxford, and Bethesda 2001, pp. 283-97.

Real, Hermann J.: *Voyages to Nowhere: More's* Utopia *and Swift's* Gulliver's Travels, in: *Eighteenth-Century Contexts: Historical Inquiries in Honor of Phillip Harth*, ed. by Howard D. Weinbrot, Peter J. Schakel, and Stephen Karian. Madison, WI 2001, pp. 96-113.

Rembert, James A. W.: *Swift and the Dialectical Tradition*. Houndmills, Basingstoke, Hampshire, and London 1988, pp. 63-72.

Rodino, Richard H.: *Swift Studies, 1965-1980: An Annotated Bibliography*. New York and London 1984.

Rogers, Pat: *The Augustan Vision*. London 1974.

Ruberg, Uwe: *Vom Aufstieg im Mittelalter: das Konzept der Himmelsleiter in Text und Bild*, in: *Geisteswissenschaften wozu? Beispiele ihrer Gegenstände und ihrer Fragen*, ed. by Hans-Henrik Krummacher. Wiesbaden 1988, pp. 211-44.

Sabine, George H. (ed.): *The Works of Gerrard Winstanley*. New York 1965 [1941].

Sir Richard Blackmore: *Prince Arthur: An Heroick Poem*. London 1695

Suits, Conrad: *The Rôle of the Horses in* A Voyage to the Houyhnhnms, in: *University of Toronto Quarterly*, 34 (1964-65), pp. 118-32.

Swift, Jonathan: *"The Battle of the Books": eine historisch-kritische Ausgabe mit literarhistorischer Einleitung und Kommentar*, ed. by Hermann Josef Real. Berlin and New York 1978.

Swift, Jonathan: Poems. London 1656. Quoted from: Dirk F. Passmann and Heinz J. Vienken: *The Library and Reading of Jonathan Swift*, I, 475-76.

The Works of Francis Osborn, Esq; ... in Four Several Tracts, 9th ed. London 1689.

Thompson, Paul V. and Dorothy Jay Thompson (eds.): *The Account Books of Jonathan Swift*. Newark and London 1984.

Washington, Gene: *Natural Horses > The Noble Horse > Houyhnhnms*, in: *Swift Studies*, 3 (1988), 91-95.

Weinbrot, Howard D.: *"'Tis well an Old Age is out": Johnson, Swift, and his Generation*, in: *Reading Swift: Papers from The Sixth Münster Symposium*, ed. by Kirsten Juhas, Hermann J. Real, and Sandra Simon. Munich 2013, pp. 595-620.

Williams, Harold (ed.): *Journal to Stella*, 2 vols. Oxford 1948.

Woolley, David (ed.): *The Correspondence of Jonathan Swift*, 5 vols. Frankfurt am Main 1999-2014.

"A Dialogue between the Two Horses" – A Seventeenth-Century Verse Satire and its Contexts

Kirsten Juhas
Westfälische Wilhelms-Universität, Münster

Talking horses have belonged to the repertory of the animal fable from ancient times. Even if language skills are a common feature of all animals in the fable since the animals represent human follies and virtues, it is interesting to know what horses stand for in the Aesopian fables, which became popular throughout seventeenth- and eighteenth-century Europe.[1] The most prominent translator and rewriter of Aesop's fables in England was Sir Roger L'Estrange, whose collection of fables was first published in 1692, passed through several editions, and was still printed into the next century. While the horse is repeatedly portrayed as a proud and powerful animal looking down on the ass, the boar, and the stag, it has to pay a high price for its position, enslavement to Mankind.[2] As a warhorse, it has the chance to participate in glorious deeds, but it also has to be prepared to sacrifice its life for its master. A case in point is the Aesopian fable "A Horse and a Hog", in which the hog calls the horse a fool for making "Haste to be Destroy'd." Feeling provoked, the horse decides to teach the hog a lesson: "That Consideration, says the Horse, may do well enough in the Mouth of a Wicked Creature that's only Fatted to be Kill'd by a Knife, but whenever I'm taken off, I'll leave the Memory of a Good Name Behind me." As L'Estrange explains in the moral added to the fable, the example of the horse shows that "an Honourable Death is to be Preferr'd before an Infamous Life."[3]

II

The close companionship between rider and horse in battle also found its expression in equestrian statues, the most famous being the one of Marcus Aurelius now preserved in the Capitoline Museums in Rome. Equestrian statues are intended to illustrate the *virtus*

[1] Cf. Thomas Noel: *Theories of the Fable in the Eighteenth Century,* New York and London 1975, p. 30.
[2] Cf. Sir Roger L'Estrange: *A Horse and an Asse*; *A Boar and a Horse*; *A Stag and a Horse,* in: *Fables of Aesop and Other Eminent Mythologists: With Morals and Reflexions,* London 1704, pp. 36-41 (XXXVII), pp. 56-58 (LVI); pp. 56-58 (LVII).
[3] Sir Roger L'Estrange: *A Horse and a Hog*, ed. cited, pp. 268-69 (CCXCIX).

bellica, to honour the rider and celebrate his virtues as well as to commemorate his deeds and victories.[4]

The earliest English example is the near life-size statue of Charles I by Hubert Le Sueur of 1633, exhibited at Charing Cross in London (Figure 1).[5] It was commissioned by the Lord Treasurer, the first Earl of Portland, for his garden at Roehamptom in 1630. The Lord Treasurer died before the statue could be delivered, and in 1655, during the Interregnum, it was sold by Parliament to John Rivet, a brazier, who was instructed to break it up. Rivet, however, preserved the statue, producing some knives and forks of brass to show that he had done what he was ordered to do. After the Restoration, the new Lord Treasurer Thomas Osborne, soon to be Earl of Danby, bought the statue and had it erected at Charing Cross on a newly made stone pedestal in 1675. It is still to be seen in this very spot today, sitting to the south of Nelson's Column in Trafalgar Square, looking down Whitehall, to the place of Charles I's execution in January 1649.

For sixty-one years, the statue of Charles I had a counterpart at Stocks Market, the site of the present Mansion House, representing his son, Charles II (Figure 2). On 29 May 1672, the King was presented with a marble statue on the double occasion of celebrating His Majesty's forty-second birthday and the twelfth anniversary of his enthronement in London on 29 May 1660. It was set up by Sir Robert Viner (1631-88), a wealthy goldsmith, who was to become Lord Mayor of London in 1675. In contrast to other equestrian statues consisting of two component parts – horse and rider – this one has an additional element: the horse is shown trampling on a cowering figure whose left hand is raised in self-protection, and who is usually taken to represent Oliver Cromwell, the former Lord Protector of the Commonwealth of England, Scotland, and Ireland. The fact that the cowering figure is wearing a turban reveals the statue's provenance. The mounted figure is believed to have originally represented Jan (Johann, or John) Sobieski (1629-96), King of Poland from 1674-96, trampling a Turk beneath his horse's feet in order to commemorate his heroic deeds at the Battle of Vienna.[6] When Robert Viner bought the statue, he had the rider transformed into Charles II, and the Turk into Cromwell. In the latter case, however, the conversion remained incomplete since the turban on the Turk's head was overlooked, thus metamorphosing Cromwell into an

[4] Cf. Victoria Avery: *Virtue, Valour, Victory: The Making and Meaning of Bronze Equestrian Monuments (*ca. *1440* – ca. *1640)*, in: *Praemium Virtutis III: Reiterstandbilder von der Antike bis zum Klassizismus*, ed. by Joachim Poeschke, Thomas Weigel, and Britta Kusch-Arnold, Münster 2008), p. 204.

[5] For the following information, I am indebted to various sources: Henry B. Wheatley: London Past and Present: Its History, Associations, and Traditions, 3 vols, London 1891, l. 355-57; The statue of Charles I and site of the Charing Cross, in: *Survey of London: Volume 16: St Martin-in-the-Fields I: Charing Cross* (1935), ed. by G. H. Gater and E. P. Wheeler, pp. 258-268. Available at: <http://www.british-history.ac.uk/report.aspx?compid=68141>, accessed 8 September 2013; Story of a statue, available at: <http://www.englishcivilwar.org/2011/12/charles-i-statue.html>, accessed 8 September 2013.

[6] This story has lately been questioned by Matthew Birchwood in his monograph *Staging Islam in England: Drama and Culture, 1640-1685,* Cambridge 2007. Birchwood points out that the statue was unveiled in London "a full eleven years before [Sobieski's] defeat of the Ottomans at Vienna, upon which his fame was principally based" (pp. 3-4). He thinks that Viner acquired a generic statue.

Ottoman sultan. In contrast to the statue of Charles I, that of his son was generally ill-received by the public, being reviewed by a critic as "a thing in itself [...] exceedingly ridiculous and absurd."[7] It is no coincidence that the statue was taken down in 1736 when clearing the site for Mansion House. Today, it is located at Newby Hall, Ripon, the Yorkshire seat of the Viner family.

III

Both statues provoked a number of poetic responses, one by Edmund Waller entitled "On the Statue of King Charles I at Charing Cross, in the Year 1674", and three are ascribed to the poet, satirist, and politician Andrew Marvell (1621-78). Two of these responses focus on one of the statues ("The Statue in Stocks-Market" and "The Statue at Charing Cross"), while in the third poem, the two statues, or rather, their equestrian parts, start talking to each other ("A Dialogue between the Two Horses"). All three are written in the same metre and style, and presumably by the same author, most likely Marvell, although definitive proof is lacking.[8] All three poems reveal an intimate knowledge of the political intrigues of the time, knowledge which Marvell would have possessed as a Member of Parliament for almost twenty years (1659-78). What is more, there are traces of Marvell's disillusion with Charles II in nearly all of the satires attributed to him, such as "The Kings Vowes" and "Upon His Majesties Being Made Free of the City" as well as in his later *Account of the Growth of Popery and Arbitrary Government in England* (1677).

"The Statue in Stocks-Market" was probably written two years after the statue had been set up, around October 1674, when the statue had been covered up for alterations.[9] The satire was first printed in *State Poems* in 1689, and its speaker voices a deeply felt indignation at Sir Robert Viner's birthday present for Charles II:

> Now it appears from the first to the last
> To be all a revenge and a malice forecast,
> Upon the King's birthday to set up a thing
> That shews him a monster more like than a king.
>
> When each one that passes finds fault with the horse,
> Yet all do affirm that the king is much worse,
> And some by the likeness Sir Robert suspect
> That he did for the King his own statue erect.[10] (ll. 9-16)

[7] James Ralph: *A Critical Review of the Publick Buildings, etc. of London* (1734), p. 12, cited in: *The Poems and Letters of Andrew Marvell*, ed. by Herschel M. Margoliouth, 2 vols, Oxford 1971, I. 395.
[8] Cf. *The Poems and Letters of Andrew Marvell*, ed. by Herschel M. Margoliouth, 2 vols, Oxford 1971, I. 395, I, 394.
[9] Cf. ibid.
[10] Ibid. I, 188-90 (p. 188).

All this seems to be pure irony, since the "disfigured" (l. 17) statue of Charles II, which makes him look like a "monster" (l. 12), as the speaker calls it, originally showed the Polish king, Jan Sobieski. Besides, the speaker of the poem not only finds fault with the statue itself, but he also satirically comments on the appropriateness of the place where it had been erected, a market for fruit and vegetables:[11]

> But a market, they say, does suit the king well,
> Who the Parliament buys and revenues does sell,
> And others to make the similitude hold
> Say his Majesty himself is bought too and sold.
>
> This statue is surely more scandalous far
> Than all the Dutch pictures that caused the war,
> And what the exchequer for that took on trust
> May be henceforth confiscate for reasons more just. (ll. 21-28)

These lines allude to the outbreak of the Third Anglo-Dutch War (1672-74), which was part of the larger Franco-Dutch War (1672-78) fought by France, Sweden, and England, among others, against the United Provinces. Although England, the Dutch Republic, and Sweden had entered into the Triple Alliance against France in 1668, on 1 June 1670, Charles II signed the secret Treaty of Dover with France, which made England a pensioner of France and forced it into joining the French attack on the United Provinces on 28 March 1672 (O.S.).[12] The line "his Majesty himself is bought too and sold" (l. 24) is likely to refer to Charles' receiving subsidies from Louis XIV. Among the trivialities supplying pretexts for the war was a portrait of Cornelius de Wit, brother to Johann de Witt, the Grand Pensionary of Holland, into which the painter had inserted some ships on fire in a harbour. The English took this to be Chatham, where the Dutch had destroyed the English navy in the Second Anglo-Dutch War, and accordingly, they felt insulted.[13]

In "The Statue in Stocks-Market", the criticism of the statue amounts to a criticism of Charles II as a warmonger, spendthrift, and nepotist:

[11] Stocks Market used to be a market for the sale of meat and fish until it was destroyed in the Great Fire of London. After the Fire, it became a market for fruit and vegetables (Wheatley and Cunningham: *London Past and Present*, III, 316).

[12] Cf. the gloss on "*the beginning of the second* Dutch *War in* 1672" in Swift's *Preface to Temple's* Letters, ed. by Kirsten Juhas and Hermann J. Real, with the assistance of Dirk F. Passmann, and Sandra Simon (Online.Swift/Ehrenpreis Centre for Swift Studies, Münster, October 2011, updated November 2013, <http://www.anglistik.uni-muenster.de/Swift/online.swift/works/templesletters/>).

[13] Cf. *The Poems and Letters of Andrew Marvell*, ed. cited, I, 396 (*ad* l. 26); cf. also *Poems on Affairs of State*, ed. by Lord, *et al.*, I, 268 (*ad* I. 26).

Sure the king will ne'er think of repaying his bankers,
Whose loyalty now all expires with his spankers.
If the Indies and Smyrna do not him enrich,
They will scarce afford him a rag to his breech.

But Sir Robert affirms we do him much wrong;
For the graver's at work to reform him thus long.
But alas! He will never arrive at his end,
For 'tis such a king as no chisel can mend. (ll. 49-56)

The reference to Smyrna is loaded. In March 1672, before the declaration of war, a squadron under Sir Robert Holmes made a piratical attack on the Dutch Smyrna fleet in the Channel that failed ignominiously.[14] The poem suggests this failure to be symptomatic of Charles II's reign, of a king "as no chisel can mend" (l. 56).

The poem's counterpart on the statue of Charles I, entitled "The Statue at Charing Cross", also refers to the statue of Charles II, which had been erected three years earlier:

To comfort the hearts of the poor Cavaleer
The late King on Horseback is here to be shown:
What a doe with the Kings and the Statues is here:
Have wee not had enough already of one?[15] (ll. 17-20)

Like "The Statue in Stocks-Market", "The Statue at Charing Cross", which was probably written in the summer of 1675 and which was first printed in *State Poems* of 1698, attacks the reign of Charles II, summed up in the last lines of the poem:

So the Statue will up after all this delay,
But to turn the face to Whitehall you must Shun;
Tho of Brass, yet with grief it would melt him away,
To behold every day such a Court, such a son. (ll. 53-56)

The long delay in erecting the statue was blamed on the statue's buyer, Lord Treasurer Danby, the main target of the satire. The Earl of Danby was a key figure at the time. According to Gilbert Burnet, "he got into the highest degree of confidence with the King, and maintained it the longest, of all that ever served him."[16] The Lord Treasurer's dealings and policies were controversial as well as unpopular, and they provoked opposition; they even led to his being thrown into the Tower of London from 1678-84. Among Danby's dishonest practices excoriated are his illegal stopping of the pensions ("Does the Treasurer think men so Loyally tame / When their Pensions are stopt to be

[14] Cf. *The Poems and Letters of Andrew Marvell*, ed. cited, l, 397 (*ad* I. 51); *Poems on Affairs of State: Augustan Satirical Verse, 1660-1714*, ed. by George deF. Lord, *et al.*, 7 vols, New Haven and London 1963-75), I, 269 (*ad* I. 51); and David Ogg: *England in the Reign of Charles II*, 2nd ed., 2 vols, Oxford 1956, I, 356.

[15] *The Poems and Letters of Andrew Marvell*, ed. cited, I, pp. 199-201 (200).

[16] Gilbert Burnet: *History of his Own Time*, 2 vols, London 1724-34, I, 351; II, 4.

fool'd with a sight?" [ll. 21-22]), three prorogations of Parliament ("As the Parliament twice was prorogued by your hand, / Will you venture soe far to Prorogue the King too?" [ll. 35-36]), which threatened Marvell's livelihood, as well as Danby's buying of voters, a typical case of bribery ("So many voters he had / As would the next tax reimburse them with use" [ll. 51-52]), of whom he is known to have had a list.[17] The fact that Danby bought the statue is shown to be but one of his many schemes "to win over public opinion in favour of the new Parliament shortly to be convened."[18]

The whole poem reads like a dissection of Danby's tactics throughout his career.[19] The satire reaches its highest point of ridicule when Danby's wife, Lady Bridget, a domineering woman, who was taken to be responsible for her husband's love of money and who was thought to be behind most of his political manoeuvres,[20] suggests having "a Monarch of Gingerbread" (l. 48)[21] instead of a bronze equestrian statue:

> To buy a King is not so wise as to sell,
> And however, she said, it could not be denyed
> That a Monarch of Gingerbread would doe as well. (ll. 46-48)

IV

In terms of fairy tale, it is but a small step from a gingerbread man to talking horses. "A Dialogue between the Two Horses" is not only the longest of the three verse-satires, but also the most radical one in tone and content, going as far as to voice republican sentiments. Therefore, and due to the poem's not being included in the Bodleian Marvell Manuscript (MS. Eng. Poet. d. 49), some editors have doubted Marvell's authorship.[22] However, the poem was ascribed to Marvell in *State Poems* of 1689, 1697, and in later issues, as were the other two poems of the trio. None of the extant nine

[17] *Poems on Affairs of State*, ed. by Lord, *et al.*, I, 273 (*ad* l. 50). According to an anecdote, Danby also tried to bribe Marvell, offering him one thousand pounds. However, Marvell refused the attempt and rejected the money (cf. Hilton Kelliher: *Andrew Marvell: Poet and Politician, 1621-78,* London 1978, pp. 88-89).

[18] Kelliher: *Andrew Marvell*, p. 104.

[19] Cf. Nigel Smith: *Andrew Marvell: The Chameleon,* New Haven and London, p. 294.

[20] Mark Knights: *Osborne, Thomas, first duke of Leeds (1632–1712)*, in: *Oxford Dictionary of National Biography Online*, (<http://www.oxforddnb.com/view/article/20884>, accessed 22 October 2013); cf. also Smith: *Andrew Marvell*, ed. cited, p. 294.

[21] Gingerbread may also mean "something showy and unsubstantial", and especially in the expression 'knight', 'lord', 'man', or in this case, "Monarch of Gingerbread", it is an obsolete form of "burlesque or ironical laudation" (OED).

[22] Whereas Margoliouth considers the poem authentic and includes it in his two-volume edition of *The Poems and Letters of Andrew Marvell*, Lord argues against Marvell's authorship and excludes it from his 'complete' edition (I, 414). Lord assumes the satire to have been written by John Ayloffe (cf. *Poems on Affairs of State*, ed. by Lord, *et al.*, I, 274). The most recent edition of *The Poems of Andrew Marvell*, edited by Nigel Smith, only lists it among the "Poems of Uncertain Attribution" (revised edition, London and New York 2013, p. 462). The editor provides the additional information that it is to be found in the Bodleian Library manuscript "MS Douce 357" (pp. 462, 431).

manuscript copies of "A Dialogue between the Two Horses" identifies Marvell as the author of the satire. Since the last eight lines are absent in two of the manuscripts, they may be an afterthought.[23] They allude to a Royal Proclamation for the suppression of coffee houses issued on 29 December 1675 and revoked on 8 January 1676:[24]

> Let the Citty drink Coffee and Quietly groan
> They that Conquered the Father won't be slaves to the Son:
> 'Tis wine and Strong drink makes tumults increase;
> Chocolet Tea and Coffee are liquors of peace.
> No Quarrells or oathers amongst those that drink 'um;
> Tis Bacchus and the Brewer swear Dam 'um and sink 'um
> Then, Charles, thy edict against Coffee recall;
> Theres ten times more Treason in Brandy and ale.[25] (ll. 181-88)

The closing appeal to Charles II for the revocation of the coffee-house act chimes in with the poem's general criticism of the present and the former king.

"A Dialogue between the two Horses" has a tripartite structure: the dialogue proper, an Introduction and a Conclusion, the two latter functioning as a kind of frame. Having listed numerous 'authenticating' examples of talking animals from various literary sources and the Bible, the Introduction turns to the Catholic practice of image worship, which is derided as religious superstition and associated with pagan rites:

> *Introduction.*
> Wee read in profane and Sacred records
> Of Beasts that have uttered Articulate words:
> When Magpyes and Parratts cry 'walke Knave walk',
> It is a clear proofe that birds too may talke;
> Nay Statues without either windpipe or Lungs
> Have spoken as plainly as men doe with Tongues:
> Livy tells a strang story can hardly be fellow'd
> That a sacraficed ox, when his Gutts were out, Bellow'd:
> Phalaris had a Bull which grave Authors tell ye
> Would roar like a Devill with a man in his belly:
> Fryar Bacon had a head that spoke made of Brass,
> And Balam the Prophet was reprov'd by his Asse:
> At Delphos and Rome Stocks and Stones now and then, sirs,
> Have to Questions return'd oracular Answers:
> All Popish beleivers think something divine,

[23] *The Poems and Letters of Andrew Marvell*, ed. cited, I, 415.

[24] For the text of the Proclamation, cf. *The London Gazette*, 27-30 December 1675, printed in *English Historical Documents, 1660-1714*, ed. by Andrew Browning, London 1966 [1953], pp. 482-83; for further information on Charles II's "Coffeehouse Politics," cf. Brian Cowan: *The Social Life of Coffee: The Emergence of the British Coffeehouse,* New Haven and London 2005), pp. 195-98.

[25] *The Poems and Letters of Andrew Marvell*, ed. cited, I, 208-13, p. 213.

When Images speak, possesses the shrine:
But they that faith Catholick ne're understood,
When Shrines give Answers, say a knave's in the Roode;
Those Idolls ne're speak, but the miracle's done
By the Devill, a Priest, a Fryar, or Nun. (ll. 1-20)

That the speaker should start with a remark on talking parrots ("walke Knave walk" [l. 3]) sets the jocose tone of the poem, reminiscent of Samuel Butler's *Hudibras*.[26] The next example of the sacrificed ox that bellowed "when his Gutts were out" (l. 8), ascribed to Livy, has not been definitely identified yet.[27] It is probably based as much on hearsay as the legend of the Sicilian tyrant Phalaris (*c*.580 BC), who is said to have roasted his enemies to death in a brazen bull with a fire underneath.[28] The cries of his victims made the bull "roar like a Devill with a man in his belly" (l. 10). Roger Bacon's "head that spoke made of Brass" (l. 11) occurs in the comedy *Friar Bacon and Friar Bungay* (1589) by the Elizabethan playwright Robert Greene, and the biblical story of Balaam's ass from Numbers 22:23-35 is a commonplace example of talking animals.

Associating the Greek and Roman oracles with Catholic image worship ("All Popish beleivers think something divine, / When Images speak, possesses the shrine" [ll. 15-16]) was a common feature of Protestant anti-Catholic propaganda in the seventeenth and eighteenth centuries.

If the Roman Church, good Christians, oblige yee
To beleive men and beasts have spoke in effigie,
Why should wee not credit the publique discourses
Of a Dialogue lately between the two Horses,
The Horses I mean of Woolchurch and Charing,
Who have told many truths well worth a mans hearing,
Since Viner and Osburn did buy and provide 'um
For the two mighty Monarchs that doe now bestride 'um.
The stately Brass Stallion and the white marble Steed
One night came togeather by all is agreed,
When both the Kings weary of Sitting all day
Were stolne of Incognito each his own way,
And that the two Jades after mutuall Salutes
Not onely discoursed but fell to disputes. (ll. 21-34)

[26] *Hudibras*, ed. by John Wilders, Oxford 1967, p. 17 (I, i, ll. 543-46).
[27] *The Poems and Letters of Andrew Marvell*, ed. cited, I, 416 (*ad* l. 8). For the passage that comes closest to the incident, cf. Titus Livius: *Titi Livii Historiarum libri: ex recensione Heinsiana*, 3 vols, Leiden 1634, II, 80 (XXI, 63, 12-14).
[28] For sources, cf. the running commentary to Swift's *Battle of the Books*, s.v. "For *Phalaris* was just that Minute dreaming, how a most vile *Poetaster* had lampoon'd him, and how he had got him roaring in his *Bull*" (*The Battle of the Books*, ed. by Hermann J. Real, with the assistance of Kirsten Juhas, Dirk F. Passmann, and Sandra Simon [Online.Swift/Ehrenpreis Centre for Swift Studies, Münster, October 2011, updated November 2013 <http://www.anglistik.uni-muenster.de/Swift/online.swift/works/battleofthebooks/>).

As in the two poems before, the buyers of the statues, Sir Robert Viner and Thomas Osborne, first Earl of Danby, are explicitly mentioned. But instead of imagining them speaking to each other, or showing the two monarchs on horseback in discourse, it is "the stately Brass Stallion and the white marble Steed" (l. 29) that break their stony silence as soon as their riders leave them "Incognito each his own way" (l. 32). Thereby, Marvell, if we credit him with this idea, not only joins the tradition of talking horses beginning with Homer's Xanthus, but he also faintly echoes the Pygmalion myth, the most prominent story about a living and talking statue.

As in the two earlier poems on the statues, Charles II's reign and moral conduct are severely attacked, and in this, the two horses agree from the very start (*Ch.* stands for the horse from Charing Cross; *W.* for the horse in Stocks-Market, also called Woolchurch Market, from the church nearby):

> *Ch.* My Brass is provok't as much as thy stone
> To see Church and state bow down to a whore
> And the King's Chiefe minister holding the doore:
> *W.* To see dei Gratia writ on the Throne,
> And the Kings wicked life say God there is none;
> *Ch.* That he should be styled defender o'th faith,
> Who beleives not a word, the word of God saith;
> [...]
> *W.* That a King should consume three Realms whole Estates
> And yet all his Court be as poore as Church Ratts;
> *Ch.* That of four Seas dominion and Guarding
> No token should appear but a poor Copper farthing;
> *W.* Our worm-eaten Navy be laid up at Chatham,
> Not our trade to secure but foes to come at 'um,
> [...]
> *Ch.* Yet baser the souls of those low priced Sinners,
> Who vote with the Court for drink and for Dinners.
> *W.* 'Tis they who brought on us the Scandalous Yoak
> Of Exciseing our Cups and Taxing our Smoak.
> *Ch.* But thanks to the whores who have made the King Dogged
> For giving noe more the Rogues are prorugued.
> *W.* That a King shou'd endeavour to make a warr cease
> Which Augments and secures his own profitt and peace.
> *Ch.* And Plenipotentiaryes send into France
> With an Addleheaded Knight and a Lord without Brains.
> *W.* That the King should send for another French whore,
> When one already hath made him soe poor. (ll. 40-46, ll. 59-64, ll. 85-96)

The "whore" Church and State supposedly bow to in the opening lines of the dialogue is Charles II's Catholic mistress Louise-Renée de Penancoët de Kéroualle (1649-1734), better known as the Duchess of Portsmouth. Their affair, which started in 1671, was the talk of the day: "She hath more power over [the King] than can be imagined", Henry

Sidney noted in his *Diary of the Times of Charles the Second*.[29] The phrase "whore" is only one out of many derogatory epithets of the time resulting from the Duchess' being suspected of working in the French and Catholic interests.[30] The poem's satiric suggestion "That the King should send for another French whore, / When one already hath made him soe poor" (ll. 95-96) alludes to the King's new French mistress, Hortense Mancini, Duchesse de Mazarin (1646-99), who came over from France in November 1675 and from then on competed with the Duchess of Portsmouth for the King's favour. The horses not only criticize Charles on moral grounds, but they also condemn his costly and inane warmongering, the corruption at Court and in Parliament, as well as the royal tax politics.[31] Moreover, they question Charles' motives upon sending English ambassadors to the peace negotiations in Nijmegen, doubts that were more than justified: Instead of ratifying the treaty with the United Provinces, Charles chose to side with France, a move, which Sir William Temple, the senior of the three ambassadors and here (somewhat unjustly) styled an "Addleheaded Knight" (l. 94) should never get over during his lifetime.[32]

Unlike "The Statue at Charing Cross", "A Dialogue between the Two Horses" does not spare Charles I either, mocking him as a martyr of the Church:

> *W.* Thy Priest-ridden King turn'd desperate Fighter
> For the Surplice, Lawn-Sleeves, the Cross and the mitre,
> Till at last on a Scaffold he was left in the lurch
> By Knaves who cry'd themselves up for the Church. (ll. 117-20)

Interestingly, it is the horse of the statue in Woolchurch Market, or Stocks-Market, carrying Charles II that turns out to be more outspoken and decidedly anti-royalist than its counterpart at Charing Cross. In characterizing their masters, the two horses resort to animal imagery: Charles II is depicted as a goat, whereas his father figures as a lion:

> *W.* The Goat and the Lyon I Equally hate
> And Free men alike value life and Estate.
> Tho Father and Son are different Rodds,
> Between the two Scourges wee find little odds.
> Both Infamous Stand in three Kingdoms votes,

[29] Henry Sidney, Earl of Romney: *Diary of the Times of Charles the Second*, ed. by R. W. Blencowe, 2 vols, London 1843, I, 15.

[30] *Poems on Affairs of State*, ed. by Lord, *et al.*, II, 291: "Portsmouth, that pocky bitch, / A damn'd Papistical drab", one satire ran, "An ugly deform'd witch, / Eaten up with the mange and scab. / This French hag's pocky bum / So powerful is of late, / Although it's both blind and dumb, / It rules both Church and State" (ll. 17-24).

[31] In 1670, the Commons granted "an additional Excise on beer and ale" (Ogg: *England in the Reign of Charles II*, I, 350). "Taxing our smoke" refers to the hearth tax or chimney money (*Poems on Affairs of State*, ed. by Lord, *et al.*, I, 279 n 88).

[32] The other two ambassadors were Sir Leoline Jenkins and John Lord Berkeley (or Barclay). For Temple and Jenkins, cf. Limojon de St Didier: *Histoire des négotiations de Nimegue,* Paris 1680, pp. 7, 12, and *passim*; for Berkeley, pp. 16, 73.

This for picking our Pocketts, that for cutting our Throats.
Ch. More Tolerable are the Lion Kings Slaughters
Than the Goats making whores of our wives and our Daughters.
The Debauch'd and the Bloody, since they Equally Gall us,
I had rather Bare Nero than Sardanapalus.
W. One of the two Tyrants must still be our case
Under all that shall Reign of the false Scottish race.
Ch. De Witt and Cromwell had each a brave soul.
W. I freely declare it, *I am for old Noll.* (ll. 125-38; my emphasis)

The 'goat' has been a symbol of lechery and lust since classical antiquity. By 1600, "As lecherous as a [He-] Goat" was proverbial.[33] As is well known, the list of the 'goatish' Charles II's mistresses is long, as is the list of his illegitimate children, acknowledged and unacknowledged.[34] In contrast to the goat, the lion bears more positive connotations; proverbial sayings include "as fierce (valiant) as a lion."[35] Lions are royal attributes, appear in various coats of arms, including that of the Kings and Queens of England, and as a result the British Lion stands for the whole nation. Nevertheless, it is a dangerous animal. More particularly, the line on "the Lion Kings Slaughters" (l. 131) refers to the accusation brought against Charles I at his trial, namely that of having made war against his own subjects.[36]

In addition to reducing father and son to animals, the horses equate them with notorious historical emperors. Charles I figures as Nero (AD 37-68), the cruel tyrant who, according to Louis Moréri's *Great Historical, Geographical and Poetical Dictionary* of 1694, "spent his Life in the most extravagant Enormities, horrid Crimes, and monstrous Abominations that ever entred the deprav'd Imagination of Man."[37] Charles II is compared to Sardanapalus, the last Assyrian emperor-king, who was notorious for having lead "a most voluptuous and effeminate Life, to that degree that he was used to sit and Spin in a Womans Habit amongst his Concubines."[38] That the horse statue from Charing Cross should prefer its own rider, Charles I, seems 'natural'. Surprisingly, however, it also praises the Dutch Pensionary, Johan De Witt, as well as the Lord Protector Oliver Cromwell, one of those responsible for the death of its rider. This seditious thought is only superseded by the Woolchurch horse's declaring for "old Noll" (l. 138), Cromwell, that is, as he was called by his followers. This may be considered to be an intended witticism of the poem's author since, as far as the statues

[33] Morris Palmer Tilley: *A Dictionary of the Proverbs in England in the Sixteenth and Seventeenth Centuries: A Collection of the Proverbs Found in English Literature and the Dictionaries of the Period,* Ann Arbor 1950, G167.
[34] The best-known of Charles II's seventeen mistresses was the actress Nell Gwyn(n) (1650-87) (for the total number of seventeen, cf. Anne Somerset: *Ladies in Waiting: From the Tudors to the Present Day,* London 1984, p. 131).
[35] Tilley: *A Dictionary of the Proverbs in England in the Sixteenth and Seventeenth Centuries*, L 308.
[36] Moréri: *The Great Historical, Geographical and Poetical Dictionary*, s.v. "Charles I."
[37] Moréri, *The Great Historical, Geographical and Poetical Dictionary*, s.v. "Nero."
[38] Moréri, *The Great Historical, Geographical and Poetical Dictionary*, s.v. "Sardanapalus."

are concerned, it is this very same horse which tramples upon the figure of Cromwell with the turban and now claims to be one of his most ardent followers.

In the course of the poem, the horses' politics get more and more confused. Before calling for a (new) rebellion, they show symptoms of a Tudor nostalgia, praising Elizabeth I ("old Besse" [l. 150]) as the best regent in the history of England:

> *W*. A Tudor a Tudor! Wee've had Stuarts enough;
> None ever Reign'd like old Besse in the Ruff.
> [...]
> *Ch*. But canst thou Divine when things shall be mended?
> *W*. When the Reign of the line of the Stuarts is ended.
> *Ch*. Then, England, Rejoyce, thy Redemption draws nigh;
> Thy oppression togeather with Kingship shall dye.
> *W*. A Commonwealth a Common-wealth wee proclaim to the Nacion;
> The Gods have repented the Kings Restoration. (ll. 149-62)

When read without the immediate context of the poem, this is strong republican propaganda. Together with "the unmitigated hatred and contempt toward both kings, the disparagement [...] of monarchy itself, and the allusions to cruel and decadent Roman emperors", the unmistakable call for a commonwealth has made editors doubt Marvell's authorship of the poem.[39]

However, there are several aspects which need to be considered before jumping to conclusions: first, as a young man, Marvell was "Cromwell's poet", and he wrote several poems on the Lord Protector, the two most important ones being "An Horatian Ode upon Cromwel's Return from Ireland" and "The First Anniversary of the Government under Oliver Cromwell." Second, "A Dialogue between the Two Horses" is a satire. The satiric mode is generally characterized as an aggressive form of speaking, being directed *ad hominem*, attacking the vices and follies of discernible individuals: "In order to force their audience into acknowledging the abuses only they perceive, satirists exaggerate and misrepresent, and they customarily resort to distortion, hyperbole, and caricature."[40] The mere fact that the horse which tramples upon Cromwell should in reality be his admirer is a case in point. Third, on a symbolical level, the horses' call for a rebellion by which they would unhorse their riders is a most original poetic idea, whether it comes from Marvell or not. Finally, it is important to read the dialogue proper in relation to the poem's frame, especially in relation to its conclusion:

[39] *Poems on Affairs of State*, ed. cited, I, 274.

[40] Hermann J. Real: *An Introduction to Satire,* in: *Teaching Satire: Dryden to Pope*, ed. by Hermann Josef Real, Heidelberg 1992, pp. 12-13.

Conclusion
If Speech from Brute Animals in Romes first age
Prodigious events did surely presage,
That shall come to pass all mankind may swear
Which two inanimate Horses declare.
But I should have told you, before the Jades parted,
Both Gallopt to Whitehall and there Horribly farted,
Which Monarchys downfall portended much more
Than all that the beasts had spoken before.
If the Delphick Sybills oracular speeches,
As learned men say, came out of their breeches,
Why might not our Horses, since words are but wind,
Have the spirit of Prophecy likewise behind?
Tho' Tyrants make Laws which they strictly proclaim
To conceal their own crimes and cover their shame,
Yet the beasts of the field or the stones in the wall
Will publish their faults and prophesy their fall.
When they take from the people the freedome of words,
They teach them the Sooner to fall to their Swords. (ll. 163-80)

Throughout the poem, the language has already been somewhat gross, the term 'whore' appearing no less than four times in the dialogue. The image of the farting horses in the conclusion ("But I should have told you, before the Jades parted, / Both Gallopt to Whitehall and there Horribly farted" [ll. 167-68]) puts the poem into the tradition of the grotesque and the scatological, capping it by a bawdy pun "Why might not our Horses, since words are but wind, / Have the spirit of Prophecy likewise *behind*?" (ll. 173-74; my emphasis) The speaker of the poem also mocks the belief that the Delphic Oracle originated from a chasm in the earth, from which the vapours inspiring the Delphic sybils ascended, profanely degrading their prophecies to physical flatulence ("If the Delphick Sybills oracular speeches, / As learned men say, came out of their breeches" [ll. 171-72]).[41] At first sight, these obscene puns undermine the authority of the equine speakers. Upon closer examination, however, the conclusion asserts their criticism of the present king who is attacked as a tyrant who "makes laws [...] to conceal [his] own crimes and cover [his] shame" (l. 177), another possible allusion to the coffee-house act of December 1675. At the end, the poem proclaims freedom of speech and warns the King (and likewise the reader) against the dangers of a new civil war, a warning that echoes the horses' heated call for a rebellion in the conclusion of the dialogue proper. Yet, as the proverbial saying "words are but wind" implies, the threatened downfall of the monarchy remains as notional as the linguistic capacity of "the two inanimate Horses" (l. 166).

[41] For a description of the chasm, cf., for example, *Diodorus of Sicily*, ed. and trans. by Charles L. Sherman, 12 vols, London and Cambridge, MA 1963), VII, 309-11 (XVI, 26, 2-3).

V

History has shown that neither the horses' seditious talk nor their breaking wind led to the overthrow of the King. Charles II died a natural death in 1685, and although one of his successor's, William III, died of a complication from a broken collarbone following a fall from his horse in 1702, the English monarchy is still thriving today, and on 22 July 2013, a new heir to the throne was born, Prince George of Cambridge. As if to hail his birth in advance, a high bronze statue of a boy on a rocking horse was unveiled on the Fourth Plinth in Trafalgar Square on 23 February 2012 (Figure 3).[42] Like "A Dialogue between the Two Horses" which undercuts "the self-confident civic authority […] proclaimed" by the equestrian statues of Charles I and Charles II,[43] this work of art, entitled "Powerless Structures, Fig. 101", questions "monuments predicated on military victory or defeat", as the two Scandinavian artists, Michael Elmgreen and Ingar Dragset, stated in an interview.[44] They intend to acknowledge "the heroism of growing up" instead of "celebrating military victory and commemorating fame", thereby criticizing and opposing the historical function of equestrian statues.[45] In addition, this piece of contemporary art may be understood as a comment on "the obsession of youth that permeates our culture."[46] Besides, it indirectly reflects the minor role horses generally play in everyday (urban) life.

Even if the outspoken horses of "A Dialogue" claim to possess prophetic qualities, they could certainly not foresee the amount of change in culture, government, and society from the seventeenth to the twenty-first century. Therefore, it would be interesting to know what an updated version of "A Dialogue between the Two Horses", namely between Charles I's horse and its new rocking counterpart, would be about. This is up to our imagination.

[42] I would like to thank Dr Sabine Baltes: *Hürth*, for drawing my attention to the statue.

[43] Birchwood: *Staging Islam in England*, p. 1.

[44] "Fourth Plinth Rocking Horse Unveiled," BBC News online of 23 February 2012. Available from: <http://www.bbc.co.uk/news/entertainment-arts-17140952>, accessed on 10 November 2013.

[45] Florence Waters: *Bronze statue of a boy on a rocking horse adorns Trafalgar Square's Fourth Plinth,* in: *The Telegraph*, 23 February 2012. Available from: <http://www.telegraph.co.uk/culture/art/art-news/9100356/Bronze-statue-of-a-boy-on-a-rocking-horse-adorns-Trafalgar-Squares-Fourth-Plinth.html>, accessed on 10 November 2013.

[46] Alastair Sooke: *Elmgreen and Dragset's Fourth Plinth, Review*, in: *The Telegraph*, 23 February 2012. Available from: <http://www.telegraph.co.uk/culture/art/art-reviews/9101444/Elmgreen-and-Dragsets-Fourth-Plinth-review.html>, accessed on 10 November 2013.

Figure 1: Charles I by Hubert Le Seueur (1633) ©Philip Halling

Figure 2: Charles II – unknown provenance

Figure 3: source wikimedia commons

Bibliography

Avery, Victoria: *Virtue, Valour, Victory: The Making and Meaning of Bronze Equestrian Monuments (*ca. *1440* – ca. *1640)*, in: *Praemium Virtutis III: Reiterstandbilder von der Antike bis zum Klassizismus*, ed. by Joachim Poeschke, Thomas Weigel, and Britta Kusch-Arnold. Münster 2008, pp. 199-233.

Birchwood, Matthew: *Staging Islam in England: Drama and Culture, 1640-1685.* Cambridge 2007.

Browning, Andrew (ed.): *The London Gazette*, 27-30 December 1675, printed in: *English Historical Documents, 1660-1714*. London 1966 [1953.

Burnet, Gilbert: *History of his Own Time*, 2 vols. London 1724-34.

Cowan, Brian: *The Social Life of Coffee: The Emergence of the British Coffeehouse.* New Haven and London 2005.

de St Didier, Limojon : *Histoire des négotiations de Nimegue.* Paris 1680.

deForest Lord, George, *et al.* (eds.): *Poems on Affairs of State: Augustan Satirical Verse, 1660-1714*, 7 vols. New Haven and London 1963-75.

Fourth Plinth Rocking Horse Unveiled, in: BBC News online of 23 February 2012. Available from: <http://www.bbc.co.uk/news/entertainment-arts-17140952>, accessed on 10 November 2013.

Gater, G. H. and E. P. Wheeler (eds.): *The statue of Charles I and site of the Charing Cross*, in: *Survey of London: Volume 16: St Martin-in-the-Fields I: Charing Cross* (1935), pp. 258-268. Available from: <http://www.british-history.ac.uk/report.aspx?compid=68141>, accessed 8 September 2013.

Kelliher, Hilton: *Andrew Marvell: Poet and Politician, 1621-78.* London 1978.

Knights, Mark: *Osborne, Thomas, first duke of Leeds (1632–1712)*, in: *Oxford Dictionary of National Biography Online.* Available from: <http://www.oxforddnb.com/view/article/20884>, accessed 22 October 2013.

Margoliouth, Herschel M. (ed.): *The Poems and Letters of Andrew Marvell*, 2 vols. Oxford 1971.

Moréri: *The Great Historical, Geographical and Poetical Dictionary*, s.v. "Charles I."

Moréri: *The Great Historical, Geographical and Poetical Dictionary*, s.v. "Nero."

Moréri: *The Great Historical, Geographical and Poetical Dictionary*, s.v. "Sardanapalus."

Noel, Thomas: *Theories of the Fable in the Eighteenth Century*. New York and London 1975.

Ogg, David: *England in the Reign of Charles II*, 2nd ed., 2 vols. Oxford 1956.

Poems on Affairs of State, ed. by Lord, *et al.*, I, 274.

Ralph, James: *A Critical Review of the Publick Buildings, etc. of London* (1734), cited in: *The Poems and Letters of Andrew Marvell*, ed. by Herschel M. Margoliouth, 2 vols. Oxford 1971.

Real, Hermann J., with the assistance of Kirsten Juhas, Dirk F. Passmann, and Sandra Simon (eds.): *The Battle of the Books*. Available from: Online.Swift/Ehrenpreis Centre for Swift Studies, Münster, October 2011, updated November 2013 <http://www.anglistik.uni-muenster.de/Swift/online.swift/works/battleofthebooks/>.

Real, Hermann J.: *An Introduction to Satire,* in: *Teaching Satire: Dryden to Pope*, ed. by Hermann Josef Real. Heidelberg 1992, pp. 7-19.

Sherman, Charles L. (ed. & transl.): *Diodorus of Sicily*, 12 vols. London and Cambridge, MA 1963, VII.

Sidney, Henry, Earl of Romney: *Diary of the Times of Charles the Second*, ed. by R. W. Blencowe, 2 vols. London 1843.

Sir Roger L'Estrange: *Fables of Aesop and Other Eminent Mythologists: With Morals and Reflexions*. London 1704.

Smith, Nigel (ed.): *The Poems of Andrew Marvell*, revised edition. London and New York 2013.

Smith, Nigel: *Andrew Marvell: The Chameleon*. New Haven and London 2010.

Somerset, Anne: *Ladies in Waiting: From the Tudors to the Present Day*. London 1984.

Sooke, Alastair: *Elmgreen and Dragset's Fourth Plinth, Review,*in: *The Telegraph*, 23 February 2012. Available from: <http://www.telegraph.co.uk/culture/art/art-reviews/9101444/Elmgreen-and-Dragsets-Fourth-Plinth-review.html>, accessed on 10 November 2013.

Story of a statue. Available from: <http://www.englishcivilwar.org/2011/12/charles-i-statue.html>, accessed 8 September 2013.

Swift, Jonathan: *Preface to Temple's* Letters, ed. by Kirsten Juhas and Hermann J. Real, with the assistance of Dirk F. Passmann, and Sandra Simon. Available from: Online.Swift/Ehrenpreis Centre for Swift Studies, Münster, October 2011, updated November 2013, <http://www.anglistik.uni-muenster.de/Swift/online.swift/works/templesletters/>.

Tilley, Morris Palmer: *A Dictionary of the Proverbs in England in the Sixteenth and Seventeenth Centuries: A Collection of the Proverbs Found in English Literature and the Dictionaries of the Period*. Ann Arbor 1950.

Titus Livius: *Titi Livii Historiarum libri: ex recensione Heinsiana*, 3 vols. Leiden 1634.

Waters, Florence: *Bronze statue of a boy on a rocking horse adorns Trafalgar Square's Fourth Plinth,* in: *The Telegraph*, 23 February 2012. Available from: <http://www.telegraph.co.uk/culture/art/art-news/9100356/Bronze-statue-of-a-boy-on-a-rocking-horse-adorns-Trafalgar-Squares-Fourth-Plinth.html>, accessed on 10 November 2013).

Wheatley, Henry B.: *London Past and Present: Its History, Associations, and Traditions*, 3 vols. London 1891.

Wilders, John (ed.): *Hudibras*. Oxford 1967, I, i, ll. 543-46.

On the Wings of Pegasus: Sissy Jupe and National Velvet

Francesca Orestano
University of Milan

Horses, stars

According to Lemprière's classical dictionary, Pegasus was a winged horse which sprung from the blood of Medusa when Perseus cut off her head.[1]

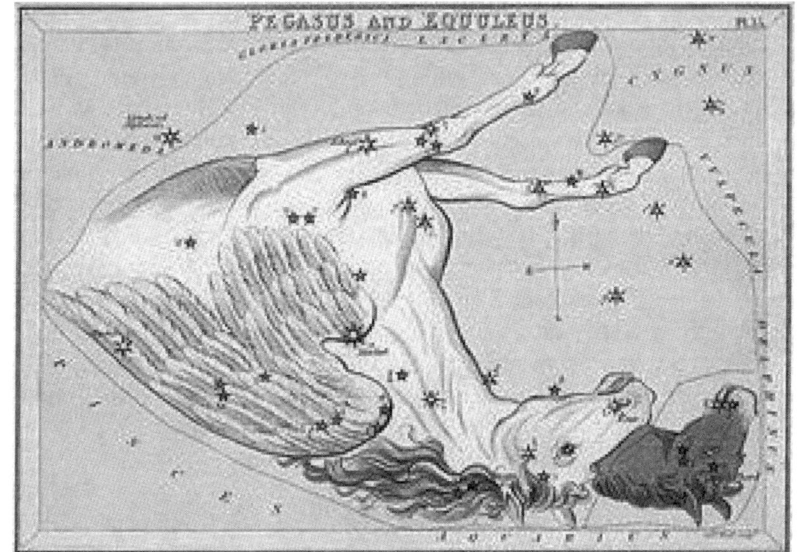

Fig. 1: Pegasus, the constellation, http://commons.wikimedia.org/wiki/File:Sidney_Hall_-_Urania's_Mirror_-_Pegasus_and_Equuleus_(best_currently_available_version_-_2014)_-_original.jpg

Pegasus received his name from being born, according to Hesiod, near the sources (πήγή) of the ocean. After he had been born, "he left the earth and flew up to heaven, or rather, according to Ovid, he fixed his residence on Mount Helicon, where by striking the earth with his foot, he raised the spring which was called Hippocrene."[2] He then

[1] John Lemprière: *A Classical Dictionary containing a Copious Account of all the Proper Names Mentioned in Ancient Authors with The Value of Coins, Weights, and Measures, used among the Greeks and Romans; and a Chronological Table*, London 1818, p. 557.
[2] John Lemprière: *A Classical Dictionary*, ed. cited, p. 557.

became the favorite of the Muses. Eventually Pegasus continued his flight up to heaven and was placed among the constellations by Jupiter. The right place for Pegasus is, indeed, among the stars, and thus he becomes the constellation described by the astronomer Ptolemy. As a side quote, the horses Ben-Hur leads to victory in the eponymous 1880 novel and 1959 movie[3] also bear the name of four stars: Aldebaran, Rigel, Altair and Antares.

The mythical Pegasus, source and emblem of poetical inspiration to the extent that Ovid would call the Muses 'Pegasides', does not stand without connection with the fictional characters evoked in these notes, Sissy Jupe and National Velvet, or Cecilia Jupe and Velvet Brown to give them their full name. The former a Victorian character, the latter almost born one century later, they are placed by their authors in strong proximity with the quadruped and thus invested – at once physically and metonymically – by the force of the mythical horse. Inspired or affected by a Pegasus, whose presence touches their lives in different ways, these characters derive from the horse inspiration and strength, flying at once over the difficulties of life and jumping over the high fences of a national competition.

In the literary plots I am going to examine, the horses are prominent figures, indeed co-protagonists to say the least, confirming the role that animals would obtain within the context of Victorian and early twentieth-century British literature, as well as the cultural shift occurring in those decades.[4] Actually the connection between young female characters and horses suggests the presence of a gendered issue which touches at once the heroines of these stories and their horses, and allows us to focus on cultural aspects and changes occurring between the XIXth and the XXth century : thus in *Hard Times* (1854) by Charles Dickens, and *National Velvet* (1935) by Enid Bagnold (1935), the horses – named Pegasus, and The Piebald, or Pie, – offer their full support to the weak, timid, ugly girls they escort into life, and victory. Such relationships indicate the cultural changes occurring between 1854 and 1935, with the rise of a new girl – akin to the new woman riding her bicycle, or driving a car – a girl able to compete, and to win.

Horses in children's literature and Victorian popular culture

During the second half of the eighteenth century, when children's literature was developing its full cultural impact, the relationship between animals and human characters had been the object of a number of it-narratives with a strong moral purpose, such as Dorothy Kilner's *The Life and Perambulations of a Mouse* (1784), *Fabulous Histories* (later known as *The Story of the Robins*) by Sarah Trimmer (1786), and the anonymous *Memoirs of Dick, the Little Poney, Supposed to Be Written by Himself; And Published for the Instruction and Amusement of Good Boys and Girls* (1800). Educa-

[3] Respectively Lew Wallace: *Ben-Hur: A Tale of the Christ* (1880) and the movie *Ben Hur* by William Wyler (1959). They belong to Sheikh Ilderim: the names of the stars are all Arabic in origin.

[4] Harriet Ritvo: *The Animal Estate. The English and Other Creatures in the Victorian Age*, Cambridge, MA 1987. Also cf.: *Victorian Animal Dreams: Representations of Animals in Victorian Literature and Culture,* edited by Deborah Denenholz Morse and Martin A. Danahay, Aldershot, Ashgate 2007.

tional patterns enforced by Mrs Laetitia Barbauld, then another prominent writer for children, suggested that the child had to learn "that the horse is an animal, & Billy is better than a Horse and such like", a statement provoking the criticism of Charles Lamb: "instead of that beautiful interest in wild tales [...] Science has succeeded to Poetry."[5] And this attitude, which we may call scientific, gained over the romantic holistic entanglement with nature and merged with the period's misogyny, to the extent that animals – especially pets – and women are physiologically connected not only by their (supposed) physical inferiority but also by the space of domesticity which they are meant to share, both subordinate to a male authority. Not casually in 1851 a manual seals within the pages of a popular booklet the joint destinies of women and pets: Jane Webb Loudon's *Domestic Pets: Their Habits and Management* places women and dogs, cats, parrots, Guinea pigs, rabbits and squirrels within the domestic scene, all elegantly caged into the master's household. The gendered relationship existing between women and household pets is also clearly indicated by the implied readership of Loudon's manuals, a public of women readers, whom she constantly addressed in writings aimed at female gardeners, budding women botanists, and household decorators.[6]

The horse, however, does not belong to the domestic environment, but rather enjoys a different species of domesticity – a domesticity displaced to a different environment. Traditionally viewed as a beast of burden (and thus protected since 1824, and under the Queen's aegis from 1840, by the *Royal Society for the Prevention of Cruelty against Animals*, RSPCA), the horse is a creature of the street, harnessed to the cart or to the ubiquitous coach, until gradually superseded by the railway. The horse is also the protagonist of horse-racing, a popular national sport,[7] involving thousands of spectators, requiring careful selection of thoroughbred champions, and a lot of betting. But the horse was also present on the Victorian cultural and literary scene as a performing animal, in the so-called equestrian circus entertainment. In this context, the horse is not just a slave, or a champion, but an actor, sharing with the equestrian artist or instructor the applause of the public. Moreover, within the surrogate family of the circus, made of instructors, clowns, jugglers, performing ladies, and despite this displaced domesticity, the horse is a regular member of the equestrian group, often in conjunction with a young woman rider, whose grace and beauty complement those of the quadruped: both are attired in fancy costume, harnessed with tinsel and feathers, for a joint feat of dexterity and charm.

In Charles Dickens' times the most popular place of amusement was Astley's Royal Equestrian Amphitheatre, between Westminster Bridge Road and Lambeth Palace

[5] Charles Lamb, letter of October 1802, cited in: Tess Cosslett: *Talking Animals In British Children's Fiction, 1786-1914*, Aldershot, Ashgate 2006, p. 27.

[6] Among the books by Jane Webb Loudon many can be cited, specifically addressing women: *Young Ladies Book of Botany* (1838); *Gardening for Ladies* (1840); *Botany for Ladies* (1842); *The Ladies Magazine of Gardening* (1842); *The Ladies Companion to the Flower Garden* (four volumes, 1840–44).

[7] On the subject cf. Kate Fox: *Watching the English. The Hidden Rules of English Behaviour*, London 2004, esp. pp. 249-250.

Road, rebuilt after a fire in 1843.[8] Founded in the last decade of the XVIII century, this equestrian activity enlarged and improved its London premises under the direction of Philip Astley, self-styled as 'professor of the Art of Riding' and author of *Astley's System of Equestrian Education*, published in 1801. A popular Victorian entertainment, with clowns and jugglers and performing animals, Astley's Equestrian Amphitheatre would be represented in 1808 in Rudolph Ackerman's popular series of aquatints entitled *The Microcosm of London.* Dickens mentions Astley as early as *Sketches by Boz*, devoting a whole chapter of the London scene section to this cherished amusement of his own childhood, still very popular also in years to come with its 'grand' riding-masters and equestrian performances.

Fig. 2: Astley's Amphitheatre from R. Ackerman's *Microcosm of London,* http://commons.wikimedia.org/wiki/File:Astley's_Amphitheatre_Microcosm_edited.jpg

The Royal Equestrian Amphitheatre fascinated whole families, parents and children alike, who would flock to the show, enjoying the graceful equestrian act of a Miss Woolford: "Another cut from the whip, a burst from the orchestra, a start from the horse, and round goes Miss Woolford again on her graceful performance, to the delight of every member of the audience, young or old."[9] This popular entertainment is described by Dickens with the usual vividness of touch and detail, as he follows the direction of the eyes of the spectators assessing at once their social class and response to the performance. Boz, however, has to remark that the glowing characters and costumes

[8] This popular entertainment, which had horses as the principal actors on the scene, is mentioned in *Sketches by Boz,* Scenes, 11; in TOCS, when Kit takes his family there for entertainment (39, 72); in *Bleak House* (21) when Mr George enjoys the performance of the Emperor of Tartary.

[9] Charles Dickens: *Sketches by Boz* (1836), London & Glasgow n.d., with Illustrations by T. H. Robinson, Ch. XI, "Astley's", p. 124.

which look so full of glitter and charm by the lamps over the ring, in daytime assume a discolored, cheap, and threadbare aspect. The illusion fades by daylight, while in the evening the show must go on, and every act, albeit repeated over and over, and always identical, will always fill the spectators with wonder.[10] This last aspect in which the magic of the show is contrasted against the unflattering perception during daytime will feed into the leading motif Dickens weaves in his novel *Hard Times* (1854) – in which the circus horse, a Victorian Pegasus, functions as a symbolic foil and core of Dickens' critique of Victorian society. The circus – Sleary's Horsemanship – is contrasted against Coketown, the magic of illusion against the rational, scientific, statistical assessment of life. The static, numeric system is cast against a poetical glimpse of heaven.

Pegasus in Coketown

Pegasus is the name of the horse whose nature, representation, description, and performance Charles Dickens evokes at the very beginning (and at the philosophical crux) of *Hard Times*[11] – also defined a condition-of-England novel insofar as it exposes the circumstances and the problems arising in factory districts, and the huge gap between the two nations living in England, the rich, and the poor working classes.

In the manufacturing towns of the North, as the young Friedrich Engels would report from Manchester in the early 1840s,[12] schools were meant to provide 'HANDS' to the factories: fodder to the mill. Hence a practical system of education was implemented, the Bell and Lancaster system, in which facts – facts – facts – counted more than anything else. In Coketown, – the imaginary, but realistic manufacturing city where the story told by Dickens is set – the opening question from the schoolmaster to the children is "Give me your definition of a horse."

There is not a more poignant and effective way for a writer who intends to expose the evils of society than showing them imparted to innocent children as if they were excellent and impregnable values. The "plain, bare, monotonous vault of a schoolroom" (*HT*, 47) is the place where only facts have to be learned by heart; the girl from the circus, Sissy Jupe, "Girl number twenty", is asked to give her definition of a horse. She is a new girl in the school, and Mr Gradgrind inquires about her father. The answer is "He belongs to the horse-riding, if you please, sir." But this activity must not be mentioned in the practical world of Coketown, entirely employed as factory hands. Thus Gradgrind tries to pin down Sissy's father activity by asking "Your father breaks horses, don't he?" And when Sissy answers that he breaks horses in the ring, here is another allusion to a world, to a 'there,' that must not be taken into consideration in 'here', by the practical kids of Coketown.

> "You mustn't tell us about the ring, here. Very well, then. Describe your father as a horse-breaker. He doctors sick horses, I dare say?"

[10] For this aspect of Dickens' careful recording of the culture of his age, cf. Paul Schlicke: *Dickens and Popular Entertainment*, London 2003.
[11] Charles Dickens: *Hard Times*, ed. by David Craig, Harmondsworth 1982. All subsequent references to this edition indicated as *HT*.
[12] Friedrich Engels: *The Condition of the Working Class in England*, Harmondsworth 1987.

> "Oh yes, sir."
> "Very well, then. He is a veterinary surgeon, a farrier, and horsebreaker. Give me your definition of a horse."
> (Sissy Jupe thrown into the greatest alarm by this demand.)
> "Girl number twenty unable to define a horse!" said Mr. Gradgrind, [...]. "Girl number twenty possessed of no facts, in reference to one of the commonest of animals! Some boy's definition of a horse. Bitzer, yours." (*HT*, 49)

The timid Sissy, although knowing very well what a horse is, and what a horse can do, and perform, is overwhelmed by her shyness and the stringent questions of Gradgrind. Thus she cannot describe a horse, if not with a telling silence. A local boy, instead, Bitzer, well inured to the system of the school, has the right answer:

> Quadruped. Graminivorous. Forty teeth, namely twenty-four grinders, four eye-teeth, and twelve incisive. Sheds coat in the spring; in marshy countries, sheds hoofs too. Hoofs hard, but requiring to be shod with iron. Age known by marks in mouth. (*HT*, 50)

The boy Bitzer is correct. His is the right answer. Sissy Jupe, on the contrary, is scolded by Mr Gradgrind. She cannot voice her love for the kind animal, nor her feelings for the artist who is part of her circus family. Again Sissy, girl number twenty, is questioned by a government officer: "Would you paper a room with representations of horses?" The children ignore the correct answer, which is soon imparted from the authority of the teacher: rooms should never be papered with representations of horses because: "Do you ever see horses walking up and down the sides of the room in reality? – In fact? Do you?" (*HT*, 51).

Thus we realize that the horse, in Coketown, is the core toward which cluster all the tensions operating in the place. The horse is a hard fact according to the empiricist agenda, where figures of teeth and legs are to describe it. But the horse is also placed in Coketown, where, as far as Sissy, the circus girl, is concerned, horses evoke sublime wonder, and lack of articulation; whereas for the children of Coketown the horse is an unusual fanciful show, so that they cluster near the circus trying to get a glimpse of the equestrian performance. According to Coketown school authorities horses cannot ignore the gravity law: whereas for Sissy (and for the other children as well) horses are able to defy gravity, to soar, to fly, and lightly walk up walls and up the ether. Sissy's inability to explain her first-hand knowledge of the rich and complex nature of the animals who work with her father, is obliquely justified when the children of the very rational Mr Gradgrind, his metallurgical Louisa and his mathematical Tom, are caught peeping at the equestrian act of Sleary's Horse-Riding circus: from a cranny in the tent they try to catch at least the dancing hoofs of a very graceful equestrian Tyrolean flower-act, performed by the daughter of the manager (*HT*, 56). Reason, mathematics, metallurgy, facts and figures, gravity itself, are soon forgotten and defeated by the spectacular acts of the circus performer, her picturesque costumes, the romantic halo enfolding her life, and the strange holistic relationship which holds the circus family – human animals and non-human animals – together.[13]

The circus is indeed the last testimony of a romantic attitude, already tinged with nostalgia for a way of life made of gipsy caravans, seasonal tours, fantastic shows eliciting that "spontaneous overflow of powerful feelings" which again, in a symbolic topography, take us directly back to the poetical fountain of the Muses' spring, from which our feelings gush – and where we meet Pegasus, the source of poetical inspiration, once again.

The capitalist Mr Bounderby and the intellectual Mr Grandgrind, struck by his own children's extravagant behavior, visit Sleary's horsemanship. The circus family is camping at a poor inn, under the sign of the Pegasus Arms:

> The name of the public-house was the Pegasus' Arms. The Pegasus' legs might have been more to the purpose; but, underneath the winged horse upon the sign-board, the Pegasus' Arms was inscribed in Roman letters. Beneath that inscription again, in a flowing scroll, the painter had touched off the lines:
> Good malt makes good beer,
> Walk in, and they'll draw it here;
> Good wine makes good brandy,
> Give us a call, and you'll find it handy.
> Framed and glazed upon the wall behind the dingy little bar, was another Pegasus – a theatrical one – with real gauze let in for his wings, golden stars stuck on all over him, and his ethereal harness made of red silk. (*HT*, 70)

Pegasus is painted on the sign of the inn, with a kind of cheap surrogate for his noble wings, made of red gauze, and tinsel stars that look like gold. There is no escaping the mass-production trend of Victorian times, the cheapening of craftsmanship in factories, the replacement of substance with theatricality and make-believe. But what Dickens suggests here is that substance after all is not of paramount importance: the poetical lightness of an equestrian show will alleviate the gravity of facts. As Sleary says, "People must be amuthed" (*HT*, 82) – all the more so when they live in a place like Coketown, where hard facts and the dark factory seem the only life companions.

Thus the magic Pegasus even when placed in Coketown, with fake stars and gauze wings, will operate its magic, as long as people can spend a night at the circus. The ability to enjoy the flight of Pegasus, and the fancy equestrian Tyrolean performance, sets the circus spectators on a different plan, apart from the capitalist tycoon who considers the circus a waste of time, a wart on the edge of his prosperous manufacturing town. Dickens' eye, while catching the shabby and worn apparel of the performers, also dwells on the genial make-believe, and the glowing impression that a few worn costumes may produce on spectators, on children, willing to suspend their disbelief and dream about the flying horse.

Thus the figure of Sissy Jupe, linked through her father to Sleary's horsemanship, helps me drawing the fundamental opposition between the horse as quadruped

[13] Michael Hollington: *Dickens and the Circus of Modernity*, in: *Dickens and Modernity,* ed. by Juliet John, London, pp. 133-149.

graminivorous, and the horse as a source of poetical inspiration, the starry Pegasus of this story. Dickens is well aware of this antinomy when he places all his circus actors under the sign of Pegasus: as if they were the last inspired artists of the age, and bearers of an outworn poetical tradition who must not be forgotten or ignored. The mythical Pegasus, the favorite of the Muses who is symbolically, emblematically, and even teleologically set among the stars of poetical inspiration, provides fantasy, lightness, and light, even in the poorest context, marked with darkness and the weight of facts. Within the context of Victorian culture a timid girl is the only advocate of his supreme power.

End of the century and modern horse and pony stories

To proceed from *Hard Times* to the horse and pony story, which gained the first bout of popularity at the end of the nineteenth century, we have to dwell briefly on Ann Sewell's *Black Beauty* (1877). *Black Beauty* is the successful story of a horse told in the first person, using equine language, duly translated into English, but nevertheless offering a riches-to rags-to riches story – the 'anagnorisis' story of a hero which is lost to his social origin, but eventually, owing to a white star mark, is recognized and saved from death. *Black Beauty* (1877) provides the reader with a biography set in English but translated from equine language. The talkative Black Beauty recalls his life, from being a colt up to old age, and the frightening dangers eventually impending upon a tired and spent cab horse. The story has been likened by Tess Cosslett to slave narratives, and indeed it contains more than a political innuendo, so that the equine world almost acquires the aspect of a convenient scenery or context in which issues related to human society are discussed by the author, a ventriloquist lending her voice to Black Beauty.

But the stories I am going to examine do not portray an anthropomorphized animal, whose memoirs are offered under the genre of autobiography. Horses are horses, and they are wont to perform in that role; their language cannot be translated from equine into English; and yet despite, or because of the realistic portrayal of the animal, a very strong relationship between horse and humans is engendered. After *Black Beauty*, horse stories seem to become increasingly popular.[14] I am referring here to books that flourish in the 1920s and 1930s, often telling a story about a girl, and her horse, or pony, set in the domestic rural context of Great Britain (I won't go into American or Australian horse and pony stories).

A cultural shift is evident here. These stories present a middle class family, often short with money. The conventions of the genre require a girl lacking in self-confidence, a horse that needs training, or a horse who seems worthless, owing to negligence or ill-treatment. The gradual process during which both horse and girl mutually acquire confidence and skills constitutes the bulk of the story, and the happy ending coincides with the successful performance at a show where they win a prize. In time, all this will become conventional, even formulaic. Books like *Moorland Mousie*

[14] Theresa Mangum: *Animal Angst: Victorians Memorialize Their Pets*, in: *Victorian Animal Dreams: Representations of Animals in Victorian Literature and Culture,* Aldershot, Ashgate 2007, pp. 15-34; Alison Haymonds: *Pony Books,* in: *The International Companion Encyclopaedia of Children's Literature*, 2 vols., ed. by Peter Hunt, London 2004, vol. I, ch. 36, pp. 481-489.

(1929) by Muriel Wace, a.k.a 'Golden Gorse', about an Exmoor pony, *Riders of Tomorrow* (1935) by Captain J. E. Hance, *A Pony for Jean* by Joanna Cannan (1936), *Janet and Felicity the Young Horse Breakers* (1937) by Monica Edwards and her *Wish for a Pony* (1947), are pioneers and models in a genre in which almost invariably a timid girl from a not so well-off family takes care of a neglected pony, or horse, and by dint of care, affection and training manages to 'convert' the horse into a docile performer and a champion. It is worth emphasizing that these books do frequently contain a lot of practical information: how to deal with the horse, inside and out of the stable; how to care, to feed, to train, to ride the horse. Thus they manage to compound the amount of useful advice horse lovers may need, with the dreams of glory typical of all sports literature – a sublimated quintessence of the medieval chivalry contests, taking place in a modern riding arena, or track. In other words, horse and pony books acquire popularity because they are halfway between the *Bildungsroman* and the practical manual about horse keeping and riding. According to Haymonds,

> Yet the pony story succeeds [...] and remains popular because it stays within the small, highly specialized society of horse lovers. Although the world of horses is perceived as upper class and privileged, the families in these stories are not always middle –class [...] and [...] obsessed with the costs, care, riding and love of horses – and these concerns are as relevant in the twenty first century as they were in the 1940s.[15]

Actually this is so because horse-racing, eventing, and jumping, manages to be one of those cultural pursuits in which Englishness, as stated by Robin Fox, shows its apparent disdain for class and caste, and its capability for a much-cherished cultural encompassing of social and class distinctions.

National Velvet

The successful author, dramatist and rider Enid Bagnold, Lady Jones (1889-1981), achieved great popularity with the novel entitled *National Velvet,* published in 1935.[16] The 1944 movie, with the young promising stars Elizabeth Taylor and Mickey Rooney, would seal its popular success. First of all *National Velvet* is a charming family portrait, set in rural England, near the chalky coast of Sussex and the green tufted hills behind. This is England in the Thirties, in a small healthy community near Worthing. The father is the village butcher, Mr Brown; his wife Araminty is a towering fat woman, who once had swum the Channel; there are four sisters, blond and lean like gazelles, and the youngest, Velvet, is the protagonist of the story – plus Donald, a mischievous baby brother, a young man, Mi Taylor, who works with Mr Brown, a few dogs, canaries, and an old pony, Miss Ada.

Velvet is the one who dreams about horses: riding them, jumping, winning. In a box she keeps paper horses cut from magazines, and pretends she is riding them; she rides

[15] Alison Haymonds: *Pony Books, ed.* cited, p. 482.

[16] Enid Algerine Bagnold, Lady Jones, CBE, also wrote *A Diary Without Dates* (1917) about her war experiences as a nurse, a few plays, among which *The Chalk Garden* (1955), and her *Autobiography* (1969). Cf. Anne Sebba: *Enid Bagnold, A Life*, New York 1986.

through the streets of the village; she rides when in bed, pretending she is clearing fences; her first and last prayer is "Oh, God, give me horses, give me horses! Let me be the best rider in England!" [17] She is fourteen, very thin, with "short pale hair, large protruding teeth, a sweet smile and a mouthful of metal" – hers is "the look of a sapling-Dante" (*NV*, 1-2).

As if by magic, in one single day, one old, eccentric and wealthy customer of her father's, Mr Cellini, decides to bequeath his five horses to Velvet. On the very same day another magic event occurs: Velvet wins the village lottery, with a one shilling ticket, the prize being a difficult, unmanageable piebald horse. The Piebald horse keeps escaping from the field where he is kept, jumping over stone walls to run at great speed into the sea-village's twisted streets. This is his first apparition:

> The sound of hoofs striking on the metalled road came out of the darkness, and down the street, all alone, galloped a horse. […] Something black and white and furious raced down the street. […] With a striking of hoofs, flying off the flints, a piebald horse, naked of leather, wild and alone, slid almost to its haunches and stood stock still, shaking and panting. He lowered his head. "A suitor for Velvet!"(*NV*, 24-25)

Stars are sparkling under the hoofs of the Piebald; even before the story of Velvet and Pie starts, there is the hint of an empathy negotiated through the senses, entirely built on the interpretation of the horse's attitudes and gestures, rather than on the fiction of an equine language. Going to the field where the Piebald is, with her sisters and Mi Taylor, who knows quite a lot about races and racing, Velvet realizes the enormous potential of the horse.

> He was white in bold seas, and black in continents, marked in such a way that when he moved his white shoulders and his white quarters flashed, and his black body seemed to glide. […] Velvet went among the hot grasses towards him. She knew him. She had already ridden him in her dream. […] She walked steadily and straight and began to talk in low tones. He raised his head and looked at her as firmly as she looked at him. She paused. He walked several paces towards her with confidence. No quirk or tremor or snort of doubt. […] The piebald, whose desires were gone, had kept his pride. He walked after Velvet like a stocky prince. Thick-necked, muscular, short and proud. (*NV*, 48)

Mi remarks that he has "Bin gelded late", a detail that previous children stories wholly erase. Indeed the horse emanates a very strong physical, almost sexual, attraction. When Velvet leaves the field of their first encounter, the horse decides to gallop after her, jumping a high stone wall.

> It was five feet two at the end of the field, with a fine downhill take-off. The horse sailed over it like a dappled flying boat, It was a double spring. As he was high in the air he saw also to his hind feet and drew them up sharply.
> "[…] AND to spare," said Mi quietly, nodding his head. "A horse like that'd win the National." (*NV*, 49)

[17] Enid Bagnold: *National Velvet* (1935), New York 1971, p. 14.

Thus Velvet dreams of taking part in the Grand National. "If I won that piebald [...] I might ride him in the Grand National myself." (*NV*, 51). With a bit of luck, her mother's strong support and savings, and with Mi's technical help, Velvet's dream will come true.

Two remarks are due here. The Grand National, annually held at Aintree Racecourse in Liverpool since 1839, is perhaps the oldest and most challenging handicap steeplechase competition in England. It covers over seven kilometres with thirty fences over two circuits, much larger and deeper than those found in similar competitions. Among the fences the Beecher's Brook was modified after 1989, due to too many horse casualties.[18] Other fences have also been reduced in height over the years, and the entry requirements for the race have been made stricter. After 1975, women jockeys were allowed to enter the race.[19]

Second: an "Author's Note" at the end of the novel explains that before 1931, when the competition in the novel is wont to take place, any horse could be entered in the Grand National: "and for all I can find in the Rules a zebra could have entered, provided he was the proper age." (*NV*, 215). Thus Velvet and Mi – she being a female and not an accredited male rider – will enter The Piebald for the Grand National race, pretending she is the Russian jockey James Tasky. Velvet has tried the horse and it is worth now to quote the passage about their first jump:

> They went at the wall together. [...] both knitted in excitement, the horse sprung to the surge of her heart as her eyes gazed between his ears at the blue top of the flint wall. She bent slightly and held him firm and steady, her hands buried in the flying mane firm on the stout muscles of his neck. She urged him no more, there was no need, but sat him still. He was a natural jumper. She did not attempt to dictate to him. They cleared the wall together, wildly, ludicrously high, with savage effort and glory, and twice the power and the force that was needed. (*NV*, 90)

From this moment onwards, the story predictably unfolds toward the grand moment of the competition, when Velvet, hair cropped and pretending to be a male, enters the course and wins the race. Yet just after the finishing line Velvet slides to the ground, from sheer exhaustion, and at the hospital the deception is discovered. The astounding news rapidly spread all over England, Europe, the US, the world: "A girl had won the Grand National" (*NV*, 173). It does not matter whether Velvet will be disqualified, and not awarded the silver cup and the rich prize money. She is the winner: "They had bitten off a piece of dream together, and like winged children accomplished it. [...] There was going to be trouble for her and Mi, though pure white glory for The Piebald." (*NV*, 177). After the race, they return to the village, and Pie is placed in his field as usual, tranquilly cropping, but showing his heavenly nature: "The Piebald was flashing his

[18] The image of the Beecher's Brook fence is the first illustration in the booklet *British Horses and Ponies*, by Lady Wentworth, London 1947, in the popular Britain in Pictures Series.

[19] Information about the Grand National and its history from the website http://www.grand-national.net/history.htm (accessed June 30, 2014).

colours under stars by the gate." (*NV*, 184). And when the marketing of gadgets, postcards, tiepins, powder-puffs, brown silk material, mechanical piebald horses, suggests to the reader the mass-culture dissemination of the event, the story will eventually come full circle: "There was a cartoon in one of the evening papers of Velvet coming over Beecher's sitting between the wings of Pegasus." (*NV*, 197).

The story of this modern Pegasus is similar, yet different from that of the Victorian Pegasus, owing to its cultural implications. The dissimilarity may be accounted for by describing on the one hand the interaction between Pegasus and Sissy Jupe as a source of poetical inspiration, which dictates to Sissy the right words to counteract the crude logic and figures of Coketown; while, on the other hand, the interaction between the Pie and Velvet affects the senses, and establishes a strong link between human and non-human animal. In her essay "The Turn to Affect: A Critique" Ruth Leys offers as an epigraph a meaningful passage: "If you don't understand try to feel. According to Massumi it works."[20]

The reference is to Brian Massumi and affect theory, which came out of the dissatisfaction with dominant modes of analysis in the humanities. The privilege granted to language seemed to prevent other modes of awareness to come to the surface of critical discourse. Thus affect theory tries to rescue and explain sensations, emotions, non-verbal interaction, and the ways in which the body can bear information and transmit it, over and beyond the information contained in any linguistic system. Affect sets itself side by side with signification, meaning, language – and in this function I find in this critical option the ideal tool to describe the relationship between Velvet and the Pie.

The full cultural potential of the story, as well as the emotions affecting the relationship between the horse and the young rider, are further displayed in the successful *National Velvet*, a 1944 MGM movie based on the novel by Enid Bagnold. Directed by Clarence Brown, screenplay by Helen Deutsch, it stars Mickey Rooney as Mi Taylor, and a young Elizabeth Taylor as Velvet. Shot in California, it won two Oscars in 1945. In 2003, *National Velvet* was selected for preservation in the United States National Film Registry by the Library of Congress as being "culturally, historically, or aesthetically significant." [21] Despite several departures from the original novel, the movie captures the intensity of Velvet's dreams, the simple charm of the domestic life in the village, and her strong relationship with the horse.[22]

A Contemporary Tail

A recent investigation in one of the major bookstores in England reveals that horse and pony stories have by no means ceased to exert their full fascination over young girls –

[20] Ruth Leys: *Critical Inquiry* 37:3 (Spring 2011), pp.434-472; Brian Massumi: *Parables for the Virtual: Movement, Affect, Sensation,* Durham, N.C. 2002; *The Affect Theory Reader*, ed. by Melissa Gregg and Gregory J. Seigworth, Durham, NC 2010.

[21] *America's Film Legacy: the Authoritative Guide to the Landmark Movies in the National Film Registry,* ed. by Daniel Eagan, New York 2010, p. 380.

[22] This kind of relationship is reiterated in the movie *Champions* (1984), the story of the horse Aldaniti and Bob Champion. In 1981 they won the Grand National, despite the fact that Aldaniti had suffered a chronic leg problem, and Champion a heavy chemotherapy for cancer.

and girl readers. They occupy a special shelf, in long rows of books, mainly paperbacks. I am just going to quote a few titles to indicate the growing success and essential features of the formula.

The story entitled *The One Dollar Horse*, by Lauren St John,[23] is classed as chick-lit and contains the same powerful messages of optimism which used to characterize children's literature and especially girl stories. Casey Blue, the protagonist, has a difficult life in East London; her father is just out of jail; but, again, a wild and starving horse is saved by Casey, and with this horse, Storm, she will realize her dream, to take part in the Badminton Horse Trials. Partly a fairytale, partly realistically told, the story shows how by dint of a mutual training of horse and rider victory can be achieved. A sequel already exists with *Race the Wind, One Dollar Horse Book 2,* by the same author, published in 2013.

Pippa Funnell, champion rider and author of pony tales, provides young girl readers with the Tilly's Pony Tails series. The protagonist, Tilly Redbrow, loves horses, dreams about them just like Velvet Brown, and learns to ride and care for them at Silver Shoe Farm, where she meets her champion horse, Magic Spirit. We are told that these Ten Perfect Pony Tales by Pippa Funnell are warm and engaging, yet also packed with Pippa's expert advice on everything you ever want to know about horses. Among her titles, *Pickle: The Show Pony* (2010), *Nimrod: The Circus Pony* (2011), *Moonshadow: The Derby Winner* (2011), *Free Spirit. The Mustang* (2012), and many more. The list could indeed be made longer by quoting other recent series addressing young horse-mad girls – suffice it to say that the genre is well established, and that with all the cultural changes affecting present times, Pegasus still inspires and affects. These stories offer at once the realization of a wild dream, and the instructions which foster mutual well-being with a close, confident physical relationship between horse and rider.

Bibliography

Bagnold, Enid: *National Velvet* (1935). New York 1971.

Dickens, Charles: *Hard Times*, ed. by David Craig. Harmondsworth 1982.

Dickens, Charles: *Sketches by Boz* (1836). London & Glasgow n.d., with Illustrations by T. H. Robinson.

Eagan, Daniel (ed.): *America's Film Legacy: the Authoritative Guide to the Landmark Movies in the National Film Registry*. New York 2010.

Engels, Friedrich: *The Condition of the Working Class in England.* Harmondsworth 1987.

Fox, Kate: *Watching the English. The Hidden Rules of English Behaviour.* London 2004.

Gregg, Melissa and Gregory J. Seigworth (eds.): *The Affect Theory Reader*. Durham, NC 2010.

Haymonds, Alison: *Pony Books,* in: *The International Companion Encyclopaedia of Children's Literature*, vol. 1, ed. by Peter Hunt. London 2004.

Hollington, Michael: *Dickens and the Circus of Modernity*, in: *Dickens and Modernity,* ed. by Juliet John. London 2012.

http://www.grand-national.net/history.htm (accessed June 30, 2014).

Lady Wentworth: *British Horses and Ponies*, London 1947.

[23] Lauren St John: *The One Dollar Horse*, London 2012

Lamb, Charles: *Letter of October 1802*, cited in: Tess Cosslett: *Talking Animals In British Children's Fiction, 1786-1914.* Aldershot, Ashgate 2006.

Lemprière, John: *A Classical Dictionary containing a Copious Account of all the Proper Names Mentioned in Ancient Authors with The Value of Coins, Weights, and Measures, used among the Greeks and Romans; and a Chronological Table*. London 1818.

Leys, Ruth: *Critical Inquiry* 37:3 (Spring 2011), pp.434-472.

Mangum, Theresa: *Animal Angst: Victorians Memorialize Their Pets*, in: *Victorian Animal Dreams: Representations of Animals in Victorian Literature and Culture.* Aldershot, Ashgate 2007, pp. 15-34.

Massumi, Brian: *Parables for the Virtual: Movement, Affect, Sensation.* Durham, NC 2002.

Morse, Denenholz, Deborah and Martin A. Danahay, (eds.): *Victorian Animal Dreams: Representations of Animals in Victorian Literature and Culture.* Aldershot, Ashgate 2007.

Ritvo, Harriet: *The Animal Estate. The English and Other Creatures in the Victorian Age.* Cambridge, MA 1987.

Schlicke, Paul: *Dickens and Popular Entertainment*. London 2003.

St John, Lauren: *The One Dollar Horse.* London 2012.

Writing/Riding on non-anthropocentric Horses

Susanne Peters
University of Magdeburg

1. The readability of animal stories

Narratives that fit into the genre specifics of popular and young adult or adolescent fiction mostly unfold on archetypal, uncluttered patterns. Their story worlds are peopled with manageable amounts of characters, who negotiate limited sets of dilemma or ethical conflicts.[1] The straightforward development of plot offers the reader orientation, namely a resolution of emotional and other entanglements and sometimes even a moral evaluation of the actions at the end. They can be described – using Roland Barthes' distinction – as 'readerly' texts, which make less demand on the reader, are more straightforward, and whose meaning is more immediately evident.[2] In addition to that, they also appear to follow some basic principles of 'tellability', a concept that pertains to discourse-independent individual interest in telling a good story which leads to the presumed emotional, intellectual and/or aesthetic involvement of the audience, and we can add, the reader.[3]

The fact that such stories are fairly easy to decode may help explain their appeal to the young and to those enjoying a good story, if a little on the simple (though not

[1] The generic distinction between young adult fiction and texts that are marketed as popular fiction is not always easy to gauge. The by now classical difficulty of allocating Lewis Carroll's *Alice's Adventures in Wonderland* to the domain of children's or adults' fiction is a case in point here – perhaps this is an indication that attempts to distinguish between the two types of fiction (if that is indeed what they are) might only yield limited epistemological insight. However, as this issue is not at the forefront of my essay, we might consider Wall's suggestion to categorise this type of fiction according to its addressees. Wall argues that "a story can contain single address (i.e. children only), double address (children and adults in alternative moments in the narrative), or dual address (both age-based audiences addressed simultaneously)." Cf. David Herman, Manfred Jahn and Marie-Laure Ryan: *Routledge Encyclopedia of Narrative Theory*, London, New York 2005, p. 59, and Barbara Wall: *The Narrator's Voice: The Dilemma of Children's Fiction*, New York 1991.

[2] Roland Barthes: *S/Z*. Translated by Richard Miller, New York 2000.

[3] Labov's concept of tellability "presupposes that stories exist in a virtual state in the mind of the storyteller, before they are actualised as texts in the storytelling (or writing) performance." I use Labov's concept of tellability in a broader sense to comprise the reader's expectation as well. Cf. Herman, Jahn and Ryan: *Routledge Encyclopedia*, ed. cited, p. 589, and William Labov: "The Transformation of Experience in Narrative Syntax", in: *The Discourse Reader*, ed. by Adam Jaworski and Nicolas Coupland, London 1999, pp. 221-235.

simplistic) side. Stories need not be intellectually warped, simple texts can be equally enlightening in regard to the proposition and solution of conflicts. Thus, the presumed lack of sophistication of popular and/or adolescent fiction should not be conceived as a deficiency. Rather, it appears more profitable to look at how they manage to elicit reader response and encourage empathy in both groups of addressees.

It is a common feature of these stories that their protagonists must undergo rites of passage: they leave their protected childhood homes and set out on hazardous journeys through life, they cover great distances – though the conception of space (as well as that of time) naturally varies according to the species involved, and they meet friend and foe. Their quest, particularly in the stories selected for this essay, is that of survival, with long periods of danger broken up by brief phases spent in relative safety. Pain, fear and redemption (Christian undertone intended, see below) seem to alternate in these stories, while their endings often present tableaus of a somewhat belated, subdued happiness, with the experience of trauma still weighing heavily on their minds and obviously on those of their readers.

The question whether popular books either for youngsters or for grown-ups or both are didactic rests on the issue of the moral guidance that they provide. As empathy and sensibility is something that can be learned from books – and language didactics has long since convinced us that this is the case, moreover, that it is an important legitimization for using fiction especially in the foreign language classroom[4] – popular fiction is a very rewarding place to look for training material.

Turning to the question of animal agency, we notice that animals often feature major roles in such texts. They can be 'people in fur', distinctly humanoid in their character traits or they serve as supportive companions to humans, or indeed they make an appearance as narrators, telling their own story.[5] Animals are often agents which help the young human to become a socially responsible and emotionally responsive individual. This may be a reason why many stories couple young humans and young animals, usually domesticated or companion animals such as dogs and horses. Furthermore, and even more to the point of this essay, the psychology of human-animal stories is also revealing in terms of our view on these animals and what place we ascribe them in our culture. What can be gained by interpreting human-animal stories does not rest with the reader's lesson in empathy. Larger issues are at stake and need to be addressed, as the following sections will show.

[4] Cf. Lothar Bredella and Werner Delanoy (eds.): *Challenges of literary texts in the foreign language classroom*, Tübingen 1996.

[5] This phenomenon has hitherto been theorized mainly in contexts of children's fiction proper. Cf. Maria Nikolajeva: *The Rhetoric of Character in Children's Fiction*, Lanham 2002. The purpose of employing talking animals can perhaps best be described along the continuum of anthropocentric presence: 'People in fur' are found at one end, while animals presented in a realistic fashion "have their consciousness cast in human speech" (cf. Herman, Jahn and Ryan: *Routledge Encyclopedia*, ed. cited, p. 59, where the horse Black Beauty is briefly mentioned under this category). In addition, anthropomorphic characters "can be used to mask differences in class, race, and ethnicity as well as to appeal to children through fantasy." Ibid.

2. Questioning the human-animal divide

Where do we turn to if we want to find out about the place animals hold in our culture? Our dealings with our fellow creatures on Earth appear to be motivated not by mutual benefit as some will argue in the context of the economic necessity to earn one's keep, but by the question of how we as humans can profit (quite often in the monetary association of that verb) from them, whether by keeping and breeding them for pleasure, food or work – and the proverbial 'beast of burden' is a case in point – there's always some foremost human interest to be discovered. In this sense, animal stories are also concerned with the question of what it means to be a human being. Moreover, companion animal stories – of smaller pets, but also those that feature domesticated animals such as horses, which will be of particular interest here – also allow us to historicize human-animal relations.

The stories I discuss here for that purpose are Anna Sewell's all-time bestseller *Black Beauty* (1871-1877), selling more than fifty million copies to date[6], a book that has suffered countless adaptations for the television screen as well as the cinema. Each new horse-loving generation has its own version of *Black Beauty*, most of them more on the sentimental or even melodramatic side than the original, which was written to alleviate ignorance and to provide know-how on horse-keeping and horse-handling to those in sore need of it. The classic *Black Beauty* will be read in a similiar context with a text that has recently gained wide media attention, Michael Morpurgo's *War Horse*, written roughly a hundred years and two world wars later (1982). The exceptional media attention that both these stories continue to attract has far removed them from their original contexts. Yet it is not the exploration of their adaptability to a variety of different visual genres that is of interest here (see Anja Müller's contribution) – it is their narrative perspective that seems to be finely tuned to the plight of the animal suffering at the hands of humankind. The books are very similar in cleverly employing a narrative technique that is rather successful: Although the stories are told from the perspective of the animals, we do not hear them 'speak' the human language. Neither do they babble or prattle, but rather, they appear to philosophize without directly mimicking oral human speech. This I deem significant because in real life, animals do not speak either, although they sometimes appear to possess a sophisticated consciousness which we might then imaginatively access via literature. To conceptualize this kind of narrative voice is perhaps closely related to the precepts of a 'natural' narratology.[7] Direct speech is turned into perceiving and interpreting – internally representing – human and other animal action. The horses feel and and they think, but they do not speak in human voices.

The stories appeal not only to youngsters, but to grown-ups as well. Perhaps this is due to the fact that we humans are more and more sensitized to the issue of how we humans treat animals – especially those we come into close contact with. A growing

[6] According to a survey in *The Times*, 2 February 2008. (Retrieved from Wikipedia's entry on "Black Beauty").

[7] Cf. Monika Fludernik's study *Towards a 'Natural' Narratology*, London, New York 1996, where she considers the originary connection between narrativity and orality and defines narrativity as independent from plot and negotiating experientiality.

number of scientific studies suggest to us that quite possibly, there is no great human-animal divide in existence, at least not in the way we have come to think of our relationship to animals over thousands of years of regardless exploitation. Whether we perceive this distinction to be ever diminishing and therefore humiliating to our pride is another issue, but the concern for human-animal relationships amounts to an assessment of a humanistic culture of responsibility. Consideration, respect and allowing animals to be beings-in-themselves, independent from our knowledge of them, signifies how much we value the animal Other, in our present day and also how we have valued them in the past. In terms of such a political zoology we might formulate, translating Roland Borgards' dictum "tell me where you place animals, and I tell you something about the way your culture functions."[8]

It may be difficult to think ourselves outside the boundaries of our species identity, but we are under a "fundamental obligation to honour the claims of others as the claims exceed anthropocentric moral and legal frameworks."[9] Although avoiding anthropocentrism may never be fully achieved for the simple reason that we can never slip into the consciousness of an Other (as some will argue), we need to remember that fiction can do what we cannot do in real life. Still, in one compelling aspect, the relationship between humans and animals is indeed conceived as mutual: As we communicate with the animals, they communicate with us. And quite often in the history of humankind, this has been perceived as a sign of witchcraft.[10] Swift's account of Gulliver's journey to the land of the Houyhnhnms can serve as an illustration (a deeper analysis is to be found in Herman Josef Real's contribution). There, the horse that he meets shortly after his landing, appears to be speaking "in some language of his own" (271) and, after a while, the species confer freely with one another. The humanoid creatures on the island, the Yahoos, are, on the other hand, and quite contrary to the horses, described as howling and ugly brutes. While the horses, according to their mediator Gulliver, have the ability to speak, even to philosophize, and seem to be the gatekeepers of morality *per se*, the Yahoos are rendered speechless. The elegance of the horse's refined movements is contrasted with the clumsiness of the Yahoos in human shape. The anthropocentric register is displaced into the (anthropomorphic) horse, endowed with reason and offered for identification (at least to Gulliver himself), while the human race is depicted as odious, barbarous and without language or at least the capacity for interspecies communication. In Swift's novel, the human becomes the Other: Literature is indeed capable to giving up anthropocentric solipsism.

Thus works of literature of all ages have managed to replace the prevailing anthropocentrism – regardless of whether it is attached to humans or appear in the

[8] Cf. Roland Borgards: *Tiere in der Literatur – eine methodische Standortbestimmung*, in: *Das Tier an sich,* ed. by Herwig Grimm and Carola Otterstedt, Göttingen 2012, pp. 87-118, 96.

[9] Cf. Natalie Hansen: *Horse stories: rethinking the human-animal divide*, Ann Arbor: 2009, p. 13.

[10] John Dando: *Maroccus extaticus: or, Bankes bay horse in a trance*. From the original trait printed in 1595. Ed. by Edw. F. Rimbault, London 1843. Retrieved from Münchener Digitalisierungszentrum (Bayerische Staatsbibliothek). http://en.wikisource.org/wiki/Maroccus_Extaticus.

disguise of anthropomorphised animals – by ‘pathocentric’ or even ‘holistic’[11] points of view, that render the distinction between animals and humans less clear-cut and widen our perspective on the world to encompass the subjectivity of animals.[12] The fact that two species are able to communicate successfully with each other is, I believe, a sure sign of both being capable of empathy and reason – if we understand reason as a fundamental principle of life and a prerequisite of survival.

As postcolonial discourse has shown, logocentrism (or even phallogocentrism), as the overarching philosophical paradigm that still guides Western understandings of the nature of humans and serves as the prime base for conceptualising reason, is aligned with white male supremacy. It has been stigmatized in the context of the necessary deconstruction of imperialist power that paid no heed to indigenous rights of place. In a similar vein, human-animal studies strive to deconstruct the supremacy of humankind over the animal kingdom (somctimes widened to encompass the biosphere) and further our understanding and theorising of mutual interspecies communication. And perhaps there can be no better place to illustrate how this is possible than literature, the testing ground of communicative possibilities without the restrictions of reality and under no obligation to depict something as true. The stories under examination here are thus seen to focus on the granting of primary subject status to the nonhuman animal via the construction of narrative perspective. The stories, as a ‘laboratory’, or alternative world in which to probe ethical questions, exemplify how acts of supposed human supremacy lead to irresponsibility and disregard of the nonhuman animal. They render such supremacy void. Taking the unaccustomed perspective of a horse, it becomes possible to spell out the message of these texts which is to reject our continuous exploitation of nonhuman partners in life. Just why it should be viable to take up that perspective the following analysis will show. However, the outcome will be a bit of a mixed blessing: the stories as stories can never be anything but anthropomorphic, the stories *do* anthropomorphise horses, which *do* represent human qualities worth striving for but hard to achieve. The crux of representation cannot after all be argued away, though it can be restricted, because these animals also *do* speak for themselves; and as agents, they also represent themselves in their demand for fairness and respect.

[11] Both terms are used in environmental ethics: “Pathocentrism is based on the assumption that all life is of the same origin and thus related. As a consequence, all living beings have the capacity to experience pain. In Christian tradition, this leads back to an ‘ethics of compassion’.” Holism is defined as contrary to individualistic and particularly anthropocentric points of view and encompasses biocentrism, ecocentrism and deep ecology. Cf. http://ulrich-menzel.de/forschungsberichte/water-and-international-relations-presentation_karafyllis. Retr. 6.7.2014.

[12] Mc Hugh has argued that there is always an underlying metaphoric streak in employing literary animals: animals represent – perhaps until the early 19th century, but this is subject to further research – human characteristics. In her analysis of romantic poetry, as of Keats’ “Ode to a Nightingale”, she demonstrates that the crux is representation: what does the nightingale stand for when it can never be itself in a literary text? Cf. Susan Mc Hugh: *Literary Animal Agents*, in: *PMLA* 124:2 (2009), pp. 487-495.

3. "Horseness is the whatness of allhorse"[13]

With respect to the literary horse's 'essence', it is their admirable physical qualities, their initial beauty and elegance that are the most striking, and significantly, the colour of their coat which is mostly black or dark. White horses are sometimes connected with the devil or to some evil motif, as is the horse in Theodor Storm's *Der Schimmelreiter*, or, within the boundaries of popular fiction, the white killer horse in Albert G. Miller's *Fury*. The Apocalypse, though, employs a different colour symbolism. There, Christ returns to earth on a white horse to conquer the world,[14] while the black, the chestnut and the dun horse symbolize death, war, and famine. Colours signify different meanings at different times and in different cultures, while it is only the black or dark horse that seems to raise consistently positive connotations throughout literary history. Still, colour discussed in this context is metaphoric, while the horse stands for something else, never for itself.

Literary horse protagonists are also noble and fast-moving, strong-willed, intelligent, and sensitive; they comply to a Christian work ethic, are hard-working and honourable. More or less immediately after the stories begin, they are separated from their mothers, and sold on to become animal slaves never to fully regain their liberty. In the course of their lives, they get hurt, they grow sick, and finally, old and frail. In the context of the human-animal divide, this very much resembles not only the human way of life, but all life cycles on Earth.

The narratives are of the adventurous kind with frequent shifts of setting. They are of an episodic structure with a plot more or less determined by downwardly spiralling movements until the final 'rescue' at the end. The stories alternate between danger, mishap, and temporary relief. This continues until they eventually find peace with some former owner or groom who recognizes their long-lost animal friend, purchases him, puts him out to pasture and gives him his *Gnadenbrot*. Thus, their sense of time and timing, too, appears humanoid.

Black Beauty is part companion part working animal when the story begins, then he moves down the social ladder to becoming an inner city cart horse, and finally, back to something he was at the beginning, though much reduced by age and bad experience, as well as in general visual appeal. Joey in *War Horse* is a farm animal before becoming a trained war horse in the First World War. At the end of the war, he is shipped back to England and allowed to spend the rest of his days in peace. The horses represent economic value to their owners, which necessitates a master-servant relationship between human and animal, as this wise comment to Black Beauty serves to demonstrate:

[13] James Joyce: *Ulysses*, episode 9 (Scylla and Charybdis), Penguin student edition 1986, p. 153. It is Stephen's thought representation that references the famous dispute between Plato and Aristotle about the question whether there is an ideal world behind our actual one which is only the representation, or whether what we perceive is all there is and ever will be.

[14] In Kenneth Branagh's film version of Shakespeare's *Henry V* (1989), Henry rides to the battle of Agincourt on a white horse, possibly an allusion to Henry's identification with Christ.

> [My mother] told me the better I behaved, the better I should be treated, and that it was wisest always to do my best to please my master. "But," said she, "there are a great many kinds of men; there are good, thoughtful men like our master, that any horse may be proud to serve; but there are bad, cruel men, who never ought to have a horse or dog to call their own. Beside, there are a great many foolish men, vain, ignorant and careless, who never trouble themselves to think, these spoil more horses than all, just for want of sense; [...] but a horse never knows who may buy him, or who may drive him; it is all a chance for us, but still I say, do your best, wherever it is, and keep up your good name." (*Black Beauty*, 13f.)

Many horse protagonists are male. In Christian mythology the female horse, the mare, is connected to the powers of darkness, etymologically still recognizable in the term 'nightmare'. Regardless of whether the authors of the narratives under consideration here were aware of that, the preference of and desire for masculine power seems rather obvious. Concurrently, the horses' environments are almost exclusively peopled by male humans, who act as grooms, teachers, and masters. Women are predominantly decorative. In *Black Beauty*, they are vain creatures who show no concern for horses and treat them cruelly, in particular with regard to the bearing-rein, an 18th and 19th century fashionable and unnatural, painful way to pull horses' heads up as they were pulling coaches. In *War Horse*, there is a little girl who cares for Joey and treats him well, but this is 'just' a girl, who has no agency in the male-dominated story world (and she is written out of the story as another victim of the war). The absence of women in these stories is quite remarkable, particularly because it is them who provide the greatest share of their readership. Thus, characterization and plot development do indeed very closely resemble human agency and storytelling.

4. "Some language of his own": Beauty and Joey as narrators and reflectors

There is a long tradition of talking animals in the history of literature. The ability to narrate the story of one's life is a sure sign of agency and reason. However, it is not only the speaking horse that comes into the question. In inter-species communication, we might also look at the humans talking to horses. In modern times, horse whisperers are sought to cure problem horses, while equitherapy is supposed to cure humans and help them rediscover their psychological balance. Not not only does the talking animal come into consideration, the human conversing with the animal is also a point in question – here we need to look at the reciprocity of human-animal communication. Yet, it was Michel de Montaigne who rejected the definition of language in 17th century France in purely human terms: "[...] they may reckon us to be brute beasts for the same reason that we reckon them to be so [...] How could they not speak to one another? They certainly speak to us, and we to them." [15]

Black Beauty as well as *War Horse* are narrated by the horses themselves. Can we interpret that fact in terms of the construction of an ethics of literary horses? In reality, as we all know, horses do not speak the human language, but in literary texts, diegetic

[15] Michel de Montaigne: *An Apology for Raymond Sebond*, trans. and ed. M.A. Screech, London 1993, p. 17.

animals can. Here is an example, in which Black Beauty comments on humans and one of their less desirable character traits:

> I must now say a little about Reuben Smith, who was left in charge of the stables when York went to London. No one more thoroughly understood his business than he did, and when he was all right, there could not be a more faithful or valuable man. He was gentle and very clever in his management of horses, and could doctor them almost as well as a farrier, for he had lived two years with a veterinary surgeon. He was a first-rate driver; he could take a four-in-hand, or a tandem, as easily as a pair. he was a handsome man, a good scholar, and had very pleasant manners. I believe everybody liked him; certainly the horses did; the only wonder was that he should be in an under situation, and not in the place of a head coachman like York: but he had one great fault, and that was the love of drink. (*Black Beauty*, 100)

In Marpurgo's *War Horse*, the most common narrative device is to let the horse narrate some events in a factual manner, and then adapt that situation to use the horse as focaliser who listens carefully to what the humans have to say to each other or to the animals, as in this example:

> It was some months later, on the way back from cutting the hay in Great Meadow along the sunken leafy road that led up into the farmyard that Albert first talked to us about the war. His whistling stopped in mid-tune. "Mother says there's likely to be a war", he said sadly. "I don't know what it's about – something about some old duke that's been shot at somewhere. Can't think why that should matter to anyone, but she says we'll be in it all the same. But it won't affect us, not down here. We'll go on just the same. At fifteen I'm too young to go, anyway – well, that's what she said. But I tell you, Joey, if there is a war I'd want to go. I think I'd make a good soldier, don't you? Look fine in a uniform, wouldn't I? And I've always wanted to march to the beat of a band. Can you imagine that, Joey? It if comes to that, you'd make a good war horse yourself, wouldn't you, if you ride as well as you pull, and I know you will. We'd make quite a pair. God help the Germans if they ever have to fight the two of us." (*War Horse*, 15)

Here, the horse listens to Albert's explanation of why nations go to war while the narrative achievement is that of exposing the absurdity of war itself. While the horse's natural inability to comprehend what has been said meets with the boy's naivety, it serves to epitomize the craziness of war. The comprehending horse is as much an impossibility as is the misappropriation of war by assuming it is about chasing some Germans. It is not in the nature of either participants in this little talk to grasp the real meaning of war. Yet both will soon be forced into it as the story evolves.

The horses Black Beauty and Joey are well-meaning, freedom-loving, noble, beautiful, strong and fast-moving animals. In this they are depicted to be superior to humans. Their male teachers more often than not use cruelty in their exertion of power over them. The alternation between safety and danger, being well-fed and going hungry, liberty and constraint secure an easy to follow, archetypal pattern of narration that allows for a postponement of a happy ending while safeguarding that it will if only partially, come in the end. Using a horse as narrator thus not only ensures greater empathy from the reader, but at the same time serves to expose human folly. Thus the horse is a powerfully ambivalent agent who engages us emotionally and may raise an awareness of our responsibility towards animals in our care. Yet, we need to remind ourselves that literary horses are a construct, that it is not the horses who *feel*, but the actual readers of their stories who *feel*. What we now ask is: if horses and humans are set in a common frame of action, does that automatically entail the objectification of the animal? Are we never to escape our anthropocentric views on the animal world?

5. "Horse sense is the thing a horse has which keeps it from betting on people":[16] Theorising the horse

If horses can be discussed as representatives of cultural change in systems of thought, can such a change be found in the rejection of the objectification of the horse as demonstrated by the horse as narrator? In order to attempt a preliminary answer to this question, I will sum up my findings so far and suggest to approach the stories from three critical angles that build upon each other and perhaps lead to a more comprehensive understanding of contemporary human-animal relations in popular fiction.

a) Reader response

How is the reader's response to these stories elicited? Looking at the bonds between text and reader, one finds that the reader – and especially the young one – may easily identify with the horses and more particularly, with their noble character traits, especially their sensitivity, strength, foresight, and so on. Regardless of their melodramatic potential, the identification of which is a very personal judgement anyway, reading about the horses' suffering, their hunger, pain and fear may, on the other hand, produce a cathartic effect in the reader. Eliciting reader response may also touch upon didactic issues, such as the role of ignorance in our dealings with the animals. According to her biographer, Anna Sewell wrote her book also to provide knowledge about the proper care for horses.[17] In all cases, our response to the stories is emotionally charged. Our empathy towards the poor protagonists and their cruel fate may then indeed help change our attitudes towards the animal Other, furthering greater understanding. An approach in terms of reader response will ultimately diminish the human-animal divide, and because of that – although this may seem paradoxical – it can be argued that this makes it even harder to see the plight of the maltreated animal at the hands of humans. If we thus continue to look at animals through our anthropocentric vision – and the interest in reader-response is precisely that – we will always look at animals in an attempt to see ourselves rather than allowing them to be beings-in-themselves. The diminishing of the human-animal divide via constructing the thinking, reflecting horse is a double-edged sword, because we can also argue that the visible difference between human and animal is a prerequisite to awaken a human sense of responsibility to the ever inferior creature. If, on the other hand, we insist on the

[16] This phrase is attributed to W.C. Fields.

[17] Cf. Adrienne Gavin: *The Autobiography of a horse?: Reading Anna Sewell's Black Beauty as autobiography*, in: *Representing Victorian Lives,* ed. by Martin Hewitt, Leeds 1999, pp. 51-62.

similarities and highlight these, we care for them not more than we care for our fellow human beings – but then we *do* care for them. The insistence on the human-animal divide opens the door to a misanthropically informed biocentrism, in which the human is not regarded to be at the top of our hierarchical chain of beings.

b) Gender

To look at these texts from a gender-conscious perspective allows us to focus on the characteristic absence of females in the books.[18] As we engage with a world crowded by males (human as well as nonhuman) the prevalence of male characteristics easily effaces femininity. In terms of gender politics, this appears to be odd, particularly with a view to the largely female readership, and taking into account the well-documented general preference of teenage girls for horses and riding. In a corresponding vein, a gender conscious perspective surely also allows us to focus on the masculinity of the horse as main protagonist and the positive connotation of their power and intelligence, while human masculinity is often constructed rather negatively in these texts (and associated with dumbness and ignorance). The male horse becomes the better man. There are large numbers of men who abuse horses – usually those who also abuse women–, though some are wise, calm, patient and friendly in their dealings with both species. Continuing this line of argument, one would discuss the common denominator between femininity and animality, which would be the position of the inferior a point which takes us back to the argument about the highlighting or downtoning of similarities between humans and animals and its possible consequences. Horses, as much as women, are usually the victim, not the perpetrator. However, this approach might limit our insights into broader ethical concerns in our enquiry into the nature and indeed justifications of our dealings with literary horses.

c) Post anthropocentric human-animal studies

Human-Animal studies is a relatively new approach that examines human-animal relations across established disciplines within the context of questioning human logocentric supremacy. It is informed by the former strongholds of postcolonial and feminist criticism and their ideas of the deconstruction of thinking in hierarchical terms. It is a viable approach in our context because it allows us to read the stories as a) non- (or post)- anthropocentric constructions of the horse, and b) to bring the ethical plight of animal abuse to the fore, which is the underlying message of these texts and c) it challenges the primary justification of economic trajectories in our dealing with horses. As Kenneth Shapiro notes, human animal studies interrogates "the various ways in which nonhuman animals figure in our lives and we in theirs", investigating the "impressively variable forms of bonds, attachments, interactions, and communications" between human and nonhuman animals – relationships that "can be symbolic, factual or fictitious, historical or contemporary, and beneficial or detrimental to one or both

[18] Cf. also Kristen Guest: *Black Beauty, "Masculinity, and the Market for Horseflesh",* in: *Victorians Institute Journal* 38 (2010), pp. 9-22, especially on Victorian cultural context.

parties." The task then is to reflect on and describe "the limitations and complexities" of these relationships.[19]

In a historicising gesture, one would have to point out that *Black Beauty* was written and set at a time when horses represented economical value and genteel living; but that is still the case today, although at least in our western culture, the horse is no longer a working animal. *War Horse* is set at a time when no one thought about the justification of taking animals to a crazy World War I which cost many millions of human lives. Both texts were written with the clear aim to help alleviate the position of horses in human-animal relationship, while largely subscribing to the imposed hierarchy of order, in which horses had to earn their keep.

In Sewell's novel, the message is limited, yet clear: mend ignorance and stop cruelty, and in Malpurgo's text, the message is foremost an anti-war one, a call for the fair treatment and honouring of the horse veterans of war. Neither text can be described as substantially melodramatic, and even if they are considered to be sentimental, they still claim to be true in their depiction of human-animal relationships. Although they are to be seen in the context of the time in which they were written, they point towards some greater understanding that may only be achieved in the future. And as we reflect on this, we do not diminish or disregard the texts' status as fiction: on the contrary, the individualised horse is an eloquent messenger with a voice that may help bridge the human-animal divide, if only tentatively. The literary horse is situated in the text to negotiate subject as well as object positions, an ideological construct grounded in biological nature that allows us to rethink our relations to nonhuman animals in theriotopological terms.

Bibliography

Barthes, Roland: *S/Z*. Transl. Richard Miller. New York 2000.

Borgards, Roland: *Tiere in der Literatur – eine methodische Standortbestimmung,* in: *Das Tier an sich,* ed. by Herwig Grimm and Carola Otterstedt. Göttingen 2012, pp. 87-118.

Bredella, Lothar and Werner Delanoy, (eds.): *Challenges of literary texts in the foreign language classroom*. Tübingen 1996.

Cline Kelly, Anne: *Gulliver as pet and pet keeper: Taking Animals in Book 4*, in: *ELH* 74:2 (2007), pp. 323-349.

Dando, John: *Maroccus extaticus: or, Bankes bay horse in a trance*. From the original trait printed in 1595. Ed. by Edw. F. Rimbault. (London 1843). Retrieved from Münchener Digitalisierungszentrum (Bayerische Staatsbibliothek). http://en.wikisource.org/wiki/Maroccus _Extaticus

De Montaigne, Michel: *An Apology for Raymond Sebond*, trans. and ed. by M.A. Screech. London 1993, p. 17.

Fludernik, Monika: *Towards a 'Natural' Narratology*. London, New York 1996.

[19] Quoted in Carol Freeman, Elizabeth Lane and Yvette Watts: *Considering Animals Contemporary Studies in human-animal relations*, Farnham 2011, p. 3. Kenneth Shapiro: *Human-Animal Studies: Growing the Field, Applying the Field*. Ann Arbor 2008, p. 3.

Gavin, Adrienne: *The Autobiography of a horse?: Reading Anna Sewell's Black Beauty as autobiography*, in: *Representing Victorian Lives,* ed. by Martin Hewitt. Leeds 1999, pp. 51-62.

Guest, Kristen: *Black Beauty, "Masculinity, and the Market for Horseflesh"* in: *Victorians Institute Journal* 38 (2010), pp. 9-22.

Hansen, Natalie: *Horse stories: rethinking the human-animal divide*. Ann Arbor 2009.

Herman, David, Manfred Jahn and Marie-Laure Ryan: *Routledge Ecyclopedia of Narrative Theory*. London, New York 2005.

http://ulrich-menzel.de/forschungsberichte/water-and-international-relations-presentation_karafyllis. Retr. 6.7.2014.

Joyce, James: *Ulysses*. Penguin student edition 1986.

Labov, William: *The Transformation of Experience in Narrative Syntax*, in: *Language in the Inner City*. Philadelphia 1972.

Lothar Bredella and W. Delanoy (eds.): *Challenges of literary texts in the foreign language classroom*. Tübingen 1996.

Mc Hugh,Susan: *Literary Animal Agents*, in: *PMLA* 124:2 (2009), pp. 487-495.

Morpurgo, Michael: *War Horse*. New York 2010.

Nikolajeva, Maria: *The Rhetoric of Character in Children's Fiction*. Lanham 2002

Sewell, Anna: *Black Beauty*. Penguin 2011.

Swift, Jonathan: *Gulliver's Travels*. Penguin Classics 1985.

Wall, Barbara: *The Narrator's Voice: The Dilemma of Children's Fiction*. New New York 1991.

The Different Faces of *War Horse* – Media Change and Cultural Implications

Anja Müller
University of Siegen

Michael Morpurgo's novel *War Horse* (1982) is first and foremost a novel commemorating the Great War. In several interviews, former children's laureate Morpurgo explained how his novel evolved from the idea to capture the experiences of ordinary people and to render an empathetic portrait of the universal suffering caused by the First World War. The decision to hinge his representation on a horse is sometimes connected to Morpurgo's learning about the immense number of equine casualties during the war, sometimes to the representational opportunities deriving from this particular choice of perspective. However, it is certainly safe to argue that the enormous success which *War Horse* is enjoying today is hardly due to the print version of the rather conventional horse biography, but to its adaptations for the stage and the movie screen. The following essay is going to examine these different media appearances and adaptations of Michael Morpurgo's *War Horse*: the original novel for children published in 1982; Nick Stafford's stage adaptation, in association with Handspring Puppet Company, which first premiered in the National Theatre's Olivier auditorium on 9 October 2007;[1] and the movie by Steven Spielberg of 2011, which was nominated for six Oscars, among them best film,[2] but did not win any. I shall first analyze how Morpurgo's horse biography uses the horse as a reflector of moral implications. In the stage version, the representation of the horses as abstract puppets with almost life-like movements, effectively contributes to the highly emotional response of audiences to the play. This emotionally loaded subtext also differs considerably from the rather detached perspective in Morpurgo's novel, which largely eschews the usual anthropomorphic take of horse biographies. Spielberg, in contrast, uses an anthropomorphized life horse as the alter ego of his human protagonist. When comparing the respective representations of horses in these three versions of *War Horse*, my interest lies with how 'horseness' is embodied on page, stage and screen, how the figure of the horse is juxtaposed with human beings, and to what effect this happens. I shall argue that, as the

[1] Since then, the play has been running successfully in London's West End (New London Theatre), on Broadway, and it is now being exported throughout Europe.

[2] The other nominations were Best Achievement in Cinematography (Janusz Kaminski), Best Achievement in Music Written for Motion Pictures, Original Score (John Williams), Best Achievement in Sound Mixing (Gary Rydstrom, Andy Nelson, Tom Johnson, Stuart Wilson), Best Achievements in Sound Editing (Richard Hymns, Gary Rydstrom) and Best Achievement in Art Direction (Rick Carter, Lee Sandales).

different adaptations employ the possibilities and conventions the respective media offer, the three versions of *War Horse* reflect on different cultural meanings and significances of the relationship between horse and man.

The story of *War Horse* is simple: The bay hunter Joey is bought by Devonshire farmer Ted Narracott out of a drunken whim and is raised and trained by the farmer's son Albert. Horse and boy develop a close friendship, which is interrupted when Ted sells the horse to the army at the outbreak of the First World War. There, Joey makes friends with the horse Topthorn. Both horses are sent to the Western front, where they endure increasing hardships as cavalry and draught horses on both sides of the frontline. When both horses are conscripted to the drudgery of pulling German guns, Topthorn eventually dies from exhaustion. Joey only barely survives, after a frantic escape has him trapped in barbed wire in No Man's land. Released by the joint efforts of an English and a German soldier, Joey is taken to a military hospital where he is eventually reunited with Albert, who had joined the army, too, hoping against all odds that he would find his beloved horse again. At the end of the war, after a few minor complications have been solved, Joey and Albert can return back to Devon together.

As mentioned above, *War Horse* hardly owes its great popularity to this rather conventional story of horse-and-boy friendship. The chief interest of Morpurgo's horse biography lies clearly with the attempt to represent and commemorate World War I for young readers.[3] One of Morpurgo's inspirations to have a horse as protagonist was the fact that the casualties of the war included eight million horses. Among the British forces about a million of horses had been listed, of which only 60.000 returned.[4] For Morpurgo, such figures highlight the universality of suffering during the war, which affected not only human beings of different nationalities, but human and non-human beings alike. Deciding to present the war not from a human being's but from a horse's perspective, Morpurgo has opted for an alternative viewpoint to drive home an empathetic agenda. With his choice of an equine narrator for this particular topic, he clearly endorses Jeremy Bentham's concept that man's relation to the animal world should not be determined by an alleged superiority of rational man, but by sympathy and empathy because animals suffer physical and emotional pain like human beings:

[3]Another novel by Morpurgo dealing with this topic is *Private Peaceful*. In the sequel to *War Horse*, *Farm Boy*, Morpurgo briefly resumes the Word War topic, but then shifts to a more general concern of the impacts of mechanization on British farm life in peace time. In this novel, the horses embody the notion of a foregone, rural English past.

[4] Cf. Simon Butler: *The War Horses: The Tragic Fate of a Million of Horses Sacrificed in the First World War*, Wellington 2011, p. 11.

> What else is it that should trace the insuperable line? Is it the faculty of reason, or, perhaps, the faculty of discourse? But a full-grown horse or dog is beyond comparison a more rational, as well as a more conversable animal, than an infant of a day, or a week, or even a month, old. But suppose the case were otherwise, what would it avail? the question is not, Can they reason? nor, Can they talk? but, Can they suffer?[5]

Nevertheless, despite this empathetic agenda, Morpurgo also attempts at sustaining clear distinctions between man and horse in his novel. In an interview recorded for the National Theatre's *Making of War Horse* DVD, Morpurgo contends that his major difficulty when writing the novel was to get the narrative voice right. First-person animal narrators are a common trope in horse biographies, Anne Sewell's *Black Beauty* being the most prominent example. But in a novel on the Great War that emphasises its realistic mode of representation, a first-person animal narrator is somewhat incongruous with stark realism. It may not only undermine the overall credulity of the novel, but it also borders all too closely on sentimentalism. Both effects can severely impede the development of empathy in the reader, who may easily overlook the seriousness of the war topic in view of the conventional sentimentalism of traditional horse biographies. However, Morpurgo also perceived a great narrative potential in a first-person horse narrator, because he believed if he only got the narrative voice right, the horse could become a highly effective focalizer that allows the reader to come close to the people surrounding it and thus witness their plight on both sides of the front. Besides, being devoid of national jingoism, the horse could provide a credible neutral perspective on the different sides involved in the war.

How, then, can one get a horse's voice right for a realistic narrative? Most importantly, Morpurgo's horses do not talk. They neither talk to human beings (like in the US comedy series *Mister Ed*), nor do they talk amongst each other (like in Sewell's *Black Beauty*). Of course, Joey does tell his story to the reader, but his narrative voice only exists on the level of fictional discourse. On the level of communication in the fictional story, horses do not speak. Communication and emotional expression among horses is described through reported acts of body language, movement, or animal sound such as neighing, snorting, nudging, tension of muscles, pawing, pricking ears or lashing tails. Following Joey's limited perspective, the reader can only conjecture from these descriptions of the animals' physical reactions what their thoughts or emotions may be, and the more familiar readers are with the body language and behaviour of horses, the more information can they derive from the descriptions. The human characters in the story do the same, projecting their own interpretations onto the horses. Joey himself does not give any hints whether one's reading of a horse's body language is right or no. What may come across as a rather dry way of storytelling with little depth in characterization, can be relegated to this choice of a realistic animal narrative voice that retains the animal's alterity.[6]

[5] Jeremy Bentham: *An Introduction to the Principles of Morals and Legislation.* 1789. Oxford 1907. Web, ch. 17, §1, xvii.6, fn. 122.

[6] This would, of course, presuppose that animals lack emotional or psychological depth and, especially, are unable to perceive more than physical manifestations of emotional reactions.

The horses' alterity, as manifest in their lack of speech, almost inevitably impedes successful communication between horse and man. Although Joey's account does render human dialogue, the meaningful units of human language for the horse are volume, pitch and intonation; words as such are hardly significant in themselves. Similarly, the actions of human beings often appear threatening to the horses and easily create confusion or panic. The corresponding reactions on the horses' side are, in turn, interpreted as wilfulness, stupidity or obstinacy by the human beings. In Morpurgo's novel, man and horse thus exist within two different systems of perception and communication, but as our culture has domesticated the horse and rendered it subservient, successful communication becomes a necessity. Directing the readers' sympathy to those characters who at least try to comprehend the horses' needs and manage to interact, the novel suggests that the achievement of mutual understanding based on trust and, ideally, friendship between two distinct beings, is a great moral imperative. In view of the novel's topic of war, the alterity of the horse and the resulting difficulties in communicating between horse and human being very obviously become symbolic of the alterity perceived among different groups of human beings themselves. The plea for a co-existence in mutual acceptance and empathetic effort that is insinuated in *War Horse*, is projected from animal-human relationships to interhuman relations.

The horse in Morpurgo's novel thus fulfils a number of narrative and symbolic functions. As a focalizer, it provides a "vision of the shattered worlds" (Morpurgo in *Making Of*) left by World War I. When Joey describes a battlefield, he can only do so by rendering his perception of incoherent noises and sights. This mode of description serves to illustrate poignantly the terror of a war that cannot be explained logically. The alterity of the horse, combined with the necessity to understand the communications of the animal other, becomes a symbol of the importance of mutual understanding if conflicts or wars ought to be prevented. Last but not least, the horse narrator is a completely neutral observer of the war. Joey moves across the frontlines swiftly and smoothly, serving first in the British cavalry, then pulling a German ambulance cart; he finds temporary peace working for a French farmer and his granddaughter, before pulling German guns. After an attack, he runs panic-stricken into the barbed wire of No-Man's Land and is released through the united efforts of a British and a German soldier. A tossed coin decides who is to have the horse, and as the Tommy wins, Joey returns to the British side. Through all these encounters, Joey displays no national interests or preferences. The opposing parties are assessed from his neutral perspective which is solely interested in people's ability to treat other beings with compassion and respect and thus to instil trust. Who started the war is of as little interest to the equine narrator as who should win it. Morpurgo, who is known for the explicit morals of his books for children, very consciously deploys the disinterested animal perspective as a representative of a cultural ideal of peacefulness.

Another idealizing connotation of the horse comes into play in the passages when Morpurgo alludes to the horse as a loaded cultural signifier of natural beauty. In one scene, for instance, a German officer remarks: "the world has gone quite mad. When noble creatures such as these are forced to become beasts of burden, the world has gone

Apparently, for Morpurgo, the horse is thus an object of emotional and empathetic investment rather than an active subject enacting empathy itself.

mad."[7] This comment goes beyond the laments about using horses as cannon fodder in the Great War, because it not only perceives the horse as a military device (one of the first shocking insights of the Great War was the uselessness of the once glorious cavalry in an increasingly mechanized warfare with machine guns and tanks), but as an outstanding creature whose worth precisely does not depend on its useful instrumentalization. This veritable aesthetic quality of the horse is pronounced in another episode, when young German soldier Rudi rigidly contradicts his companion Karl, for whom horses "are just four legs, a head and a tail, all controlled by a very little brain that can't think beyond food and drink." To this, Rudi retorts: "There's a nobility in his eye, a regal serenity about him. Does he not personify all that men try to be and never can be? I tell you, my friend, there's divinity in a horse [...]. God got it right the day he created them. And to find a horse like this in the middle of this filthy abomination of a war, is for me like finding a butterfly on a dung heap. We don't belong in the same universe as a creature like this."[8] Although Morpurgo's novel generally insists on the ordinariness of the horses in order to make them representatives of ordinary people, his human characters frequently insist on the aesthetic significance horses have come to adopt. This aesthetic quality of a living animal contrasts sharply with the degradation and corruption of human beings that has come to fore in the destructiveness of the Great War – a war that does not only destroy man, the man-made world and nature, but also puts an end to ideas of human perfection or the concept that man is a creator of beauty.

Although the horse can represent noble beauty and perfection in Morpurgo's novel, we do not encounter, however, another horse type of former tales of war, that would incorporate precisely these qualities, namely the 'noble steed' or 'noble charger', that is, the heroic war horse. Morpurgo's novel here distinguishes itself from traditional narratives of veritable horse warriors. If one compares *War Horse* with General Jack Seely's memoir *My Horse Warrior* on the eponymous horse that had accompanied him through World War I, one finds many parallels to Morpurgo's novel in the description of the hardships the horses had to endure during the war. But contrary to kind-hearted Joey, who had been dragged from his Devon farm to the war, Seely describes his gelding Warrior as a veritable soldier with an "unflinching courage"[9], who was disappointed when he "could [...] never go at the enemy, as all creatures long to do when they are attacked"[10] – apparently forgetting that horses are no predators but potential prey and hence prone to flight rather than attack. Seely's anthropomorphic projection of human soldiers' ideals even leads him to assert: "my stout-hearted horse not only kept his own fear under control, but by his example helped beyond measure his rider and his friend to do the same."[11]

Morpurgo's novel is not only devoid of such inappropriate conjectures about horses' emotions, it skirts any notion of heroism altogether. What might potentially be regarded

[7] Michael Morpurgo: *War Horse,* London 1982, p. 74.
[8] Ibid. pp. 112-113.
[9] Jack Seely: *Warrior: The Amazing Story of a Real War Horse*. Introd. Brough Scott. Newbury 2011. Originally published as *My Horse Warrior* (1934), p. 131.
[10] Ibid. p. 107.
[11] Ibid. p. 68.

as heroic deeds in *War Horse* is rendered almost paradoxical through the narrative voice and thus clearly strives to avoid heroic stereotypes. When Joey and Topthorn survive a cavalry charge by jumping barbed wire, the casualties and the futility of the charge are emphasised over their desperate action. When the horses pull a German ambulance car, saving wounded soldiers from the front, one of the soldiers gives them an Iron cross he has found on the battlefield and comments: "I bet you are the first English in this war to win an Iron Cross, and the last I shouldn't wonder."[12] True glory, the novel insists, lies in everyday work, kindness, friendship and trust, especially if these are still exchanged among human beings in war time. If Morpurgo glorifies anything, it is the work of the farmer who cultivates the land to procure nourishment for himself and the community.[13] Horses are the natural helpers in this rural world, which was destroyed by the Great War in a violent culmination of technological destructiveness.

Accordingly, Morpurgo's major target in his novel is to commemorate the fate and suffering of those ordinary people and creatures who are integral to what he perceives as a functioning community. In the prologue to the novel, he raises the topic of memory as he describes a picture of Joey in an old village school: "Some in the village, only a very few now and fewer as each year goes by, remember Joey as he was. His story is written so that neither he nor those who knew him, nor the war they lived and died in, will be forgotten."[14] At the end of the novel, the story returns to this issue of memory: Before the British troops return home after armistice, all horses must be sold. Albert and his friends try to buy Joey but are outbid by the French farmer at whose place Joey had worked for a while. The old man insists on buying the horse because he had promised his granddaughter Emilie, who had meanwhile died, to find her beloved horses. Upon hearing Albert's story, however, he returns Joey to Albert on the following condition: "I want my Emilie to live on in people's hearts. I shall die soon, in a few years, no more; and then no one will remember my Emilie as she was. […] She will just be a name on a gravestone that no one will read. So I want you to tell your friends at home about my Emilie […]. That way she will live for ever and that is what I want."[15] With this appeal to remember, the novel arrives at narrative closure. The insistence on commemoration connects man and horse: both deserve to remain unforgotten because of their common suffering in the war.

The popularity which *War Horse* had achieved after its stage adaptation has definitely contributed to the memory culture of the Great War – as was reflected, for instance, in an exhibition on War Horses in London's Army Museum, accompanying the stage production in winter and early spring 2013. However, when National

[12] Michael Morpurgo: *War Horse*, ed. cited, p.180.

[13] Accordingly, Emilie's grandfather, the French farmer where Joey and Topthorn spend a brief time of happiness between the frontlines, asserts: "We must live as we have always lived, cutting our hay, picking our apples and tilling our soil. We cannot live as if there will be no tomorrow. We can live only if we eat, and our food comes from the land. We must work the land if we want to live and these two [the horses] must work with us. They don't mind, they like the work." (ibid. p. 91). With the final sentence, the horses are integrated into this ideal prospect of a peaceful community, uniting all beings without considering nationality or species.

[14] Ibid. p. 2.

[15] Ibid. p. 180-181.

Theatre's associate director Tom Morris had suggested to adapt Morpurgo's novel together with the South African Handspring Puppet Theatre company, director Nicholas Hytner at first objected that theatre, especially a huge stage like the Olivier, was meant for epic storytelling in words. *War Horse*, on the contrary, would be "a play where the protagonist is a puppet and does not talk."[16] Adapting the narrative perspective of the novel therefore became a major challenge. Whereas Morpurgo had to get the horse's voice right, the stage production was concerned with representing the physical appearance of the horses without disneyfying anthropomorphism. "Horses need to be horses"[17], Stafford insisted, therefore the horse puppets had to emulate animal behaviour as closely as possible and to underscore the alterity of the animal. The production should preserve the horseness of the horse in horse puppets.

The result can aptly be described as "pure theatre", working on the basis of the audience's willing suspension of disbelief. The life-size horse puppets use cane frames and coloured polyester georgette fabrics to render a horse's shape, hinting at skeletal construction and muscular structure.[18] They represent a horse, while simultaneously revealing the construction of a horse's body as well as their own construction as horse puppets. This is enhanced by the fact that each puppet is operated by three players – for the head, the heart and the tail – who are always visible on stage. Rather than attempting to create the illusion of a real horse, the play makes the audience aware of how the puppet is constructed and how it functions. The remarkable theatrical effect of National Theatre's *War Horse* derives from the transformation which the horse puppets undergo during the performance. The puppets' material is transformed into real horse bodies through the audience's imagination; the players' presence is gradually obliterated during the act of beholding the horse figures. This transformation prepares the ground for the deep empathetic affect the play succeeds in creating, so that the audience is ready to invest considerable time in a play without a speaking protagonist. According to Jennifer Parker-Starbuck, this transformation also makes the audience perceive in the puppets a certain authenticity of the horses' bodies, which allows us to regard the figures in *War Horse* as horses, as animals – in other words, the puppets achieve to create true 'horseness' on stage.

Several instances in the puppeteers' and puppets' performance help to achieve this goal. For Handspring, the first maxim is to make a puppet breathe. Accordingly, the 'heart' players consistently keep the animal puppet animated, and the constant sound of the horses' breath in the play helps to convey emotions much more effectively than any speaking horse could. Breathing for and with the horse is for the puppeteers an important means of communication with each other and with the audience. An even greater contribution to the 'horseness' of the puppets is achieved through movement. As body language must replace verbal dialogue when it comes to interactions with the horses on stage, the movements of the puppets are integral to the willing suspension of disbelief in the audience. When operating the horses, the puppeteers create the idea of

[16] *Making of War Horse*. National Theatre and Seventh Art, 2009. DVD.

[17] Ibid.

[18] Cf. Mervyn Millar: *The Horse's Mouth: How Handspring and the National Theatre made War Horse*, 2nd ed. London 2011, pp. 58-62 on the process of finding the appropriate design for the puppets.

the horse's weight; when moving legs, rump or head, the muscular structure and strength of the animal are taken into consideration. Impressive care has been taken to get even the horses' gait patterns right. A similar realism of movement applies to the head, ears and tail. Handspring explains that they decided to work with rod puppets because the players can control movements very precisely, which is important if one wishes the puppet to interact with other characters[19].[20] From the audience's perspective, this means that one can focus on very subtle movements, for example of the ears, in analogy to the very minute muscle contractions an animal might use to communicate. With such a reductive representation, avoiding "movement noise"[21], the production manages to create authentic 'horseness' for their puppets.[22] The horses thus communicate on stage with a language of their own that is rendered accessible to the audience, and which is purely theatrical. During the live event of a theatrical performance "there's not much imagination required to project a horse into the puppet"[23], to forget about the puppeteer's presence, to join the game of make believe and allow the strong emotional, empathetic reaction the play intends to evoke via its representation of horses.

I argue that the immense success of *War Horse* as a play rests largely on this immediate emotional response to the imagined physical presence of the horse puppets and their authenticity. The puppets unite recognizable realism and imaginative investment. They thus appeal to an individual response as much as to a collective recognition of common associations or symbolic values connected with horses, such as strength, beauty, pride, gentleness, innocence, trust and companionship. In other words, they operate with the cultural significance of the horse on a highly emotional basis. Besides, *War Horse* is not any horse biography, but a story about commemorating the Great War. The play's empathetic effect rests on two pillars: the representation of the horse and the evocation of a remembering community, as it surfaces in the representation of the village or in the use of folk song. Within this context of conjuring up the idea of bonding and belonging, the relationship of man and horse becomes a cultural signifier of symbol of community. This community exceeds the mythological symbols of animal-human fusion, as they are expressed in the figure of the centaur, which often served as a model for ideal horsemanship. The bond between man and horse in *War Horse* is of both an individual and a collective, or communal nature, and it rests on the ordinariness of its creatures as well as on the notion that two utterly different beings can nevertheless enter into a companionship through mutual trust. This trust-based companionship is depicted again and again as maybe not an antidote against war (war is shown to be too incomprehensible to be understood – and prevented through

[19] cf. *Making of War Horse*, ed. cited.

[20] String puppets, on the other hand, are more poetic and dreamy and good for flying motions, but inconvenient for the precise interactions that are needed for War Horse.

[21] Ibid.

[22] Last but not least, the puppets' eyes add depth to the figures. Although they are immobile, the eyes pick up the light on stage, the audience consequently focuses on them, and the illusion of depth that is created through a trick of light and reflection enables the audience to imagine themselves in the head of the horse – to the extent even that some audience members claim to perceive eye movement, too.

[23] Kit Harington in ibid.

mere rational considerations), but as what can preserve humanity in times of extreme inhumanity.[24] Since togetherness and community can be considered to be the leitmotifs of National Theatre's *War Horse*, the aim of the production is to create the notion of a collective. Nick Stafford claims: "What is going on is much more complex in the emotional sense than just being sentimental."[25] The friendship of horse and man, the stunning co-operation of the puppeteers, the interaction of puppets and characters, the songs, all these staged communities eventually absorb the audience, too, into an imagined community, united by a common act of viewing and listening, a common act of empathy, a common memory of the Great War and, finally, a common experience within the shared theatre space. It is only appropriate that this experience of community is hinged on the representation of a horse – an animal known for its essential dependence on a herd and hence its willingness for bonding.

When I mentioned that National Theatre's *War Horse* was more complex than being merely sentimental, in the final section of this paper, I shall suggest that, alas, the same does not apply to Steven Spielberg's movie. This is not to disparage the film entirely or to denigrate film adaptations of novels in general. I only contend that Spielberg's employment of the horse in his movie version of *War Horse* results largely in the sentimental effect which both novel and stage production tried to avoid. Why is it, one may ask, that the depiction of real horses suffering on the big screen becomes sentimental, whereas merely imagining a horse from a drily told narrative or watching puppets on a stage not only evokes a more intense empathetic investment but also produces 'horseness' to a much greater effect? In an article published in *Theatre Journal*, Jennifer Parker-Starbuck has explained how the technological conditions of Spielberg's film rather obliterate our perception of the film horse as an authentic horse than create authenticity. Apparently, watching the body of a real horse in a film does not automatically create 'horseness' – the fictional character of the medium film transforms the real horse's body into something that may resist 'horseness'. In addition to Parker-Starbuck's observations, I would argue that Spielberg's particular adaptation of *War Horse* as a story about courage[26] and extraordinary individuals, who overcome all odds through strength and will power, reduces the potential significance of the horse. One major reason for this reduction is that, contrary to the novel and the stage production, Spielberg's *War Horse* contains two plot strands: Joey's story is complemented with that of Albert Narracott and his father Ted. Morpurgo's Ted Narracott is a farmer whose struggle for financial survival has led him to drink and, in the state of inebriation, sometimes do irresponsible things. Buying Joey is a mere whim of intoxication, and Ted rarely changes his disparaging attitude towards the horse until the war. The stage play adds a competitive tension between Ted Narracott and farmer Arthur Warren for

[24] It is hardly surprising that even Jack Seely's otherwise quite jingoistic memoirs about Warrior emphasise this companionship between man and horse as their major leitmotif.

[25] *Making of War Horse*, ed. cited.

[26] So Spielberg in the Bonus clip on the German DVD. In a similar vein, the extended trailer to the movie ended with Captain Nicholson (played by Benedict Cumberbatch) sitting on Joey and encouraging his soldiers before the impending cavalry attack to "Be brave".

additional dramatization in its first scenes, but does not develop this plotline further.[27] Spielberg, on the other hand, transforms Ted Narracott into a covert hero – a distinguished Boer War veteran, who takes no pride in having killed. His purchase of Joey and his later bet that Joey will plough are acts of defiance against his class superiors. Unlike his wife, Ted sees hidden qualities in Joey and firmly believes in the horse. Albert shares his father's stubborn courage, but is frequently irritated by Ted's behaviour. Nevertheless, Albert keeps his father's regimental badge and ties it to Joey's halter as a protective charm, when Joey is sold to the army.

Joey, in turn, is singled out as a remarkable horse from the beginning of the film. His stamina and unyielding spirit relate him at once to the Narracotts. At the beginning of the movie, the viewers are shown how Albert meets Joey while the latter is still a foal in a field with his mother. Their bonding thus starts already before Joey's purchase by Ted; it is indeed presented like a fated companionship. Later on, after being sold to the army, Joey finds in Topthorn a father figure who helps him come to terms with the army drill. The tables turn when the two horses are used for pulling carts, and it is now the farm horse Joey who can persuade the charger Topthorn to yield his pride and accept a collar. When Topthorn's strength falters while pulling German guns, Joey takes his place. The respective scenes show how the horse Joey is deliberately taking decisions and managing to communicate his intentions successfully to the human beings around him.

The reunion between Albert and Joey at the end of the movie is the reunion of two wounded war veterans who both had eventually stepped into the places of their fathers. This parallel (without the father-son subplot) had already been established in the stage adaptation, which had included scenes with Albert fighting in the trenches and being temporarily blinded by gas. However, whereas the stage plot of Albert in the war was solely driven by the goal of his reunion with Joey, in Spielberg's movie Albert's war experience prepares his reconciliation with his father. Significantly, when Albert is finally reunited with Joey, he does not only get his horse back, but also his father's regimental badge. The doubling of Joey's and Albert's plotlines in the movie makes the horse's plot subservient to the boy's – the horse is reduced to a reflection of the human protagonist.

This reduction of the horse corresponds with the significance the horse assumes in Spielberg's movie. Whereas novel and stage production struggled with the limitations of their media to represent a real horse, but finally succeeded in quite authentic representations of the horse as animal, Spielberg apparently pursues different strategies and goals. While using real horse actors, he consistently anthropomorphizes these horses and thus does not present them as animals. This anthropomorphization is achieved by the above mentioned handling of plotlines, establishing analogies between human and animal biographies. It is extended to the horses' behaviour patterns, including their body language. Where Handspring's human puppeteers strive to make their puppets move like horses, the real horses employed in Spielberg's movie are veritable horse actors whose frequent looks into the camera are no coincidence. The

[27] This tension includes their rival bidding for Joey at the auction and the bet whether Joey can be made to plough. In later versions of the play, Arthur has transformed into Ted's brother.

actions and interactions of the film horses are overt, performed acts following a human script and not the script of animal behaviour.[28]

In Morpurgo's novel, the horse is an innocent and defamiliarizing lens through which man must look in order to perceive the horrors of war properly. Spielberg, on the other hand, is heavily indebted to the *bildungsroman* tradition of earlier horse biographies like *Black Beauty* and their anthropomorphic handling of animals. As a consequence, the horse's main function is to symbolize human qualities, while its 'horseness' is downplayed.[29] The audience may feel pity with the horse's suffering, but their empathetic investment will rather be directed to the human characters. Albert is introduced as a second focalizer, as if one could not trust that the horse focalizer alone were sufficient. By introducing a human focalizer for the war, however, the attempts at neutrality in Morpurgo's novel and its stage adaptation are lost. Both novel and play show how people from different countries make friends with the horses; the novel even takes great pains to explain callous behaviour towards the horses as the general result of the war. Spielberg's *War Horse* does not make any difference to his previous war movies in taking clear sides with the British. With four exceptions to the rule (who are either outsiders, speak English and/or end up dead),[30] the movie makes a point in locating cruelty, callous and wilfully destructive behaviour on the German side. Whereas Morpurgo and Stafford represent the Great War (like any war) as first and foremost a human catastrophe, Spielberg cannot refrain from identifying a culprit. Instead of presenting a neutral, innocent, horse perspective, Spielberg's War Horse remains anthropomorphic even in its judgmental view on World War I.

Accordingly, the cultural significance of Spielberg's Joey is confined to mirror one particular human individual rather than a community. The typical Spielbergian motif, the story of a remarkable individual mastering the odds of life, is projected onto the remarkable horse Joey. The anthropomorphized horse is a stand-in and projection screen for the human individual, mirroring the qualities of the human being to which it belongs, and without which it will remain unaccomplished. Ironically, the very

[28] The extended scene in which Albert trains Joey to come at the sound of a particular whistle is not only essential for preparing the later recognition scene between Albert and Joey in the hospital. It is also a key for the understanding of the significance of the horse in Spielberg's War Horse. What we are witnessing in this scene is a moment of training: Joey is a clever horse, but he is essentially a well-trained horse that can accommodate within the human world and even comply with their means of communication. Similarly, the scene in which Albert patiently trains Joey to accept a collar, is another initiation of the horse into the human world: the acceptance of the collar and the willingness to plough will make Joey useful for human beings – and only as such a useful horse, his survival will be guaranteed. Later on, he will pass on this 'knowledge' to Topthorn.

[29] Added to this is the cultural significance of the horse in the tradition of the U.S. American Western, where the horse may symbolize the cowboy's trusty companion in the conquest of the frontier – or, in more recent movies like *Hidalgo* or Disney's *Spirit*, the mustang comes to stand for a lost tradition of the American West. In both instances, the U.S tradition tends to focus on strong individual (usually male) horse characters that can easily represent the American Dream of rugged individual and self-preserving strength.

[30] The latter, namely the two young German soldiers, are actually gleaned from Private Peaceful, another WWI novel for children by Michael Morpurgo.

individuality of Joey is undermined by the fact that Spielberg employed fourteen different horse actors for the role. Even if the development over different age stages in the horse biography might call for more than one horse actor, and even if human actors also have their doubles, such a high number of animal actors is unusual and implies the exchangeability and lack of individuality that is, in fact, attributed to the horse.[31] It also implies that the audience is supposed not to discriminate between different animal individuals either, although the differences between the employed horses are sometimes hard to overlook. This attitude of presupposed indiscrimination also prevents the audience's imaginative investment that happens in Morpurgo's novel or Stafford's stage version, where the acknowledged individuality of the animal figures effected a bonding that could compensate for some less credible events. As Spielberg's movie lacks such an investment, the horse figure, despite being a real horse, apparently loses its significant power and merely renders the movie sentimental. Crucial dramatic scenes, like the ploughing contest, the encounter with the tank or Joey's being trapped in barbed wire become mere sensational episodes, craving for dramatic effect and lacking credulity. Is it by coincidence that the No Man's land scene was rendered through CGI?[32] Where the puppets on the National Theatre's stage highlighted the horse's alterity to man and allowed the audience to perceive and re-appropriate the impressive physicality of the horse's body, the exchangeable film horse becomes trivial and no longer challenges the audience's imaginative investment. This gratuitous horse as it were also works against the notions of community and collective memory that were so important for the novel and the play. The movie fails to adequately render this important aspect and leaves us with a horse that has little more cultural significance than the sentimental value of an animal serving as man's projection screen.

I would suggest, however, that the use of the horse figure we can perceive in Spielberg's *War Horse* has less to do with the film as a medium but with Spielberg's particular deployment of the horse in his movie. The choices that affect the cultural significance of the horse in the movie are less determined by the idiosyncrasies of film and have more to do with how the underlying narrative of the movie relates the aspects of community and individualism, and, most importantly, how it adapts and appropriates the issue of animal alterity. Comparing the three media realizations of war horse Joey, in the novel, on stage and on screen, the horse's cultural significance apparently hinges on its function for the community. To become a projection screen for our human concerns, it seems as if cultural representations of the horse must retain traces of animal alterity, of 'horseness' as it were, and thus must retain enough blanks to allow us to inscribe our desires and ideas into the animal body that is so different from ours and that still invites us to bond. The cultural significance of the horse seems to unfold from this shifting balance between preserving the horse's alterity and the impulse to appropriate this alterity of the animal other through anthropomorphization.

[31] Cf. also Parker-Starbuck, pp. 387-389.

[32] Of course, this may also have been a precaution taken to fulfil the standards of the American Humane Society, which puts its "no animals were harmed" stamp on the movie credits. Yet, as Parker-Starbuck convincingly explains, the coincidence of exchangeable horse bodies and the use of CGI for the most extremely dramatic and anthropomorphic scenes, can hardly be overlooked.

Bibliography

Bentham, Jeremy: *An Introduction to the Principles of Morals and Legislation*. 1789. Oxford 1907. Web.

Butler, Simon: *The War Horses: The Tragic Fate of a Million of Horses Sacrificed in the First World War*. Wellington 2011.

Gefährten. Dir. Steven Spielberg. Dreamworks. 2012. DVD. (Original: *War Horse*. 2011)

Making of War Horse. National Theatre and Seventh Art, 2009. DVD.

Millar, Mervyn: *The Horse's Mouth: How Handspring and the National Theatre made War Horse,* 2nd ed. London 2011.

Morpurgo, Michael: *War Horse*. London 1982.

Parker-Starbuck, Jennifer: *Animal Anthologies and Media Representations: Robotics, Puppets and the Real of* War Horse, in: *Theatre Journal* 65.3 (2013), pp. 373-393.

Seely, Jack: *Warrior: The Amazing Story of a Real War Horse*. Introd. Brough Scott. Newbury 2011. Originally published as *My Horse Warrior* (1934).

Stafford, Nick and Michael Morpurgo: *War Horse*. Oxford Playscripts. Oxford 2009.

The Horse as Symbol of Social Change in Canadian Literature: Re-Reading Robert Kroetsch's *The Studhorse Man*

Martin Kuester
University of Marburg

While horses play an important role in classical European works of literature such as Jonathan Swift's *Gulliver's Travels* or even Miguel de Cervantes' *Don Quixote*, these quadrupeds are of course also a traditional element in Canadian – and especially Western Canadian – culture and literature. In the case of Robert Kroetsch's postmodern novel *The Studhorse Man*, which was awarded the Canadian Governor General's Award for English-language fiction in 1969, they even stand for social and medical change in mid-twentieth-century Canadian society, as I will show in these pages.

We should not forget, however, that horses, however natural they may appear to us who were brought up on a diet of Western movies replete with "Indians" riding across the plains and hunting buffalo while at the same time being pursued by gunslinging cowboys are a European import to North America.[1] But then, so is, one might argue, the novel as a literary genre. Still, in our contemporary view of Canada and the Canadian West, the horse as an icon is of utmost importance. As the Canadian poet, novelist and literary theorist Robert Kroetsch once pointed out, the horse plays a central part in "classical" prairie novels such as Sinclair Ross' *As For Me and My House* (first published in the 1940s) as well as in the fiction of contemporary Prairie writers such as the Saskatchewan novelist Sharon Butala:

> By design or accident, we have found in the image of the horse the dramatic juncture of sky and earth; in novels as widely different in content and intention as Sinclair Ross' *As For Me and My House* and Sharon Butala's *The Gates of the Sun* the horse figures our predicament – and reminds us that the novel had its beginning in another landlocked and open landscape. Don Quixote, in the country that apparently gave the horse to our landscape, gave us the story of Don Quixote, his feet not quite on the ground, his head not quite in the sky.[2]

Horse and cowboy represent the image of the North American West, although of course the American and Canadian versions of the West differ to a certain extent, ranging from

[1] For alternative views, cf. Scott Sonner: *Are Wild Horses Native to the U.S.? A Federal Court Seeks Answer,* in: *LA Times Greenspace.* June 5, 2011. Accessed Dec. 24, 2013. Available from: http://latimesblogs.latimes.com/greenspace/2011/06/wild-horses-nevada-blm-native-species.html

[2] Robert Kroetsch: *The Cow in the Quicksand and How I(t) Got Out: Responding to Stegner's* Wolf Willow, in: *A Likely Story: The Writing Life,* Red Deer 1995, pp. 71-2.

the American Wild West Frontier we know from TV and movie westerns and the supposedly more civilized Canadian "Mild West"[3] settled under the supervision of the supposedly benevolent Mounties. Postmodern authors sometimes parodically play with the significance of these stereotypical views and choose to have a cow*girl* ride east into the sunrise rather than having a cow*boy* going west into the setting sun. This is the case in George Bowering's postmodern novel *Caprice*, but this is by far not the only novel in which traditional expectations regarding equine animals and human society are challenged. For example, one of the Sisters brothers in Patrick de Witt's 2011 novel seems to be alluding to the 1972 hit song "A Horse With No Name" (written by Dewey Bunnell and recorded by the band *America*) when he remarks that he does not "believe in naming horses." He prefers "horses without histories and habits and names they expected to be addressed by."[4]

Horses in Canadian literature often stand for the traditional lifestyle of the agrarian West. However, the traditional views of a farmer tilling the land of the endless Prairies or of a teacher going to his one-room country school in a horse-drawn sled or buggy are things of the past that we nowadays encounter only in works of early twentieth-century Prairie realism represented by writers such as Frederick Philip Grove or W. O. Mitchell. Horses also play a pivotal role in Sinclair Ross' classic novel *As For Me and My House* that Kroetsch refers to in the above quotation. In this novel, the somewhat unreliable first-person narrator Mrs. Bentley is rather unhappy as the wife of the Prairie small town minister Philip Bentley. As Kroetsch reminds us in his afterword to the New Canadian Library edition of the novel, Philip's Christian "name would make him a lover of horses"[5], and horses are not only an important means of transport in the Prairies suffering from drought and depression but also a symbol of sexual attraction.[6]

In his own novel *The Studhorse Man*, Robert Kroetsch conjures up the by now almost obsolete image of a stallion that is taken from farm to farm, in this case by a studhorse man named Hazard Lepage. Hazard is trying to sell the sexual services of his last stallion to farmers who see little sense in raising a new generation of horses when farm work can also be done – and more economically – with machinery that is driven by gasoline. This is of course especially true in a province like Alberta, where huge oil resources are about to be discovered. Kroetsch clearly depicts the studhorse man's conundrum in the very first sentences of the novel:

> Hazard had to get hold of a mare. He was desperate. In an area centered on a string of seven towns he was the only remaining studhorse man, yet in the previous season he had traveled the hundreds of miles of dirt roads in a two-wheeled cart, pulled by his old gelding, leading his beautiful blue beast of a virgin stallion – and he had found not one farmer with a mare that wanted covering.[7]

[3] Francis, Daniel: *The Mild West: The Myth of the RCMP*, in: *National Dreams: Myth, Memory, and Canadian History,* Vancouver 1997.
[4] Patrick De Witt: *The Sisters Brothers,* London 2011, p. 5.
[5] Robert Kroetsch: *Afterword* As For Me And My House. By Sinclair Ross. Toronto 1989, p. 218.
[6] Cf. Barbara Mitchell: *Paul: The Answer to the Riddle of* As For Me And My House, in: *Studies in Canadian Literature* 13.1 (1988). Web. Accessed May 14, 2014. Available from http://journals.hil.unb.ca/index.php/scl/article/view/8076/9133.
[7] Robert Kroetsch: *The Studhorse Man.* 1969. Edmonton 2004, p. 5.

The time of the horse seems to be threatened on the prairies, and this is a feeling that is also voiced in Sharon Butala's *The Gates of the Sun*, the second novel Kroetsch had mentioned in the essay quoted above. Butala's archetypal cowboy, Andrew Samson, also feels that his days of ranching are coming to an end:

> He sighed and turned his attention to the horses. With tractors and trucks being used more all the time there was less and less call for horses. Especially for a mixed, wild herd like his. He squinted in the brilliant light as he watched them grazing. Below him, near the bottom of the hill he had parked on, a curious bunch had gathered and stood, their tails and manes blowing in the wind, their ears pointed. If he moved, they would run.[8]

According to Kroetsch's fellow Albertan writer Aritha van Herk, the studhorse man "is the grandfather of all persistent car salesmen"[9] in his attempts to "sell" the service of his studhorse to more or less unwilling ranchers in the Alberta foothills of the Rocky Mountains. His situation is a typically Canadian one, if one believes Margaret Atwood's thesis that survival is *the* most important theme in Canadian literature.[10] As Kroetsch describes the situation of Hazard, who has been breeding horses in the province of Alberta ever since a Native Canadian gave him a beautiful horse just after he returned to Canada from the European battlefields of the Great War: "He was a truly desperate man. Extinction or survival was quite simply to be the fate of the breed of horse he alone had preserved through six generations [...]."[11]

But the Hazard's last stallion – called Poseidon – is not the only male in need of female company. As van Herk puts it, "The cock that Hazard Lepage peddles is presumably that of his stallion, Poseidon; but the cock that gets the most action is his own."[12] In the novel, we follow Hazard on his quest for the ideal mare which doubles as the almost endless Odyssean – i.e., less than direct – journey towards his thirteen-year fiancée Martha Proudfoot, a woman who not only runs a hotel but who is also a horse breeder (and whose ranch cum hotel thus would also be Poseidon's ideal haven).

It is not necessary in the context of the argument of this paper to exactly follow Hazard's re-enactment of Odysseus' Mediterranean travels on dry Prairie land, even though several authors have established enlightening parallels between Homer's epic and episodes in Hazard's quest.[13] This quest takes place towards the end of the Second World War, and Hazard's attempt at earning the money he needs for the acquisition of a mare by collecting "BONES FOR WAR"[14] comes to an end because the market dries up as soon as the Americans cross the Rhine. This event signals that the end of the war on the European battlefield is near. As Tad Proudfoot puts it, gas rationing will end soon and "[Hazard's] horses will really be worthless now."[15] Horses have now become so

[8] Sharon Butala: *The Gates of the Sun*. 1986. Toronto 1994, p. 246.

[9] Aritha van Herk: Introduction. *The Studhorse Man*. By Robert Kroetsch, Edmonton 2004, p. v.

[10] Margaret Atwood: *Survival: A Thematic Guide to Canadian Literature*, Toronto 1972.

[11] Robert Kroetsch: *The Studhorse Man,* ed. cited, p.5.

[12] Aritha von Herk: Introduction, ed. cited, p. vi.

[13] Cf. Aritha van Herk, Peter Thomas, Carol R. Beran, and many others.

[14] Robert Kroetsch: *The Studhorse Man,* ed. cited, p. 5.

[15] Ibid. p. 12.

worthless, in fact, that they are brought to a slaughterhouse in Edmonton, and this tendency will not even be turned around by Hazard's setting hundreds of them free and thus causing a major disturbance in the city centre.

Before Hazard is – however briefly – reunited with Martha Proudfoot, the Penelope figure of his Odyssean quest, and before he is able to – perhaps – become the father of a daughter called Demeter, the stations of his carnivalistic quest include archetypal points of reference representing Albertan politics, culture, geography and society. These include the Alberta Legislature in Edmonton, a home for the incurably ill in the same city, an ugly lady in rural Alberta who is hungry for male attention, a river to be crossed without a bridge, a schoolhouse that is burned down by Hazard's Doukhobor anarchist friend, a traditional wedding in rural Alberta, a coyote hunt, a recuperative stay with a beautiful rancher and horse breeder, Marie Eshpeter, who in the end seems to be more interested in Poseidon's semen than in Hazard's affection, and an all too brief stay in the bed of a church caretaker, which is cut short by a house fire.

In front of the Alberta Legislature, Hazard and his horse Poseidon are confronted with artistic recreations of their respective ideals: of a lady (Queen Victoria?) sitting on a bronze horse:

> Poseidon snorted in wonder and fear at the poised and perfect bronze beast, approached, turned to lash out viciously with his heels, reared up himself just as the tall bronze stallion reared.
>
> Two strong males contending for one mare could not have been locked into a more desperate equilibrium.[16]

While Poseidon attacks his artistic counterpart, Hazard – at least temporarily – gives in to the seductive lures of a curator working in the museum that is housed in the legislature.

Although Hazard's quest for the ideal mare to be "served" by Poseidon is of almost epic proportions (at least from his own perspective), Kroetsch does not provide a traditional epic narrator's voice. Far from providing Hazard's exploits with a reliable epic voice that one would expect on the basis of Mikhail Bakhtin's definition of the monologic epic, Kroetsch gives us the most unreliable voice of Demeter Proudfoot. Demeter is a male narrator somewhat erroneously named after a female goddess by "my dear mother, pretending to knowledge and believing Demeter to be a masculine name."[17] He composes his epic sitting in a bathtub in a mental hospital. We as readers observe him reconstructing an epic search that is set in a world that he can only see through a contraption of mirrors. He justifies his narrative activity by idiosyncratically reinterpreting events that led him to believe he had become Hazard's official successor as the last studhorse man: "It was decreed there […] that I, in the final analysis, through my devotion and concern, should save the Lepage horse from extinction."[18] And he

[16] Robert Kroetsch: *The Studhorse Man,* ed. cited, p.32

[17] Robert Kroetsch: *The Studhorse Man,* ed. cited, p. 74.

[18] Ibid. p. 182.

concludes: "That morning I was D. Proudfoot, Studhorse Man."[19] Unsurprisingly, his activities then result in his being institutionalized.

In general, the distinction between stallion and studhorse man becomes somewhat difficult. When Demeter in his delusion takes over Hazard's mansion, in which the studhorse man had lived together with his stallion Poseidon, he feels he has to defend the horse against both Hazard and Martha, Hazard's fiancée, who seem to have lost sight of the ultimate goal of breeding the ideal horse. Then he suddenly hears an "exquisitely piercing mortal cry, the cry half horse, half man, the horse-man cry of pain or delight or eternal celebration at what is and what must be."[20] The cry probably signals Hazard's death, but possibly also the "little death" of orgasm. And in spite of Poseidon's obvious rage, Demeter will not kill him, as once again stallion and studhorse man become one: "And then it was too late for me to fire; the two heads were together, the man's, the stallion's."[21]

Hazard is a typical (or rather, because of his limited reliability, a not so typical) example of Kroetsch's duality of competing narrative voices in his novels.[22] In her seminal chapter on Robert Kroetsch as "Mr Canadian Postmodern", Linda Hutcheon in *The Canadian Postmodern*[23] distinguishes between Kroetsch's "creative characters" (such as the "ambiguously creative" Hazard Lepage) and his "ordering interpreters" (such as Demeter Proudfoot). But we must not forget that Demeter is not beyond ordering through a posture of madness.

Robert Kroetsch's personal interest in horses seems to be somewhat problematic. At least he (or his persona?) claims in his long autobiographical poem *Seed Catalogue* that as a child he managed to fall off a horse standing still.[24] But one of the lasting concepts of literary analysis of Prairie literature that he developed is the *horse-house* dichotomy. In his seminal essay "The Fear of Women in Prairie Fiction: An Erotics of Space", the horse stands for the male principle of movement while the house stands for the home-making female concept. As Kroetsch puts it, "We conceive of external space as male, internal space as female. More precisely, the penis: external, expandable, expendable; the vagina: internal, eternal."[25] And in the same essay, he states that

[19] Ibid. p. 184.

[20] Ibid. p. 198.

[21] Ibid. p. 201.

[22] Cf. Martin Kuester: *Kroetsch's Fragments: Approaching the Narrative Structure of His Novels, in: Postmodern Fiction in Canada*, ed. by Theo D'haen und Hans Bertens, Amsterdam 1992, pp. 137-160; Martin Kuester: *Tales Told in the Bathtub: Robert Kroetsch's Historiographic Metafiction*, in: *Historiographic Metafiction in Modern American and Canadian Literature*, ed. by Bernd Engler and Kurt Müller, Paderborn 1994, pp. 399-410.

[23] Linda Hutcheon: *The Canadian Postmodern: A Study of Contemporary English-Canadian Fiction,* Toronto 1988, p. 160.

[24] Robert Kroetsch: *Seed Catalogue* (1977), in: *Completed Field Notes: The Long Poems of Robert Kroetsch,* Edmonton 2000, p. 29.

[25] Robert Kroetsch: *The Fear of Women in Prairie Fiction: An Erotics of Space (1979)*, in: *The Lovely Treachery of Words: Essays Selected and New,* Toronto 1989, p. 73.

> On: in. Motion: stasis. A woman ain't supposed The basic grammatical pair in the story-line (the energy-line) of prairie fiction is house: horse. To be *on* a horse is to move: motion into distance. To be *in* a house is to be fixed: a centring unto stasis. Horse is masculine. House is feminine. Horse: house. Masculine: feminine. to move. Pleasure: duty.[26]

This dichotomy, which Kroetsch also sees at work in Sinclair Ross' *As For Me and My House* to which I alluded at the beginning of this essay, is of course deconstructed by a man who shares his mansion with horses as Hazard does, even cleaning up after them in a housewifely fashion before he leaves the house. In van Herk's words, "This binary might appear simplistic were it not followed by Kroetsch's conclusion that the male on the horse, in approaching the house of the female, is the one 'who must make the radical change', he who must give up his precious and treacherous name. Any equivalence between naming and authority is turned upside down."[27] Susan Rudy Dorscht also sees Kroetsch's general urge to "undermine Western philosophical discourse" in "a doubled sexual identity": "Demeter/Hazard is a he/she who, in speaking, gestures toward the multiplication of meaning inherent in signification."[28] Rudy Dorscht's final reading after seeing that Demeter Lepage, Martha's daughter fathered by either Hazard or Eugene Utter, is not only "something of a lover of the horse" and the dedicatee of Demeter Proudfoot's "portentous volume"[29]: "The studhorse man is a woman."[30]

Yet another way of deconstructing the horse-house dichotomy is suggested by Kroetsch in "The Fear of Women in Prairie Fiction", and this is a solution probably not unknown to Hazard – who has horses living in his mansion, his old house, in which he "felt secure" while "it was the road he dreaded"[31] – either:

> The most obvious resolution of the dialectic, however temporary, is in the horse-house. Not the barn (though a version of resolution does take place there), but whore's-house. Western movies use that resolution.[32]

The equine species is thus almost doomed to extinction in industrialized society, especially after oil is discovered in the province of Alberta, thus rendering horses even more redundant in an increasingly motorized society. Even Demeter's attempt to metaphorically link "the organ of copulation of a horse" to the three-part structure of "the contemporary spaceship, a kind of trinity of woe"[33] seems to be in vain. Temporarily, however, horsedom gains a new lease on life by becoming the basis of a new and more permissive paradigm in liberal Western society. As Kroetsch's not always reliable narrator, Demeter Proudfoot (who received his ill-fitting first name

[26] Ibid. p. 76.

[27] Aritha van Herk: Introduction, ed. cited, p. vi.

[28] Susan Rudy Dorscht: *Women, Reading, Kroetsch: Telling the Difference,* Waterloo, Ont. 1991, pp. 61, 62.

[29] Robert Kroetsch: *The Studhorse Man*, ed. cited, p. 204.

[30] Susan Rudy Dorscht: *Women, Reading, Kroetsch,* ed. cited, p. 69.

[31] Robert Kroetsch: *The Studhorse Man,* ed. cited, p. 10.

[32] Robert Kroetsch: *The Fear of Women,* ed. cited, p. 76.

[33] Robert Kroetsch: *The Studhorse Man,* ed. cited, p. 68.

because his mother took it to be a masculine one and who tells his story sitting in a bathtub in a mental hospital), lets us know, "From the urine of pregnant mares [...], scientists are able to extract the female hormone known as estrogen. With estrogen, in turn, they have learned to prevent the further multiplication of man upon the face of the earth"[34], and "it was the Lepage stallion [...] that filled the vacuum left by the near extinction of the horse."[35] Significantly enough, it is the former anarchist Doukhobor Eugene Utter who then marries Martha, Hazard's fiancée, and sells the Pregnant Mares' Urine to an American company. Martha's daughter, perhaps even the daughter of Hazard conceived the one and only time he and Martha consummate their relationship, is ironically called Demeter, too.

In *The Studhorse Man*, the horse, its changing role and impact stand for one of those epistemic breaks that Kroetsch sees as central elements of the decentring movement of postmodernism, although it may also be seen as an example of Kroetsch's "romantic-reactionary response to 'the general process of enlightenment' that characterizes the last four hundred years of Euro-American history."[36] As part of his Weberian "disenchanted" reading of the novel, Zichy even suggests an even more all-encompassing context in which the horse and its function in the old and new world orders play a role going beyond the mere plots of Hazard Lepage and/or Demeter Proudfoot:

> Near the end of the novel, the narrator manages to link the development of artificial insemination and the contraceptive pill with the thermonuclear bombing of Hiroshima, and the moral paradox of a scientific progress that is at least the sibling if not the actual offspring of war can be seen as confirming Weber's description of the "general process of enlightenment" as indeed "nihilistic", and of "scientific rationalization" as a major contributor to the destructive "reduction of religious ethics and ultimate beliefs to rational calculation and this-worldly action."[37]

Or, as Rudy Dorscht puts it in a somewhat less philosophically or sociologically oriented interpretation of "disenchantment":

> Sexual desire, procreation, and birth control become metaphors for textual play, dissemination, and the fixing of meaning. Homologically, the "pill" arrests the pregnancy of signification and sterilizes language. It is not in the sterilizing but in the "teazing" (in both the sexual and textual senses [...]) out of the possibilities of

[34] Ibid. p. 202.

[35] Robert Kroetsch: *The Studhorse Man,* ed. cited, p. 203;
Francis Zichy insists in his excellent and exhaustive – although "occasionally Demeteresque" (38) – study of *The Studhorse Man* that "the widespread folk myth that pregnant mare's urine is the source for the hormones in the Pill is factually incorrect" and that "even Demeter's statement, as of 1969, that 'with estrogen [scientists] [...] have learned to prevent the further multiplication of man upon the face of the earth' is only half true at best" (Francis Zichy: *Disenchanted Modernity in Robert Kroetsch's* The Studhorse Man, New York 2010, p.29).

[36] Francis Zichy: *Disenchanted Modernity,* ed. cited, p. 2.

[37] Ibid. p. 3.

> meanings and of multiple sexual subject positions, that *The Studhorse Man*'s gesture toward the future of human sexual/textual relations lies.[38]

But the horse stands here not only for the innovation and epistemological change that liberated sexuality means for the role of women but also for the shift from traditional conservative to a more liberal (perhaps even promiscuous) society, for Canada's move from – as Kroetsch has put it in another context – "Victorian into Postmodern" without ever having been modern.[39] Whether this move into a society in which – to all too briefly summarize the concept of postmodernism – "anything goes" is positive or negative remains a question, but not to Demeter. Demeter gives us, as Zichy shows, "a bitterly acerbic comment on an emerging culture of self-realization through sexual liberation."[40] Demeter's description of the consequences of the use of the urine of the mares impregnated by the stallion Poseidon give us an utterly negative, Swiftian or rather Gulliverian perspective of the future of mankind as yahoos: "Scurrilous, barbarous, stinking man would soon be able, in the sterility of his own lust, to screw himself into oblivion, to erase himself like a rotting pestilence form the face of God's creation."[41]

How to come to a conclusion regarding Robert Kroetsch and the function of the horse in his novel? The horse in *The Studhorse Man* may well be seen as a symbol of epistemic change from realism to postmodernism, from Weberian work ethic to postmodernism's playfulness as it may be seen to express itself in sexual promiscuity. Perhaps we can even see Kroetsch as the melancholic conservative that Francis Zichy makes him out to be: Hazard as Swiftian yahoo (i.e. Gulliver) who has moved in with his stallion Poseidon: "Demeter's misanthropic, Gulliveresque meaning is that the horse is more real than the man; the animal is natural but the human is perverse."[42]

These intertextual connections to Swift that I started out with at the beginning come full circle in a poem included in Kroetsch's last volume of poetry published before his death in 2011, which is sardonically entitled *Too Bad*. While the book as a whole – according to the information given on the front flap – represents "a candid walk through the tortuous corridors of the poet's remembering", the poem "Time to Spare"[43] brings together the two elements of Kroetsch's horse/house metaphor in a way that may well be seen as having Swiftian overtones. After all, in *Gulliver's Travels* Swift's horse-like houyhnhnms were not only capable of speech, but they were also much more intelligent and philosophical than the human-like yahoos. In his poem, Kroetsch's speaker buys a horse and builds a ranch, then decides that his house should no longer play a central role in his life, and so he now lives "with a horse in a pasture." Unfortunately, though, the wisdom of the horses is not immediately available to all humans. This would not be surprising for Kroetsch as he – as a critic and theorist – always insisted on the importance of the concept delay. Delay/ing is of utmost importance not only in the

[38] Susan Rudy Dorscht: *Women, Reading, Kroetsch,* ed. cited, p. 69.
[39] Robert Kroetsch: *A Canadian Issue*, in: *Boundary 2* 3.1 (1974), p. 1.
[40] Francis Zichy: *Disenchanted Modernity,* ed. cited, p. 7.
[41] Robert Kroetsch: *The Studhorse Man,* ed. cited, p. 204.
[42] Francis Zichy: *Disenchanted Modernity,* ed. cited, p. 129.
[43] Robert Kroetsch: *Too Bad: Sketches Towards a Self-Portrait,* Edmonton 2010, p. 92.

poststructuralist Derridean concept of *différance* but also in the literary-sexual act of writing/reading the long poem, as Kroetsch pointed out in his important programmatic essay punningly entitled "For Play and Entrance: The Contemporary Canadian Long Poem": "In love-making, in writing the long poem – delay is both – delay is both technique and content. Narrative has an elaborate grammar of delay."[44]

And another version of this delay is what Kroetsch's persona is ironically confronted with in "Time to spare":

> Right now I am waiting. Just simply waiting.
> My horse, in a month, hasn't spoken a word.

Kroetsch's old-age candidness has (to) come to terms with the fact that horses, signs and symbols can – but do not have to – transport a deeper meaning, that they can – but do not have to – speak to us. I trust this does not necessarily undermine the general message of this essay.

Bibliography

Atwood, Margaret: *Survival: A Thematic Guide to Canadian Literature*. Toronto 1972.

Beran, Carol R: The Studhorse Man: *Translating the Boundaries of Text*, in: *Great Plains Quarterly* (1994). DigitalCommons@University of Nebraska – Lincoln. Paper 830.

Butala, Sharon: *The Gates of the Sun*. 1986. Toronto 1994.

De Witt, Patrick: *The Sisters Brothers*. London 2011.

Francis, Daniel: *The Mild West: The Myth of the RCMP*, in: *National Dreams: Myth, Memory, and Canadian History*. Vancouver 1997, pp. 29-51.

Hutcheon, Linda: *The Canadian Postmodern: A Study of Contemporary English-Canadian Fiction*. Toronto 1988.

Kroetsch, Robert: *A Canadian Issue*, in: *Boundary 2* 3.1 (1974): pp. 1-2.

Kroetsch, Robert: *For Play and Entrance: The Contemporary Canadian Long Poem,* in: *Open Letter* 5.4 (*Robert Kroetsch: Essays*) (1983), pp. 91-110.

Kroetsch, Robert: *Seed Catalogue* (1977). *Completed Field Notes: The Long Poems of Robert Kroetsch*. Edmonton 2000, pp. 29-46.

Kroetsch, Robert: *The Fear of Women in Prairie Fiction: An Erotics of Space* (1979), in: *The Lovely Treachery of Words: Essays Selected and New*. Toronto 1989, pp. 73-83.

Kroetsch, Robert: *The Studhorse Man*. 1969. Edmonton 2004.

Kroetsch, Robert: *Too Bad: Sketches Towards a Self-Portrait*. Edmonton 2010.

Kroetsch, Robter: *The Cow in the Quicksand and How I(t) Got Out: Responding to Stegner's Wolf Willow*, in: *A Likely Story: The Writing Life*. Red Deer 1995, pp. 65-86.

Kroetsch, Roebrt: *Afterword*. As For Me and My House. *By Sinclair Ross*. Toronto 1989, pp. 217-221.

Kuester, Martin: *Kroetsch's Fragments: Approaching the Narrative Structure of His Novels,* in: *Postmodern Fiction in Canada*, ed. by Theo D'haen und Hans Bertens. Amsterdam and Antwerpen 1992, pp. 137-160.

[44] Robert Kroetsch: *For Play and Entrance: The Contemporary Canadian Long Poem,* in: *Open Letter* 5.4 (*Robert Kroetsch: Essays)* (1983), p. 91.

Kuester, Martin: *Tales Told in the Bathtub: Robert Kroetsch's Historiographic Metafiction,* in: *Historiographic Metafiction in Modern American and Canadian Literature*, ed. by Bernd Engler and Kurt Müller. Paderborn 1994, pp. 399-410.

Lecker, Robert: *Robert Kroetsch.* Boston 1986.

Mitchell, Barbara: *Paul: The Answer to the Riddle of* As For Me and My House, in: *Studies in Canadian Literature* 13.1 (1988). Web. Accessed: May 14, 2014. Available from: http://journals.hil.unb.ca/index.php/scl/article/view/8076/9133.

Rudy Dorscht, Susan: *Women, Reading, Kroetsch: Telling the Difference.* Waterloo, Ont. 1991.

Sonner, Scott: *Are Wild Horses Native to the U.S.? A Federal Court Seeks the Answer,* in *LA Times Greenspace.* June 5, 2011. Web. Accessed Dec. 24, 2013. Availabe from: http://latimesblogs.latimes.com/greenspace/2011/06/wild-horses-nevada-blm-native-species.html.

Thomas, Peter: *Robert Kroetsch.* Vancouver 1980.

Van Herk, Aritha: *Introduction.* The Studhorse Man. *By Robert Kroetsch.* Edmonton 2004, pp. v-xvi.

Zichy, Francis: *Disenchanted Modernity in Robert Kroetsch's* The Studhorse Man. New York 2010.

Equestrian Ballet as a Representative of Cultural Change in Europe, *c.*1500-1700

Barbara Ravelhofer
Durham University

Between the fifteenth and the seventeenth century, significant changes became evident in the way horses were perceived, treated, and put to use. These changes tell us not only how humans valued them but also how humans saw themselves. The seventeenth century was a cognitive watershed: philosophers such as Locke and Descartes redefined the individual in ways that are fundamental for our modern understanding of selfhood. In the language of the period we can trace emergent ideas of an abstract, autonomous self alongside notions of a self that was collective, interpersonal, and viscerally physical – a self that defined itself in relation to the animal world: "animal", after all, is etymologically related to Latin "anima", soul.[1] Literature of the period offers rewarding insights into the construction of human 'selves': King Lear was not the only one who asked "Who is it that can tell me who I am?" and arrived at the conclusion that man was, ultimately, a creature among many.[2] By looking closely at one of humanity's favourite fellow creatures, this essay considers, then, important, related questions: how did poets, philosophers, and equestrian experts relate to horses? What was the impulse behind wanting an animal to practise an art, and why did the equestrian arts develop across early modern Europe in the first place, teaching a horse to execute movements which it would never perform by nature?

From jousting to hippodrama: a short history of equine performance

In the Middle Ages, tournaments highlighted the nobility's equestrian prowess and also prepared riders and horses for the battlefield. Some interesting conclusions can be drawn from attempts to re-enact such medieval practices in modern-day Germany, for instance, at a medieval festival in Landshut, Bavaria. At Landshut, specially trained riders run at the ring and the quintain, and joust in armour weighing well over 30kg, forged after original items in regional museums. All this requires many rehearsals. The 'knights' find that they achieve the best results if they have worked closely with a

[1] Laurie Shannon: *The Eight Animals in Shakespeare; Or, Before the Human*, in: *PMLA*, 124/2 (2009), pp. 472-79; Bruce Boehrer: *Animal Studies and the Deconstruction of Character*, in: *PMLA*, 124/2 (2009), pp. 542-47.

[2] William Shakespeare: *The History of King Lear* (1608), in: *King Lear: A Parallel Text Edition*, ed. by René Weis, London 1993, 1.4.218.

particular horse, possibly over several years.[3] Each knight has a squire to lead the animal and run with it towards the barrier as it is breaking into a gallop. Frequently, horses will nonetheless shy away. Most horses need to be replaced because they so utterly dislike the experience of charging towards a rapidly approaching opponent. We find this fact reflected in romances of the sixteenth century, for instance, in Sir David Lindsay's *Squyer Meldrum* (first pb. *c.*1582), based on the life of the Scottish baron William Meldrum. Here the English champion Talbot loses a challenge against Meldrum because his charger is "loath to run".[4] The reality of jousting shows the challenge of wearing heavy armour and balancing a tilting lance while keeping control of an unwilling mount in full career. Historic re-enactments sharpen our awareness of why steady war horses, those "trampling coursers"[5] of Spenser's poetry, were so prized. It is very difficult indeed to make a horse do what it does not wish to do.

In the mid-sixteenth century, the programme of equestrian display diversified. Elaborate entertainments became fashionable which, apart from mock battles and pageants, included dressage performances to the sound of drums and trumpets rather than a full-frontal crashing of harnesses. With regard to Renaissance England, Kirby Farrell has argued, military changes had

> shrunk the scale of aristocratic heroism and made the armored knight a pompous sitting duck on the battlefield. In Shakespeare's day, English nobles still pumped up their heroic self-esteem by jousting, but the cult of chivalry was already becoming an exercise in bravura histrionics and solemn doublethink.[6]

The preference of European courts for refined forms of courtly display was nowhere more interestingly in evidence than at Dresden. As the seventeenth century progressed, Saxony's capital set new standards for rich ostentation, exotic disguise, and inventive variations of the chivalric programme.

[3] Over the 1980s and 1990s, the performer playing the role of Duke Sigmund of Tyrol was a frequent tournament winner thanks to his stolid if shortish mount named "Wiggerl".

[4] "Bot Talbartis Horse, with ane mischance/ He outterit and to ryn was laith,/ Quhairof Talbart was wonder wraith." Sir David Lindsay: *Squyer Meldrum*, ed. by James Kinsley, London 1959, l. 506-8.

[5] "An armed knight, vpon a courser strong,/ Whose trampling feet vpon the hollow lay/ Seemed to thunder." Edmund Spenser: *The Faerie Queene*, ed. by A. C. Hamilton, London, corr. ed., 1980, book III, canto 8, st. 15.

[6] Kirby Farrell: *Post-Traumatic Culture: Injury and Interpretation in the Nineties,* Baltimore 1998, p. 48.

Fig 1: Queen Semiramis. Tournament costume for a Saxon Prince, embroidered atlas, *c.*1672. Dresden, Rüstkammer, inv. No. I 44. Photo: Elke Estel and Hans-Peter Klut.
By permission of the Staatliche Kunstsammlungen, Dresden.

This costume was made for a Saxon prince who rode out as Queen Semiramis in about 1672.[7] Its sleeves and collar imitate the colour of skin; this was meant to suggest bare arms and cleavage. The use of delicate fabrics – red, azure, white and yellow flowers on green silk lined with gold lace – and the excellent state of the costume's conservation suggest that no serious bruising was involved in the spectacle. Dresden also invented and popularized another kind of equestrian divertissement: the ladies' running for the ring ("Damenringrennen"). The lady, comfortably placed in a sledge or chariot and escorted by her cavalier, aimed with her lance at a target, usually a ring suspended between two pillars. The first such event of note took place in 1709; the underlying idea was to integrate the lady as an active partner in festive court culture.[8]

Attention also turned, however, to the horses as performers in their own right. Riding schools became a feature at courts such as Naples, Paris, Madrid, or Parma from the sixteenth century onwards. These establishments produced highly trained animals able to execute a wide range of complicated steps and postures to a specific rhythm. The tradition survives in select locations, for instance, the Écurie Royale at Versailles, or Vienna's Hofreitschule, where riders still train with carefully selected Lipizzan horses

[7] Reproduced in *Eine gute Figur machen: Kostüm und Fest am Dresdner Hof*, ed. by Claudia Schnitzer and Petra Hölscher, Dresden 2000, fig. 7, p. 44. See also Claudia Schnitzer: *Höfische Maskeraden: Funktion und Ausstattung von Verkleidungsdivertissements an deutschen Höfen der Frühen Neuzeit*, Tübingen 1999, p. 180.
[8] *Eine gute Figur machen,* ed. by Claudia Schnitzer, ed. cited, p. 182.

in a demanding programme lasting several years.[9] Owing to great cost, the maintenance of such schools was, and remains, an elite pastime.

Dressage books prescribed many movements for horses; the terminology was close to that used in the repertoire of human dancers. Trainers strove to teach horses quasi-human steps (as far as four legs rather than two would allow); one example is the Italian *capriola* (French *capriole*), a dexterous jump imitating the capers of a goat (Italian 'capra') which became fashionable in the sixteenth century and still survives in classical ballet. In practising the *capriola*, the human dancer produced some nimble leg movements while in mid-air. Jehan Tabourot, an author familiar with the better circles around Paris and Lengres, published a treatise on dances of his time. His *Orchésographie* (1589) appeared under the pseudonym Thoinot Arbeau; in the work, a teacher instructs a pupil called Capriol in the ways of proper dancing, and the reader learns with Capriol and his master, following their socratic dialogue. *Orchésographie* explains the jump as follows: "there are many dancers so agile that while executing the *saut majeur* they move their feet in the air and such capering is called *capriole*".[10] The *capriole* was also documented in Italian dance manuals from the second half of the sixteenth century. It occurred, among others, in courtly dances as practised in Rome, Naples, or Venice. Dancing masters of the time advised that only skilled performers should attempt the *capriole*; it was the domain of male courtiers wishing to show off their strength and agility in *gagliardas*, athletic dances involving assiduous jumping. First evidence of a *capriole* for female dancers occurs much later, in French professional ballet of the later seventeenth century.

[9] Georg Kugler and Wolfdieter Bihl, *Die Lipizzaner der Spanischen Hofreitschule,* Vienna 2002; Mathilde Windisch-Graetz: *The Spanish Riding School,* London 1956, p. 22; Helen Watanabe-O'Kelly: *Triumphall Shews: Tournaments at German-Speaking Courts in Their European Context, 1560-1730,* Berlin 1992; *Les écuries royales du XVI*e *au XVIII*e *siècle*, ed. by D. Roche, Versailles 1998; Giles Worsley: *The History of* haute école *in England*, in: *The Court Historian*, 6 (2001), pp. 29-47.

[10] Thoinot Arbeau [Jehan Tabourot]: *Orchesography*, ed. by Julia Sutton, transl. by Mary Stewart Evans, New York 1967, p. 91.

Fig. 2. An author ascending to Olympus, on a Pegasus executing a heavenly *capriole.* William Cavendish, *La methode nouvelle* (Antwerp, 1658). Shelfmark F.165.bb.6.1.
By permission of the Syndics of Cambridge University Library.

In the equestrian *capriole*, the horse jumped, its hind legs parallel in an almost horizontal position, while drawing its forelegs under, as illustrated above.[11] René de Menou's *La Pratique du Cavalier* (1614) spent a full 26 pages explaining how to teach progressively in eleven lessons those jumps "qui sont hauts, & eslevez tout d'un temps, & le cheval estant en l'air à la fin de sa hauteur, avant que de tomber à terre". Menou advised that this risky jump, which could easily lead to injury, should be reserved for especially strong and light horses. The *capriole* was to be taught with many caresses to encourage the creature.[12]

One of the finest seventeenth-century books on dressage was authored by William Cavendish, Duke of Newcastle, husband of the prolific writer Margaret Cavendish and England's foremost equestrian expert at the time. Cavendish prided himself on being a practical rather than a bookish man; even so, he routinely acquired Continental books through agents. Thomas Hobbes, no less, procured him Galileo's latest works.[13] Cavendish's library shows a reader deeply steeped in European performance culture of his day, ranging from French *ballet de cour* to banqueting, Italian horsemanship, music, and mannerist architecture. The catalogue attests to the presence of Isaac de Caus, Vitruvius, Serlio, Gastoldi's *Balletti* (1598), and Puget de la Serre's accounts of

[11] For a definition of the jump see Windisch-Graetz: *The Spanish Riding School*, ed. cited, p. 25.
[12] René de Menou: *La pratique du cavalier. Par ou il est enseigné la vraye methode qu'il doit tenir pour mettre son cheval à la raison, & le rendre capable de paroistre sur la carriere, obeïssant à l'ordre des plus justes proportions de tous les plus beaux airs & manages,* Paris 1614, pp. 109, 115.
[13] Hobbes to Cavendish, 26 January 1634. *The Manuscripts of the Duke of Portland, Preserved at Welbeck Abbey*, vol. 2, ed. by Historical Manuscripts Commission, London 1893, p. 124.

festivities at the court of Louis XIII.[14] Christoforo di Messisbugo's *Modo d'ordinar banchetti* (1596) was apt literature for a man who laid on the most expensive royal entertainment recorded under the early Stuarts. James Shirley's court masque *The Triumph of Peace* (1634), a £2000 extravaganza, is commonly credited with this record. It was, however, dwarfed by Cavendish's legendary receptions in honour of Charles I and Henrietta Maria at his Nottinghamshire estates in 1633 and 1634. Complete with alfresco banqueting, tilting, and musical theatre, these racked up almost £ 20,000. Years later the Earl of Clarendon recalled Cavendish's "stupendious" hospitality "which (God be thanked) [...] no man ever after in those days Imitated".[15] As for horsemanship, the ducal library boasted Cesare Fiaschi's *Modo dell'imbrigliare* (1563), Nicholas Morgan's *Horsemanship* (1609), Gervase Markham's *The English Horseman* (1616), Thibault's *Academie de l'espée*, Melchiori's *Equestria* (1621), and Soleysel's *Parfait mareschal* (1672). Several books indicate an interest in animal language and metamorphosis, such as *Philomythie, Wherein Outlandish Birds, Beasts, and Fishes are Taught to Speake English* (1616), and Bulwer's *Man Transform'd, or, The Artificial Changeling* (1650). Bulwer is now better known for another work (also in Cavendish's library): *Chirologia, or the Natural Language of the Hand* (1644) explained the precise meaning of rhetorical hand movements, and is the first point of call for theatre historians wishing to reconstruct the gestures of early modern English stageplayers. All these books give us a palpable idea of the mental horizon of a man who was equally interested in spectacle, drama, and cross-communication between humans and animals.

A royalist, Cavendish went into exile when King Charles' armies were defeated. He lived for many years in Antwerp, where he rented the house of Rubens, built a riding school in the backyard, and trained a number of horses in *haute école* to a standard that attracted a host of visitors from across Europe. During this time, he wrote the imposing book *La methode nouvelle* [...] *de dresser les chevaux.* It was first published in Antwerp in 1658 in a luxury folio format. Circulating in French, German, and English versions, the work saw at least eleven editions before 1745. *La methode nouvelle* offers state-of-the-art insights into practical and theoretical aspects of *haute école*. Woodcuts and engravings illustrate training spaces, accessories such as bridles, as well as equine steps and postures and their choreographic arrangements. For Cavendish, these had a deeper sense: the horses were literally his world, as becomes clear from his vision of a "universal choreography" composed of a square and a circle, which were considered as

[14] All listed in: *Bibliotheca Nobilissimi Principis Johannis Ducis de Novo-Castro, &c.* London 1719, now Cambridge University Library. The library comprises the holdings of collections of William and Henry Cavendish as well as John Hollis, late Dukes of Newcastle; I confine my list to the items which (I confidently believe) entered the collection under William. For further evidence of the latter's interest in Continental music see Lynn Hulse: *Apollo's Whirligig: William Cavendish, Duke of Newcastle and His Music Collection*, in: *The Seventeenth Century*, 9/2 (1994), pp. 213-46.

[15] Edward Hyde, Earl of Clarendon: *The History of the Rebellion and Civil Wars in England, Begun in the Year 1641* [...] *Volume the First,* Oxford 1702, book I, p. 61. For estimates of Cavendish's entertainments see Margaret Cavendish: *The Life of William Cavendish Duke of Newcastle*, ed. by C. H. Firth, 2nd ed. London 1906, p. 78; and Cedric Brown: *Courtesies of Place and Arts of Diplomacy in Ben Jonson's Last Two Entertainments for Royalty*, in: *The Seventeenth Century*, 9/2 (1994), pp. 147-71.

two of geometry's perfect figures in philosophical writing of the time.[16] The quadrature of a circle was the result of perfect communication between animal and human, and exemplified the harmonious collaboration between horse and rider.

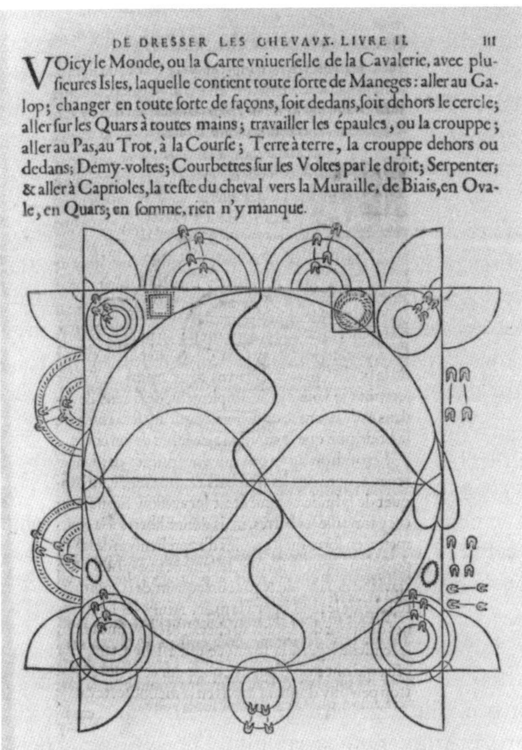

DE DRESSER LES CHEVAVX. LIVRE II. 111

VOicy le Monde, ou la Carte vniuerſelle de la Cavalerie, avec pluſieures Isles, laquelle contient toute ſorte de Maneges: aller au Galop; changer en toute ſorte de façons, ſoit dedans, ſoit dehors le cercle; aller ſur les Quars à toutes mains; travailler les épaules, ou la crouppe; aller au Pas, au Trot, à la Courſe; Terre à terre, la crouppe dehors ou dedans; Demy-voltes; Courbettes ſur les Voltes par le droit; Serpenter; & aller à Caprioles, la teſte du cheval vers la Muraille, de Biais, en Ovale, en Quars; en ſomme, rien n'y manque.

Fig. 3: Cavendish's universal choreography. William Cavendish, *La methode nouvelle* (Antwerp, 1658), p. 111. Shelfmark F.165.bb.6.1.
By permission of the Syndics of Cambridge University Library.

Cavendish was representative of a more kindly way with horses that set in towards the end of the sixteenth century and is, for instance, evident in the way Menou advocated the teaching of the *capriole*. Peter Edwards has compared this "more progressive and caring" approach favourably to the brutal times of Henry VIII; indeed, critics have drawn parallels between the improved treatment of animals and that of children in education.[17] Interestingly, dressage manuals of the period often compared the manège to a classroom, with the young horse being coaxed to desired movements by "loving

[16] Anne Conway, *The Principles of the Most Ancient and Modern Philosophy*, tr. J[odocus?] C[rull?] ([London]: printed in Latin in Amsterdam by M. Brown, 1690, and reprinted at London, 1692), pp. 156-57.

[17] Peter Edwards: *Horse and Man in Early Modern England,* London 2007, pp. 51, 54; Joan Thirsk: *Horses in Early Modern England: For Service, for Pleasure, for Power,* Reading 1978, p. 18; Erica Fudge: *Brutal Reasoning: Animals, Rationality, and Humanity in Early Modern England,* Ithaca 2006, pp. 138-39.

speeches & gentle usage", in the words of a manual published in 1609.[18] As with the horses, so with the riders: both were regarded as in need of gentle education. The French riding master to Louis XIII, Antoine de Pluvinel, whom Cavendish admired, proposed a riding academy which would educate the indolent young gentry to proper behaviour and vigorous engagement in matters of the state. Apparently, Cavendish nurtured similar ideas; he had already obtained didactic experience in the 1630s as the tutor of the future Charles II, to whom he had dedicated a treatise on how to govern well.[19] Lucy Worsley and Tom Addyman propose that Cavendish planned an equestrian academy after the French model in Clerkenwell, London.[20] If so, the Civil War put an end to such ambitions.

Pluvinel was also more directly connected with Cavendish because the latter bought at least one young dressage horse from the Paris riding school. Intriguingly, it was Hobbes who negotiated the purchase of "Le Superbe", a young Spanish stallion. When the animal arrived at Cavendish's Nottinghamshire estates, however, it sorely disappointed its new owner due to a chap-fallen expression and a lack of dressage technique. Hobbes remarked in a letter from Paris:

> [For his fault of gaping], they confesse it [...] For his feet they obstinately deny that he has any fault in them at all, and do suppose that the journey may have hurt him. That he has no other [steps] but corvettes, is a thing your Lordship was made acquainted with before. The greatest fault is his price. Which [...] is a very good reason why he should henceforward be called Le Superbe.[21]

We no longer know how much Cavendish had spent on Le Superbe but some comparative prices of the period may give us an idea. In the times of Charles I and Cromwell a coach horse might have cost between £6 5^{s} and £31 5^{s}. During the Civil War, the Parliamentarian Army purchased troop horses for about £7 each; status-conscious cavaliers, on the other hand, showed off their £50 mount.[22] Horses of Le Superbe's quality were far more expensive. Around 1610, Lord Herbert of Cherbury was offered £200 for his Spanish jennet, a diplomatic gift of the Duke of Montmorency which had originally cost 500 crowns (possibly an equivalent of 15kg of silver or over 1 kg of gold) when it was imported from Spain. Cavendish himself had seen prize horses sold for as much as £100-200 in the 1660s.[23] To give a modern-day equivalent for top-

[18] Nicholas Morgan: *The Horse-Mans Honour* (1609), pp. 168, 173-74. Listed in: *Bibliotheca Nobilissimi*, ed. cited, p. 44, no. 276.

[19] *The Little Book*, ed. by Gloria Italiano Anzilotti as *An English* Prince. *Newcastle's Machiavellian Political Guide to Charles II,* Pisa 1988.

[20] Lucy Worsley and Tom Addyman: *Riding Houses and Horses: William Cavendish's Architecture for the Art of Horsemanship*, in: *Architectural History*, 45 (2002), p. 221.

[21] Thomas Hobbes to Cavendish, Paris, 15/25 August 1635, in: *The Correspondence. Volume I: 1622-1659*, ed. by Noel Malcolm, Oxford 1994, pp. 28-29. The horse's price is not stated.

[22] Edwards: *Horse and Man*, ed. cited, p. 153; table of purchase prices 1620-59, p. 221.

[23] *The Life of Edward, First Lord Herbert of Cherbury, Written by Himself*, ed. by J. Shuttleworth, London 1976, pp. 49, 52. My thanks to Luca Einaudi for the silver estimate. In the 1660s, Cavendish knew that prize horses sold at fairs for £100-200; Joan Thirsk: *Horses in Early Modern England*, ed. cited, p. 58.

class dressage stallions, the catalogue of Paul Schockemöhle's equestrian establishment commands a stud fee of €4,000 for the seed of three-time World Champion Totilas, "best dressage horse of all times" and "living legend", whose foals are being sold for as much as €200,000.[24]

Le Superbe eventually prospered under his new owner. Cavendish came to regard his horse as the perfect dancer:

> He went in Corvets forward, backward, sidewayes, on both Hands; made the Cross perfectly upon his Voltoes; and did Change upon his Voltoes so Just, without breaking Time, that no Musitian could keep Time better.[25]

Cavendish was in good company: early modern opinion regarded horses as particularly musical and excellent dancers.[26] Indeed, humans were sometimes unfavourably compared to their equine counterparts. The city comedy *The Lady of Pleasure* (1635) poked fun at would-be gentlemen who, when still, resembled stuffed mannequins, and when moving, were far outdone by superior horses.[27] (It may not have been a coincidence that the play's author, James Shirley, looked to Cavendish for patronage.) In Cavendish's youth, the travelling entertainer John Banks came to fame with his stallion Morocco. Morocco was, supposedly, able to count and indeed, as a French source claimed, danced, "after an infinite number of level turns", "the Canary with great art and dexterity".[28] The Canary is known from late-sixteenth-century French and Italian dance books. Originally derived from the Canaries, it featured a characteristic *canario* step sequence. The dancing master Fabritio Caroso described several versions of the latter in his famous book *Il ballarino* (1581) and used it in a number of choreographies to add mediterranean colour, for instance, in a *Spagnoletta*.[29] Arbeau's *Orchésographie*

[24] Paul Schockemöhle: *Stallion Collection 2013*, catalogue of the stud, p. 51; see also www.schockemoehle.com.

[25] William Cavendish: *La methode nouvelle,* Antwerp 1658, engraving no.7; *A New Method*, sig. b2^{v}. A painting of Le Superbe, now in a private collection, has been reproduced in Peter Edwards: *Les écuries des monarques anglais aux XVIe et XVIIe siècles*, in: *Les écuries royales*, ed. by D. Roche, pp. 154-65.

[26] For instance, the sixteenth-century horsemaster Cesare Fiaschi. Writing about the art of spectacle in the 1680s, the Jesuit Jean-François Ménestrier noted that horses were excellent dancers.

[27] As Lady Celestina scolds a presumptuous suitor, "you dare not/ Out of your guilt of being the ignobler beast,/ But give a horse the wall (whom you excel/ Only in dancing of the brawl, because/ The horse was not taught the French way)." James Shirley: *The Lady of Pleasure*, ed. by R. Huebert, Manchester 1986, 3.2.299-303.

[28] "Apres une infinité de tours de passe-passe, il luy fait danser les Canaries avec beaucoup d'art & de dexterité." Apuleius: *Les metamorphoses, ou l'asne d'or*, transl. by J. de Montlyard, Paris 1601/1623, p. 254; Montlyard had inserted a section on Morocco. Cited from Philip Butterworth: *Magic on the Early English Stage,* Cambridge 2005, p. 69.

[29] "Questa si fa tirando indietro, ò spingendo innanzi ad ogni passo l'uno de i piedi schizzandolo, ò strasciando sì innanzi come indietro: et da questo modo di strascinar, ò schisciar di piedi, ha preso cotal nome." *Della schisciata al canario*, in M. Fabritio Caroso: *Il ballarino,* Venice 1581; facs. rpr. New York 1967, fol. 16^{r}, rule LII.

defined the canary dance as "strange and fantastic with a strong barbaric flavour". Its characteristic step included scraping the foot forwards and backwards along the ground "as if one were treading down spittle or killing a spider".[30] Conceivably, then, Morocco scraped one hoof back and forth again, before stomping decisively.

Horses are rarely documented in indoor theatricals; such locations might have made them nervous and bad-tempered. When Henry, Prince of Wales prepared for his first masque, *Oberon* (1611), he wanted to enter the stage as a fairy prince in a triumphal chariot drawn by two horses. His concerned father, James I, however, demanded a change for reasons of safety, and so Henry eventually appeared in the company of two polar bear cubs led by attendants.[31] Occasional mishaps afflicted the French courtly stage, for instance, in *The Ballet of the Dowager of Bilbao*, performed before Louis XIII in 1626, where the entry of the Grand Turk (the dancer Marais) and his harem (which included the King's brother as one of the "sultanes") was ruined by the participating horse. Marais rode in when his mount committed, in the words of a commentator, an "embarrassing indignity" on stage.[32]

Yet there were spectacular exceptions. In *Les amours de Jupiter et de Junon* (1625), the god Hypodame was played by Monsieur de Pluvinel, who directed eight horses in a ballet by the mere sound of his voice, to the general admiration of the assembled audience:

> Le Dieu Hypodame, dompteur des chevaux, voulant faire paroistre les merveilles de son industrie en une si royale Assemblee, faict danser un ballet, en cadence au son de sa voix, comme au son d'un instrument, en presence des Dieux, à huict chevaux, de la race de ceux d'Appollon; mais avec un telle mesure, que l'Ordre, qui estoit un des admirateurs; ne sçeut dire que des loüanges, à l'honneur de ce Dieu.[33]

The fact that the account of this ballet was in Cavendish's library, and that Cavendish relied on the Pluvinel riding school for his own stables, should make us ponder Cavendish's training philosophy and ambitions. It was not the whip but the voice which prompted, in Paris and in Nottinghamshire, the horses' successful performance.

Another rare example took place on the occasion of a Medici-Farnese wedding in Parma's generously proportioned theatre in 1628, where, apparently, three horses descended from the heavens for some indoor jousting. As Frederick Hammond writes about this feat, "the Ferrarese were celebrated horse trainers, but lowering three live

[30] Thoinot Arbeau: *Orchesography*, ed. cited, p. 181.

[31] B. Ravelhofer: *"Beasts of Recreacion": Henslowe's White Bears*, in: *English Literary Renaissance*, 32/2 (2002), pp. 287-323.

[32] *Ballet de la douairière de Billebahaut* (1626), stage design reproduced in: Marie-Françoise Christout: *Le ballet de cour au XVIIe siècle,* Geneva 1987, p. 130, fig. 116; Michel de Marolles: *Les mémoires de M. de M. Abbé de Villeloin (1656-57)*, cited from: *Dance Music from the Ballets de Cour 1575-1651,* ed. by David J. Buch, Stuyvesant, NY 1993, p. xvi.

[33] Puget de la Serre: *Les amours de Jupiter et de Junon, avec les magnificences de leurs nopces,* Paris 1625, pp. 29-30.

mounted horses from the flies of a theater still staggers the imagination".[34] *L'Ermiona*, a spectacle performed in Padua in 1636, included tournaments and a ballet. Flanked by blind Cupids, a knight on horseback descended to the sound of violins. His richly plumed mount neighed lustily in response to the trumpets; then the pair crossed the stage towards the audience. The spectactors were mesmerized by this novelty. Later on, more horses erupted from backstage and engaged with each other with 'puntualità cavalleresca'.[35] It is difficult to assess the practicalities of this equestrian spectacle. The famous stage designer Alfonso Chenda, also known as Il Rivarola, must have devised some elaborate machinery for lifting and lowering animals. We cannot discount the possibility that an artificial horse might have been involved in the descent, but a real one seems far more likely, given the dynamics of the ensuing action, and the fact that the chief performer had specially been sent for from Modena, where he had built a reputation for equestrian feats.

We see here the early modern expressions of what has been called, in Arthur Saxon's felicitous phrase, "hippodrama"[36] – an integrated form of entertainment that fused circus, theatre, pantomime, dance, and music. Hippodrama was in its purest form a Victorian creation, but its seventeenth-century roots were not forgotten by its foremost practitioner, the trainer, acrobat and contortionist Andrew Ducrow. In Ducrow's establishment around 40 horses and ponies cavorted with artists, ballet dancers, and assorted exotic animals. In one of his numbers, "Classical Picturesque History of Ancient and Modern Equitation", Ducrow appeared as "the celebrated Duke of Newcastle, training his horse in the presence of Louis XIV".[37] Highlight of the 1835 season was the guest trainer Laurent Franconi with his steed Blanche. Blanche absolved the full *haute école* programme but was also able to (among other feats) smoke and waltz.[38] "What a beautiful creature is Franconi's horse Blanche," wrote one effusive newspaper critic, "how gentle, how tractable, how graceful, and really clever. It is a pleasure to see this horse, because we know that no torture, no flogging, could have trained it to such exploits. It must have been a superior instinct and natural cleverness in the animal."[39]

[34] Frederick Hammond: *Music and Spectacle in Baroque Rome: Barberini Patronage under Urban VIII,* New Haven 1994, p. 205.

[35] Marchese Pio Enea Obizzi: *L'Ermiona,* Padua 1638, plate of knight descending on horseback following p. 88, account pp. 89-90, 103-4.

[36] A. H. Saxon: *Enter Foot and Horse: A History of Hippodrama in England and France,* New Haven 1968.

[37] A. H. Saxon: *The Life and Art of Andrew Ducrow & the Romantic Age of the English Circus,* Hamden 1978, pp. 278-79.

[38] Playbill for 29 June 1835, V&A. Blanche was trained for three years for this. A. H. Saxon, *The Life*, ed. cited, pp. 287-88 and note 43.

[39] Henry Mayhew in the *Figaro in London* for 11 July [1835], cited in: A. H. Saxon, *The Life*, ed. cited, p. 288.

The purposes of dressage: carpet dancers, soldiers, or polished subjects?

Why did men like Cavendish take the trouble to teach horses complicated movements in the first place? For some, manège was purely an idle pastime. Christopher Clifford, who dedicated his treatise on horsemanship to the poet and Protestant war hero Sir Philip Sidney, scoffed at those who "make their horses more fit to daunce on a carpet, then for anie other kinde of service", and resolved "onelie to teach those, whose noble mindes delight in armes".[40] Yet Cavendish held that manège did serve practical purposes in battle. Certainly, synchronised movements such as the equestrian *caracole* helped the advance of a band of cavalry musketeers; whether finer arts such as the *capriole* were practical in combat remains unclear. In any case, it must have been helpful for a rider to be able to rely on a well-disciplined horse that was able to move in a coordinated group. Basic formations are evident in strategic literature of the Civil War period, for instance, John Vernon's *The Young Horse-Man* [...] *Wherein is plainly demonstrated* [...] *the Exercise and Discipline of the horse, very usefull for all those that desire the knowledge of warlike Horse-man-ship* [*sic*] (1644). Vernon's book included illustrations of double ranks which might offer strategic advantage, with floor patterns for the organised movement of mounted troops.[41]

Among critics, a persuasive minority concedes an element of usefulness in dressage training.[42] For Kate Van Orden, the art paved the way from the armed man to the gentleman, as "the *ballet à cheval* showed off a synchronization associated both with the spectacles of the court and with the latest techniques of military discipline".[43] In the early modern period, the finer disciplines often needed justification; apologies of dressage were reminiscent of the arguments in favour of dancing. Utilitarian beauty was often invoked in seventeenth-century texts defending ballet. Not only did the art serve as a non-verbal body language; it also enhanced a person's proper, graceful bearing, and a facility in mounting a horse and wielding arms, for the benefit of the nation. A document announcing the foundation of the Academie royale de la danse in 1663 stressed military accomplishment and "politesse" as positive outcomes: dancers served their prince in both battle and ballet.[44]

Rulers frequently imagined themselves as the sun of their courts in early modern Europe. A solar Charles I recurs in literature of the period; in one typical lament on the

[40] Christopher Clifford: *The Schoole of Horsmanship,* London 1585, "To the Reader", sig. [¶ii]^r.

[41] John Vernon: *The Young Horse-Man, or The Honest Plain-Dealing Cavalier. Wherein is plainly demonstrated, by figures and otherwise, the Exercise and Discipline of the horse, very usefull for all those that desire the knowledge of warlike Horse-man-ship* [*sic*], London 1644.

[42] For instance, Helen Watanabe O'Kelly: *Triumphall Shews: Tournaments at German-Speaking Courts in Their European Context, 1560-1730,* Berlin 1992.

[43] Kate van Orden: *From* Gens d'Armes *to* Gentilshommes: *Dressage, Civility, and the* Ballet à Cheval, in: *The Culture of the Horse: Status, Discipline, and Identity in the Early Modern World*, ed. by K Raber and T. Tucker, Basingstoke 2005, p. 214.

[44] The discipline offered "avantage à la Nation, soit pour la politesse ou pour la facilité des exercices militaires", and made dancers "plus propres à servir leur Prince dans les batailles, & à luy plaire dans les divertissemens". Anonymous pamphlet *Etablissement de l'Academie Royale de danse en la ville de Paris,* Paris 1663, pp. 8, 10.

King's absence, "the Suns withdrawing leaves one world, / Into a Winters Tyrannie t'be hurld".[45] In equestrian display, the sun sometimes materialized in a chief rider. When Frederick of Denmark visited Dresden in 1709, August the Strong of Saxony impersonated Apollo at a nightly tilting, wearing a sun mask made of gilt copper, modelled after his face.[46]

Fig. 4. Sun mask worn by August the Strong of Saxony at a tournament in 1709. Artist: Melchior Dinglinger. Dresden, Rüstkammer, Inv. No. N 171. Photo: Jürgen Karpinski.
By permission of the Staatliche Kunstsammlungen, Dresden.

When August entered Cracow for his coronation as King of Poland in 1697, his horse was caparisoned with flaming suns, made of red glass mounted on silver foil and encased in gilt brass, surrounded with rays of small crystals. Louis XIV, the sun king, was also partial to the role of Apollo, not only when dancing in ballets but also when guiding horses. Popular iconography of the time showed Louis XIV on a celestial ride in a chariot drawn by four horses; the king kept the bridle in one hand, while the other rested on a lyre. The posture was suggestive of relaxed control; a god effortlessly in charge, sitting at the centre of much commotion around him.[47]

[45] Mildmay Fane: *Upon a Journey of His Majesty's into Scotland, and His Safe Return*, a revised, darker version of a poem originally written in 1633, in: *Otia Sacra,* London 1648, II, p. 142; also Dale B. Randall: *Winter Fruit: English Drama, 1642-1660,* Lexington 1995, p. 16.
[46] *Eine gute Figur machen*, ed. by C. Schnitzer, ed. cited, fig. 110, p. 210.
[47] *Hortus Regius*: "Louis XIV dans un char trainé par quatre chevaux apparait porté sur les nuages au-dessus du Jardin du Roi", engraving by G. Rousselet (1665), Bibliothèque Nationale de France, Reserve FOL QB-201(47), Hennin 4313. Based on a gouache by Joseph Werner (1637-1710), *Louis XIV en Apollon dans le char du soleil précédé par l'Aurore et accompagné par les*

Fig. 5. G. Rousselet, *Hortus regius* (1665). Bibliothèque Nationale de France, Reserve FOL QB-201(47), Hennin 4313.
By permission of the Bibliothèque Nationale de France.

A monarchy of hearts: *La contesa dell'aria e dell'acqua* and the visual arts

One of the finest equestrian ballets of the seventeenth century was performed as part of the imperial festival *La contesa dell'aria e dell'acqua* (1667), which celebrated the wedding of the Austrian emperor Leopold I to Margherita of Spain. Versions in several languages were printed in Vienna, and thus *La contesa dell'aria* gives us perhaps the most widely publicised horse ballet of the early modern period. The riders, including the Emperor himself, had rehearsed for five months to pull it off.[48] Alessandro Carducci had devised the equestrian part; the court's chief violinist, Johann Heinrich Schmelzer, had composed the music, and Carlo Pasetti had designed the scenery, including a temple

Heures. Musée national du château de Versailles. Reproduced in *Les Écuries royales*, ed. by D. Roche, ed. cited, p. 264.

[48] Francesco Sbarra: *La contesa dell'aria e dell'acqua* (*Sieg-Streit deß Lufft und Wassers* in the German version), Vienna 1667, on the occasion of the wedding of Leopold I and Margaret of Spain; see also Paul Nettl: *Equestrian Ballets of the Baroque Period*, in: *Musical Quarterly*, XIX (1933), pp. 74-83; Egon Wellesz: *Die Ballett-Suiten von Johann Heinrich und Anton Andreas Schmelzer*, in: *Sitzungsberichte der Kaiserlichen Akademie der Wissenschaften in Wien*, vol.176/5, Vienna 1914, with a transcription of the music score for the horse ballet.

and a gigantic, richly furnished pageant car. Francesco Sbarra's account offered full details of the event, including audience reactions.

All participants wore headgear with billowing white and blue plumes; these formed, Sbarra enthused, a heaven which announced the appearance of his Majesty. Leopold emerged in a garment of silver and gold brocade encrusted with jewels, and embroidered with marguerites in honour of the bride's name. Sbarra paid much attention to Leopold's "fierce" courser Speranza ("Hope"). The horse carried both physical and metaphorical weight. As Sbarra claimed, Speranza

> fully understood its good fortune to serve the Emperor. With a noble mien, svelte appearance, delicate head and vivacious eye, it was so gracious, so lithe and agile, so obedient, and so quick to respond, that, bearing the name of Speranza, it surpassed all others [...]. It did not champ on its bit, which had not been made of rigid iron, but bright gold. [...] This superb courser which could boast that it bore the riches of Peru on its back, more powerful than Atlas, without staggering under its glorious weight, sustained all the heavens of human greatness.[49]

In their magnificent entry, the participants won "the absolute possession of the monarchy of hearts" (sig. G2^{v}). A cortège of over 300 persons followed the Emperor, "animated by the desire to serve the august Caesar, ready to give their all" in a visceral tribute (sig. H^{r}). A chorus announced the horse ballet, and a symphony of hundred wind instruments allowed the Emperor and four squadrons to take position. According to Sbarra, altogether 600 participants moved about in exquisite figures on horseback and by foot to clear the space for the ballet.

The first figure enraptured the audience with a lively *courante*. Leopold's horse started the ballet with corvets; it became apparent to all that it perfectly understood the music, an evident sign of its well-composed spirit. The foremost experts of horsemanship were deeply impressed by the way in which the courser managed to end each movement on the beat ("cadenza"), which was "by all accounts the most difficult operation a horse can execute" (sig. H^{v}). Schmelzer had included some echo effects in his music, which gave the riders the opportunity to pause a little, and allowed the audience to enjoy the figures better.

By and large, wind instruments and a simple score with a regular rhythm and straight beats dominated the equestrian ballet, which enabled riders' groups to stop for effects resembling a *tableau vivant*. This kind of music was typical of equestrian ballet as it facilitated the prompting of specific movements and the keeping of time; contemporary specialists stressed the need for such tunes.[50] Yet there was one exception: a stately *allemande*, played by over hundred string instruments.[51]

[49] Sbarra: *La contesa dell'aria e dell'acqua*, ed. cited, sig. G^{v}-G2^{r}. My translation; I have condensed Sbarra's voluble prose.

[50] Pierre de la Noë: *La cavalerie françoise et italienne,* Lyon 1621, p. 145.

[51] Sbarra: *La contesa dell'aria e dell'acqua*, ed. cited, appendix, *Arie per il balletto à cavallo*, no. 4.

Fig. 6: Johann Heinrich Schmelzer, *Allemande* for the equestrian ballet. Francesco Sbarra, *La contesa dell'aria e dell'acqua* (Vienna, 1667), score no. 4. Shelfmark Hn 4° 32.
By permission of Herzog August Bibliothek Wolfenbüttel.

The *allemande* aimed at an overall effect of steady motion: the ensemble executed intricate chains, imitating the regular movements of the spheres. From a practical point of view, this slower moment in the ballet allowed the horses to catch breath after so much exertion, and enabled the audience to identify individual riders and admire them (sig. I^{v}).

A lively *sarabande* announced the last part of the ballet. Leopold was at the centre of a star, his cavaliers forming the rays. In a fast-moving serpentine pageant, the performers retreated to a chorus of 200 voices.

Fig. 7. Emperor Leopold I as star at the centre of the equestrian ballet in *La contesa dell'aria e dell'acqua* (Vienna, 1667), fig. 12. Shelfmark Hn 4° 32.
By permission of Herzog August Bibliothek Wolfenbüttel.

We have to be careful not to take Sbarra's superlative account at face value; even so, it is telling. Sbarra stressed the no-less-than-planetary effect of the Emperor on riders and spectators, and he took care to record spectators' reactions; this means that the audience really mattered to the chronicler and the court that had commissioned the report. Furthermore, Sbarra devoted much space to the horses both in terms of visual appearance and mental capacity. As the imperial courser Speranza demonstrated, the horses were endowed with quasi-rational powers. Allegedly they even understood the deeper meaning of the ballet and the representative functions of their own dance. For the Emperor's horse, the bit had lost its original controlling function and turned into a decorative item worn by a freely obedient creature. The Emperor did not command service; he had obedience thrust upon him.

How should we read this "absolute monarchy of hearts"? Post-Foucauldian criticism has stressed the centralizing tendencies of absolutist spectacle. Rudolf Zur Lippe's theory on baroque ballet, developed in the 1970s, is still influential today.[52] In such a reading, ballet, whether human or equestrian, subdues the individual performer. Dancers are not just displaying themselves but displaying themselves *for* someone and are thus subject to the audience's controlling gaze. Zur Lippe argued that courtly choreographies functioned very much like baroque garden vistas: they enabled the viewer to take a total survey of performers and their motions, the so-called *Überblick* ("total gaze" or "super gaze"; this notion is nicely captured in the abovementioned engraving showing Louis

[52] The classic study on that topic is Rudolf Zur Lippe: *Naturbeherrschung am Menschen*, 2nd ed., 2 vols, Frankfurt am Main 1981.

XIV riding in a chariot above an orderly landscape, fig. 5). The *Überblick* fostered an absolutist mentality because, Zur Lippe might argue, observers gained a pleasing sensation of command over the spectacle. In the case of *La contesa* it was wielded by the imperial bride, Margherita: the riders controlled their mounts, and Margherita's imperious eye controlled the riders (including her future husband).

But perhaps more subtle dynamics were at work here as well. The account of *La contesa* is at pains to stress the voluntary nature of the spectacle. Audience and participants cannot help but *love* Leopold and his bride. This may be verbal propaganda on Sbarra's part; after all, the text was commissioned work – and yet, why should we exclude the possibility that the parties involved did enjoy a splendid occasion and nursed benevolent fellow feelings? Perhaps *La contesa* staged a collective transference: we love the emperor on his horse, because we are him. Temporarily, disagreements are set aside because we are enraptured by something beautiful of which we are made to feel a part. Of course, such moments are fleeting, but for a short while they suggest a utopian vision of what a perfect commonwealth could be like, with animals and humans living in harmonious concord.

Writing from a safe distance some time after 1660, the exiled English regicide Edmund Ludlow reflected that the main difference between his and the King's party was "whether the King should govern as a god by his will, and the nation governed by force like beasts: or whether the people should be governed by law made by themselves, and live under a government derived from their own consent".[53] In *La contesa*'s universe, beasts were no longer governed by force. Brute creation gladly subordinated itself. What better to express voluntary consent than dancing horses? As argued earlier, it is hard to make a horse do what it does not wish to do. The dressage expert Giovanni Battista Galiberti stressed that a horse had to learn by free will; the key term "volentieri" pervades his treatise *Il cavallo del maneggio* (1650). Manège horses, Galiberti said, were the most sensitive of their species, and therefore any severe chastisement would ruin their "gaillardise", their high spirit.[54] The charm of equestrian ballet lies in its graceful character; Leopold beguiles his audience because Speranza follows willingly, not because he has flogged his horse into submission.

From the Elizabethan courtier and poet Philip Sidney we learn that the horse was "a peerless beast", a "courtier without flattery".[55] Sidney, who had taken lessons with one of the horse masters of Austria's imperial court in 1574, understood that training required skill and patience, and challenged the rider as much as the creature itself. The learning process went both ways. When a ruler engaged in equestrian display, he submitted himself to a test: Leopold had to work hard for five months to impress his audience with his effortless horsemanship. Elizabeth LeGuin, a rider herself, rightly points out that current criticism has a problem with "discipline", reducing it to mere "coercion". Equestrian ballet shows that there is more to discipline: all participants –

[53] *The Memoirs of Edmund Ludlow Lieutenant-General of the Horse in the Army of the Commonwealth of England*, ed. by C. H. Firth, 2 vols. Oxford 1894, I, p. 18, cited from Randall: *Winter Fruit*, ed. cited, pp. 17-18.

[54] *Il cavallo del maneggio. Del Signor Giovanbatista Galiberti,* Vienna 1650, pp. 13, 112.

[55] Sir Philip Sidney: *An Apology for Poetry*, ed. by Geoffrey Shepherd, Manchester 1973, p. 95.

riders, horses, musicians – must be attuned to each other, or the harmonious overall impression will fail:

> Thus Louis XIII or the Emperor Leopold, astride magnificent horses before their noble audiences, were demonstrating to their subjects nothing so crude as a capacity for domination but rather – and this is a most crucial distinction – a capacity for command: command as distinct from domination, command as a reciprocal condition, command as predicated upon a knowledge of when to listen as well as when to tell.[56]

Such "reciprocal" qualities are made visible in equestrian portraiture and statuary, whether Emperor Marcus Aurelius on horseback, or Van Dyck's canvasses of a mounted Charles I.[57] Kenneth Gross reflects on how the visual arts juxtapose rider and horse: these are radically different, yet "subtly mirror or infect each other". The human is placed in

> proximity to an inhuman but still kindred form of natural energy, intelligence, violence, and beauty. It represents human identity and power linked to the ever-present threat of losing control; it recommends a mode of holding, a mode of staying in place that yet entails physical and mental mobility.[58]

If statues and paintings bring out the subtle willing and yielding between horse and human, equestrian ballet achieves this even more pointedly thanks to its dynamic audio-visual display, which highlights and underscores those "kindred forms of natural energy". Equestrian ballet is fiercely interrelational. It banks on good communication: between creature and rider, between performers and audiences, and between humans of different hierarchical levels. It can only function if all participants, including animals, receive considerate treatment.

Equestrian ballet and the cognitive sciences

By placing animals at the centre of such complex interactions, equestrian ballet affirms that even they belong. It suggests that animals have advanced cognitive capacities. The situation was not as clear cut in early modern thought. At one end of the spectrum, Descartes famously argued that beasts might be compared to sophisticated machines without a mind. His *Discours de la méthode* (1637) stated that animals

> have no reason at all, […] nature […] acts in them according to the disposition of their organs, just as a clock, which is only composed of wheels and weights, [and]

[56] Elizabeth LeGuin: *Man and Horse in Harmony*, in: *The Culture of the Horse*, ed. by K. Raber and T. Tucker, Basingstoke 2005, pp. 193-94.
[57] Walter Liedtke: *The Royal Horse and Rider. Painting, Sculpture and Horsemanship 1500 – 1800,* n. pl. 1989.
[58] Kenneth Gross: *The Dream of the Moving Statue,* Ithaca 1992, p. 174.

> is able to tell the hours and measure the time more correctly than we can do with all our wisdom.[59]

The Cartesian line of thought fuelled later utilitarian, empirical ages, and sanctioned experiments on animals such as vivisection.[60] The prominent medical scientist Claude Bernard (1813-78) held that a man of his profession had to be totally absorbed by his research if he wished to discover the secrets of the living body, that "machine vivante": "he no longer hears the cries of the animals, he no longer sees the blood that flows, he only sees his idea and the organisms that conceal the problems he wishes to discover".[61] (Such attitudes ultimately prompted the first antivivisection society in Europe, founded by Bernard's estranged wife and daughter.)

Yet plenty of evidence from the later sixteenth to the mid-eighteenth century suggests that the Cartesian worldview was by no means universally held.[62] Michel de Montaigne credited animals with reasonable abilities. Cavendish, who corresponded with Descartes in the 1640s, fervently disagreed with the philosopher; as he put it, "if he [the horse] does not think (as the famous philosopher DES CARTES affirms of all beasts) it would be impossible to teach him what he should do".[63] Descartes might have retorted with a mechanical cause-and-effect explanation: the animal simply reacted to prodding, in the way a body moves when given an impulse. His *Abrégé de musique* (1618) argued that dance music, with its regular beats, did not appeal to any intellect; rather it fed the instinct and impelled humans and animals alike to move.[64] For Descartes, animals did not absorb the finer points of music which nourished the human soul. Yet dressage horses seemed to exist in a league of their own if we are to believe testimonies of festivals and prodigies such as Morocco, Le Superbe, Speranza, or (later) the redoubtable Blanche. Long before *Gulliver's Travels*, seventeenth-century satirical literature preferred clever horses to humans, who made asses of themselves. In a French pamphlet of the 1640s, Mazarin's horse felt compelled to give sound advice to its

[59] René Descartes: *Discours de la méthode – Discourse on the Method: A Bilingual Edition*, ed. & transl. by. George Heffernan, Notre Dame 1994, part V, section 11, pp. 80-83.

[60] See Erica Fudge: *Brutal Reasoning*, ed. cited, pp. 158-59.

[61] "Le physiologiste n'est pas un homme du monde, c'est un savant, c'est un homme qui est saisi et absorbé par une idée scientifique qu'il poursuit; il n'entend plus les cris des animaux, il ne voit plus le sang qui coule, il ne voit que son idée et n'aperçoit que des organismes qui lui cachent des problèmes qu'il veut découvrir." Claude Bernard: *Introduction à l'étude de la médecine expérimentale,* Paris 1865, II, ch. 2, §3, p. 180.

[62] For critics disputing the Cartesian stereotype, see Keith Thomas: *Man and the Natural World: Changing Attitudes in England 1500-1800,* London 1984, p. 35; Erica Fudge: *Brutal Reasoning*, ed. cited, p. 174; Denis Lopez: *L'animal du XVIIe siècle: fond de tableau théologique, mythologique, philosophique (quelques points d'ancrage)*, in: *L'animal au XVIIe siècle*, ed. by Charles Mazouer, Biblio 17, Tübingen 2003, pp. 11-25.

[63] William Cavendish: *La methode nouvelle*, sig. 2^r. Translation from the work's 1743 edition, *A General System of Horsemanship*, ed. by W. C. Steinkraus and E. Schmit-Jensen, London 2000, p. 12; Erica Fudge: *Brutal Reasoning*, ed. cited, pp. 154-55, on the epistolary exchange in 1646.

[64] "Il suit de là, de plus, que les bêtes peuvent danser en mesure, si elles sont instruites et dressées, parce qu'il ne faut pour cela qu'une impulsion naturelle." René Descartes: *Abrégé de musique: compendium musicae*, ed. by F. de Buzon, Paris, 2nd ed. 2012, p. 62.

master, who was clearly in sore need of it.[65] The philosopher Anne Conway chose the horse as an example in her rebuttal of Descartes. It was

> a Creature indued with divers degrees of perfection by his Creator, as not only strength of body, but [...] a certain kind of knowledge, how he ought to serve his Master, and moreover also Love, Fear, Courage, Memory, and divers other Qualities which are in Man: [...] An Horse in divers Qualities and Perfections draws near unto the Nature and *Species* of a Man, and that more than many other Creatures; Is therefore the Nature of a Man distant from the Nature of an Horse, by Infinite Degrees, or by Finite only?[66]

Conway not only suggested the presence of an animal soul but anticipated Darwin's idea that the elementary difference between humankind and other animals might be one of degree, and that we might be closer to our equine fellow creatures than we might think.

Conclusion

As *haute école* shows, we should not think of the seventeenth century as an epoch in which a switch was suddenly turned in 1637 towards a Cartesian worldview. Horses were accorded a degree of rational capacity in literature, philosophy, and spectacle of the period. This capacity was, in the view of specialists of horsemanship, evident in the dexterity of equine movements, an ability to keep time, an appreciation of music, and even an ability to understand the deeper purposes of a certain performance. Equestrian ballet was the perfect art form to enact, in a harmonious vision, early modern notions of a human self that was collective, interpersonal, and viscerally physical – a self that defined itself also in relation to the animal world and communicated with it. The horse played, as it were, the role of an emotional but not ungifted sidekick, a trusty Watson to the cerebral Holmes that was its rider.

Whether training methods were, in practice, always non-violent is difficult to tell; for certain, the literature on horsemanship emphasized gentle treatment. Did equestrian ballet express a deeper yearning for civilised interaction in a peaceful universe? The sixteenth and seventeenth centuries were marked by devastating religious wars in Europe. Or did *haute école* represent the ultimate, sublimated form of oppression? "Voluntary" is the key term when we trace the history of equine – and human – performance in spectacle from the medieval to the early modern period.[67] Based on choice, not force, "voluntary" behaviour was deemed rational, positive, and beautiful, but as the notion spread it also came under scrutiny. It was Montaigne's best friend,

[65] "Mais enfin qu'ils sçachent que Dieu/ Fait maintefois en temps & lieu/ Le Cheval raisonner en Homme/ Lors qu'on voit presque aussi brutal,/ Cher Maistre, sans que ie vous nomme,/ L'homme raisonner en Cheval." *Advis burlesque du cheval de Mazarin. A son maistre,* Paris, p. 6.

[66] Anne Conway: *The Principles*, ed. cited, pp. 59, 62.

[67] See also Karen Raber on "volition" in Cavendish's horsemanship: *"Reasonable Creatures": William Cavendish and the Art of Dressage*, in *Renaissance Culture and the Everyday*, ed. by P. Fumerton and S. Hunt, Philadelphia 1999, pp. 42-66.

Étienne de La Boétie, who coined the term "voluntary servitude", probably some time in the 1550s.[68] La Boétie noted that humans were liable to act with anticipatory obedience, and took a dim view of spectacle, which, in his view, was instrumentalised by regimes of voluntary servitude to amuse and thus govern a multitude.[69] Unlike humans, animals, La Boétie believed, had a natural instinct for liberty, even domesticated ones: the horse recoiled at the bridle, and birds lamented in their cages. So why was man different?

> Since even the animals made for man's service cannot accustom themselves to serve, without protesting a contrary desire, what evil has denaturalised man, born truly to live freely, from remembering his original estate and wishing to recover it?[70]

More than hundred years ahead of Hobbes' *Leviathan*, La Boétie understood that one person's power relied on a group's consent, but group power could also lead to group pressure and individual inertia. It is the achievement of absolutist spectacle that it transposed conflicts of power and interest to a space where they could be resolved, if only temporarily. Absolutist performance was not about unquestioned obedience: a ruler could only demonstrate total command if challenge was possible, and what better to represent this challenge than an animal not bound by human conventions of allegiance. Equestrian ballet, with its unspoken willing and yielding, exemplified voluntary servitude in its most pleasing, charming expression. Perhaps horses had become as unnatural as humans, plying their nimble *caprioles* and flashing golden bridles. Maybe they had turned from trampling coursers into carpet dancers. But they exemplified that non-violence was, ultimately, more productive.

This essay explores further some issues raised in my article "Understanding Horses: Equestrian Ballet and Early Modern Political Thought", in *Shakespeare. Satire. Academia: Festschrift in Honour of Wolfgang Weiß*, ed. Sonja Fielitz and Uwe Meyer (Heidelberg: Winter, 2012), pp. 101-22. The author would like to thank Robert Carver, John McKinnell, and Kirby Farrell for their suggestions.

[68] Étienne de La Boétie: *De la servitude volontaire ou Contr'un*, ed. by N. Gontarbert, Paris 1993. No dated manuscripts of this treatise have survived. Written probably after 1548 and before 1562.

[69] "Les theatres, les jeus, les farces, les spectacles, les gladiateurs, les bestes estranges, les medailles, les tableaus, et autres telles drogueries c'estoient aux peuples anciens les apasts de la servitude, le pris de leur liberté, les outils de la tirannie: ce moien [...] avoient les anciens tirans, pour endormir leurs subjects sous le joug." Étienne La Boétie: *De la servitude volontaire*, ed. cited, p. 109.

[70] "Puisque les bestes qui ancore sont faits pour le service de l'homme, ne se peuvent accoustumer à servir, qu'avec protestation d'un desir contraire: quel mal encontre a esté cela, qui a peu tant denaturer l'homme, seul né, de vrai pour vivre franchement, et lui fair perdre la souvenance de son premier estre, et le desir de le reprendre." Ibid. p. 93.

Bibliography

Advis burlesque du cheval de Mazarin. A son maistre. Paris 1649.

Anzilotti, Gloria Italiano (ed.): *An English* Prince. *Newcastle's Machiavellian Political Guide to Charles II.* Pisa 1988.

Arbeau, Thoinot [Jehan Tabourot]: *Orchesography*, ed. by Julia Sutton, transl. by Mary Stewart Evans. New York 1967.

Bernard, Claude: *Introduction à l'étude de la médecine expérimentale.* Paris 1865.

Bibliotheca Nobilissimi Principis Johannis Ducis de Novo-Castro, &c. London 1719.

Boehrer, Bruce: *Animal Studies and the Deconstruction of Character*, in: *PMLA* 124/2 (2009), pp. 542-47.

Brown, Cedric: *Courtesies of Place and Arts of Diplomacy in Ben Jonson's Last Two Entertainments for Royalty*, in: *The Seventeenth Century*, 9/2 (1994), pp. 147-71.

Buch, David J. (ed.): *Dance Music from the Ballets de Cour 1575-1651.* Stuyvesant 1993.

Butterworth, Philip: *Magic on the Early English Stage.* Cambridge 2005.

Caroso, M. Fabritio: *Il ballarino.* Venice 1581, facs. ed. New York 1967.

Cavendish, Margaret: *The Life of William Cavendish Duke of Newcastle*, ed. by C. H. Firth. 2nd ed. London [1906].

Cavendish, William, *A General System of Horsemanship*, ed. by W. C. Steinkraus and E. Schmit-Jensen. London 2000.

Cavendish, William: *La methode nouvelle.* Antwerp 1658.

Christout, Marie-Françoise: *Le ballet de cour au XVIIe siècle.* Geneva 1987.

Clifford, Christopher: *The Schoole of Horsmanship.* London 1585.

Conway, Anne: *The Principles of the Most Ancient and Modern Philosophy*, transl. by J[odocus?] C[rull?]. Amsterdam 1690, repr. London 1692.

de La Boétie, Étienne: *De la servitude volontaire ou Contr'un*, ed. by N. Gontarbert. Paris 1993.

de la Noë, Pierre: *La cavalerie françoise et italienne.* Lyon 1621.

de la Serre, Puget: *Les amours de Jupiter et de Junon, avec les magnificences de leurs nopces.* Paris 1625.

de Menou, René: *La pratique du cavalier. Par ou il est enseigné la vraye methode qu'il doit tenir pour mettre son cheval à la raison, & le rendre capable de paroistre sur la carriere, obeïssant à l'ordre des plus justes proportions de tous les plus beaux airs & manages.* Paris 1614.

Descartes, René: *Abrégé de musique: compendium musicae*, ed. by F. de Buzon. Paris, 2nd ed. 2012.

Descartes, René: *Discours de la méthode – Discourse on the Method: A Bilingual Edition*, ed. and transl. by George Heffernan. Notre Dame 1994.

Edwards, Peter: *Horse and Man in Early Modern England.* London 2007.

Edwards, Peter: *Les écuries des monarques anglais aux XVIe et XVIIe siècles*, in: *Les écuries royales*, ed. by D. Roche. Versailles 1998, pp. 154-65.

Etablissement de l'Academie Royale de danse en la ville de Paris. Paris 1663.

Fane, Mildmay: *Otia Sacra.* London 1648.

Farrell, Kirby: *Post-Traumatic Culture: Injury and Interpretation in the Nineties.* Baltimore 1998.

Fudge, Erica: *Brutal Reasoning: Animals, Rationality, and Humanity in Early Modern England.* Ithaca 2006.

Galiberti, Giovanni Battista: *Il cavallo del maneggio.* Vienna 1650.

Gross, Kenneth: *The Dream of the Moving Statue.* Ithaca 1992.

Hammond, Frederick: *Music and Spectacle in Baroque Rome: Barberini Patronage under Urban VIII.* New Haven 1994.

Historical Manuscripts Commission (ed.): *The Manuscripts of the Duke of Portland, Preserved at Welbeck Abbey*, vol. 2. London 1893.

Hobbes, Thomas: *The Correspondence. Volume I: 1622-1659*, ed. by Noel Malcolm. Oxford 1994.

Hulse, Lynn: *Apollo's Whirligig: William Cavendish, Duke of Newcastle and His Music Collection*, in: *The Seventeenth Century*, 9/2 (1994), pp. 213-46.

Hyde, Edward, Earl of Clarendon: *The History of the Rebellion and Civil Wars in England, Begun in the Year 1641* [...] *Volume the First*. Oxford 1702.

Kugler, Georg, and Wolfdieter Bihl: *Die Lipizzaner der Spanischen Hofreitschule*. Vienna 2002.

LeGuin, Elizabeth: *Man and Horse in Harmony*, in: *The Culture of the Horse*, ed. by K Raber and T. Tucker. Basingstoke 2005, pp. 175-96.

Liedtke, Walter: *The Royal Horse and Rider. Painting, Sculpture and Horsemanship 1500 – 1800*. N. pl. 1989.

Lindsay, Sir David: *Squyer Meldrum*, ed. by James Kinsley. London 1959.

Lopez, Denis: *L'animal du XVIIe siècle: fond de tableau théologique, mythologique, philosophique (quelques points d'ancrage)*, in: *L'animal au XVIIe siècle*, ed. by Charles Mazouer, Biblio 17. Tübingen 2003, pp. 11-25.

Morgan, Nicholas: *The Horse-Mans Honour*. London 1609.

Nettl, Paul: *Equestrian Ballets of the Baroque Period*, in: *Musical Quarterly*, XIX (1933), pp. 74-83.

Obizzi, Pio Enea: *L'Ermiona*. Padua 1638.

Raber, Karen: *"Reasonable Creatures": William Cavendish and the Art of Dressage*, in: *Renaissance Culture and the Everyday*, ed. by P. Fumerton and S. Hunt. Philadelphia 1999, pp. 42-66.

Randall, Dale B.: *Winter Fruit: English Drama, 1642-1660*. Lexington 1995.

Ravelhofer, B.: *"Beasts of Recreacion": Henslowe's White Bears*, in: *English Literary Renaissance*, 32/2 (2002), pp. 287-323.

Roche, D. (ed.): *Les écuries royales du XVIe au XVIIIe siècle*. Versailles 1998.

Rousselet, G: *Hortus Regius*. N. pl. 1665.

Saxon, A. H.: *Enter Foot and Horse: A History of Hippodrama in England and France*. New Haven 1968.

Saxon, A. H.: *The Life and Art of Andrew Ducrow & the Romantic Age of the English Circus*. Hamden 1978.

Sbarra, Francesco: *La contesa dell'aria e dell'acqua*. Vienna 1667.

Schnitzer, Claudia, and Petra Hölscher (eds.): *Eine gute Figur machen: Kostüm und Fest am Dresdner Hof*. Dresden 2000.

Schnitzer, Claudia: *Höfische Maskeraden: Funktion und Ausstattung von Verkleidungsdivertissements an deutschen Höfen der Frühen Neuzeit*. Tübingen 1999.

Schockemöhle, Paul: *Stallion Collection 2013*. Mühlen 2013.

Shakespeare, William: *King Lear: A Parallel Text Edition*, ed. by René Weis. London 1993.

Shannon, Laurie: *The Eight Animals in Shakespeare; Or, Before the Human*, in: *PMLA* 124/2 (2009), pp. 472-79.

Shirley, James: *The Lady of Pleasure*, ed. by R. Huebert. Manchester 1986.

Shuttleworth, J. (ed.): *The Life of Edward, First Lord Herbert of Cherbury, Written by Himself*. London 1976.

Sidney, Sir Philip: *An Apology for Poetry*, ed. by Geoffrey Shepherd. Manchester 1973.

Spenser, Edmund: *The Faerie Queene*, ed. by A. C. Hamilton. London, corr. ed. 1980.

Thirsk, Joan: *Horses in Early Modern England: For Service, for Pleasure, for Power*. Reading 1978.

Thomas, Keith: *Man and the Natural World: Changing Attitudes in England 1500-1800.* London 1984.

van Orden, Kate: *From* Gens d'Armes *to* Gentilshommes: *Dressage, Civility, and the* Ballet à Cheval, in: *The Culture of the Horse: Status, Discipline, and Identity in the Early Modern World*, ed. by K Raber and T. Tucker. Basingstoke 2005, pp. 197-222.

Watanabe-O'Kelly, Helen: *Triumphall Shews: Tournaments at German-Speaking Courts in Their European Context, 1560-1730.* Berlin 1992.

Wellesz, Egon: *Die Ballett-Suiten von Johann Heinrich und Anton Andreas Schmelzer*, in: *Sitzungsberichte der Kaiserlichen Akademie der Wissenschaften in Wien*, vol.176/5. Vienna 1914.

Windisch-Graetz, Mathilde: *The Spanish Riding School.* London 1956.

Worsley, Giles: *The History of* haute école *in England*, in: *The Court Historian*, 6 (2001), pp. 29-47.

Worsley, Lucy, and Tom Addyman: *Riding Houses and Horses: William Cavendish's Architecture for the Art of Horsemanship*, in: *Architectural History*, 45 (2002), pp. 194-229.

Zur Lippe, Rudolf: *Naturbeherrschung am Menschen*, 2nd ed., 2 vols. Frankfurt am Main 1981.

Theory Meets Practice: The Dimension of 'Presence' in Freestyle Dressage

Sonja Fielitz
University of Marburg

As Barbara Ravelhofer has made us aware in her contribution, 'horse ballet' is by no means a recent phenomenon, but was well established in the 17th century. At the beginning of the 21st century, we meet the very phenomenon once again, but this time transferred to the world of sports[1], i.e., to the discipline of dressage riding, and here, the special test of Freestyle Dressage. Freestyle Dressage (in German "Dressur-Kür") is a form of dressage competition where the horse's paces are set to music. The music is carefully chosen according to the horse's type, personality, and sometimes even name such as (in the 1990s Isabel Werth's) "Gigolo". Movements and prescribed figures are carefully choreographed to meet the technical requirements of the particular level of the test, and this to individually composed music that highlights the aesthetic as well as technical strengths of horse and rider. In mutual and trust-based understanding, the team of rider and horse interpret their music by enhancing the horse's way of moving and matching the tempos of its gaits. On an international level, Freestyle Dressage was officially established in 1996 as one of the final tests within the Olympics, and the Grand Prix Freestyle is performed at World Equestrian Games.

There is no doubt that dressage riding implies a high level of aesthetic excellence, and its special form of Freestyle Dressage has all the more proved to offer extremely great audience appeal[2]. Its four-legged performers, i.e. the horses, are generally characterized as 'noble', if not divine[3], and a dressage test is generally associated with

[1] From a theoretical point of view, Michael Bakhtin's basic claim that festivity allows an escape from the norms of everyday life has made critics claim sport to be a carnivalesque activity. This view, however, seems to be problematic, because sport is always an *orderly* activity that can be seen as meeting a (post-Cartesian) human desire for a structured and meaningful world. In most cases, the rules of games, tests, and matches appear to be clearer and hence in many ways more satisfying than those which govern our ordinary lives. Most sports allow their participants to achieve a recognizable goal due to the performance of clearly defined tasks. The idea that sport is a phenomenon always inextricably linked to the world of carnival and thus outside the rules of normative social life, does not persist. With reference to horses and equestrian sport in particular, they have long become 'partners' that help to emotionally enrich and also define the lives of individuals, social groups, and even whole nations.

[2] Cf. Ravelhofer's "The charm of equestrian ballet lies in its graceful character."

[3] As embodied in a flood of paintings and prints since the beginning of the 18th century. In addition, horses have been associated with courage, doctility, patience, perseverance, strength, and benevolent disposition.

the impression of elegance, grace, as well as energy, and tension of muscles. In Freestyle Dressage, rider and horse are perfectly in tune with each other as well as their music, thus creating a unique overall impression of harmony and aesthetic beauty. The two performers swaying in the same rhythm of movements and thus in harmonious concord achieve an absolute synthesis of two bodies. "The fascination of sports involving animals […] relies on the sense that these nonhuman elements are somehow coupled to the human body" and thus enable humans "to go beyond the limits of an exclusively human performance".[4] What is more, this entity has a special effect on their audience, who are, as Ravelhofer has called it above and with reference to the 16th century, "enraptured by something beautiful of which we are made a part." The moment of "enrapture" has not changed over the centuries, and even 400 years later, all participants of the cultural event of Freestyle Dressage are not only fascinated but even 'touched' by the performance and united in their combined physical energy:

> Wer die Harmonie in der Darbietung in der Grand-Prix-Kür und der musikalischen Untermalung sieht, muss bereits als Außenstehender begeistert nicken, und [Hubertus] Schmidt darf noch dazu den Einklang zwischen Pferd und Sound am eigenen Leib spüren.[5]:

For a literary critic it is not enough, of course, to identify the phenomenon, but rather find a way to come to terms with it. How can we, from a critical point of view, explain the phenomenon of 'being touched' by a performance in Freestyle Dressage? Spectators perceive it with their eyes and ears, and (other than the rider) without touching anything physically with their hands. And, as a second step (with particular respect to the target of our volume to identify horses as signifiers of cultural change): why did Freestyle Dressage become increasingly popular in the late 1980s and why was it established as an individual test in international competitions, such as Olympic Games or World Equestrian Games in the 1990s? Did this development in equestrian sports possibly reflect, or even contribute to shape a cultural change in man-animal relations?

Equestrian Culture Today

Despite the transfer of equestrian culture into our daily language with well-known metaphors such as "keeping pace", "hitting one's stride", "kicking up one's heels", and proverbial expressions such as "it's ill to set spurs to a flying horse", "look not a given horse in the mouth", "many stumble at a straw, and leap over a block", and "when the seed is stolen shut the stable door"[6], equestrian expertise, which had been almost all-pervading since Classical Antiquity, has almost vanished in modern Western cultural awareness. Since the 19th century, the railway, the automobile and the plane have inevitably taken over as means of transport and have clouded our view of how

[4] Hans Ulrich Gumbrecht: *In Praise of Athletic Beauty*, Cambridge, Mass. 2006, p. 174.
[5] "Die Kür wird mit den Augen gehört." http://www.welt.de/print-wams/article131623, accessed 11 June 2014.
[6] Cf. Anthony Dent: *Horses in Shakespeare's England*, London 1987, p. 5. Cf. also the essay by Christoph Schubert in this volume.

important the horse used to be in everyday life of our forefathers.[7] Over the centuries, as this collection of essays for the first time shows, horses have been employed in and shifted to a variety of cultural and literal discourses and have fulfilled numerous functions – metaphorically as well as practically. What has not changed over the last 400 years, however, is the awareness that horse riding (and the horse as one of the very few living 'sports kits'), does always imply an emotional partnership between man and beast. As His Royal Highness, The Duke of Edinburgh, has stated:

> The equestrian sports [...] are unique among all the human sports in that they involve a direct partnership between horse and rider (resp. horse and driver). There are many other sports involving animals in one way or other, but in none of them do man and animal compete as a team. The dog has probably been man's companion for even longer, but only the horse among all the animals has helped man to fight, to move, to cultivate, and to play.[8]

'Feeling' Horses

As Stanley Wells and Paul Edmondson have reminded us in their contribution, Sir Philip Sidney was one of the first, but by no means the only one in the 16th century, to confirm the sensual quality of the relationship between man and horse. In his *Defense of Poesy* (1595), he recalls his own training of horsemanship by Pietro Pagliano, whose "strong affection" of horses made an everlasting impression on him:

> Skill of gouvernment was but a *Pedanteria*, in comparison, then would he adde certeine praises by telling what a peerlesse beast the horse was, the only servicable Courtier without flattery, the beast of most beauty, faithfulnesse, courage and much more, that if I had not bene a peece of a Logician before I came to him, I thinke he would have persuaded me to have wished my selfe a horse.[9]

Shakespeare's as well as Marlowe's works abound in multi-sensual references to horses, and, as our collection of essay demonstrates, the sensitive quadrupeds furthermore feature prominently in the works of later canonised British authors such as Dickens, Marvell, and Swift[10] as well. As delineated above, riders as well as spectators have all experienced these intense moments of being bodily 'touched' by a dressage performance, but from the perspective of a literary critic (and active dressage rider in my case) we might still feel the need to somehow come to terms with the phenomenon of 'feeling' Freestyle Dressage. It is difficult to 'grasp' it with our 'ordinary' means of

[7] "Today the equestrian portrait is a thing of the past [...] if a head of state rides a horse today it is widely appreciated as a quaint personal pursuit." Walter Liedtke: *The Royal Horse and Rider. Painting, Sculpture, and Horsemanship 1500-1800*, New York 1989, p. 13.

[8] Quoted in Liedtke: *Forword.*

[9] Philip Sidney: *The Defence of Poesie*, London, 1595. The Scholar Press Facsimile. Menston 1969, B1v.

[10] Cf. the essays by Roy Eriksen, Francesca Orestano, Kirsten Juhas, and Hermann Josef Real in this volume.

criticism and interpretation which appear to be almost inevitably interconnected with the dimension of language and rationality. Bodily sensations, as Bruce R. Smith puts it in the context of the theatre, however, do not have an immediate and transparent relationship to language:

> What comes in between the toucher and the touched remains a mystery to the rational mind – indeed, it defies the rational mind. […] Neither the rational mind nor the feeling body can get at it; neither the rational mind nor the feeling body can account for the whole, for the phenomenon.[11]

Having thus acknowledged the phenomenon, does not free us, however, from further investigation of why we are 'touched' by a performance. Smith focusses on the auditory dimension of a theatrical performance and provides a mostly scientific explanation for its effect:

> With respect to sound, we still share an understanding that the speaking actor uses lungs, larynx, tongue, teeth, and lips to set up sound waves of certain frequencies in the ambient air, waves that strike the listeners' ear drums and are decoded by the listeners' brains as phonemes of speech. Other aspects of sound – volume, pitch, rhythm, cadence, timbre, non-semantic sounds – register more subliminally and may not be consciously noticed at all. […] In both cases, however, we recognize that sound *touches* [italics in the original] us: it invades our bodies and, if loud enough, reverberates in our gut.[12]

Since a dressage test is a type of theatrical performance as well, Smith's theses can well be applied to it. His "that sound *touches* us and invades our bodies" can be related to the musical score of Freestyle Dressage, which will still be closer examined below. As one of his examples, Smith applies his theory to Shakespeare's scene of Gloucester's blinding in *King Lear* and explains the phenomenon as follows:

> Confronted with this scene of cruelty, the spectator can move between the out-flowing of passion in the inflicting of torture and the inner-ebbing of passion in the experience of pain. The result of these transactions is a kinesthetic experience: neither sight nor hearing but a crawling in the flesh. If one is touched *here* by what is being represented *there*, it is because the air between here and there has been activated by two sorts of movement: light rays reflected from the actors' moving bodies and sound waves set in motion by the actors' moving tongues. Between the sixteenth century and now there may be different explanations of light rays and sound waves […] and of the biochemicals that transmit sensations and impulses within the human body […] but the basic phychophysics of the transactions remain the same: movement across space. And so do the media: air or ether, nerves or 'sinews'.[13]

[11] Bruce R. Smith: *Phenomenal Shakespeare,* Chichester 2010, xviii.
[12] Ibid, p. 143f.
[13] Ibid., p. 156.

Smith's approach of a "kinesthetic experience", of "waves", and "biochemical" certainly is *one* possible attempt of 'grasping' the phenomenon of 'feeling' any performance. Air being activated by movements, light rays and sound waves, as well as psychophysics[14], however, appear to be very much based on the natural sciences, and neglect the strengths of the humanities in order to explain the phenomenon of being inwardly touched.

Presence Effects

Despite Smith's debatable approach, his "being touched *here*" by what is performed "*there*", as well as his emphasis on "movement across space" are important keywords which suggest another cultural discourse that has found increasing interest since the 1990s, i.e., presentism[15]. Theories of presentism offer an alternative to Smith's approach by a far less scientific and much more philosophical basis. In his *Production of Presence. What Meaning Cannot Convey*[16] Hans Ulrich Gumbrecht, for instance, focuses on the rational as well as bodily dimensions of our existence and reminds us of the (almost exclusive) dominance of the Cartesian view of the world since early modernity. Against this background, he proposes his intuition[17] of 'presence' which might help us overcome the status of rational interpretation within the humanities. In the intellectual framework he develops, the long-neglected bodily dimension of our existence is brought back to the focus of our (critical) interest.

Gumbrecht suggests that all cultures can be analysed as complex configurations of the two ideal types of (modern) meaning culture and (medieval) presence culture. "In a meaning culture the dominant human self-reference is the mind, consciousness or *res cogitans*, whereas the dominant self-reference in a presence culture is the body" (*PP*, 80). And he further lines out:

> What is 'present' to us (very much in the sense of the Latin form *prae-esse*) is in front of us, in reach of and tangible for our bodies. […] That any form of communication implies such a production of presence, that any form of communication, through its material elements, will 'touch' the bodies of the persons who are communicating in specific and various ways may be a relatively trivial observation – but it is true nevertheless that this fact had been bracketed (if not – progressively forgotten) by Western theory building ever since the Cartesian *cogito* made the ontology of human existence depend exclusively on the movements of the human mind. (*PP*, 17)

[14] In his essay "Hearing Green", Smith suggests that phonetic linguistics may help us imagine a reception of sound in which the "passions 'hear' sensations before reason does. Bruce R. Smith: *Hearing Green*, in: *Reading the Early Modern Passions. Essays in the Cultural History of Emotion,* ed. By Gail Kern Paster, Katherine Rowe, Mary Floyd-Wilson, Philadelphia 2004, pp. 147-168.

[15] Cf. also *Presentism: Essential Readings,* ed. by Ernani Magalaes and Nathan Oaklander, Lanham, MD 2010.

[16] Published in Stanford, CA 2004. In the following abbreviated as *PP*.

[17] Cf. *Präsenz Interdisziplinär. Kritik und Entfaltung einer Intuition. Mit einem Vorwort von Hans Ulrich Gumbrecht,* ed. by Sonja Fielitz, Heidelberg 2012.

Similar to Smith's "movements in space" (see above), Gumbrecht does not mainly refer to a temporal but to a spatial relationship and its objects as well.

> If the body is the dominant self-reference in a presence culture, then [...] space, that is, the dimension that constitutes itself around bodies, must be the primordial dimension in which the relationship between different humans and the relationship between humans and the things of the world are being negotiated. Time, in contrast, is the primordial dimension for any meaning culture, [...] because it takes time to carry out those transformative actions through which meaning cultures define the relationship between humans and the world. (*PP*, 83)

What we should do, according to Gumbrecht, is to integrate (medieval) 'presence culture' into our contemporary and rationally based 'meaning culture', and this not by excluding the respective other: "Presence and meaning always appear together, however, and are always in tension" (*PP*, 105)[18], respectively, as Gumbrecht calls it, in a process of 'oscillation'.

'Oscillation' and Dressage Riding

As indicated above, an aesthetic experience, such as a theatrical (or in our case, an equestrian) performance, results from an "oscillation (and sometimes as an interference) between 'presence effects' and 'meaning effects'" (*PP*, 2).[19]

In contrast to Smith (who did also establish a spatial dimension), Gumbrecht does not see biophysics and the air as the channel of transmission of signs, but rather the physical contact of human bodies: "If we attribute a meaning to a thing that is present, that is, if we form an idea of what this thing may be in relation to us, we seem to attenuate, inevitably, the impact that this thing can have on our bodies and our senses" (*PP*, xiv).[20] And he pleads for a more immediate approach to the world:

[18] Cf. also: "Every human contact with the things of the world contains both a meaning- and a presence component" (*PP*, 109 and "Essential is the point that, within this specific constellation, meaning will not bracket, will not make the presence effects disappear, and that the – unbracketed – physical presence of things (of a text, of a voice, of a canvas with colors, of a play performed by a team) will not ultimately repress the meaning dimension." (*PP*, 108). "[O]ur desire for presence will be best served if we try to pause for a moment before we begin to make sense – and if we let ourselves be caught by an oscillation where presence effects permeate the meaning effects" (*PP*, 126).

[19] In its ultimate consequence, and as Rainer Maria Rilke has famously put it in his sonnet "Archaischer Torso von Apollis" ["Torso of an Archaic Apollo"] of 1908, the aesthetic experience of a work of art can indeed have so much impact on a recipient that it calls for a change in his or her life: "denn da ist keine Stelle, / die Dich nicht sieht. Du musst Dein Leben aendern" ["until there is no place / that does not see you. You must change your life" (transl. C.F. MacIntyre)].

[20] Cf. also: "Presence effects [...] exclusively appeal to the senses" (*PP*, xv).

> Are we not precisely longing for presence, is our desire for tangibility not so intense – because our own everyday environment is almost insuperably conscious-centered? Rather than having to think, always and endlessly, what else there could be, we sometimes seem to connect with a layer in our existence that simply wants the things of the world close to our skin. (*PP*, 106)[21]

By applying Gumbrecht's and Smith's theories to Freestyle Dressage as an undoubtedly highly corporeal event being acted out in space, we indeed come closer to 'grasping' the fascination of Freestyle Dressage. Smith's focus on sound, that is in our case, music, is met by Gumbrecht's "The presence component will always dominate when we are listening to music." (*PP*, 109) In a comparison of the two approaches, Gumbrecht's philosophically-based theory appears to be much more appropriate for the phenomenon to be investigated here. Vice versa, our focus on horses might even be apt to enrich and go beyond it. Gumbrecht restricts himself exclusively to human beings, but presence effects in Freestyle Dressage happen with, through, and to the bodies of two performers, i.e., an animal and a human being. As developed above, in Freestyle Dressage, a human and an equine body produce presence effects: by touching each other in their harmonious swaying to the musical score of their performance they become one bodily and aesthetic entity.

The horses' three gaits easily correspond to musical rhythms, because their walk covers four beats, their trot two beats, and their canter three beats. Thus, a horse's movements can very well be accentuated by a musical score of the same amounts of beats. What is more, in the space of an arena (even if dressage events usually do not draw ten thousands of spectators such as football matches), the sounds of the horse's hooves are not heard in isolation but are elements in a larger environment of sounds, that is, the musical score, the horse's snorting, and also the spectator's reactions. The latter project their sounds such as by jingling keys, coughing, whispering, etc. into the atmosphere as well, and this at the same time that they are listening to what their environment and the performers, i.e. horse and rider, are communicating to them. In an overall synthesis, human-produced sounds mix with the sounds produced by horses. Spectators as well as riders and horses are absorbed into a community united by the common act of viewing, listening and feeling.

[21] Our contemporary desire to engage with the means by which objects can 'speak' for themselves and 'address' us is not only evident in texts and their performances, but also in the fine arts. The museum as an archive-like institution where knowledge is displayed to the visitor who is meant to observe the noteworthy objects of the past from a spatial distance, appears to have come to an end. Instead, museums have meanwhile turned into places of experience where the claim is that the visitor does no more look at a collection 'from the outside', that is, from a certain distance but experiences it (ideally with its sights, sounds and smells) 'from within'. Distant gazing has been substituted by (the longing for) physical contact.

Oscillation and Freestyle Dressage

As delineated above, Gumbrecht's theory of 'presence' sees an oscillation of presence effects and meaning effects as constitutive of the feeling of being inwardly touched by a performance.[22] And here may lie another reason for the fascination of Freestyle Dressage to its spectators. A Freestyle Dressage test consists of two parts, that is, a technical and an artistic section (each making up 50% of the overall score). The former is made up of scores for each of the compulsory movements, and competence and (seeming) ease in the execution of the movements is crucial to a successful test. Thus, in contrast to figure skating, for instance, Freestyle Dressage adjusts not only one, but two individual bodies "at a specific moment and within a given time limit to a sequence of predefined complex forms. To impress the judges means above all to fulfill their expectation that certain forms will be precisely executed. By contrast, pushing the limits of the sport means going for ever higher levels in the complexity of the forms involved."[23] And it is especially the latter element that moves Freestyle Dressage beyond the level of mere technical perfection. It is the exciting, creative and complex combinations of the prescribed requirements (such as, for instance, a double pirouette after a diagonal in extended canter) that exceed the criteria of the judges' expectations of perfection and create the unique aesthetic and artistic fascination of this discipline.

The components of the artistic score, are usually divided into five sections (with a coefficient of four at international competitions), that is, rhythm, energy and elasticity, harmony between horse and rider, choreography, degree of difficulty, and choice and interpretation of the music. An oscillation in Gumbrecht's sense is thus – in an additional dimension – realized by the choreography incorporating all the technical requirements for the required level but also the inventiveness of creative and surprising choices highlighting the horse's strong points. Thus, presence effects are not only created by two individual bodies (equine and human) becoming one, but in the case of Freestyle Dressage also by the interplay of the technical and artistic sections. By this interplay of technical excellence on the one hand, and aesthetic movements and impressions on the other hand, horse and rider establish a particular intimate connection of their two bodies by the constant phenomenon of (aesthetical) movement as registered in music, as well as (technical) precision in figures. Using this technique, Freestyle Dressage meets what Kent Cartwright[24] in the field of drama has called "the rhythm of engagement and detachment."[25] Similarly, Jean Howard[26] speaks of "the orchestration

[22] The feeling is even heightened when music is employed (see above).

[23] Hans Ulrich Gumbrecht: *Praise*, p. 181f.

[24] Kent Cartwright: *Tragedy and Its Double: The Rhythms of Audience Response,* Pennsylvania State University 1991.

[25] Ibid., p.3. Cf. also Cartwright's "The shifting pattern of spectatorial engagement and detachment – sometimes called 'aesthetic distance' – constitutes dramatic response." (10) "By 'engagement' I mean the spectator's surrender of self-awareness" (11). For him, "engagement and detachment dance together." (16) "In the symbiotic rhythm of distance, engagement participates ('What's next?') while detachment stands chorus ('Why that?')." (17)

[26] Jean E. Howard: *Shakespeare's Art of Orchestration: Stage Technique and Audience Response,* Urbana 1984. Howard focuses on the sensory dimensions of the Bard's art and has developed that

of speed and sound that governs the rhythm of the audience's theatrical experience in shaping its perception of and responses to the progressive flow of stage events."[27] With reference to the contradicting moods and movements in Shakespeare's plays, she recognizes an alternation of engagement and detachment, "that is in musical terms, a crescendo-decrescendo-rhythm, and changes of key, the audience experience Shakespeare's plays as a "series of dynamic movements, differing in tempo, tone, and atmosphere."[28] Just as a theatrical performance, Freestyle Dressage also oscillates between a detached (noting only the technical section) and an engaged (noting the artistic section) external vision, culminating for the spectators in a comprehensive vision of the overall performance, that is, the interplay of technical and artistic merits. It thus almost ideally meets Gumbrecht's philosophy of presence. By a constant oscillation between positions of detachment and intimacy, rider and horse evoke a pattern of (rational) reflection and (sensual) fascination in their audience and thus provide a narrative of bodily experience, The performance by rider and horse covers both temporal succession and spatial arrangement and thus fulfils Gumbrecht's oscillation between meaning culture (time) and presence culture (space). In faithful co-operation and mutual acceptance, man and horse become part of an aesthetic totality, and the aesthetic effect is a matter of emotion *as well as* of intellect. By its dynamic interplay of outer observation (technical part) and inward impressions and sensations (artistic part), horse and rider in Freestyle Dressage perfectly testify to Gumbrecht's presence culture, "where […] humans want to relate to the surrounding cosmology by inscribing themselves, that is, by inscribing their bodies into the rhythms of cosmology." (82)[29]

Conclusion

As I have tried to develop, the philosophy of 'presence' could be a rewarding approach in order to come to terms with the question of why we are inwardly 'touched' by Freestyle Dressage. Those of us who as active riders have had the privilege of feeling these unique and unforgettable moments of intensity on horseback while two bodies become one swaying in the rhythm of cosmology will agree to Gumbrecht's intuition that the Cartesian dimension should not cover the full complexity of our existence. We should rather take the time to think about and react to the consequences the dominance the Cartesian worldview has produced.

the recurring techniques that underlie Shakespeare's art of orchestration are verbal diversity, the technique of counterpoint, the simultaneous juxtaposition of two strands of action and speech, as in an eavesdropping encounter. (cf. 13).

[27] Howard, p. 24.

[28] Howard, p. 167.

[29] With reference to Heidegger's philosophy, Gumbrecht sees the experience of 'presence' as being gained by "[p]erhaps […] singling out […] strong individual feelings of joy or of sadness – and by concentrating on them; with our bodies and our minds; by letting them push the distance between us (the subject) and the world (the object) up to a point where the distance may suddenly turn to an unmediated state of being-in-the-world" (*PP*, 137).

> Once we understand our desire for presence as a reaction to an everyday environment that has become so overly Cartesian during the past centuries, it makes sense to hope that aesthetic experience may give us back at least a feeling of our being-in-the-world, in the sense of being part of the physical world of things (*PP*, 116).

What remains, is the initial question, why the 'horse ballet' of the 17th century came returned to the stage, this time in sports, in Western culture at the end of the 20th century. Against the background I have outlined, the answer may lie in the 'bodily turn' of the late 1990s.[30] In this wake (also implying the rise of animal studies), the horse increasingly came to be seen as a sensual partner of man and acting as a cultural signifier of pleasure for a broader public.

Let us then, as a final thought, keep enjoying the rare moments of intensity that happen to us and allow ourselves "to be quiet for a moment from time to time amid the technological and epistemological noise of our general mobilization [...] for we find ourselves in an environment that will not let us pause for more than *moments of presence* [italics in original]." (*PP*, 141) Freestyle Dressage, it would seem to me, is the perfect means to do so.

Bibliography

"Die Kür wird mit den Augen gehört." http://www.welt.de/print-wams/article131623, accessed 11 June 2014, 18:40.

Cartwright, Kent: *Tragedy and Its Double: The Rhythms of Audience Response.* Pennsylvania State University 1991.

Dent, Anthony: *Horses in Shakespeare's England.* London 1987.

Fielitz, Sonja (ed.): *Präsenz Interdisziplinär. Kritik und Entfaltung einer Intuition. Mit einem Vorwort von Hans Ulrich Gumbrecht.* Heidelberg 2012.

Gumbrecht, Hans Ulrich: *In Praise of Athletic Beauty*. Cambridge, Mass, 2006.

Gumbrecht, Hans Ulrich: *Production of Presence. What Meaning Cannot Convey.* Stanford, CA 2004.

Howard, Jean E.: *Shakespeare's Art of Orchestration: Stage Technique and Audience Response.* Urbana 1984.

Liedtke, Walter: *The Royal Horse and Rider. Painting, Sculpture, and Horsemanship 1500-1800.* New York 1989.

[30] Cf., for instance: Antonio R. Damasio: *The Feeling of What Happens: Body and Emotion in the Making of Consciousness,* New York 1999; *The Body in Late Medieval and Early Modern Culture,* ed. by Darryll Grantley and Nina Taunton, Aldershot 2000; *Environment and Embodyment in Early Modern England,* ed. by Mary Floyd-Wilson and Garrett A. Sullivan Jr., Basingstoke 2007; *The Empire of the Senses: The Sensual Culture Reader*, ed. by David Howes, Oxford 2005; Gail Kern Paster: *Humoring the Body: Emotions and the Shakespearean Stage,* Chicago 2004; Alan Petersen: *The Body in Question. A Socio-Cultural Approach,* London 2007;, Michael C. Schoenfeldt: *Bodies and Selves in Early Modern England: Physiology and Inwardness in Spenser, Shakespeare, Herbert and Milton,* Cambridge 1999. For the theatre cf., for instance, Bert O. States: *Great Reckonings in Little Rooms,* Baltimore 1987; Alice Rayner: *Ghosts: Death's Double and the Phenomena of the Theatre,* Minneapolis 2006.

Magalaes, Ernani and Nathan Oaklander (eds.): *Presentism: Essential Readings.* Lanham, MD 2010.
Sidney, Philip: *The Defence of Poesie*. London 1595. The Scholar Press Facsimile. Menston 1969, B1v.
Smith, Bruce R.: *Hearing Green*, in: *Reading the Early Modern Passions. Essays in the Cultural History of Emotion,* ed. by Gail Kern Paster, Katherine Rowe, Mary Floyd-Wilson. Philadelphia 2004, pp. 147-168.
Smith, Bruce R.: *Phenomenal Shakespeare.* Chichester 2010.

Neoclassical Poetics and the Art of Horsemanship

Rolf Lessenich
University of Bonn

Socrates' aristocratic disciple Xenophon, philosopher, soldier, historian, and author of two Greek treatises of horsemanship, described the various tempers of horses, from spirited to dull, and the different techniques of riding and bitting that they require. The Greek myth of Pegasus, the Muses' horse, also suggested the linking of equestrian and poetic art from ancient Greece and Rome to Renaissance and Enlightenment Europe. In his Horatian *Essay upon Poetry* (1682), John Sheffield, Earl of Mulgrave, compared the poetic genres to dressage horses of various tempers and in need of different techniques of horsemanship:

> A higher flight, and of a happier force,
> Are Odes, the Muses most unruly Horse,
> That bounds so fierce the Rider has no rest,
> But foams at mouth, and speaks like one possest
> The Poet here must be indeed Inspired,
> And not with fancy, but with fury fired.[1]

In the ensuing critique of Abraham Cowley's Metaphysical mode, Mulgrave refers to the Neoclassical ideal of a balance existing between poetical fancy (imagination corresponding to equestrian impulsion) on the one hand and poetical judgment (meaning reason, or equestrian restriction) on the other: "Judgment yields, and Fancy governs there."[2] As Xenophon's spirited horse must, however, never be one that bolts, carrying away its rider, so a spirited piece of poetry must never evade the control of its author, not even an ode.

In his Horatian *Essay on Criticism* (1711), Alexander Pope stressed the need of the poet to control his writing, using the image of the rider controlling his spirited horse, a possible reference to Mulgrave. The Pegasus of a spirited poet may sometimes "boldly deviate from the common Track" and "*snatch a Grace* beyond the reach of Art"[3], just as a spirited horse may sometimes deviate from the hoof-beat during a horseshow in a manège. As William Warburton later pointed out in his commentary, Pope here

[1] Early of Mulgrave: *An Essay upon Poetry*, 1682, lines 115-20, in: *Critical Essays of the Seventeenth Century* II, ed. by J.E. Spingarn, Oxford 1908, 1957, p. 289.
[2] Ibid. Line 128, in: II, p. 290.
[3] Alexander Pope: *An Essay on Criticism*, 1711, lines 151 and 155, in: *The Poems of Alexander Pope,* ed. by John Butt, London 1963, p. 147.

apologetically referred to the authority of Quintilian.[4] Just as (in Pope's traditionalist Augustan view) the husband's reason must control his wife's impulsive fancy in the interest of an ideal balance of partnership, so the rider's art must responsibly control his spirited horse's impulsion:

> For *Wit* and *Judgment* often are at strife,
> Tho' meant each other's Aid, like *Man* and *Wife*.
> 'Tis more to *guide* than *spur* the Muse's Steed;
> Restrain his Fury, than provoke his Speed;
> The winged Courser, like a gen'rous Horse,
> Shows most true mettle when you *check* his Course.[5]

A few lines later, Pope expresses his typically Augustan assumption that the rule of balance was a rule of reason and not the mere dictate of French Neoclassicism, a rule inherent in nature and discovered in classical Antiquity after the Dark (pre-classical) Ages, lost again in the equally Dark Middle Ages, and rediscovered in the second Augustan peak of modern enlightened civilization. If Newtonian nature was regularly created *natura naturata*, it was the duty of the artist (meaning poet as well as horseman) to render that regularity visible without giving an impression of artificiality. Pope's double reference was to the proverbial "ars est celare artem" as well as to René Rapin's formulation "la nature réduite en méthode":[6]

> Those RULES of old *discover'd*, not *devis'd*,
> Are *Nature* still, but *Nature Methodiz'd*;
> *Nature*, like *Liberty*, is but restrained
> By the same Laws which first *herself* ordain'd.[7]

The fate of Xenophon's two treatises of horsemanship seemed to confirm this cyclic Enlightenment view of history. In the Middle Ages, Xenophon's two books had fallen into oblivion, along with the classical Greek and Latin treatises of horsemanship by Simon of Athens and Pliny the Elder, and were almost lost forever. It was not until the Renaissance that Xenophon's treatises were printed in the complete Xenophon edition of 1516, initiating what has aptly been called the revival of scientific equitation.[8] The first English translation of Xenophon's *On Horsemanship* was by John Astley, a distinguished Elizabethan courtier and politician (1584). Modern treatises on the art of horsemanship, all based on Xenophon, began to appear: Federico Grisone (1550),[9]

[4] Quintilian: *Institutio Oratoria*, ca AD 95, book II, chapter 13.

[5] Alexander Pope: *An Essay on Criticism*, lines 82-87, ed. cit. p. 146.

[6] René Rapin: *Réflexions sur la Poétique d'Aristote*, 'De la poétique en général', Paris 1674, chapter 12. An English translation by Thomas Rymer was published in London in the same year and again in 1694.

[7] Alexander Pope: *An Essay on Criticism*, lines 88-91, ed. cit. p. 146.

[8] Charles Chevenix Trench: *A History of Horsemanship*, London 1970, pp. 101-153.

[9] Federico Grisone: *Ordini di cavalcare e modi di conoscere le nature de' cavalli*, Venice 1551.

Cesare Fiaschi (1556), Antoine de Pluvinel (1623),[10] and William Cavendish, first Duke of Newcastle (1658).[11] Like Xenophon, these authors were all noblemen and soldiers. The horsemanship that Xenophon described first served military needs, to which horseshow and parade were subordinated. The riding masters and theorists of the leading Napolese School,[12] Giovanni Battista Pignatelli, Federico Grisone, and Cesare Fiaschi of Ferrara, were teachers of the European Renaissance nobility who sent their sons or riding masters to Italy for equestrian training as part of a Renaissance aristocrat education in the arts. As the cases of Puvinel and Newcastle show, refined horse dressage remained a privilege of both the continental and the English aristocracy. Against his Napolese teacher Pignatelli, who still taught harsh medieval methods in the training of horses, Pluvinel, riding master of King Louis XIII of France, developed a non-violent, more elegant and natural method for training horses; and Newcastle, royalist cavalry commander in the English Civil War and pre-Restoration refugee in Spanish Antwerp, asked for more refined and artificial training of cavalry soldiers in their riding schools. In his *Aeneid*, Virgil had already given a poetical account of horseshows in ancient Troy, where cavalry soldiers paraded their horses and their skill to the public – a passage that Richard Berenger quoted in full, together with a translation into English heroic couplets.[13] With the spread of artillery and the shedding of heavy armour, however, more elegant horses had to be bred as their agility in the field needed to be improved. Thus, in the course of the seventeenth and eighteenth centuries and beginning in Italy, military riding schools built more and more manèges where the modern art of dressage developed, transforming into a non-military, recreational sports discipline. The first occurrence of the word 'manège' in English dates to 1705, when Joseph Addison, in his *Remarks on Several Parts of Italy*, wrote: "I saw here the largest Manege that I have met with anywhere else." In fact, the acceptance of dressage riding in England lagged behind Italy and France due to the English preference for racing, hunting, and steeple chasing. As the name indicates, the old Royal Mews in Charing Cross (now Trafalgar Square) had been built for hawks, falconers, and their horses and was finally demolished in 1830. It had no manège. In 1683, the Royal Court introduced the position of Gentleman of the Horse, subordinate to the older Master of the Horse, evidently a riding teacher for the royal family and their nobles. Gentleman-like education of the horses came to replace enforced mastery. It was, however, not until 1763-66 that King George III had Sir William Chambers build the new Royal Mews (now in Buckingham Palace Road), holding a so-called Riding House. George III, like King Louis XV of France, was known to love and practise dressage riding for his amusement. He also admired François Robichon, the theoretical founder of the modern art of dressage. And the above-mentioned Richard Berenger, his Gentleman of the Horse, published a learned two-volume *History and Art of Horsemanship* (1771) in which, following Robichon, he argued for the moderns in the *querelle des anciens et des modernes*. The rough military art of Xenophon and the

[10] Antoine de Pluvinel: *Le Manège Royal*, posth. Paris 1623.

[11] Duke of Newcastle: *Méthode et invention nouvelle de dresser les chevaux*, Antwerp 1658.

[12] Meaning the Kingdom of Naples rather than the city.

[13] Richard Berenger: *The History and Art of Horsemanship*, London 1771, lines. 87-93.

ancient Greeks had yielded to the refined horsemanship of the moderns: “All art is progressive, and receives addition and improvement in its course […].”[14]

As in the writing and reading of literature, commoners soon became riding masters and spectators; witness François Baucher - a wine-merchant’s son who became director of the Duc de Berry’s two manèges in Le Havre and Rouen in 1820 and published his seminal *Dictionnaire d'Équitation* in1833. The demand increased for more public access to the manèges of the aristocracy, as in Vienna’s *Hofreitschule*, and even for non-aristocratic manèges like Philip Astley’s famous 1780 Amphitheatre in London (which also served as a circus and an illegitimate theatre). Significantly, Astley had been a low-ranking military breaker-in of battle horses, distinguished in the French and Indian War in America as part of the Seven Years War 1756-63, not a gentlemanly trainer of dressage horses for the courts of the aristocracy.

The art of horsemanship thus became democratized having been more and more refined and aestheticized in royal, imperial, or ducal manèges that were closed to the public. As François Robichon put it, horsemanship was a fine art in which the rider should make the horse perform all the movements it would naturally execute on the pasture, only in regular geometrical figures and on regular outlined hoof-beats in manèges for horseshows, *la nature réduite en méthode*. Robichon, a Norman nobleman of some distinction, became master of the Académie Équestre de Caën in the castle of La Guérinière, founded in 1727, then master of the Manège des Tuileries, founded by King Louis XV, who was also the founder of the École de Cavalerie in Saumur. Robichon de La Guérinière’s seminal *École de Cavalerie* (two volumes Paris 1729-31), the equestrian bible of modern dressage riding, went a step beyond Grisone by demanding that the dressage act should not only reproduce but improve upon the horse’s natural movements – a requirement in exact accordance with Pope’s “*Nature* to Advantage drest”,[15] in order to make the internal regularity of nature visible in artistic mimesis:

> La théorie nous enseigne à travailler sur de bons principes; & ces principes, au lieu de s’opposer à la nature, doivent servir à la perfectionner par le secours de l’Art.[16]

This was the origin of the horse’s six-step training scale as we know it today, with emphasis on a relaxed, balanced, and harmonious partnership between horse and rider encompassing: rhythm and regularity (*Takt*), relaxation (*Losgelassenheit*), contact (*Anlehnung*), impulsion (*Schwung*), straightness (*Geraderichten*), and, ultimately, collection and concentration (*Versammlung*). The rider should train every horse on a general, rational model inherent in nature, respecting each horse’s individual character to ‘help’ it with the sensitive contact of seat, hand, and legs, rather than dominating with curb bit, voice, and whip:

> *Aids* or *helps*, are the means which the rider employs to govern his horse, and put him in motion. These means consist in the different motions of the [rider's] hands and legs.[17]

[14] Richard Berenger: *The History and Art of Horsemanship*, London 1771, I. 2.
[15] Alexander Pope: *An Essay on Criticism*, 1711, line 296, ed. cit. p. 153.
[16] François Robichon: *Ècole de Cavalerie*, edition Paris 1736, I. 111.

To call this art of horsemanship "Baroque" instead of Neoclassical, as a modern German translation does, is misleading.[18] The art of riding described by Pope and Robichon is based on ease and naturalness, *ars est celare artem*, whereas the Baroque art of the earlier seventeenth century cultivated conceit and artificiality, *ars est praesentare artem*. Mythological court masques featuring horses in unnatural movements, set to music and accompanied by fireworks, such as the equestrian show *The King's Entertainment at Welbeck* presented by Newcastle to Charles I on 21 May 1633, or the horse ballet *La contesa dell'aria e del'acqua* performed in Vienna on the occasion of the marriage of the German Emperor Leopold I and the Spanish Infanta Margarita Teresa on 24 and 31 January 1667, were Baroque. In contrast, in his *Analysis of Horsemanship* (1799), John Adams, riding master to the Duke of York, a propagator of French Neoclassical dressage in England, declared that "nothing distinguishes a gentleman more than ease, grace, and elegance on horseback"[19], meaning natural ease and natural movements (*sprezzatura*) of both horseman and horse, and confirmed the analogy of dressage riding and writing:

> Having said as much as I think necessary in defence of the Manege, or Horsemanship, I shall only add one simile, to conclude the subject: - the Art of Penmanship, from its analogy to the word Horsemanship, is the first that presents itself [...].[20]

Naturalness, elegance, and ease were the chief aims of Neoclassical riding and writing. When a horse first feels the weight of its rider, it carries him on its weaker forehand, thus losing the natural movements impelled by the stronger hind legs. The Neoclassical art of dressage consisted in restoring and improving such natural movements by training the horse to learn to bear the rider's weight on its hind legs, regaining its impulsion, concentration, and the relaxed, elegant movements of its forehand (as in extended trot). This meant further acceptance of the reins and curb bit without stiffening the crest, and thus to show the strength and beauty of all its muscles in perfect balance between impulsion and restriction. Newcastle's art of horsemanship, by contrast, was Baroque and artificial, as seen in his illustrations of large groups of horses submissively kneeling around their master-king and before their mistresses, with the whole culture of the early Stuart court (including its court masques) being Baroque in its maxim of *ars est praesentare artem*.[21] Shows featuring horses performing such unnatural performances in circuses, such as those Philip Astley established in late eighteenth century London and Paris, were a democratized offspring of aristocratic Baroque horse ballets, *gesunkenes*

[17] François Robichon: *École de Cavalerie*, 1729-31, transl. William Frazer: *The Art of Horsemanship*, Calcutta 1801, p. 40.
[18] *Barockes Reiten: La Guérinières École de Cavalerie*, ed. by Bent Branderup, Brunsbek 2006.
[19] John Adams: *Analysis of Horsemanship, Teaching the Whole Art of Riding in the Manège*, 'Preface', London 1799, p. VII.
[20] Ibid. 'Introduction', p. XXVI.
[21] Duke of Newcastle: *Méthode et invention nouvelle de dresser les chevaux*, Antwerp 1658, transl. John Brindley: *A General System of Horsemanship in All Its Branches*, London 1743, lines 14-15.

Kulturgut.[22] However, beauty is found in unadulterated nature, Pope said, though only in the divinely planned harmony of the whole, not in peculiar parts or skills, meaning 'monstrous' Gothic and Baroque as opposed to Neoclassical Palladian buildings, as well as the false art of clowns and circuses he mentions in context with his critique of Baroque Metaphysical poetry:

> In Wit, as Nature, what affects our Hearts
> Is not th' Exactness of peculiar Parts;
> 'Tis not a *Lip*, or *Eye*, we Beauty call,
> But the joint Force and full *Result* of *all.*
> […]
> No monstrous Height, or breadth, or Length appear,
> The *Whole* at once is *Bold* and *Regular.*[23]

Augustan horse paintings confirm this ideal of balance being analogous to that of a Palladian building or a piece of Augustan poetry, individualized though it may be by 'Denham's strength' or 'Waller's sweetness': boldness controlled by regularity, variety by unity, or, in equestrian art, impulsion by restriction. The most outstanding Augustan painter of horses was George Stubbs (1724-1806). Though paintings of wild animals, including horses, were ranked low in the artistic hierarchy and commissioned for commensurate prices, Stubbs specialized in them, aware that nature was the matrix of all art of training. He spent almost two years (1756-58) dissecting horses to study their anatomy, delineated his dissections, and published a highly acclaimed series of engravings, *The Anatomy of the Horse* (1766). When he painted the horses of noblemen it was rather for the benefit of his income than for artistic preference. Yet even then he preferred to portray the prancing horse on the pasture without its rider, as he did for Lord Rockingham's racehorse Whistlejacket (1762), painted in a levade of which the equivalent in equestrian dressage was nothing but a polished artistic reproduction.[24]

English Neoclassical aesthetics, however, differed from their French model in so far as they insisted on more liberty from the beginning, in accordance with the English construction of nationhood at the time of Charles II and Louis XIV: English liberty versus French slavery. In 1660, the English court retuned from exile in France with rather mixed memories of the French King's - and his Cardinal Mazzarin's - hospitality. Thus, from its rebirth after Cromwell's Puritan dictatorship, the English Neoclassicism of John Dryden, and later of Alexander Pope, tilted the balance in favour of imagination, impulse, and passion to the detriment of reason and rule as slavishly observed by the French, the slaves of Horace, Boileau, and Louis XIV:

[22] For the role of Philip Astley's and Charles Hughes's multi-functional circus in the Romantic-Period debate about polite culture and popular culture, cf. Rolf Lessenich: *Neoclassical Satire and the Romantic School 1780-1830*, Göttingen 2012, p. 145.

[23] Alexander Pope: *An Essay on Criticism*, lines 243-46, 251-52, in: *Poems*, ed. cit. pp. 151-52.

[24] Gerhard C. Rump: *Pferde und Jagdbilder in der englischen Kunst: Studien zu George Stubbs und dem Genre der "Sporting Art" von 1650-1830*, Hildesheim 1983.

The *Rules*, a Nation born to serve, obeys,
And *Boileau* still in Right of *Horace* sways.
But we brave Britons [...][25]

English Neoclassicism allowed for graces beyond the confines of the rules of reason, or, in the analogy of the arts of writing and riding, Pegasus, the Muses' horse, should be less strictly reigned in and less rigidly kept on the hoof-beat. Pope underscored his famous plea for more English liberty in the arts by his occasional use of enjambments and heroic triplets instead of heroic couplets. Unwittingly, English Neoclassicism thus paved the way for Preromanticism's increasing preference for impulse and spontaneity, along with derogation of rule in all the fine arts:

Musick resembles Poetry, in each
Are *nameless Graces* which no Methods teach,
And which a *Master-Hand* alone can reach.
[...]
Thus *Pegasus*, a nearer way to take,
May boldly deviate from the common Track.
Great Wits sometimes may gloriously offend,
And rise to *Faults* great Criticks *dare not mend*;
From *vulgar Bounds* with *brave Disorder* part,
And *snatch a Grace* beyond the Reach of Art.[26]

The apex of the Neoclassical art of dressage riding came at a time when it was called into doubt, so that manège and military riding began to separate. Robichon's contemporaries, King Frederick II of Prussia and the Earl of Pembroke, found fault with too much collection, all the more as the manège horse's levade, curvet, capriole, pirouette and other skills that had formerly been useful in battle, were far less effective under contemporary dense artillery fire.[27] Daredevil cavalry attacks were the requirement of modern warfare at a time when Preromanticism sought to liberate all arts from the trammels of rigid rules in favour of imagination and impetus. As throughout all history, changes in the breeding and training of horses, as well as in the art of dressage riding, were representative of wider cultural changes in systems of thought. "The whole mystique of the manège, based on collection, discipline, and an aristocratic concept of life, was totally alien to the egalitarian, romantic, permissive atmosphere"[28] of the time that led up to the French Revolution. The observance of the rules of dressage riding as first prescribed (or, in Pope's view, rather 'discovered' and 'not devised') by Xenophon and rediscovered by Robichon, together with the observance of the Neoclassical rules of the Classical Tradition of Greece and Rome, then assumed the taint of *ancien-régime* elitism and repression. Neoclassical dressage horseshows now appeared as the prerogative and pleasure of an over-refined, outdated, stiff aristocracy, with its

25 Alexander Pope: *An Essay on Criticism*, lines 713-15, ed. cit. p. 167.
26 Ibid. lines 143-45, 150-55, ed. cit. p. 149.
27 Charles Cenevix Trench: *A History of Horsemanship*, pp. 154-62.
28 Charles Cenevix Trench: *A History of Horsemanship*, pp. 161-62.

associated haughty disdain of popular culture and came under the attack of 'dissenting', rule-despising, and egalitarian Preromanticism.[29] In their treatise of horsemanship, Newcastle and Robichon had left no doubt that their concept of the relationship between rider and horse was a courtly, feudal, rational, and non-sentimental one, the rider being the master, and the horse the subject to be guided and punished into obedience. It held a high rank in the chain of being, yet one subordinate to man (and noblemen in particular):

> THE horse being, after man, the most noble of all animals (for he is as much superior to all other creatures as man is to him, and therefore holds a sort of middle place between man and the rest of the creation) he is wise and subtile; for which reason man ought carefully to preserve his empire over him [...][30]
>
> [...] aids and chastisements are employed, aids to prevent the faults a horse may commit, and chastisement to punish him when he actually doth commit them. Since horses only obey from the fear of punishment [....][31]

The anti-feudal and socially levelling cult of sensibility and the 'man of feeling', however, discredited Cartesian reason, or *le bon sens*, which had strictly distinguished between rational human beings of various ranks on the one hand and subordinate animals on the other. In *The Seasons* (1726-39), James Thomson placed the feeling heart above reason not only in the treatment of slaves, but also of animals; sheep, oxen, and horses became fellow creatures protected from domination, exploitation, and slaughter: "This the feeling heart Would tenderly suggest."[32] The distinction between the human subject regulating nature as an object yielded to man's conception of himself as part of an integral dynamic, rather than static, nature - *natura naturans* instead of *natura naturata* - prepared for the erasure of the subject-object distinction in later German Romantic Idealist philosophy. The parallel change in horticulture is evident. The formal French garden, with its symmetrically laid-out walks, parterres, flower beds and bushes cut into regular shapes, and where the gardener's scissors 'improved' nature, was gradually replaced by the English landscape garden, and later the picturesque garden. The gardener's scissors increasingly gave way to the irregularities of a dynamically shooting nature defying all rule, *natura naturans*. Impulse and imagination gained ground over reason and restriction, individuality over generality, and the mastery of man over nature came to an end.[33] Analogously, the rider dominating his horse was no longer taken for a divinely instituted hierarchy or feudal order in the "great chain of

[29] Rolf Lessenich: *Aspects of English Preromanticism*, Cologne and Vienna 1989, pp. 20-23.

[30] Duke of Newcastle: *Méthode et invention nouvelle de dresser les chevaux*, Antwerp 1658, transl. John Brindley: *A General System of Horsemanship in All Its Branches*, London 1743, I. 122.

[31] François Robichon: *École de Cavalerie*, 1729-31, transl. William Frazer: *The Art of Horsemanship*, ed. cit. p. 74.

[32] James Thomson: *The Seasons*, 'Spring', 1726-30, lines 370-71, in: *Complete Poetical Works*, ed. by J. Logie Robertson, Oxford Standard Authors, London 1908, p. 17.

[33] Laurence Fleming and Alan Gore: *The English Garden*, London 1979, 1980, pp. 47-144.

being", this being a world picture that gradually faded out as the eighteenth century progressed.[34] Preromanticism instead brought forth numerous poems and works of fiction where a faithful horse served its rider out of compassion, friendship, or even love, with the rider assuming a more passive role. It was raised to being at the same level as a faithful dog, William Hayley's "speechless friend of man"[35]. Even when incensed by an unfeeling rider trying to tame or dominate it as a master, the wild horse sensed and respected virtue so as to save the life of a good mother with her child – a literary ballad in plain popular speech illustrated by William Blake.[36] To harm it or to destroy its life in old age now appeared as an unpardonable sin, like manslaughter:

> Of creatures that to man attend,
> His pastime, or his wealth;
> The Horse we cherish as a friend,
> To sickness and to health.
> Bless them, who shield a steed from woe.
> By age from toil released!
> And hated by the proud, who shew
> No mercy to the beast.[37]

Such a 'horse of feeling' carried its rider fast and glad to his beloved girl or friend, and it tarried sadly after the farewell; it saved his life in battle and even sacrificed itself for him. The speaker of Leopold Friedrich Günther von Göckingh's Preromantic *Sturm und Drang* poem 'An sein Reitpferd' (1777) addresses his stallion as a close friend who will quickly cross every obstacle to carry him to his beloved Nantchen without the use of spurs and whip, whom he will never slaughter for old age, and whose health and happiness he will never endanger for profit. The reference to the famous racing course of Newmarket, Suffolk, links the poem to English Preromanticism:

> Mein treuer Hengst! du weißt, ich liebe dich;
> Du sollst auch alt in meinem Stalle sterben;
> Du weißt, nicht Zorn, nicht Wettlauf reizte mich,
> Mit deinem Blut die Sporen rot zu färben.[38]

In the Age of Enlightenment, such irrational manifestations of the cult of sensibility and such 'pathetic fallacies' exposed themselves to ridicule, and care had to be taken not to take rationales to extremes like Laurence Sterne's Uncle Toby refusing to kill a poor fly:

[34] Arthur O. Lovejoy: *The Great Chain of Being*, Cambridge, MA 1936.
[35] William Hayley: *The Dog*, line 1 in: *Ballads: Founded on Anecdotes Related to Animals*, London 1805, p. 1.
[36] William Hayley: *The Horse*, ibid. pp. 205-12.
[37] William Hayley: *The Fatal Horse*, lines 1-8, ibid. p. 85.
[38] Leopold Friedrich Günther von Göckingk*: An sein Reitpferd*, in *Die Lieder zweier Liebenden*, 1777, in: *Sturm und Drang Werke in drei Bänden*, ed. by René Strasser, Zürich 1966, l. 89.

> I'll not hurt thee, says my uncle *Toby*, rising from his chair, and going a-cross the room, with the fly in his hand, --- I'll not hurt a hair of thy head: Go, says he, lifting up the sash, and opening his hand as he spoke, to let it escape; - go poor Devil, get thee gone, why should I hurt thee? ---- This world surely is wide enough to hold both thee and me.[39]

Sensibility, like the Gothic, tended to be self-parodic in the sense of Romantic Irony. This was the context in which Sterne's nine-volume novel *Tristram Shandy* (1759-67), with its wealth of real and metaphorical horses, must be read. Its European-wide impact can be seen in such subversive works as Denis Diderot's *Le neveau de Rameau* (MS 1762-74) and *Jacques le fataliste* (MS 1773-75), with their pitting of naturalness and impulse against premeditated and regular art, the animal cry of the passions, considering both their advantages and drawbacks, including the danger of their lapse into absurdity and ridicule. In the words of Rameau's ingenious though erratic nephew: "We want it [art] more energetic, less mannered, more genuine."[40] Both Sterne and Diderot pleaded for a middle way, a sensibility and a fatalism that did not lapse into ridicule and absurdity: hence their novels' mixtures of the serious and the satirical. Tristram, Sterne's hobby-horsical first-person narrator, is subject to necessity as his pen guides him and thus gives the lie to the Enlightenment Neoclassical concept of an author's free will in rationally planning his regular work of art. This comic fatalism of an *ars poetica* of mere whim and chance applies to all plans in his life. He wants to visit Chantilly, the most prestigious stud for breeding horses in Europe. Lacking both control and self-control, however, he falls asleep against his rational intention, is woken up against his wishes, and sees the famous city for no other reason than an altercation with the postillion. Due to this, he is no longer in a mood to enjoy Chantilly's sights. The goal of education was control of the passions, just as the goal of dressage was control of the horse, and as the goal of writing was control of the pen. In Pope's words, "'Tis more to *guide* than *spur* the Muse's Steed." Sterne's novel, in which the horses direct their riders or carriage drivers instead of the conventional opposite, teems with lame or bolting horses, poor jades badly put together, mad hobby-horses, and references to horsemanship. It thus subverts all Enlightenment ideals of rational control. Tristram cannot regulate his passions any more than he can his pen or horses; they run riot in spite of his efforts, and he gives up, making a virtue of necessity by affirming (while simultaneously satirizing) the rising Preromantic ideals of spontaneity, originality, nature above art, and the tipping of the Neoclassical balance of imagination and reason in favour of imagination. Obedience to the rules of reason, including the rule of decorum, appears as both boring and impossible – a radical philosophical and aesthetic theory proposed with tongue-in-cheek Romantic Irony. Tristram, the chaotic writer and equally chaotic horseman, passionately proclaims his rule-despising *ars poetica et hippica* with a steeplechase rider's exclamation when he defends his anti-Fieldingesque division of the novel into chaotically irregular chapters and his bolting pen's running riot on paper in general.

[39] Laurence Sterne: *The Life and Opinions of Tristram Shandy*, 1759-67, volume II, chapter 12, Penguin Classics, ed. by Melvyn and Joan New Harmondsworth 1997, p. 91.

[40] Martin Price: *To the Palace of Wisdom: Studies in Order and Energy from Dryden to Blake*, 'Sterne: Art and Nature', New York 1964, pp. 327-36.

> [...] let that be as it will, Sir, I can no more help it than my destiny: - A sudden impulse comes across me - drop the curtain, *Shandy* – I drop it – Strike a line here across the paper, *Tristram* – I strike it – and hey for a new chapter.[41]

Bibliography

Adams, John: *Analysis of Horsemanship, Teaching the Whole Art of Riding in the Manège*, 'Preface'. London 1799.

Berenger, Richard: *The History and Art of Horsemanship*. London 1771.

Branderup, Bent (ed.): *Barockes Reiten: La Guérinières École de Cavalerie*. Brunsbek 2006.

de Pluvinel Antoine: *Le Manège Royal*, posth. Paris 1623.

Duke of Newcastle: *Méthode et invention nouvelle de dresser les chevaux*. Antwerp 1658.

Duke of Newcastle: *Méthode et invention nouvelle de dresser les chevaux*. Antwerp 1658, transl. John Brindley*: A General System of Horsemanship in All Its Branches*. London 1743.

Early of Mulgrave: *An Essay upon Poetry*, 1682, lines 115-20, in: *Critical Essays of the Seventeenth Century* II, ed. by J.E. Spingarn. Oxford 1908, 1957.

Fleming, Laurence and Alan Gore: *The English Garden*. London 1979, 1980.

Grisone, Federico: *Ordini di cavalcare e modi di conoscere le nature de'cavalli*. Venice 1551.

Hayley, William: *Ballads: Founded on Anecdotes Related to Animals*. London 1805.

Lessenich, Rolf, *Neoclassical Satire and the Romantic School 1780-1830*. Göttingen 2012.

Lessenich, Rolf: *Aspects of English Preromanticism*. Cologne and Vienna 1989.

Lovejoy, Arthur O.: *The Great Chain of Being*. Cambridge, MA 1936.

Pope, Alexander: *An Essay on Criticism*, 1711, in: *The Poems of Alexander Pope,* ed. by John Butt. London 1963.

Price, Martin: *To the Palace of Wisdom: Studies in Order and Energy from Dryden to Blake*, 'Sterne: Art and Nature'. New York 1964.

Quintilian: *Institutio Oratoria*, ca AD 95, book II.

Rapin, René: *Réflexions sur la Poétique d'Aristote*, 'De la poétique en général'. Paris 1674.

Robichon, François: *École de Cavalerie*, 1729-31, transl. William Frazer: *The Art of Horsemanship*. Calcutta 1801.

Robichon, François: *Ècole de Cavalerie*, edition Paris 1736.

Rump, Gerhard C.: *Pferde und Jagdbilder in der englischen Kunst: Studien zu George Stubbs und dem Genre der "Sporting Art" von 1650-1830*. Hildesheim 1983.

Sterne, Laurence: *The Life and Opinions of Tristram Shandy*, 1759-67, volume II, chapter 12, Penguin Classics, ed. by Melvyn and Joan. New Harmondsworth 1997.

Thomson, James: *The Seasons*, 'Spring', 1726-30, in: *Complete Poetical Works*, ed. by J. Logie Robertson, Oxford Standard Authors. London 1908.

Trench, Charles Chevenix: *A History of Horsemanship*. London 1970.

von Göckingk, Leopold Friedrich Günther*: An sein Reitpferd*, in *Die Lieder zweier Liebenden*, 1777, in: *Sturm und Drang Werke in drei Bänden*, ed. by René Strasser. Zürich 1966.

[41] Laurence Sterne: *Tristram Shandy*, ed. cit. p. 231.

Accompanying HORSE(s) through time. The Depiction of Horses from a Corpus-Linguistic Perspective

Rolf Kreyer
University of Marburg

Introduction

Literary and cultural studies approaches to any kind of phenomenon are usually based on the close scrutiny of the object of study. Claims are based on close readings of the text or the author at issue. The present paper wants to supplement this kind of research by a methodology which is usually not employed in such contexts, namely corpus linguistics. As the name already makes clear, the method was developed in linguistic research. It came into being in the early 1960s with the compilation of the BROWN corpus of written American English and, to some extent, can be understood as a counter movement to the then prevailing generative-transformational research paradigm with its reliance on intuitive data: the natives-speak researcher asks him- or herself whether a certain construction sounds right and then includes it in his/her description of the language at issue. Corpus linguistics, in contrast, is interested in how language is actually used rather than in how language could possibly be used. To this end huge (sometimes several billions of words) corpora of authentic spoken and written texts were compiled, and it was soon found that "language looks rather different when you look at a lot of it at once."[1] Today the corpus linguistic method is of key importance for modern linguistics.

More recently, the value and power of corpus linguistic methods have become increasingly appreciated in neighbouring disciplines, such as stylistics[2] or gender studies[3]. The present paper understands itself as a further contribution in this direction. It wants to explore the depiction and conceptualisation of horses in English literature from early modern times to the present. More specifically, with the help of corpus-linguistic methods the paper will provide a bird's-eye view (a 'far-away' reading, if you so wish) on the use of the lexeme *horse* and its (near-)synonyms (e.g. *steed* or *mare*) over the centuries. Hoping that "horses look rather different when you look at the lot of them at once", the paper tries to shed light on the horse as signifier of cultural change in systems of thought.

[1] John Sinclair: *Corpus, Concordance, Collocation*. Oxford 1991, p. 100.
[2] c.f. Michaela Mahlberg: *Corpus Stylistics and Dickens' Fiction*, London 2012.
[3] c.f. Paul Baker: *Using Corpora to Analyze Gender*, London 2014.

The paper is organised in three major parts. Following this introduction, the next section will provide a short overview of the corpus approach. We will then proceed to the description of the basic distribution and use of *horse* and related expressions over time. The second part of the analysis will zoom in on the use of the lexeme *horse* in comparisons and similes.

The corpus approach

A 'corpus' in the language sciences can be understood as "a body of written text or transcribed speech which can serve as a basis for linguistic analysis and description."[4] Generally, corpora are understood as representing either a particular register of a given language or a language as a whole, i.e. corpora are understood as samples on the basis of which claims concerning the totality of the language can be made (similar to a sample of voters as representatives of the whole electorate). One plausible (although not uncontroversial) assumption is that patterns that are identified in a representative corpus are patterns of language use in general and, therefore, are likely to be represented (in some way or another) in the mind of the user. The relevance of such patterns was formulated very succinctly more than 50 years ago in John Rupert Firth's famous dictum "you shall know a word by the company it keeps."[5] That is, part of the meaning of a word lies in the words and structures that frequently co-occur with that word. The fact, for instance, that the verb *to cause* has a strong tendency to take negative nouns as objects is an aspect of its meaning that goes beyond the basic meaning of the verb, which could be glossed as 'make something come to exist'. The rationale underlying the present paper is that our understanding of the word *horse*, our conceptualisation of horses, is mirrored in and depends on the way we use this lexeme (and related terms), i.e. the patterns in which it occurs.

Corpus linguistics has identified a variety of such patterns. Four of these are particularly relevant for the present paper, namely collocation, colligation, semantic preference and semantic prosody. Consider the authentic examples of *naked eye* (taken from the British National Corpus) shown below.

The mite is just visible to the **naked eye**.
The whiskers were too small to see with the **naked eye**.
Because they are so faint, not a single one is visible to the **naked eye**.
These […] cannot be seen by the **naked eye**.
Very little of the red underpainting is discernible to the **naked eye**.
We'd been prepared to buy houses with flaws invisible to the **naked eye.**
The human egg is just visible to the **naked eye**.

The data above shows distinctive patterns, first described by John Sinclair,[6] in which *naked eye* occurs. On the first position to the left (L1), we always find the definite article *the*. This is usually preceded by a preposition in L2 (*to, with*, and *by*), which is preceded by a lexical item in L3 that relates to visual perception (*see, (in)visible,*

[4] Graeme Kennedy: *An Introduction to Corpus Linguistics*, Edinburg 1998.
[5] John Rupert Firth: *Papers in Linguistics 1934–1951,* London 1957.
[6] John Sinclair': *The search for units of meaning*, in: *Textus* 9 (1996), pp. 75-106.

discernible). In addition, and usually further to the left but not necessarily in L4, we find elements that express a notion of difficulty (*just, too small, not a single one, cannot, very little* or the prefix *in-*).

The first kind of patterning, i.e. the co-occurrence of a word/phrase with another word/phrase, is called a 'collocation'. This is a very frequent kind of pattern, and it is not difficult to find other examples such as *pretty girl*, *handsome boy*, or the English *to do your homework* as opposed to the German *seine Hausaufgaben machen*. The term 'colligation' refers to the co-occurrence of a word/phrase with a particular grammatical construction or category, in this case prepositions. Another example is the noun *assumption,* which is very frequently followed by a *that*-clause. 'Semantic preference' and 'semantic prosody' are similar in that they describe the co-occurrence of a word/phrase with linguistic elements that share a particular semantic feature. In the former case, this feature, i.e. 'visual perception', is of a neutral kind (similar to the co-occurrence of *true feelings* with verbs expressing showing or revealing; cf. Sinclair 1996), whereas in the latter case we are dealing with what we could call an evaluative semantic feature, namely 'difficult'. Other examples of semantic prosody are the verbs *cause* and German *verursachen*, both of which have a high probability to occur with nouns that refer to negative events, such as *catastrophe*, *distress* or *Unfall* and *Probleme*.

Similar to the view that patterns in a corpus reveal patterns in language use, we assume that corpus patterns betray cultural patterns. That is, the way in which the word *horse* and related terms are used tells us something about how people conceptualise and think about horses. More specifically, changes in the use of these terms can be interpreted as an indication of cultural change in systems of thought.

HORSE – the broad perspective

As mentioned in the introduction, the present study first wants to provide a broad overview of how *horse* and its related terms are used from the early modern period to the 20th century. Two corpora were built: The first represents writing of 58 authors ranging from Sir Thomas More to Virginia Woolf. It contains 124 texts, totalling approximately 13 million words, all of which were available through *Projekt Gutenberg* (cf. the appendix for a complete list of authors and texts). Since access to more modern fiction is restricted, the first corpus was supplemented by the imaginative prose section of the British National Corpus, which contains roughly 16.5 million words. All in all, the findings reported in the present paper are based on almost 30 million words.

The data was analysed with the help of two programs, AntConc,[7] a freely downloadable concordancer that can be used to analyse any collection of .txt-files, and the web interface for the CQP-edition of the British National Corpus.[8] Both softwares identify any search expression in a text corpus and provide the user with the opportunity

[7] Lawrence Anthony: *AntConc (Version 3.2.2)* [Computer Software], Tokyo 2011. Available from http://www.antlab.sci.waseda.ac.jp/.

[8] Sebastian Hoffmann and Stefan Evert: *BNCweb (CQP-edition): The marriage of two corpus tools*, in: *Corpus Technology and Language Pedagogy: New Resources, New Tools, New Methods* ed. by S. Braun, K. Kohn, and J. Mukherjee (2006), pp. 177-195.

to sort the output with regard to different positions in relation to the search expression. This way, patterns of use become apparent fairly easily: sorting according to position L1, for instance, will give us a very good idea as to which adjectives are typically used to premodify the word *horse*, as can be seen in figure 1, which provides a screenshot of AntConc.

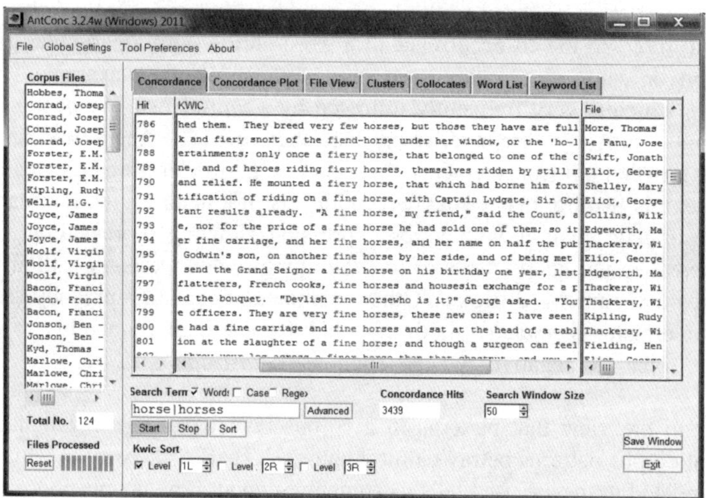

Figure 1: Concordance lines in AntConc.

Table 1 provides an overview of the search expressions. For each of the words listed, all inflectional forms were identified in the first corpus. Since the second corpus, representing the second half of the 20th century, was disproportionately large, a 1 million word random sample was created. To weed out any non-horse homonymous forms, e.g. *chestnut* as the tree or *colt* as the weapon, every concordance line was checked, and erroneous material was deleted. Figure 2 shows the distribution of the search terms across the major literary periods of English literature.

Table 1: The lemmas under analysis, and their frequencies of occurrence in the corpus.

LEMMA	**# instances (slightly rounded)**
HORSE	8300
STEED	220
COLT	90
MARE	430
NAG	55
GELDING	25
STALLION	85
BAY	4
SORREL	40
CHESTNUT	28
Total	**~9300**

The distribution that we see in figure 2 is not surprising. Firstly, across all periods the term *horse* is by far the most frequent, followed by *mare* and *steed*. All of the other terms are comparatively rare. As regards the frequency per million words, we can see a general decline from the Renaissance to the second half of the 20th century. Interestingly, we have a slight increase in the romantic period, which might be interpreted as a reaction to the onset of the Industrial Revolution with a resulting stronger focus on the countryside, landscape, nature and so on. The first major decrease from 348 in the romantic period to 272 occurrences in the Victorian era, nicely mirrors the stronger preoccupation of writers with the situation in the great cities and the life of the workforce there. For many people horses ceased to be a part of everyday life. They continue to lose their relevance in the modernist period, which is reflected in the continuing decrease (from 272 to 234 occurrences). What is surprising is that we do not see any further decrease in the second half of the 20th century. If the distribution of *horse* and related terms just depended on the relevance of horses for everyday life we would expect a further drop. The absence of such a decline is another factor that has to be taken into account if we want to explore horses as an indication of cultural change in systems of thought.

HORSE – the narrow perspective

A first hypothesis about changes in the conceptualisation and depiction of horses is instigated by the following quote from Sydney's *Defense of Poesy*:

> Then would he add certain praises, by telling what a peerless beast the horse was, the only serviceable courtier without flattery, the beast of most **beauty**, **faithfulness**, **courage**, and such more, that if I had not been a piece of a logician before I came to him, I think he would have persuaded me to have wished myself a horse. [my emphasis]

The above quote shows three possible qualities of horses that arguably may be very

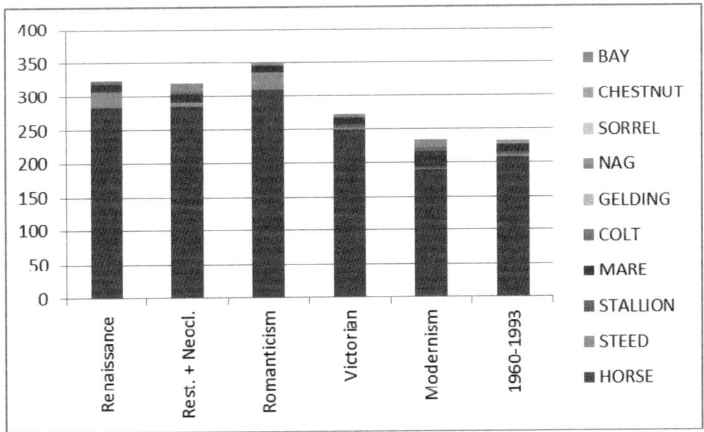

Figure 2: The distribution of *horse* and related terms across the major literary periods of English literature.

relevant in a poetic context but may seem rather irrelevant if a horse is mostly regarded as an animal used for work. It makes sense to assume that changes in the ways that we perceive and think about horses are betrayed by the attributes that we ascribe them. It seems particularly promising to start such an analysis by comparing the texts from the Renaissance to Modernism with those from 1960 onwards (henceforth corpus 1 and corpus 2, respectively), because these two groups should reflect a change (if any) in the way horses are perceived and used, i.e. as an animal that is part of everyday (work and war) life to an animal that is not. Table 2 below shows the 20 most typical adjectives immediately preceding *horse* or *horses* in corpus 1 and corpus 2.

Obviously, we find only three adjectives that occur in the top 20 in both corpora, all of which are colour terms, namely *grey*, *white* and *black*. Interestingly, colours seem to be a lot more relevant up until 1900 than after 1960: while corpus 1 features seven colours among the top 20 adjectives, corpus 2 only shows four. In addition, these latter four are basic, non-horse-specific vocabulary, whereas three of the seven colour terms in the first corpus pertain to the jargon of horse-related registers. This might be interpreted as an indication of a decrease in familiarity with horses. In line with this, we see a fairly large number of adjectives that describe the general health of horses or a particular state that a horse is in at a certain point in time, i.e. *steaming*, *wearied*, *lame*, *lean*, *fat* and *blind*. Such kind of vocabulary does not occur in the second corpus (*old* and *new* rather make reference to the time of possession). Instead we find words that make reference to the body or the build of the horse, e.g. *great*, *heavy*, *big*; the word *high* is mostly used in the idiomatic expression *get on one's high horse* and should not be considered. Again, I would like to argue that the adjectives we see in corpus 2 are of a very general kind and not specific to animals or horses, thus, again, testifying to a loss of familiarity with these animals. Interestingly, however, the modern writers make more frequent use of adjectives that show appreciation for horses. While in corpus 1 we only find one such adjective, namely *favourite*, table 2 lists four, i.e. *fine*, *good*, *best* and *great* (which admittedly is mostly used with regard to the build of the horse). A final observation can be made concerning the mental disposition of horses as reflected in the two corpora. While terms belonging to this semantic field are almost equally frequent in both compilations, three and four instances, we see slight differences when we take a closer look. The writers represented in the first corpus describe a broader range of temperaments, from *lazy* over *spirited* to *fiery*, whereas the adjectives used in the second corpus, *wild*, *frightened*, *terrified* and *nervous*, seem to focus on a possible unreliability of horses. Again, the more varied descriptions until the modernist epoch provide further evidence for a cultural change in the way horses are perceived and used.

Table 2: The 20 most typical adjectives immediately preceding *horse* or *horses* in corpus 1 and corpus 2.

Corpus 1	Corpus 2
pied	**white**
Barbary	galloping
steaming	wild
chestnut	roan
hired	**black**
bay	fresh
spirited	**grey**
wearied	spare
lazy	frightened
lame	terrified
grey	nervous
fiery	high
lean	fine
white	great
favourite	old
black	new
led	heavy
brown	good
fat	big
blind	best

In the following we take a closer look at the occurrence of *horse* in particular structures, namely comparisons and similes. These structures are especially suitable because they place a strong emphasis on those aspects that seem to be typical of horses, this way revealing important insights into our conceptualisation of horses. For instance, we say *as strong as a horse* because strength is a feature that we associate with horses. So, by looking at comparative structures and similes we get a very good idea of the central qualities that we attribute to horses. Table 3 lists the structures that were searched for together with an illustrative example. The part in bold print represents those linguistic elements that are of interest for the analysis. With the first group of search strings, for instance, we focus on any element that occurs before the prepositional phrase. With a second group of strings the focus is on the adjective that occurs within the comparative structure, and so on.

Table 3: Comparative structures and similes.

Search string	**Example**
[…] *than a/an/the * horse* **[…]** *than __/the * horses*	But those pigs are **more bloomin' nuisance** than the horses. [*My Beloved Son*]
as **[adjective]** *as a/an/the * horse* *as* **[adjective]** *as __/the * horses*	I have you here as **safe** as a horse in a pound. [*Caleb Williams*]
'**Verb phrases**' with: *like a/an/the * horse* *like __/ the * horses*	Miss Marchmont **hinnied** like a horse. [*Jacob's Room*]
like a/an/the **[adjective]** *horse* *like __/the* **[adjective]** *horses*	In short, my dear, like a **restiff** horse, […] he pains one's hands, and half disjoints one's arms, to rein him in. [*Clarissa*]

Searching for the structures above yielded a total of 29 relevant instances in the corpus containing literature from Renaissance to Modernism, and 91 cases in the data from 1960 to 1993. These 120 examples can be grouped into a fairly small range of semantic categories. The first, here called 'temperament' encompasses those cases that make reference to the fact that horses are sometimes difficult to control, either because they are of a proud nature or because they are frightened. Consider examples (1) and (2).

(1) […] the ship kept bucking and sidling like a vicious horse.
(2) Beside him Ratagan was quivering like a nervous horse […]

Other prominent categories emphasise the strength of horses, the horse as a working animal or the aspect of breaking horses as shown in the examples (3) to (5), respectively.

(3) And now she was as strong as a cart horse, and he didn't give a damn.
(4) poor old Thornbury merely trod his round like a horse in a mill.
(5) Lili pinned the seams closer, standing quietly like a broken horse to be saddled and bridled.

Two categories, namely 'breathing' and 'sound moving' describe sounds typically associated with horses. In the former category, reference is usually made to heavy breathing after exhaustion or respiratory problems. The latter focuses on the galloping of horses and the accompanying thundering sound. The category 'moving', in contrast, contains those tokens where the way horses move is in focus.

(6) The Mason only snorted and cursed like a horse with croup.

(7) The bang of the younger one's heart seemed to go right through the earth like thundering horses.

(8) Clumsily, like a fallen horse righting itself, I scrambled to my feet [...]

Finally, two minor categories encompass cases that either make reference to the reliability of horses or to the ageing of horses.

(9) [...] as true as the truest horse

(10) [...] he leant forward steadily like an old horse who finds himself suddenly out of the shafts drawing no cart.

In addition, there are a total of 21 instances that are so diverse that they cannot be grouped under a larger category; they are subsumed under the category 'other'.

The four most prominent categories in both corpora are those on the left-hand side of figure 3 (the others will be ignored). They account for 73% of all data in the Renaissance to Modernism corpus and for 60% of the data in the texts from 1960 to 1993. Focusing on these for the moment, we can see that the temperament and the breaking of horses are two aspects that have remained prominent in English literature from the Renaissance period onwards. Together, these categories account for 45% and 53% of the data in the first and the second corpus, respectively. This continuing preoccupation might be interpreted as a linguistic reflex of the continuing fascination with the wild and ferocious power of horses and the attempt of and the success in

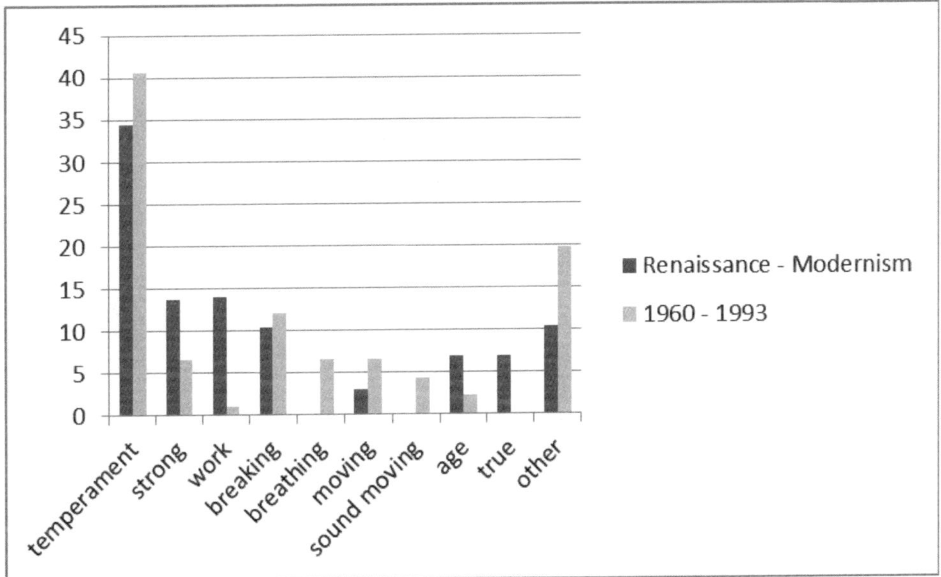

Figure 3: Thematic categories of comparative structures and similes in the two corpora under analysis.

controlling that power.

On the other hand, we see that reference to work has become a lot less frequent in the modern texts, an obvious consequence of the fact that horses as working animals are no longer a part of modern Western society. To some extent, this is also mirrored in the category 'strong': all of the instances in corpus 2 are realisations of the idiomatic expression *as strong as a horse*. From a linguistic point of view, idiomatic expressions are considered to be stored in the mental lexicon as one single unit, even though they may be analysable and transparent as in the present case. It makes sense to assume that the comparative structure is 'semantically frozen', i.e. it is used to express a high degree of strength without being fully aware of strength as a feature that is attributed to horses. It is true that three out of four instances in the first corpus are idiomatic, too, but here we also find at least one non-idiomatic use (*like a strong horse*) which points to an 'active' association of the two concepts. Presumably, this association is based on first-hand experience, which we lack in modern Western societies.

Table 4: Adjectives in the structure *like a/an/the* **[adjective]** *horse/s*.

Corpus 1		**Corpus 2**	
old	2	**balking**	**1**
unready	1	broken	1
proud	1	**crazy**	**1**
restiff	**1**	fallen	1
strong	1	**fretful**	**1**
vicious	**1**	**frightened**	**4**
		nervous	**1**
		nonchalant	1
		restive	**1**
		smart	1
		startled	**1**
		terrified	**1**
		thirsty	1
		winded	1
		over-worked	1
		unbroken	1
		galloping	1
		large	1
		thundering	1
total	7	**total**	**22**

Coming back full circle, I would like to zoom in on one of the above structures, namely *like __/a/an/the* **[adjective]** *horse/s*. In the beginning of this section we have already looked at adjectives that typically precede the noun *horse*. By focusing on the above simile we can now identify those adjectives that are most characteristic of horses, because, as was argued above, the *secundum comparatum* in comparisons and similes will usually be of a highly typical nature. Table 4 provides a list of adjectives in this construction in the two corpora under analysis.

Of particular interest are the words in bold print in table 4. They describe the temperament of horses, more specifically 'unreliable' character traits. Two out of the seven adjectives that we find in the first corpus, i.e. 29%, make reference to these traits. In the second corpus, in contrast, 11 out of the total of 22, i.e. 50%, are of this kind. In corpus linguistic terms we can state that the word *horse* has developed a semantic preference of 'mental state' or 'temperament'. However, the lexis that falls into these categories is not neutral but instantiates a rather negative semantic prosody that might be described as '(overly) sensitive' or 'unreliable'.

Conclusion

This paper wanted to explore to what extent methods from linguistics can be used to identify and describe cultural change. In particular, the aim was to trace changes in the conceptualisation of horses in English literature from early modern times to the present. In contrast to typical methods from literary or cultural studies, which are based on close 'reading' of cultural phenomena, the method of choice was that of corpus linguistics, which by its very nature adopts an extremely broad perspective and, therefore, can only provide us with a bird's-eye view. However, this drawback is counter-balanced by the huge amount of data that can be processed and analysed this way - in the present case, roughly 30,000,000 words of English literature.

The analysis has made apparent how and to what extent literature mirrors cultural change, more specifically how the way that authors use the word *horse* (and related terms) reflects changes in the conceptualisation of horses over the centuries. In particular it was shown that the changing role of horses in the 20th century reverberates in literature: the decrease in first-hand experience and familiarity with horses, almost naturally one might say, leads to a decrease in the frequencies with which horses show up in narratives. In addition, the way horses are described and, hence, conceptualised becomes narrower and less diversified. Given this development, it is remarkable that two semantic fields show a slight increase of use in the modern data, namely the fields of 'temperament' and 'breaking'. It might be argued that the horse, rampant but reigned in, is still as valid a symbol of the eternal struggle of passion and reason today as it was 400 years ago, even though the power of this symbol does not necessarily show in its instantiation in one particular piece of art but in the way the word *horse* is used in the language of literature.

In conclusion, horses do look rather different when we look at a lot of them at once but at the same time, they do look rather similar when we focus on their relevance as cultural metaphors. Even though horses play a less and less important role in modern Western societies they manage to maintain (and maybe even increase) their relevance as conveyors of fundamental human experiences.

Appendix

List of works in corpus 1

A Modern Utopia
A Modest Proposal
A Portrait of the Artist…
A Room with a View
A Sentimental Journey…
A Tale of a Tub
Adam Bede
Alice's Adventures…
Anthony and Cleopatra
As You Like It
Carmilla
Castle Rackrent
Clarissa
David Copperfield
Doctor Faustus
Dracula
Dubliners
Edward II
Emma
Essays
Evelina
Frankenstein…
Grace Abounding…
Great Expectations
Gulliver's Travels
Hamlet
Hard Times
Heart of Darkness
Henry V
Howard's End
Importance of Being Earnest
Ivanhoe
Jacob's Room
Jane Eyre
Jude the Obscure
Julius Caesar
Kim
King Lear
Lady Windermere's Fan
Legends of Longdendale
Leviathan
Life of Samuel Johnson
Lives of the English Poets
Lord Jim
Love Letters Between…
Macbeth
Major Barbara
Mansfield Park
News from Nowhere
Night and Day
North and South
Northanger Abbey
Nostromo
Oliver Twist
Oroonoko
Othello
Pamela
Past and Present
Persuasion
Pride and Prejudice
Pygmalion
Richard III
Robinson Crusoe
Romeo and Juliet
Sartor Resartus
Sense and Sensibility
Silas Marner
Sonnets
Sybil
Tess of the D'Urbevilles
The Advancement of Learning
The Adventures of Caleb Williams
The Adventures of Sherlock…
The Alchemist
The Castle of Otranto
The Expedition of Humphry…
The Fortunate Mistress
The House by the Churchyard
The Island of Dr. Moreau
The Jew of Malta
The Jungle Book
The Last Man
The Man of Feeling
The Merchant of Venice
The Mill on the Floss
The Monk
The Moonstone
The Mysteries of Udolpho
The New Atlantis
The Nigger of Narcissus
The Picture of Dorian Gray
The Pilgrim's Progress
The Return of the Native
The Spanish Tragedie
Dr Jekyll and Mr Hyde
The Way of the World
The Way We Live Now
The Woman in White
Through the Looking Glass
Tom Jones
Treasure Island
Tristram Shandy
Ulysses
Uncle Silas
Utopia
Vanity Fair
Volpone
Waverley
Where Angels Fear to Tread
Winter's Tale
Wuthering Heights

Mary Barton
Middlemarch
Midsummer Night's Dream
Moll Flanders
Mrs Warren's Profession
New Grub Street
The Tempest
The Time Machine
The Turn of the Screw
The Unfortunate Traveller
The Vicar of Wakefield
The Voyage Out
The War of the Worlds

List of authors in corpus 1

Austen, Jane
Bacon, Francis
Behn, Aphra
Boswell, James
Brontë, Charlotte
Brontë, Emily
Bunyan, John
Burney, Fanny
Carlyle, Thomas
Carroll, Lewis
Collins, Wilkie
Congreve, William
Conrad, Joseph
Defoe, Daniel
Dickens, Charles
Disraeli, Benjamin
Doyle, Arthur Conan
Edgeworth, Maria
Eliot, George
Fielding, Henry
Forster, E.M.
Gaskell, Elizabeth
Gissing, George Robert
Godwin, William
Goldsmith, Oliver
Hardy, Thomas
Hobbes, Thomas
James, Henry
Johnson, Samuel
Jonson, Ben
Joyce, James
Kipling, Rudyard
Kyd, Thomas
Le Fanu, Joseph Thomas Sheridan
Lewis, Matthew Gregory
Mackenzie, Henry
Marlowe, Christopher
Middleton, Thomas
More, Sir Thomas
Morris, William
Nash, Thomas
Radcliffe, Ann
Richardson, Samuel
Scott, Sir Walter
Shakespeare, William
Shaw, George Bernard
Shelley, Mary
Smollett, Tobias
Sterne, Laurence
Stevenson, Robert Louis
Stoker, Bram
Swift, Jonathan
Thackeray, William Makepeace
Trollope, Anthony
Walpole, Horace
Wells, Herbert G.
Wilde, Oscar
Woolf, Virginia

Bibliography

Anthony, Lawrence: *AntConc (Version 3.2.2)* [Computer Software]. Tokyo 2011. Available from http://www.antlab.sci.waseda.ac.jp/.
Baker, Paul: *Using Corpora to Analyze Gender*. London 2014.
Firth, John Rupert: *Papers in Linguistics 1934–1951*. London 1957.
Hoffmann, Sebastian and Stefan Evert: *BNCweb (CQP-edition): The marriage of two corpus tools*, in: *Corpus Technology and Language Pedagogy: New Resources, New Tools, New Methods*, ed. by S. Braun, K. Kohn, and J. Mukherjee. Frankfurt am Main 2006.
Kennedy, Graeme: *An Introduction to Corpus Linguistics*. Edinburg 1998.
Mahlberg, Michaela: *Corpus Stylistics and Dickens' Fiction*. London 2012.
Sinclair, John: *Corpus, Concordance, Collocation*. Oxford 1991.
Sinclair, John: *The search for units of meaning*, in: *Textus* 9 (1996).

Making *Horse Sense:* Phraseology and Metaphor as the Basis for Equine Cultural Models in English

Christoph Schubert
University of Vechta

1. Introduction

Human conceptualizations of natural phenomena are highly culture-specific, depending on both regional and temporal variables. This fact can already be inferred from individual entries in the *American Heritage Dictionary of Idioms*, where the phraseological expression *horse sense* is defined as follows:

> **horse sense** sound practical sense as in *She's got too much horse sense to believe his story*. The exact allusion in this term, which dates from the mid-1800s, is disputed, since some regard horses as rather stupid. However, they tended to be viewed more positively in the American West, where the term originated (Ammer 1997, 311).

Thus, horses have been important for mankind for several heterogeneous reasons, such as leisure, sports, therapy, warfare, and labour. Therefore, it does not come as a surprise that the lexeme *horse* is connected to a large number of figurative uses in English-speaking cultures. The adequate theoretical foundation for the analysis of these knowledge structures is Conceptual Metaphor Theory (CMT), which regards metaphor as a human technique of making sense of reality (cf. Fludernik/Freeman/Freeman 1999, 384). Accordingly, a metaphor originates from a transfer of specific semantic features from a source domain onto a target domain (cf. Lakoff 2006, 190). Although this mapping procedure is a general process operating across many languages, numerous metaphors are usually connected to specific cultures (cf. Kövecses 2005, 3). In the special case of HORSE metaphors and phraseology,[1] features of this animal function as concrete source domains which are mapped onto abstract target domains (cf. Lakoff/Johnson 2003, 14).

As regards the process of meaning transfer, phraseological expressions such as *put the saddle on the right/wrong horse* are closely related to metaphor from a semantic perspective (cf. Cruse 2000, 209). In addition, phraseology is intricately connected to cultural perceptions of its users and the diachronic construction of a distinct identity, for the "expressions by which a culture is implemented are passed from one generation to

[1] In line with typographic convention, source and target domains in conceptual metaphors will be printed in small capitals (cf. George Lakoff and Mark Johnson: *Metaphors We Live By,* Chicago 2003).

the next through linguistic and cultural norms of usage" (Cowie 1998, 9). Nevertheless, only a few years ago Paul Skandera still pointed out that in the research on language and culture "the study of the relation between English phraseology and culture in particular has been largely neglected" (2007, vi), so that the present paper aims to close a part of this research gap with a focus on a specific animal.[2]

Starting out from these premises, the study provides a cognitive-semantic analysis of the lexeme *horse* and its compounds with regard to their occurrence in English phraseology, concentrating on idioms, similes, proverbs, and winged words. My intention is to show that such phraseological usage both reflects and constructs cultural practices and the collective memory of a language community. As for the empirical data, lexical items were drawn from twenty widely used and influential dictionaries of idioms and quotations, as listed in the appendix. Thus, by demonstrating the wealth of figurative expressions and classifying them into distinct semantic groups, the paper wants to give an insight into the existence of equine cultural models in English.

2. Cognitive Cultural Models and Phraseology

A cognitive model is defined as the "stored cognitive representations that belong to a certain field", such as horses as a specific type of animal and mammal (Ungerer/Schmid 2006, 49). In addition, cognitive models are highly context-dependent and typically "*idealized*, in that they involve an abstraction, through perceptual and conceptual processes, from the complexities of the physical world" (Cienki 2007, 176, emphasis original).[3] Since such models are culture-specific, the conceptualization of horses in the English-speaking world is also a *cultural* model, "shared by people belonging to a social group or subgroup" (Ungerer/Schmid 2006, 51). Consequently, they underlie common perspectives on cultural practices and corresponding linguistic usage (cf. Kristiansen/Dirven 2008, 9).[4] Thus, on the basis of the theory of linguistic relativity, as established by Humboldt as well as by Sapir and Whorf, the lexicon of a language may be labelled a "storehouse of cultural data" (Teliya et al. 1998, 56). Since phraseological expressions usually have a long etymological history, they are particularly strong and persistent carriers of culture across the centuries.

As for a first glimpse at such conceptualizations, the onomasiological dictionary *Roget's Thesaurus of English Words and Phrases* is helpful. In this dictionary, which

[2] Thus, the present article belongs to the semantic subdiscipline of 'zoosemy', investigating the ways in which animal features may be figuratively transferred onto human beings (cf. Robert Kiełtyka: *On Zoosemy: The Study of Middle English and Early Modern English Domesticated Animals,* Rzeszów 2008).

[3] According to D. Alan Cruse: *Meaning in Language: An Introduction to Semantics and Pragmatics,* Oxford 2000, p. 128, the word *horse* serves as an example of one-to-one mapping with the concept HORSE, which he defines with the help of features such as typical parts ("hoof"), characteristic noise ("neigh"), dwelling ("stable"), and use ("riding"). However, since horses have played such variable roles in different human societies, it seems more adequate to speak of cognitive models in the plural.

[4] For further information on cognitive cultural models cf. the seminal book *Cultural Models in Language and Thought,* ed. by Dorothy Holland and Naomi Quinn, Cambridge 1987.

divides the knowledge of the world into seven large sections with altogether 990 subdivisions, HORSE is part of a lexical field following the sequence of "space > motion > carrier" (Kirkpatrick 1987, 132), which already underlines the meaning of the horse as a domestic animal used for labour, as prototypically indicated by the compound *workhorse*. In the lexical section 'carrier', the noun *horse* appears together with other lexemes such as *donkey*, *mule*, and *pony*, but also with *transporter*, *lorry driver*, and *ferryman*. It is only the second entry in the alphabetical section of *Roget's Thesaurus* that shows the sequence "matter > organic matter > animal" (Kirkpatrick 1987, 175), pointing toward the living being instead of the beast of burden labouring for humans.

The question arises which aspects of cultural knowledge may be the basis of specific phraseological expressions. According to Piirainen (cf. 2008, 210-213), it is possible to distinguish between five general – and partly overlapping – possibilities. First, she names 'textual dependence', which means that phraseologisms refer to influential texts such as Shakespearean plays, the Bible, or classical authors (e.g. *Trojan horse*). Second, they may go back to 'pre-scientific conceptions of the world', which include outdated ideas and superstitions (e.g. *to thank one's lucky stars*). Third, single words in idioms may function as 'cultural symbols' with figurative meanings. While Piirainen mentions the wolf as a symbol for danger in *cry wolf*, the horse can be an epitome of strength (e.g. *as strong as a horse*). Fourth, praseological expressions may refer to items of "material culture", that is to say man-made physical artefacts horses can be associated with, as in *go round like a horse in a mill*. Finally, 'culture-based social interaction' (Piirainen 2008, 212) can form the foundation of idioms, referring to customary behaviour in communities. This can be exemplified by *the grey mare is the better horse*, which pertains to gender-related interaction. Thus, by applying these categories, it becomes obvious that HORSE idioms show a wide range of cultural frameworks.

In order to define and classify phraseologisms, Fiedler uses the comprehensive term of the 'phraseological unit (PU)', which she defines as a "lexicalized polylexemic linguistic unit which is characterized, in principle, by semantic and syntactic stability, and to a great extent by idiomaticity" (2007, 28). Hence, these PUs are fixed conventionalized expressions consisting of several words, while their meanings cannot be inferred from an addition of the lexical meanings of the single constituents.[5] In addition, they are relatively fixed as far as grammatical categories such as the passive or the plural are concerned (cf. Jackson 1988, 106). Departing from these assumptions, Fiedler then defines six conventional types of PUs (cf. 2007, 39-50), which are here complemented by fitting examples with the lexeme *horse*:

[5] Along similar lines, Lipka defines idioms as "formally complex linguistic expressions whose meaning is not derivable from that of their constituents". Leonhard Lipka: *English Lexicology: Lexical Structure, Word Semantics and Word-formation,* 3rd ed., Thübingen 2002, p. 112.

1. Phraseological nominations: e.g. *hold your horses*
2. Irreversible binomials: e.g. *horse and buggy*, *horse and carriage*
3. Stereotyped comparisons (similes): e.g. *as strong as a horse*, *eat like a horse*
4. Proverbs: e.g. *if wishes were horses, beggars would/might ride*
5. Winged words: e.g. *A horse! A horse! My kingdom for a horse!* (Shakespeare, *Richard III*)
6. Routine formulae: e.g. *to horse!* (i.e. 'mount your horses')

Phraseological nominations "denote objects, people, states, processes, or relations" (Fiedler 2007, 39) and thus comprise a large number of nominal, verbal, adjectival, and adverbial idioms. Irreversible binomials are combinations of two items of the same word class which are linked by a coordinator and show a fixed sequence. Stereotyped comparisons are also called 'frozen similes' and typically contain one of the two prepositions *like* or *as*. As Jackson puts it, in such similes there is a "characteristic which we have culturally imputed" (1988, 108) to objects or living beings such as horses. A proverb is adequately defined as a "concise, well-known sentence which expresses a general truth, shared experience, a piece of advice, or a moral principle in an easy to memorize form and is handed down from generation to generation" (Fiedler 2007, 44). The specific feature of winged words is that they are clearly connected to a specific author or well-known text, showing definite textual dependence. Therefore, the term *winged words* is here used as a superordinate term for "catchphrases, slogans, sententious remarks, and quotations that enjoy currency in the language community and many contexts of speech" (Fiedler 2007, 47). Finally, routine formulae are "ready-made units for recurrent situations" (Fiedler 2007, 50) such as greetings, farewells, or military orders. It is noteworthy that all six categories are met by PUs containing *horse*, which shows their pervasive character.[6]

Another useful classification of phraseological units is proposed by Gläser (1986), taking into account both semantic and syntactic criteria. With reference to varying degrees of opacity, it is possible to distinguish between uni-, bi-, and multilateral idioms. In 'unilateral' idioms, only one constituent has a metaphorical meaning, as in *horse sense, willing horse,* or *iron horse*, where only the *horse* constituent is used figuratively, so that they could also be called "semi-opaque" (Cruse 1986, 39). If idioms are 'bilateral', two constituents have a metaphorical meaning, as in *horses for courses, a horse of another/a different colour,* or *dark horse*. In multilateral idioms, more than two constituents have a metaphorical meaning, as in *look a gift horse in the mouth, beat/flog a dead horse,* or *ride a willing horse to death*. Finally, from a syntactic point of view, idioms fulfil the functions of different word classes, so with *horse* quite many are verbal (e.g. *hold your horses*), a lot are nominal ones (e.g. *dark horse*), a few are adjectival

[6] The present study only includes phraseological units containing the lexeme *horse*, so that idioms that refer only indirectly to the mammal are not taken into account, such as *keep a tight rein, sign of good breeding,* or *feel your oats* (cf. Robert A. Palmatier: *Speaking of Animals: A Dictionary of Animal Metaphors,* Westport, CT 1995, p. 4).

(e.g. *as strong as a horse*), and very few adverbial (e.g. *straight from the horse's mouth*).[7]

3. Phraseological Units and Metaphorical Meanings of HORSE

The following remarks on phraseologisms including *horse* will chiefly concentrate on what Fiedler (2007) calls 'phraseological nominations', 'stereotyped comparisons', and 'proverbs'. This is because 'binomials' and 'routine formulae' with *horse* are quite rare, whereas 'winged words' are so frequent that they will be investigated separately in the following section. As regards equine metaphorical transfer in the phraseologisms, HORSE functions as the source domain, since particular qualities of the animal, such as physical appearance or prowess, are transferred to specific target domains. By analyzing these mappings, traditionally called the *tertium comparationis* or 'ground' of the metaphor (Leech 1969, 155), it will become clear which characteristics of horses have been culturally salient and relevant. In order to come to an objective and comprehensive result, all idioms found in the following fourteen dictionaries were taken into account: Ammer (1997), Ayto (2009), Clark (1990), Fergusson (2002), Gerbert/Zimmermann (1987), Gulland/Hinds-Howell (1986), Kirkpatrick (1993), Kirkpatrick/Schwarz (1993), McCarthy (2006), Schemann/Knight (2011), Spears (1994), Spears/Kirkpatrick (1993), Terban (2006), and Warren (1994). As far as the target domains are concerned, they can be subdivided into a number of categories referring to various physical or intellectual qualities.

Several phraseologisms are linked to PHYSICAL POWER/MOVEMENT, such as *change/swap horses in midstream*, *put the cart before the horse, don't spare the horses, wild horses couldn't drag/make sb do sth*, and *hold your horses*. These are all verbal units in which the animal is construed as a cultural symbol for transport, since this function is deeply rooted in the history of English-speaking societies. This 'carrier' notion is further confirmed by the obsolescent nominal phraseologism *iron horse* 'railway locomotive', while the exceptional physical constitution of horses is foregrounded by the prototypical simile *as strong as a horse* and the adjectival construction *enough to make a horse sick*. Obviously, this idea closely corresponds to the stereotyped comparison *as sick as a horse*, referring to a severe form of nausea that does not allow vomiting. Moreover, the bodily strength is conceptualized in a more sinister way in the noun *horseplay* and the verbal unit *drive a coach and horses through sth*, which hints at historical methods of warfare, whereas the undesirable consumption of large quantities of food surfaces in the simile *eat like a horse*. Still, the positive aspects of horses' physical presence in the phraseologisms clearly outweigh the negative concepts.

[7]Cf. Sylviane Granger and Magali Paquot: *Disentangling the Phraseological Web*, in: *Phraseology: An Interdisciplinary Perspective,* ed. by Sylviane Granger and Fanny Meunier, Amsterdam 2008, pp. 35-41; as well as Elizabeth Piirainen: *Figurative Phraseology and Culture*, in: *Phraseology: An Interdisciplinary Perspective,* ed. by Sylviane Granger and Fanny Meunier, Amsterdam 2008, pp. 213-215, for a survey of further possible typologies of phraseological units in English.

Besides the bodily notions, a few phraseologisms also reveal the target domain of INTELLECTUAL CAPACITY, as exemplified by the previously mentioned *horse sense* as well as by *straight from the horse's mouth*, which goes back to a supposed betting tip provided by the animal in the domain of horse racing. These concepts are again complemented by a number of phraseologisms denoting undesirable intellectual characteristics, as in *Trojan horse* ('deception'), *be/get on your high horse* ('arrogance'), and *you can take/lead a horse to water, but you cannot make it drink* ('stubbornness'). In addition, there are a few phraseologisms that express GENERAL ABILITY, which may pertain to qualities of either the body or the mind. Relevant instances are the nominal units *horses for courses*, *dark horse*, and *an (old) war horse*. However, undesirable and foolish social interaction may also be foregrounded, as in the verbal phraseologism *horse around/about*.

Another important semantic category manifests itself in the domain of VALUE/IMPORTANCE,[8] as demonstrated by the verbal phraseologisms *close/lock the stable/barn door after the horse has bolted/escaped*, *look a gift horse in the mouth*, *win the horse or lose the saddle*, and the proverb *if wishes were horses, beggars would/might ride*. They clearly point to the fact that the animal has always been a treasured possession or even a status symbol for their human owners. The great significance of horses in knowledge patterns of English speakers also appears in the verbal phraseologisms *back the wrong horse* ('crucial matter') and *ride a hobby horse* ('desirable pastime') as well as in the nominal expressions *a one-horse town* and *a horse of another/a different colour*, while the idiom *I could eat a horse* emphasizes the sheer size and mass of a horse's physical presence. A solitary instance that signifies an obsolete and undesirable quality can be found in the adjectival binomial *horse-and-buggy*, which directly corresponds with the diachronic change of transport systems in English-speaking cultures over the centuries.

One last major category among the target domains is INDUSTRIOUSNESS, a quality obviously ascribed to horses by their owners, making the animal a cultural paragon of a strong work ethic. The most blatant instance is the verbal simile *work like a horse*, but also the idiomatic *willing horse* and its extensions in *a willing horse never wants work*, *flog/spur a willing horse*, and *ride a willing horse to death* underline this type of metaphorical mapping. Obviously, the adjective *willing* strongly emphasizes the good-natured readiness for labour imputed to horses. Still, there is also one phraseologism that hints at possible resistance to human imposition on the horses' side, namely *every horse thinks its own pack heaviest*.

This survey of phraseological units has shown that the equine cultural models in the Anglophone world contain mainly favourable concepts. Moreover, it has become clear that some of the real-life functions of horses are more salient in phraseology than others. In particular, 'therapy' does not play a great role, and 'leisure' is mainly connected to horse racing, whereas 'labour' is the central metaphorical domain.

In addition to phraseological units, metaphorical meanings of *horse* also occur in word-formations, in particular compounds, which may be seen as the most fixed and

[8]Correspondingly, the noun *cattle* is etymologically related to *chattel* and *capital* (cf. *The Oxford English Dictionary,* 20 vols, 2nd edition, ed. by John A. Simpson and Edmund S.C.Weiner, Oxford 1989, s.v. 'cattle'.

least flexible type of phraseological nominations. Such compounds, which usually consist of two constituents, mostly show a modifier-head structure of the endocentric type, so that they can be classified both according to the position of the lexeme *horse* and according to whether the lexeme *horse* shows its literal or a metaphorical meaning. A selection of typical compounds of all four resulting categories can be retrieved from the *OED* (cf. Simpson/Weiner 1989, s.v. 'horse'), as summarized in table 1.

If the noun *horse* shows its literal meaning in the modifier constituent, it may be combined with various concepts such as body parts (e.g. *horseback*), the animal's mobile home (e.g. *horsebox*), or complex events involving the mammal (e.g. *horse racing, horse auction*). As for the metaphorical use of HORSE in the modifier, it often refers to the physical behaviour and strength of the animal in words such as *horseplay*, *horsepower*, and *horsebite*, or it may pertain to the acoustic quality of the neighing (e.g. *horse-laugh*). Alternatively, the horses may just be the affected objects of some action, as in *horse trading*, which rather negatively denotes "[n]egotiation marked by hard bargaining and shrewd exchange" (Ammer 1997, 311).

	modifier	head
literal	*horsehair, horseman, horseback, horsebox, horse-drawn, horse racing, horse-riding, horseshoe, horsefly, horse rug, horse fodder, horse auction*	*workhorse, show horse, breeding horse, brewery horse, carriage horse, cart horse, cavalry horse, circus horse*
meta-phorical	*horseplay, horsepower, horsebite, horse-trading, horse-laugh, horsefeathers, horseshit*	*hobbyhorse, vaulting horse, clothes horse, rocking horse, sea horse, charley horse, Trojan horse, stalking horse*

Table 1: Position and meaning of *horse* in compounds (selection)

If *horse* occurs in its literal meaning in the head constituent, the modifier mainly names the animal's function in relation to humans, such as the activity (e.g. *breeding horse*), the place (e.g. *circus horse*), or the instrument of labour (e.g. *cart horse*). If the head constituent of the compound contains a HORSE metaphor, the target domain often relates to objects that have a shape similar to a horse or things people can sit on. This becomes particularly obvious in the nouns *vaulting horse*, *clothes horse*, and *rocking horse*. Other metaphors may be based on various domains such as mythology (e.g. *Trojan horse*), practices in hunting (e.g. *stalking horse*), or the physical resemblance of other animals with horses (e.g. *sea horse*). Consequently, compounds both confirm the multi-faceted equine cultural models and place particular emphasis on utilitarian and functional aspects of horses.

In order to measure the significance of various ANIMAL idioms, it is helpful to compare the frequency of HORSE phraseologisms with those of other farm animals and pets.[9] An impression of the statistics is provided by a sample count based on the three

[9] For a large collection of animal metaphors cf. the comprehensive dictionary *Speaking of Animals* by Robert Palmatier, ed. cited, which also provides etymological origins.

dictionaries *Harrap's English Idioms* (*HEI*), containing about 10,000 instances, *Cambridge Idioms Dictionary* (*CID*), including about 7,000 lemmata, and *Oxford Dictionary of English Idioms* (*ODEI*), listing 6,000 examples (cf. table 2). The numbers clearly demonstrate that dogs score highest (e.g. *every dog has its day*), followed by horses and cats (e.g. *let the cat out of the bag*), while pigs (e.g. *a pig in a poke*), sheep (e.g. *the black sheep of the family*), goats (e.g. *act the goat*), and cows (e.g. *until the cows come home*) show comparatively low numbers.[10] Thus, the frequency is highest for 'man's best friend', but also the numbers of *horse* and *cat* point to a rather emotional relationship with humans, while those animals that are commonly kept for their meat, fur, or milk have lower scores.

	dog	*horse*	*cat*	*pig*	*sheep*	*goat*	*cow*
CID	31	21	17	9	5	3	2
HEI	43	27	24	7	6	3	3
ODEI	35	21	24	11	5	3	3
TOTAL	109	69	65	27	16	9	8

Table 2: Phraseological units with pets and farm animals in three dictionaries

4. Winged Words with HORSE

In addition to lexicalized phraseological units that appear in standard mono- and bilingual dictionaries, the English language also contains so-called winged words, which can be found in specific dictionaries of quotations or catchphrases. It is especially such well-known quotations from eminent texts and authors that provide insights into cultural models of a linguistic community, since they strongly contribute to the collective memory of a society.[11] In order to get a representative sample of winged words with *horse*, all examples from the following six dictionaries were taken into account: Augarde (1992), Cohen/Cohen (1988), Partington (1992), Rees (1992), Rees (1997), and Robertson (1997).

According to Partington in *The Oxford Dictionary of Quotations* (1992, iix-ix), there are several critera for including a specific quotation in the dictionary: "Fame […], memorability, significance, importance" as well as a "[c]ombination of that which is both dateless and undisputably true." Moreover, "a quotation should be able to float free from its moorings, remaining buoyant when detached from its original context. It should be apposite, pithy, wise, and of universal application" (Partington 1992, iix-ix). In contrast to most of the previously mentioned phraseologisms, these quotations have a

[10] It needs to be noted that there is some overlap here between the idioms in the different dictionaries, since I counted all the single tokens separately, not the mere types. Therefore, the table presents the absolute numbers of idioms in all the dictionaries.

[11] Obviously, also well-known titles of books including the lexeme *horse* can have this effect, as shown, for instance, by the novels *War Horse* by Michael Morpurgo (1982), *All the Pretty Horses* by Cormac McCarthy (1992), or *The Horse Whisperer* by Nicholas Evans (1995), all of which have been adapted as films as well.

clear origin, a distinct source, either from a famous book or well-known persons such as authors, thinkers, or politicians. In the *Cassell Dictionary of Catchphrases*, a 'catch-phrase' is defined as

> a phrase in frequent use and one which, for some reason, appeals to the public fancy. The catchphrase catches on because it is a more colourful and enjoyable way of expressing an idea or feeling than the conventional, straightforward one (Rees 1997, v).

It needs to be noted that not all of the quotations listed were originally produced in the English language, but it is of central importance that they are all known in the English-speaking world. An investigation of all the instances shows semantic values partly similar to the target domains of other *horse* phraseologisms, but they also highlight different aspects. It is unsurprising that the domain of PHYSICAL POWER/MOVEMENT stands out once again, as in "[h]ome, James, and don't spare the horses," which goes back to 1934 song title by the American songwriter Fred Hillebrand (cf. Augarde 1992, 141). It emphasizes the energy of horses as a means of transport, while the quotation "[h]alf the failures in life arise from pulling in one's horse as he is leaping" from Julius Hare's *Guesses at Truth* (1827) accentuates the beneficial instincts of the animal (Partington 1992, 326). In his parliamentary novel *Phineas Redux* (1874), Anthony Trollope wrote that "the best carriage horses are those which can most steadily hold back against the coach as it trundles down the hill" (Partington 1992, 704), portraying the horse as a symbol for conservative forces in politics.

The quotations also confirm the semantic categories of INTELLECTUAL CAPACITY/GENERAL ABILITY, pointing out the merits of horses. For instance, the English clergyman Thomas Fuller (1608-1661) metaphorically uses a donkey for comparison in his winged word "if an ass goes travelling, he'll not come back a horse" (Robertson 1997, 169). According to James Boswell's biography *The Life of Johnson* (1791), Samuel Johnson uttered that "[a] fly, Sir, may sting a stately horse and make him wince; but one is but an insect, and the other a horse still" (Robertson 1997, 233). Thus, again, horses appear metaphorically superior to other creatures, which contributes to the positive equine cultural models. The Irish Clergyman Father Mathew (1790-1865) uses the term *horse sense* in order to point out the eminence of horses even in comparison to humans in his statement "horse-sense is something a horse has that prevents him betting on people" (Robertson 1997, 335).

As seen in the previous chapter, horses may stand for VALUE/IMPORTANCE, which may even surpass the worth of humans, as William Penn notes in *Some Fruits of Solitude* (1693): "[m]en are generally more careful of the breed of their horses and dogs than of their children" (Partington 1992, 511). From a male patriarchal perspective, women may also be included in a list of possessions, as in the quote "[t]hree things I never lends—my 'oss, my wife, and my name" from Robert Smith Surtees' novel *Hillingdon Hall* (1845) (Partington 1992, 672). Similarly, a hierarchy of valuable belongings is suggested in "He [i.e. the husband] will hold thee, when his passion shall have spent its novel force, / Something better than his dog, a little dearer than his horse" from Alfred Tennyson's poem "Locksley Hall" (1842) (Partington 1992, 685). George Savile, the 1st Marquess of Halifax, presents a drastic perspective in the section 'Of Punishment' from his *Political, Moral, and Miscellaneous Thoughts and Reflections*

(1750). Here he points out that "men are not hanged for stealing horses, but that horses may not be stolen" (Partington 1992, 321), already arguing for pre-emptive strikes. Such quotes impressively underline the high esteem present in equine cultural models, although cultural change over the centuries has obviously led to a devaluation of horses in relation to humans.

The high value associated with horses is further supported by a semantic category that can be labelled CLOSENESS TO HUMANS. This likeness is literally expressed by the juvenile protagonist Holden Caulfield in Salinger's *The Catcher in the Rye* (1951), when he reveals his predilection for horses: "[t]ake most people, they're crazy about cars. […] I'd rather have a goddam horse. A horse is at least *human*, for God's sake" (Augarde 1992, 258, emphasis original). Similarly, the saying that "[t]here is no secret so close as that between a rider and his horse" in Robert Smith Surtees' novel *Mr Sponge's Sporting Tour* (1853) hints at a hidden equine understanding and an amalgamation of animal and man in horse racing (Partington 1992, 672). A quite subtle comprehension of human affairs by horses occurs in the poem "Smoke and Steel" (1920) by Carl Sandburg in the verses "Why does a hearse horse snicker / Hauling a lawyer away" (Augarde 1992, 260). It here appears that the animal shares the malicious joy of the lyrical speaker about the death of a member of an unpopular profession. Despite this very close association of horses with humans, however, quotations connected to pastime and leisure are again hardly in existence.

While these quotations confirm the largely positive cultural models of horses, others evoke darker and more sinister concepts, which are much more dominant in the winged words than in the previously discussed phraseological units. Obviously, a semantic category going back to classical mythology is DECEPTION from Virgil's *Aeneid*: "Do not trust the horse, Trojans. Whatever it is, I fear the Greeks even when they bring gifts" (Partington 1992, 712).[12] Although this does not pertain to a live animal, the shape of the construction obviously evokes the image of a horse. Another unpleasant association manifests itself in BODY FLUIDS, as in Naomi Royde-Smith's *Weekend Book* (1928), where the quote "I know two things about the horse and one of them is rather coarse" can be found (Partington 1992, 549). Along these lines, there also exists the famous saying that "horses sweat, men perspire and women merely glow" from the book *Nanny Says* (1972) (Rees 1992, 84). From this it is only a few steps to LUST, as condemned in the biblical quotation that "they were as fed horses in the morning: every one neighed after his neighbour's wife" from *Jeremiah* 5:8 (Cohen/Cohen 1988, 44). Consequently, all these winged words focus on unpleasant physical features of horses, adding novel facets to the cultural concept.

In contrast to the other phraseological units, winged words also show a stronger tendency towards ILLNESS of horses. A striking example appears in Patrick Kavanagh's poem "The Great Hunger" (1947): "That was how his life happened. / No mad hooves

[12] The original Latin version reads: "Equo ne credite, Teucri. Quidquid id est, timeo Danaos et dona ferentis" (*The Oxford English Dictionary of Quotations,* 4th edition, ed. by Angela Partington, Oxford 1992, p. 712). Even though the exact translation may be disputable, the central fact is that the winged word is so well-known and widespread among native speakers of English that it has been adopted by a dictionary of quotations, perpetuating the idea of a treacherous *Greek gift*.

galloping in the sky, / But the weak, washy way of true tragedy – / A sick horse nosing around the meadow for a clean place to die" (Partington 1992, 386). Here the symbol of the dying horse is clearly culture-dependent, alluding to the Irish potato famine. A related quotation can be found in the Fool's warning that "[h]e's mad that trusts in the tameness of a wolf, a horse's health, a boy's love, or a whore's oath" from Shakespeare's tragedy *King Lear* (act 3, scene 6, line 20) (Partington 1992, 596).[13]

In addition to bodily weakness, the winged words also provide a contradiction to the proverbial intelligence of horses, hinting at STUPIDITY. Famously, singer Louis Armstrong in the *New York Times* (1971) pointed out that "[a]ll music is folk music, I ain't never heard no horse sing a song" (Augarde 1992, 13), establishing a stark contrast between human art and animal life. Thus, it is only consequent to use the term as a swear word, as it happens in Shakespeare's *Henry IV, 1* (act II, scene 4, line 214), when Falstaff addresses Prince Henry with the words "Hal, if I tell thee a lie, spit in my face, call me horse" (Cohen/Cohen 1988, 321). A different aspect is highlighted in one of William Blake's "Proverbs of Hell" (1793), which reads "[t]he tigers of wrath are wiser than the horses of instruction" (Cohen/Cohen 1988, 61). In this case, the horse is a symbol of second-hand intellectual knowledge acquired through teachers, while the tigers stand for personal experience with strong emotional involvement.

Finally, since horses have always been used by humans in armed conflicts, another prominent semantic category is WAR/DEATH. For instance, in the Bible the connotations of *horse* are rather menacing, as in "[b]ehold, a pale horse: and his name that sat on him was Death" from the *Revelation of St John* 6:8 (Cohen/Cohen 1988, 57), connected to the Four Horsemen of the Apocalypse. This image is confirmed by the biblical Psalm 147:10, containing the words "[h]e delighteth not in the strength of the horse: he taketh not pleasure in the legs of a man" (Cohen/Cohen 1988, 38), as well as by Psalm 20:7, which reads "[s]ome trust in chariots, and some in horses: but we will remember the name of the Lord our God" (Cohen/Cohen 1988, 35). These ancient examples form the foundation of the equine cultural model of raw destructive power, as opposed to peace-loving religious faith. In Rudyard Kipling's poem "The Ballad of the King's Jest" (1892), horses are likewise associated with war: "Four things greater than all things are,— / Women and Horses and Power and War" (Augarde 1992, 169). As already seen in the category of VALUE/IMPORTANCE, a sexist attitude here leads to a comparison between horses and women. In poetry it is also possible to find horses associated with the afterlife, as in the verses "I first surmised the Horses' heads / Were toward Eternity" from Emily Dickinson's "Because I could not stop for Death" (1863), in which the lyrical 'I' rides in Death's carriage (Partington 1992, 244).

[13] As a footnote on *King Lear* in the *Norton Anthology* confirms, "[h]orses were supposed to be more subject to ailments than other animals" in Shakespeare's times (*The Norton Anthology of English Literature,* 6th ed. Vol. 1, ed. by Meyer Howard Abrams, New York 1993, p. 934).

5. Conclusion

Since metaphorical transfer is a technique of conceptualizing and categorizing reality, the existence of numerous phraseologisms containing HORSE is evidence of the great importance of this mammal in the history of English-speaking cultures. It could be shown that phraseological units pertain mainly, albeit not exclusively, to positive and desirable qualities of horses, such as physical strength and material value. In addition, superior intellectual qualities and features such as industriousness are attributed to horses. Many winged words stress similar merits of energy, ability, and value, but here also negative and undesirable aspects are quite noticeable, such as bodily excretion, illness, stupidity, as well as war and death. This points to the fact that the cultural model of HORSE is by no means one-sided but rather multi-faceted. As regards phraseological units with other animals, HORSE is only equalled or surpassed by mammals kept as pets in the house, that is dogs and cats.

From a diachronic perspective, it is clear that most idioms associating horses with warfare, transport, and agriculture date from times before the automobile was invented and before heavy industrialization and mechanization set in. In contrast, the semantic categories of leisure and therapy are clearly underrepresented in the examples, since these functions of horses have gained importance only in more recent times. As a result, although equine cultural models have obviously changed over the centuries, phraseology and metaphor act as preservers of diachronic cultural knowledge, which is thus perpetuated in idiomatic usage.

All that could be achieved within the scope of this paper was to give a culture-based survey of the phraseology of *horse*. Obviously, there are various criteria and parameters that provide possibilities for further analyses and future research. First, a strictly diachronic approach dealing with the origins of all phraseologisms since Old English might provide further insights into the historical development of the cultural model. Second, it would be enlightening to have a closer look at HORSE idioms and metaphors in different national varieties such as British or American English. Third, it might be useful to investigate metaphorical values of other members of the rich lexical field, such as *mare, pony, steed, filly, colt, foal, gelding,* or *stallion*. And fourth, it would be worthwhile comparing the target domains of *horse* with metaphors of other domestic or wild animals. Nevertheless, the present study could outline the wealth of equine phraseology and demonstrate that over the centuries, a coherent system of horse-related thought has been linguistically construed in Anglophone cultures.

Dictionaries of Phraseologisms

Ammer, Christine: *The American Heritage Dictionary of Idioms*. Boston 1997.
Augarde, Tony (ed.): *The Oxford Dictionary of Modern Quotations*. Oxford 1992.
Ayto, John (ed.): *Oxford Dictionary of English Idioms,* 3rd ed. Oxford 2009.
Clark, John O.E: *Harrap's English Idioms*. Edinburgh 1990.
Cohen, John M. and Mark J. Cohen: *The Penguin Dictionary of Quotations*. London 1988.
Fergusson, Rosalind: *Cassell's Dictionary of English Idioms*. London 2002.
Gerbert, Manfred and Peter Zimmermann: *Idiomatische Redewendungen Englisch–Deutsch*. Leipzig 1987.
Gulland, Daphne M. and David Hinds-Howell: *The Penguin Dictionary of English Idioms*. London 1986.
Kirkpatrick, Betty: *Concise Dictionary of Common Phrases*. London 1993.
Kirkpatrick, Elizabeth M. and Catherine M. Schwarz: *The Wordsworth Dictionary of Idioms*. Ware 1993.
McCarthy, Michael (ed.):. *Cambridge Idioms Dictionary*. Cambridge 2006.
Partington, Angela (ed.): *The Oxford Dictionary of Quotations*, 4th ed. Oxford 1992.
Rees, Nigel: *Bloomsbury Dictionary of Phrase & Allusion*. London 1992.
Rees, Nigel: *The Cassell Dictionary of Catchphrases*. London. 1997.
Robertson, Connie (ed.): *The Wordsworth Dictionary of Quotations*. Ware 1997.
Schemann, Hans and Paul Knight: *Idiomatik Deutsch–Englisch / German–English Dictionary of Idioms*, 2nd ed. Hamburg 2011.
Spears, Richard A. and Betty Kirkpatrick: *NTC's English Idioms Dictionary*. Lincolnwood 1993.
Spears, Richard A.: *NTC's American Idioms Dictionary*, 2nd ed. Lincolnwood 1994.
Terban, Marvin: *Scholastic Dictionary of Idioms*. New York 2006.
Warren, Helen (ed.): *Oxford Learner's Dictionary of English Idioms*. Oxford 1994.

Bibliography

Abrams, Meyer Howard (ed.): *The Norton Anthology of English Literature*, 6th ed. Vol. 1. New York 1993.
Cienki, Alan: *Frames, Idealized Cognitive Models, and Domains*, in: *The Oxford Handbook of Cognitive Linguistics*, ed. by Dirk Geeraerts and Hubert Cuyckens. Oxford 2007, pp. 170-187.
Cowie, Anthony P: *Introduction*, in:. *Phraseology: Theory, Analysis, and Applications*, ed. by Anthony P. Cowie. Oxford 1998, pp. 1-20.
Cruse, D. Alan: *Lexical Semantics*. Cambridge 1986.
Cruse, D. Alan: *Meaning in Language: An Introduction to Semantics and Pragmatics*. Oxford 2000.
Fiedler, Sabine: *English Phraseology: A Coursebook*. Tübingen 2007.
Fludernik, Monika, Donald C. Freeman, and Margaret H. Freeman: *Metaphor and Beyond: An Introduction,* in: *Poetics Today* 20.3 (1999), pp. 383-396.
Gläser, Rosemarie: *Phraseologie der englischen Sprache*. Tübingen 1986.
Granger, Sylviane and Magali Paquot: *Disentangling the Phraseological Web*, in: *Phraseology: An Interdisciplinary Perspective,* ed. by Sylviane Granger and Fanny Meunier. Amsterdam 2008, pp. 27-49.
Holland, Dorothy and Naomi Quinn (eds.): *Cultural Models in Language and Thought*. Cambridge 1987.
Jackson, Howard: *Words and Their Meaning*. London 1988.

Kiełtyka, Robert: *On Zoosemy: The Study of Middle English and Early Modern English Domesticated Animals*. Rzeszów 2008.

Kirkpatrick, Betty (ed.) *Roget's Thesaurus of English Words and Phrases*. Harlow 1987.

Kövecses, Zoltan: *Metaphor in Culture: Universality and Variation*. Cambridge 2005.

Kristiansen, Gitte and René Dirven: *Introduction: Cognitive Linguistics – Rationale, Methods and Scope,* in: *Cognitive Sociolinguistics: Language Variation, Cultural Models, Social Systems*, ed. by Gitte Kristiansen and René Dirven. Berlin 2008, pp. 1-17.

Lakoff, George and Mark Johnson: *Metaphors We Live By*, 2nd ed. Chicago 2003.

Lakoff, George: *The Contemporary Theory of Metaphor,* in: *Cognitive Linguistics: Basic Readings,* ed. by Dirk Geeraerts. Berlin 2006, pp. 185-238.

Leech, Geoffrey: *A Linguistic Guide to English Poetry*. London 1969.

Lipka, Leonhard: *English Lexicology: Lexical Structure, Word Semantics and Word-formation*, 3rd ed. Tübingen 2002.

Palmatier, Robert A: *Speaking of Animals: A Dictionary of Animal Metaphors*. Westport, CT 1995.

Piirainen, Elisabeth: *Figurative Phraseology and Culture,* in: *Phraseology: An Interdisciplinary Perspective,* ed. by Sylviane Granger and Fanny Meunier. Amsterdam 2008, pp. 207-228.

Simpson, John A. and Edmund S. C. Weiner (eds.): *The Oxford English Dictionary*, 20 vols. 2nd ed. Oxford 1989.

Skandera, Paul: *Preface,* in: *Phraseology and Culture in English,* ed. by Paul Skandera. Berlin 2007, pp. v-vi.

Teliya, Veronika et al: *Phraseology as a Language of Culture: Its Role in the Representation of a Collective Mentality,* in: *Phraseology: Theory, Analysis, and Applications*, ed. by Anthony P. Cowie. Oxford 1998, pp. 55-75.

Ungerer, Friedrich and Hans-Jörg Schmid: *An Introduction to Cognitive Linguistics*, 2nd ed. Harlow 2006.